THE MASTER MUSICIANS

STRAUSS

SERIES EDITED BY R. LARRY TODD

THE MASTER MUSICIANS

Titles Available

Bach • Malcolm Boyd
Beethoven • Barry Cooper
Berlioz • Hugh Macdonald
Brahms • Malcolm MacDonald
Byrd • Kerry McCarthy
Carter • David Schiff
Chopin • Jim Samson
Debussy • Eric Frederick Jensen
Handel • Donald Burrows
Liszt • Derek Watson
MacDowell • E. Douglas Bomberger
Mahler • Michael Kennedy
Mendelssohn • Philip Radcliffe
Monteverdi • Dennis Arnold
Mozart • Julian Rushton
Mussorgsky • David Brown
Puccini • Julian Budden
Rossini • Richard Osborne
Schoenberg • Malcolm MacDonald
Schumann • Erik Frederick Jensen
Strauss • Laurenz Lütteken
Tchaikovsky • Roland John Wiley
Verdi • Julian Budden
Vivaldi • Michael Talbot

THE MASTER MUSICIANS

STRAUSS

LAURENZ LÜTTEKEN

Translated by Erik Butler

OXFORD
UNIVERSITY PRESS

OXFORD
UNIVERSITY PRESS

Oxford University Press is a department of the University of Oxford. It furthers
the University's objective of excellence in research, scholarship, and education
by publishing worldwide. Oxford is a registered trade mark of Oxford University
Press in the UK and certain other countries.

Published in the United States of America by Oxford University Press
198 Madison Avenue, New York, NY 10016, United States of America.

© Philipp Reclam jun. GmbH & Co. KG 2014

All rights reserved. No part of this publication may be reproduced, stored in
a retrieval system, or transmitted, in any form or by any means, without the
prior permission in writing of Oxford University Press, or as expressly permitted
by law, by license, or under terms agreed with the appropriate reproduction
rights organization. Inquiries concerning reproduction outside the scope of the
above should be sent to the Rights Department, Oxford University Press, at the
address above.

You must not circulate this work in any other form
and you must impose this same condition on any acquirer.

Library of Congress Cataloging-in-Publication Data
Names: Lütteken, Laurenz, author.
Title: Strauss / Laurenz Lütteken.
Other titles: Richard Strauss. English
Description: New York, NY : Oxford University Press, [2019] |
Series: Master musicians |
Translated from the German published under title: Richard Strauss. |
Includes bibliographical references and index.
Identifiers: LCCN 2018027781 | ISBN 9780190605698 (hardcover : alk. paper) |
ISBN 9780190605711 (epub)
Subjects: LCSH: Strauss, Richard, 1864–1949—Criticism and interpretation.
Classification: LCC ML410.S93 L8813 2019 | DDC 780.92—dc23
LC record available at https://lccn.loc.gov/2018027781

1 3 5 7 9 8 6 4 2
Printed by Sheridan Books, Inc., United States of America

With the support of the UBS Culture Foundation and
Legat Dr Wilhelm Jerg, University of Zurich

Contents

Preface vii
Postscript to the English Translation xi
Acknowledgments xiii

Introduction: Problems 1

1 Between Patriciate and Aristocracy 19
2 The End of the Nineteenth Century: Leaving Traditional Genres Behind 32
3 The Poetry of Imagination: Lieder 49
4 Music and Life: The Kapellmeister and His Duties 69
5 Poetry of the Real: The Tone Poems 91
6 Music without Metaphysics: The Path to Opera 106
7 "The Social Achieved": Strauss and Hofmannsthal 126
8 New Mythology and the Plasticity of Music 147
9 Music and Reality 160
10 After Hofmannsthal's Death 177
11 *Metamorphosen* and the End of History 188

Appendix A: Biographical Timeline 205

Appendix B: Catalog of Works 212

Appendix C: Personalia 241

Select Bibliography 267

Index 277

Preface

SINCE THE 1950S, INCREASING DOUBT HAS COME TO BEAR ON WHETHER Richard Strauss qualifies as "modern" (and not just in a musical sense). There are many reasons for this. Even in the context of the emergent "New Music" first hailed by Paul Bekker, which reveled in proclamations and prophecies, Strauss offers an atypical example. Resolutely and persistently, he refused to provide the kind of commentary that others offered so readily. The mass of writings he left behind amounts to little more than marginalia and occasional remarks; in no way does it present a systematic account of his artistic purposes. Even the journalistic controversy surrounding *Salome* (1905) failed to move the composer to explain himself, and he positively despised such inclinations in his contemporaries. Accordingly, works of central importance—for instance, *Der Rosenkavalier* (1911)—stand without authorial explanation to accompany them. The only programmatic statement on the piece's background is a short essayistic sketch. Tellingly, it was written by Hugo von Hoffmannsthal, who gave it the paradoxical title, "Unwritten Afterword." The only time both authors felt obliged to make statements (which took very different forms) was in the context of *Die ägyptische Helena* (1928); in the event, there are highly specific circumstances for this exception.

Strauss was an avid reader, yet he hid his humanist education. His personality remained unapproachable because he did not so much as hint at how to interpret his works, although it seems that many include a sizeable biographical component. Even Hofmannsthal said that he came to understand the overarching connections in Strauss's *oeuvre* only after lengthy, oral exposition—that is, following conversations that were private and were meant to stay so. Strauss never saw fit to write down what he thought on such subjects. The only text expressing a genuine "worldview" comes from the most personal, intimate sphere: his 1892 and 1893 diary, written during his formative journey to Egypt and Greece, taken for health reasons. Strauss's contemporaries were unaware of this journal, however; it was made available by Willi Schuh only later—and then only in parts. Strauss's personal reserve proves all the more remarkable given the dauntingly systematic nature that he lent his life's work, which encompasses nearly eighty years of active composition. Unfolding between two poles—tone poems and operas—it is framed by "early" contributions to traditional, instrumental genres and explicitly classified "late works." Significantly, alongside this prodigious output was also a constant, if not uniformly intensive, stream of Lieder. Strauss's breaks with his system are rare; examples include the piano works for Paul Wittgenstein and *Intermezzo* (1924), which abandons certain principles observed elsewhere. Yet these compositions' complex relations to the overall system do not question it so much as affirm its validity.

Strauss made considerable effort to embody the roles of composer and conductor in one—a unity that had, in fact, fallen apart after Wagner. On this score, he invites comparison with Mahler. At the same time, however, Strauss differs from his contemporary for having renounced—and just as emphatically—the Wagnerian fusion of composer and librettist. Apart from a masterclass that proved just as short-lived as it was half-hearted, Strauss is the only major composer in the German-speaking world around the turn of the century to have eschewed teaching; he never sought to train pupils or gather "disciples," and he avoided a conservatory professorship to the end. He also remained unapproachable by never explaining his methods in technical terms. The only time that he deigned to offer a position—in a provisional account of his life made in conjunction with *Ein Heldenleben* (1899)—he did so indirectly, by adapting Hector Berlioz's *Traité d'instrumentation* (1904).

A further aspect of this self-occultation is evident in the strange phenomenon connecting Strauss, the great anti-metaphysician, and Anton Bruckner (1824–1896), the exemplary metaphysician of music. Endless anecdotes have been told by third parties, many of which take manifest delight in gossip and intrigue. Out of such second-hand accounts a kind of leitmotif emerges: the composer's unconscious, inborn "musicianship" and his love of playing cards. Yet the image does not reveal character traits so much as it covers them up. One may deem Strauss's pose a technique for avoiding, once and for all, the importunities of contemporaries who were positively infatuated with personal revelations. Even though he hardly suffered from a lack of self-confidence and was given to jovial moods—if not brash expressions of pride in his success—this refined intellectual screened himself off in his Garmisch library (which remains largely preserved to this day). Although a public figure through and through, Strauss kept the public at arm's length. This lifelong bearing also proves confusing inasmuch as he—and in this regard he was like Paul Hindemith, Dmitri Shostakovich, or Darius Mulhaud—demonstrated incessant, often beserker-like, creative vigor; this occasionally, as in the decade from 1909 to 1919, assumed almost incomprehensible dimensions.

The drive for unconditional, restless activity, which also found expression in self-imposed directorial and organizational tasks, qualifies as thoroughly modern. But at the same time, it was fueled by an insistent and increasingly nuanced turn to Greek antiquity. For Strauss, "heathen" antiquity—purified, as it were, through brutal and raw anti-classicism (*Salome* and *Elektra*)—eventually came to represent a corrective to the twentieth century, which had betrayed its medieval, Christian inheritance by embracing technology and science. That said, Strauss also wanted this turn to produce a commanding effect in its own right; no programmatic declarations were attached to it, even—and especially—amidst the dramatic events in the last period of his life. With a consistency and indifference that could only rouse suspicion, the composer refrained from making any statements about how he viewed the world. As such, his reserve and seclusion could not prevent entanglement in National Socialism—a complex web of attraction, rejection, and intermittent tactlessness and clumsiness that accompanied the menace facing his Jewish daughter-in-law and members of her family (some of whom were eventually murdered).

All of the above has held consequences for Strauss reception, of course. In positive and negative terms alike, the composer counts as a foreign body in the twentieth century. Unduly taxing elementary rules of logic, some interpreters have assigned him a place under the rubric of "late romanticism." Others have viewed Strauss as a traitor to modernism: a relic, or (just as problematically) an opportunist whose involvement in National Socialism discredits him beyond all hope of redemption. Such difficulties are compounded by the fact that the composer, who once seemed to have been relegated to the historical past once and for all, made a remarkable return to the repertories of opera houses and orchestras at the end of the millennium—as did some of his works that had been deemed to be of lesser merit. For some time now, Strauss's presence has not been limited to *Elektra* or *Rosenkavalier*; instead, it encompasses, if in varying articulations, almost all of his symphonic poems and works for the stage. As such, it is timely to approach the composer away from the clichés that have come to surround him. Such an undertaking is not without risk, for many of the essential materials exist only in part, or not at all. Truly nuanced scholarship on Strauss did not emerge until a few decades ago; establishing and checking source material in digital form has started, but the process is far from complete. Correspondence is available in editions of highly variable (and sometimes dubious) philological rigor; as such, no complete overview is possible. Finally, a complete edition of works—to say nothing of elucidation of the composer's highly complicated creative process—has barely started.

Yet the twentieth century, from which Strauss stood apart—or was excluded—is long over. It is time to cast a new, unprejudiced view on the composer, one that does not see him at odds with his age so much as its embodiment. Willi Schuh's biography did not necessarily remain incomplete by chance; it just might illustrate why such a nineteenth-century approach ill befits a composer like Strauss. That is, there may be deeper reasons why no biography of Strauss exists (again, in contrast to Mahler or Schoenberg) than a first glance suggests. Thus, the study at hand does not provide a biography so much as it represents a wide-ranging *essay*, in the etymological sense. The catalog of works, timeline, and personalia in the appendices, and the select bibliography, offer easy points of orientation; references to sources are limited to what is necessary. Strauss followed Wagner's example even while reversing it, and sought to fuse art and life, creative work and active biography. The approach here does not separate one element from the other; as such, it also includes narrative episodes and portraits of compositions. It may seem risky and overly provisional, indeed, it may give rise to objections. But in light of the challenge that Strauss poses even today, in the twenty-first century, such an approach is warranted—and for authentically hermeneutic reasons, too. The day when scholars had a "take" on Strauss, adopting a stance "pro" or "contra," are over; it was always nonsensical to do so, and all the more so now. As historical distance grows, the task is to sound out every possibilities for understanding both the man and his work. The book at hand is meant as a contribution, however small, to this endeavor.

Postscript to the English Translation

THE TRANSLATION AT HAND WAS MADE TWO YEARS AFTER THE BOOK'S publication in Germany. On the basis of a thorough rereading, minor adjustments have been undertaken for the *Master Musicians* series. The numerous works that have appeared since 2014 receive attention only in summary fashion. This book does not offer a traditional biography, nor does it observe a strict distinction between "life" and "work." Such an organizational scheme, although evident in most contributions to *Master Musicians*, has played less and less of a role in recent volumes. It proves unsuited for Strauss inasmuch as he persistently and intentionally sought to combine his "life" and "work"—and for reasons directly opposed to those of Wagner. Given this circumstance, the structure of the book remains as it was. The only change involves moving the first chapter of the German original to the front to serve as an introduction and abbreviating it slightly; a few illustrations have also been added. Otherwise, the text is unmodified.

Acknowledgments

NUMEROUS INSTITUTIONS GRACIOUSLY MADE MATERIAL FOR THIS book available: Geheimes Staatsarchiv Preußischer Kulturbesitz, Berlin; Stadtarchiv Dresden; Richard Strauss-Archiv, Garmisch-Partenkirchen; Richard Strauss Institut, Garmisch-Partenkirchen; Sammlung Musikgeschichte der Meininger Museen/Max Reger-Archiv, Meiningen; Bayerische Staatsbibliothek, Munich; Kritische Ausgabe der Werke von Richard Strauss, Ludwig-Maximilians-Universität München; Münchner Stadtbibliothek; Hochschule für Musik und Theater, Munich; The Pierpont Morgan Library, New York; Thüringisches Landesmusikarchiv, Weimar; Archiv, Bibliothek und Sammlungen der Gesellschaft der Musikfreunde, Vienna; Botschaft des Fürstentums Liechtenstein, Vienna; Österreichische Nationalbibliothek, Vienna; Österreichisches Theatermuseum, Vienna; Wiener Staatsoper; Zentralbibliothek. My thanks, also, to individuals who provided information on important details: Otto Biba, Vienna; Walter Brauneis, Vienna; Maren Goltz, Meiningen; Jürgen Kloosterhuis, Berlin; Thomas Leibnitz, Vienna; Jürgen May, Garmisch-Partenkirchen; Peter Poltun, Vienna; Eberhard Rick, Berlin; Hartmut Schick, Munich; Wolfgang Schuster, Caputh; Father Siegfried Thuringer, Munich; Christian Wolf, Garmisch-Partenkirchen.

For conversation and discussion, critical feedback on the manuscript, and general assistance in the writing process, I am indebted to Karol Berger, Inga Mai Groote, Michael Hampe, Hans-Joachim Hinrichsen, Isabel Mundry, Karl-Anton Rickenbacher†, Ulf Schirmer, Gabriele Strauss-Hotter, Christian Strauss, Ralf Weikert, and, in particular, Veronika Weber. Claudia Maria Korsmeier reviewed the text scrupulously, and Ulrike Thiele did an exemplary job correcting the proofs. Lion Gallusser helped with final editing and compiled the index.

A fellowship generously granted by the Wissenschaftskolleg/Institute for Advanced Study in Berlin and its rector, Luca Giuliani, permitted completion of the book. My deep and heartfelt gratitude extends to everyone named.

Berlin, February 2014

Note on the Translation

Translation into English was generously funded by the UBS Culture Foundation, to which I offer my sincere thanks. The project also received support from the Jerg Fund at the University of Zurich. Finally, I am grateful to all who made the translation possible and contributed along the way: Mirjam Beerli, Stefan Koranyi, Christian Luckscheiter, Martin Meyer, Suzanne Ryan, Larry Todd, and, especially, Erik Butler.

Zurich, February 2016

THE MASTER MUSICIANS

STRAUSS

INTRODUCTION

Problems

Images of Strauss

Many of Strauss's contemporaries would have considered him a fortunate child. Besides enjoying the advantages offered by a prosperous and musical family, he evidently possessed unbounded talent, too. The composer charted such spectacular success in youth that by the age of thirty he had achieved everything within established notions of a musical career. Besides self-confidence bordering on recklessness in composition, he demonstrated an astonishing capacity for performance—which the only serious health issue of his life, a case of pneumonia and pleurisy in 1891–1892, did nothing to diminish. Both in the boldness of his designs and the technical demands he placed on musicians, Strauss was uncompromising. His tone poems had already established his reputation as a veritable representative of "modernism." When he turned to stage works, these traits became even more pronounced; from the inception (or, at the latest, with *Feuersnot* [1901]), Strauss knew that conflicts with censors would be inevitable—and then sought them out. The operas *Salome* (1905) and *Elektra* (1909) not only shocked the public. They met with disapproval on the highest level, and Kaiser Wilhelm II took the unprecedented step of distancing himself from his own Hofkapellmeister. Still, such actions held no real consequences: Strauss continued to be handsomely remunerated, and his contracts multiplied. The single-minded nature of his creative activity, from *Guntram* (1894) on, challenged all and sundry: singers, orchestra members, directors, producers, and set designers—to say nothing of audiences. Within a few years, Strauss had become the most famous and best-paid composer in Germany. He was also the most controversial: Felix Draeseke's 1906 polemic about *Salome, Konfusion in der Musik* (Confusion in Music), gave rise to journalistic debates of unparalleled dimension.[1]

Such conflicted perceptions in the public eye proved singularly significant. Around the turn of the century, Strauss (see Figure 0.1) did not garner attention only in articles and pamphlets; he was also the figure most likely to be discussed by musicologists. In 1898, the first monograph on the composer appeared in Prague.[2] Two years later, further studies were published in Dutch and French, as well as a collection of essays in the United States.[3] In 1908, Ernest Newman (who would later achieve renown for his biography of Wagner) published a book on Strauss.[4] Numerous articles on specific works appeared in Germany, as did an array of books with a broader scope; the most important contributions were made by Gustav Brecher, Rudolf Batka, and Max Steinitzer.[5] In 1911, the year *Der Rosenkavalier* premiered, Richard Specht (1870–1932) edited a catalog of the composer's works. This volume, which provided material that Max Steinitzer (1864–1936) would use for his influential biography, is significant because it includes compositions whose whereabouts

---

1 Felix Draeseke, *Die Konfusion in der Musik: Ein Mahnruf* (Stuttgart: Grüninger, 1906); documents in Susanne Shigihara (ed.), *'Die Konfusion in der Musik' Felix Draesekes Kampdschrift von 1906 und ihre Folgen* (Bonn: Schröder, 1990).
2 Arthur Seidl, Wilhelm Klatte, *Richard Strauss: Eine Charakterskizze* (Prague: Payer, 1896).
3 Wouter Hutschenruyter, *Richard Strauss* (Haarlem: Tjeenk Willink, 1898); G. Jorissenne, *Richard Strauss. Essai critique et biologique* (Brussels: Weissenbuch, 1899); James Huneker, *Mezzotints in Modern Music: Brahms, Tschaikowsky, Chopin, Richard Strauss, Liszt and Wagner* (New York: Scribner, 1899).
4 Ernest Newman, *Richard Strauss. With a Personal Note by Alfred Kalisch* (London: Lane, 1908).
5 Gustav Brecher, *Richard Strauss: Eine monographische Skizze* (Leipzig: Seemann, [1901]); Erich Urban, *Richard Strauss* (Berlin: Gose & Tetzlaff, 1901); Rudolf Batka, *Richard Strauss* (Charlottenburg: Virgil, 1908); Max Steinitzer, *Richard Strauss: Biographie* (Berlin: Schuster & Löffler, 1911); Richard Specht, *Vollständiges Verzeichnis der im Druck erschienenen Werke von Richard Strauss: Mit Portrait und biographischen Daten sowie einer Einführung* (Vienna: Universal Edition, [1911]), 4.

Figure 0.1 Richard Strauss in 1895.

In the mid-1890s, the renowned Munich court photographer Karl Lützel took Strauss's portrait. He and his brother had opened their business around 1892 on Maffeistrasse, in the elegant center of the Bavarian capital. In 1894, Strauss was appointed royal Kapellmeister. Although the portrait should be viewed in this context, it does not depict an established artist, nor is there any indication of the musical profession. As an elegant young man with almost Bohemian traits, Strauss seems to belong to the artistic and literary milieu, not to hold an appointment at court.

Photograph. Zurich, Central Library.

remain uncertain to this day. The critic Oskar Bie (1864–1938)—who also wrote two volumes for a book series the composer founded, *Die Musik*—summed matters up in *Die moderne Musik und Richard Strauss* (Modern Music and Richard Strauss, 1906), an unconventional but illuminating discussion in the context of cultural history. Here, the composer's works are presented as the culmination of the many currents of contemporary music: "In utterly thoroughgoing fashion, Strauss is developing the most essential qualities of our new music, which, more and more, is starting to free itself from the architectonic music of the classical age: melodic harmony."[6]

Ever since the eighteenth century, the dividing line between melody and harmony had grown more and more indistinct. Such dissolution—in simple terms, the question of whether melody precedes harmony or proceeds from it—also defined nineteenth-century music. Strauss was all but guaranteed a place in debates on topics such as dissonance, orchestration, or just volume. In a poem entitled "Zwei Künstlerinnen" (Two Artists), Otto Julius Bierbaum (1865–1910) parodied this state of affairs by having the goddess of war, Bellona, marshal a world-conquering symphony against the gentle Saint Cecilia:

Bellona knitted her brow	(*Bellona zog die Stirne Kraus*
And mumbled, vexed and sore,	*Und murmelte verdrießlich:*
"A little symphony like that,	*So eine kleine Sinfonie*
Could be by Richard Strauss—	*Kann schließlich*
It would sound just as poor.	*Auch Doktor Richard Strauß.*
I need more noise and brass;	*Ich brauch noch viel mehr Blech und*
This whimpering makes me weak.	*Bei dem Gewimmer wird mir schwach;*
I long for a mighty, raucous mass	*Oh, hätt ich Massen, Massen,*
To unleash my raging soul.	*Mein ganzes Seelenungestüm*
A monstrous fugue I seek—	*In einem Fugenungetüm*
A storm that will never pass!"	*Gewaltig loszulassen.*[7])

In this send-up of a Berlin salon conversation, the great ironist of the *fin de siècle* also made it clear that Strauss—the "conquistador of music"[8]—had come to stand as a public figure *sui generis*, a favorite topic of discussion for the educated middle classes:

Bismarck, Harden Stinden, Goethe	(*Bismarck, Harden, Stinde, Goethe,*
Wagner, Bungert, Dahn, Homer,	*Wagner, Bungert, Dahn, Homer,*
Die Fledermaus and *The Magic Flute*,	*Fledermaus und Zauberflöte,*
Ludolf Waldmann, Meyerbeer;	*Ludolf Waldmann, Meyerbeer;*

---

6 "Strauß entwickelt in äußerster Konsequenz die wesentlichen Qualitäten unserer neuen Musik, die sich von der architektonischen des klassischen Zeitalters immer mehr zu emanzipieren beginnt: die melodische Harmonie." Oskar Bie, *Die Moderne Musik und Richard Strauss* (Berlin: Bard, Marquardt & Co., 1907), 72.

7 Otto Julius Bierbaum, "Zwei Künstlerinnen," in *Gedichte* (Munich: Georg Müller, 1922), 236.

8 Specht, *Vollständiges Verzeichnis*, 4.

China, Japan, Böcklin, Thumann,   *China, Japan, Böcklin, Thumann,*
Thoma, Werner, Stuck, and Knaus,   *Thoma, Werner, Stuck und Knaus,*
Johann, Eduard, and Richard Strauss   *Johann, Eduard, Richard Strauß,*
Kaiser Wilhelm, Robert   *Kaiser Wilhelm, Robert*
   Schumann . . .   *Schumann . . .*
Great! Just great!! Let me out!!!   *Mahlzeit! Mahlzeit!! Laßts mi*
                                                                                           aus!!!)

Strauss did not represent modernism, then, so much as he, with Bie, embodied its driving force—and far beyond the German-speaking world.[10] Initially, the composer's career was not impeded by tensions—in particular, the conflict between the fact that he conducted operas at court (in Munich, then in Berlin) and simultaneously displayed affinity for the Secessionist sensibility. But matters changed during and after the First World War. Now without a royal or imperial appointment, Strauss had trouble contending with the political circumstances of the Weimar era and his duties in newly republican Vienna. What is more, the course he steered with Hugo von Hofmannsthal—who viewed *fin de siècle* aesthetics with skepticism—headed in a direction different from the rest of the "New Music" (Bekker).[11] Strauss openly professed his distaste for atonal music, although he paid more attention to it than is generally assumed: in 1921 he was not just the chairman of the honorary committee at the first Donaueschingen Festival, he even instructed his grandson in Schoenberg's theory of harmony.[12]

Given these circumstances, scholars have time and again diagnosed a break, a rupture, in Strauss's *oeuvre*. In fact, the composer remained true to himself and his vision, and he continued to do so after Hofmannsthal, his most important collaborator, had died. Strauss disliked his contemporaries' embrace of atonality because it ran counter to his understanding of art, which, he held, should focus on human life. What Hofmannsthal defined as "the social"—that is, an orientation toward the actual existence of

---

9 Bierbaum, "Ein Löffel Suppe," in *Gedichte*, 411f.
10 Cf. Bie, *Die Moderne Musik*.
11 Paul Bekker, *Neue Musik* (Berlin: Erich Reiss, 1919).
12 H. H. Stuckenschmidt, *Schönberg. Leben—Umwelt—Werk* (Munich: Piper, 1989, first 1974), 68.

human beings, their communal and institutional constitution—sought to overcome the muteness of the *fin de siècle*. By making the circumstances framing life its object, art should help people find their bearing in the present, even if it could not guarantee comfort among the competing aspects of modern times. Strong tonality is a key feature of this conception of art. For Hofmannsthal and Strauss, *Die ägyptische Helena* (1928) was meant to resolve the debate once and for all: the only appropriate reaction to their peers' rejection of form was to picture human affairs at a remove, as a refracted image of antiquity. During the 1920s, this approach met with limited understanding and fell by the wayside as debates on contemporary music followed a different course. Finally, Strauss—although hardly blameless—was grotesquely misinterpreted under National Socialism, whose ideologues did not recognize (or did not wish to recognize) the real reason he had turned to "traditional" subjects. The image of his project changed yet again, and to lasting effect. (Thus, *Die Liebe der Danae*, which was produced for the first time in 1952, met with more puzzlement than appreciation.) Yet Strauss (see Figure 0.2) had not altered his perspective at any point: even in the 1930s, under dictatorial rule, his thoroughgoing agnosticism prompted him to focus on human existence. In 1954, Wilhelm Furtwängler recalled a telling exchange:

> I well remember overhearing a conversation between Richard Strauss and Joseph Goebbels, the Nazi Minister of Propaganda, in which Strauss, regarded for decades as the leader of the progressives, passionately defended the public's right to listen to what it wanted and to make up its own mind, and refused to countenance the infringement of this right by any third party.[13]

Be this as it may, debates on the avant-garde during the 1950s consigned Strauss to the historical past on the grounds that he had never belonged to the twentieth century at all. Theodor W. Adorno (1903–1969), who first engaged with Strauss's work at length in 1964, stresses this aspect in the chapter of *Aesthetic Theory* devoted to "technique":

> When Alban Berg answered in the negative the naïve question whether Strauss was not to be admired at least for his technique, he pointed up the

---

13 Wilhelm Furtwängler, *Furtwängler on Music: Essays and Addresses*, trans. Ronald Taylor (Aldershot: Scolar Press, 1991), 156.

Figure 0.2   Leonard Fanto: Richard Strauss. Bust portrait en face. Drawing.

From 1902 on, Leonard Fanto (1874–1958) oversaw costuming at the Dresden Opera. Beginning with Salome, he was in charge of the décor and costumes for numerous premieres of Strauss's works. Fanto also enjoyed renown as a portrait artist. This drawing, made in the course of preparations for the Dresden premiere of *Ägyptische Helena* and dated 3 December 1927, was reproduced in prints. In 1933, Strauss dedicated a copy "To my dear friend Clemens Krauss—who masterfully directed Arabella and other pieces—in grateful esteem." Fanto depicts the composer in a self-confident yet introverted light, as almost unapproachable.

Vienna, Österreichische Nationalbibliothek, F59 Cl. Krauss-Archiv 402.

arbitrariness of Strauss's method, which carefully calculates a series of effects without seeing to it that, in purely musical terms, one event emerges from, or is made requisite by, another.[14]

Adorno claims that the composer pursued "a conception of composition that asserts the principle of shock as fundamental and actually

---

14   Theodor W. Adorno, *Aesthetic Theory*, trans. Robert Hullot-Kentor (London: Bloomsbury, 2013), 293.

transfers the unity of the composition into the irrational suspension of what traditional style called logicality, unity." As such, "Berg's critique ... hits the mark because whoever refuses logic is incapable of the elaboration of the work that serves the *métier* to which Strauss himself was committed." The consequences are clear: "Music organized in such temporal-dynamic fashion as that of Strauss is incompatible with a compositional method that does not coherently organize temporal succession. Ends and means are contradictory."[15]

Strikingly, if not shockingly, this charge of inauthenticity—evidenced by the non-coincidence of ends and means—calls to mind objections leveled at Gustav Mahler at the turn of the century. In *Neue Musikzeitung*, for instance, Gustav Altmann had contrasted the latter's Fifth Symphony with Strauss's compositions: "Despite the exceptional art of composition and his use of the orchestra, Mahler gives me the impression of artificiality more than art."[16] Especially in the wake of Adorno's influential *Philosophy of New Music* (1948), Strauss was excluded from the very realm of "New Music." Although younger than Mahler and not much older than Schoenberg, he simply did not fit in—and was duly banished from serious scholarly debate. Worse still, both his orchestral and stage works came to be performed less and less. Paradoxically, Strauss's advocates implicitly took up Adorno's claim, contending that the composer had countered modernism's dismissive bearing by adopting the hearty outlook of a rustic, Bavarian guildsman. Conflicting views proved singularly fateful for the reception of his works and thwarted any measured assessment; to some extent, this is still the case. Two different—and contradictory—images attended Strauss all his life, and they shaped the way his works were viewed for at least fifty years following his death. With this conflict now in the past, it is time for a new and unbiased look at the facts. Such a perspective, which has been emerging in scholarly discussion since the late-twentieth century, focuses on the internal coherence of the *oeuvre* and the composer's (self-)positioning—that is, what

---

15 Ibid.
16 "Ich habe bei all der eminenten Satzkunst und Orchesterverwendung doch mehr den Eindruck von Künstlichkeit als Kunst bei Mahler...." Gustav Altmann, "Das erste elsaß-lothringische Musikfest. Straßburg, 20., 21., 22. Mai 1905." in: *Neue Musikzeitung* 26 (1905), 385.

Strauss himself considered the genuinely "modern" aspect of his works, the gesture unifying his creative life as a whole.

The Other Modernism

According to Strauss, *Ariadne auf Naxos*—an "opera in one act with a prelude," which premiered in 1916—was written as a favor to Max Reinhardt.[17] The circumstances of the work's genesis are difficult to determine, but the end result clearly reflects, under the guise of comedy, upon modern art, music, and theater. The opera amounts to an attempt at aesthetic self-positioning on the part of the composer. Branching levels of rupture shape the dramaturgy: the framing "prelude" and framed "opera" cross-fade, penetrate, and condition each other, yielding multiple layers of "theater within the theater" that reach down to the finest details. An instrumental prelude introduces the dramatic "prelude"; likewise, an overture precedes the "opera." In other words, the mythological events constituting the opera itself are not autonomous or self-evident; they are traversed throughout the work, which puts the stage itself on stage. The prelude lays the foundations for all that follows. The setting is indeterminate: "a large, sparsely furnished and poorly lit room in the manor of a great lord."[18] Here, preparations are being made for evening festivities featuring a solemn opera, a cheerful epilogue, and, finally, a fireworks display. Among the many narrative threads, the most important one concerns the unnamed young composer of the opera and Zerbinetta, the lead actress of the *commedia-dell'arte* troupe performing that evening. In other words, the central figures are an earnest artist invested in his "work" to the point of self-oblivion and a woman who, in the Dancing Master's words, is a "master of improvisation"—someone who "always plays herself" and therefore manages to do just fine in "any kind of situation."

The characters' erotic prospects are based on mistaken assumptions. The composer believes that he has found a kindred soul who has also renounced the world; addressing Zerbinetta, he holds forth that "what has no earthly existence in your soul [*das Irdische unvorhanden in deiner*

---

17 Strauss mentioned this context in a broadcast interview with Kurt Wilhelm in 1949 (uncut version in Garmisch-Partenkirchen, Richard Strauss-Institut).

18 Cf. Hugo von Hofmannsthal, *Operndichtungen. 2. Ariadne auf Naxos: Die Ruinen von Athen*, ed. Manfred Hoppe (Frankfurt: S. Fischer, 1985), 7–58.

Seele]." But in fact, the melancholy *soubrette* clings to the fullness of art and life; indeed, she believes that she has convinced her counterpart of the same. In delight that he has finally been understood—if only for a moment—the composer rhapsodizes about the metaphysical boundlessness of existence in a world he now wishes to embrace: "Now I see everything with new eyes! The depths of existence are immeasurable!" The young man's new-found sense of orientation culminates in the question of what his life's work means—that is, what is the significance of music. "Courage [*Mut*] stirs within me . . . The world is sweet, not dreadful, to the brave—and what, then, is music?" The stage directions indicate that he answers himself "with almost drunken solemnity": "Music is a sacred art, gathering all kinds of valor [*Mut*] like cherubim around a gleaming throne. That is why one art is holier than all the others, and that art is music!" His pathos-laden outpouring—*Musik* is practically a proper noun (the libretto provides no article for the word)—then comes an abrupt end. Zerbinetta makes an obscene whistle, bringing matters back to a comic register that destroys the illusion of a sanctified realm of autonomous art. The composer recognizes his error; her coarse noise has made his musical metaphysics collapse. He is forced to acknowledge that the plenitude of the world Zerbinetta affirms has nothing to do with his lofty notions. He falls into a rage and raves: "These wretches! – . . . Leaping like goats into my sanctuary!" Lamenting the incompatibility of their views, he asks, "Who made you pull me—me!— back into this world? Let me freeze, starve, perish on my own!" Then he runs off "in despair."

The tonal scheme of the scene is important. As Zerbinetta and the composer draw closer and closer, the music rings out in E major (which Wagner used to signal Wotan's departure in *Walküre*). When the luckless protagonist reaches a new understanding of life and art, the "pure" key of C major underscores his insight. But then, as the question of the meaning of art and music arises, Strauss shifts to E♭ major, which traditionally connotes the numinous and sublime. Soft, variegated murmurs from harps attend the composer's brief monologue; the motif accompanying him and the motif that is later related to Bacchus blend together. Zerbinetta returns to the stage, and the pathos is undone: the young man's motif is dashed to pieces. Instead of culminating in limpid song, the opening sequence concludes with the orchestra playing in the abrasive key of C minor. Only then does the "real" opera begin.

The same tonal constellation is featured at the end of the "actual" opera. The epiphany of Bacchus has laid the foundation for the god's final song. For the second and last time, harps play—only now the key is not E♭ major, but D♭ major. Both sequences entertain a complementary relationship, like that of the prelude and opera. The juxtaposition of keys takes up a signature pairing of nineteenth-century composition: the constellation of Wagner's *Ring*, which begins with the former and ends with the latter. After the composer storms off the stage, exasperated by Zerbinetta, he is present only through his music. Conversely, "his" opera ends with a canopy falling over Ariadne and Bacchus: the god is audible, but not visible. At precisely this juncture, Zerbinetta emerges "from the wings." The theatrical event affirms that she has carried the day. The composer disappears for good, but Bacchus remains present (in mediated form). Zerbinetta plays the key role, then, initiating the central process of transformation. The composer, who wishes to stand firm in his own world, has refused all change. Bacchus, in contrast, acknowledges that it shapes existence: "Now am I another, than I was;/Your pains have made me rich."

Scholars have often noted the self-referential nature of *Ariadne auf Naxos*—a *pièce à clef*, especially in terms of the underlying conception of music. When the protagonist succumbs to erotic confusion, he voices a metaphysics of his craft, claiming that "real life" (*Wirklichkeit*) may be found in and through music. In just a few words, the young man, who is devoted to his art to the exclusion of all else, echoes the great systems of nineteenth-century philosophical aesthetics. Hegel had grudgingly granted music a special status among the arts because it eludes conceptual thinking; Schopenhauer and Nietzsche positively rejoiced at this quality (which had already struck their late-Enlightenment forebears). For Schopenhauer, music is the self-sufficient, universal language of human existence and self-assertion. More than romantic, universal poetry expressing the inexpressible (as Wilhelm Heinrich Wackenroder had contended), it manifests the will unconditionally:

> Music is as *immediate* an objectification and copy of the whole *will* as the world itself is, indeed as the Ideas are, the multiplied phenomenon of which constitutes the world of individual things. Therefore music is by no means like the other arts, namely a copy of the Ideas, but a *copy of the will itself,* the

Figure 0.3 Hugo von Hofmannsthal/ Richard Strauss, *Ariadne auf Naxos* (first version 1912). Photograph from the first performance, Stuttgart.

Of all Richard Strauss's compositions, *Ariadne auf Naxos* came into being with the greatest difficulty. The 1912 premiere at the newly built "Little House" of the Stuttgart Court Theater, designed by Max Littmann, presented the "original version" (*Urfassung*) — that is, an adaptation of Molière followed by the opera. Strauss himself conducted, and Max Reinhardt directed. Some photographs of the production have been preserved, including the scene featuring Ariadne (Maria Jeritza, left) and Zerbinetta (Margarete Siems, right). Stylized gestures are evident, as is a décor that foregrounds the "play-within-a-play." The design illustrates Reinhardt's maxim that stage action does not "pretend" so much as it "unveils."

Stuttgart, Landesarchiv Baden-Württemberg, E 18 III Nr. 552/2.

objectivity of which are the Ideas. For this reason the effect of music is so very much more powerful and penetrating than is that of the other arts for these others speak only of the shadow, but music of the essence.[19]

Until the break with Wagner—if not before—Nietzsche stood under the spell of this all-encompassing conception. His *Birth of Tragedy* explicitly invokes *World as Will and Representation*: "Music, if regarded as an expression of the world, is in the highest degree a universal language that is related to the universality of concepts much as these are related to the particular things."[20] Nietzsche exalted Schopenhauer's connection between music and the Platonic doctrine of Ideas. Music stands, as it were, on high, above the other arts and discloses its own history next to—or outside of—"real" history. In consequence, the primacy traditionally granted to the word is upended: "Fundamentally the relationship of music to drama is the exact reverse of this: music is the true idea of the world, drama only a reflection of that idea, an isolated, shadowy image of it."[21]

Such a view represents the culmination of a long tradition of reflection shaped, since late antiquity, by competition between metaphysical claims and sensory perception (in other words, efforts to explain the world rationally, on the one hand, and examining how the mind is affected by external stimuli, on the other). Nietzsche presented a new metaphysics of the musical art surpassing all those that had come before. For him, the conflict was now resolved once and for all. By tying musical metaphysics directly to Wagner's *oeuvre*, Nietzsche assigned it a vanishing point: music gives the Idea concrete form and substance. Around the turn of the century, this view resonated not just in Europe, but across the world. (Oswald Spengler, for instance, claimed that this was why the history of "Western" music had ended with Wagner's *Tristan*.) Even if he stammers, Strauss's protagonist affirms the connection between music and metaphysics. It is telling that a *composer*—in the Nietzschean sense—makes this claim. When the young artist invokes music's potential to express the inexpressible, he

---

19 Arthur Schopenhauer, *The World as Will and Representation*, Vol. 1, trans. E. F. J. Payne (New York: Dover, 1969), 257.
20 Friedrich Nietzsche, *The Birth of Tragedy and Other Writings*, ed. Raymond Geuss and Ronald Speirs (Cambridge: Cambridge University Press, 1999), 78.
21 Ibid., 103.

dismisses the priority and preeminence that tradition has granted poetic language: the idea that music defies and transcends conceptuality. Thus, he can find nothing to say other than "but" (*jedoch*)—which he repeats five times (as the music shifts from one register to another). "The poets provide good words, after all, quite good ones—but, but, but, but, but!"[22]

With high-flown idealism, the composer links his art to courage (*Mut*): because "[t]he world is sweet, not dreadful, to the brave," music has the power to gather "all kinds of valor" around its throne.[23] These words contain a philosophical echo, too. In Schelling's *Philosophical Investigations into the Essence of Human Freedom,* "beautiful free courage" is what enables the human being possessed of "a serious disposition" to act "as . . . God instructs"—that is, it brings "man" closer to "the divine principle."[24] Such courage gives Strauss's protagonist in *Ariadne* the confidence to act. Insofar as his deeds manifest free will, they pay no heed to the world; indeed, actions such as his are supposed to create that world in the first place. The sacred realm that emerges will not tolerate disturbance from outside—that is, bacchanalian "leaps." But by the same token, this bearing admits no relationship with the Other. The composer approaches Zerbinetta because he believes that she, too, has turned away from the world; it does not occur to him that they might plunge into it together.

An avid reader of Schopenhauer and Nietzsche, Strauss was aware of what it meant to have his dramatic counterpart launch such an appeal. He distanced himself from ideas like these early in life—especially because of the privilege they granted to instrumental music. In a famous letter to Hans von Bülow (written during the 1880s), he had already declared that the fortunes of music depended on poeticization:

> If you want to create a work of art that is unified in its mood and consistent in its structure, and if it is to give the listener a clear and definite impression,

---

22 Strauss uses for this "jedoch" a sequence of thirds to prolong the dominant G (section 111) for more than six bars, until C major (as a six-four chord) is reached (section 112).

23 "Die Welt ist lieblich und nicht fürchterlich dem Mutigen. Was ist denn Musik? Musik ist eine heilige Kunst zu versammeln alle Arten von Mut wie Cherubim um einen strahlenden Thron."

24 Friedrich W. J. Schelling, *Philosophical Investigations into the Essence of Human Freedom,* trans. Jeff Love and Johannes Schmidt (Albany, NY: State University of New York Press, 2006), 58.

then what the author wants to say must have been just as clear and definite in his own mind. This is only possible through the inspiration by a poetical idea, whether or not it be introduced as a programme. I consider it a legitimate artistic method to create a correspondingly new form for every new subject.[25]

The letter goes on to critique the supposed autonomy of music—especially as exemplified by the sonata, which, Strauss declares, amounts to an empty formula that fulfilled its historical mission formula with Beethoven. (Decades later, in 1934, he would still refer with scornful irony to the "dogma of infallible form."[26]) This position stands the Nietzschean postulate of world-making art on its head. Strauss contends that music must derive its animating idea from poetry in order to achieve a valid, concrete (*plastisch*) substance. Even in youth, then, Strauss was skeptical about the exceptional status of music that philosophical idealism had trumpeted (in contrast to Mahler, who soon would claim that symphonic orchestration can give birth to a world). He first expressed his reservations apropos of instrumental music, casting doubt on its power to create objective form. When he began writing tone poems, he made it clear that music's limitations held more broadly, too.

The reservations about compositions based on poetry expressed in the letter to Bülow resemble the fundamental crisis of language that Hofmannsthal addresses in his famous "Chandos Letter" (to be discussed below). In this light, the operas on which Strauss and Hofmannsthal collaborated may be viewed as efforts to go beyond metaphysical schemes of idealization and counter voicelessness in a productive fashion. *Guntram*, which in a sense reworks *Tannhäuser*, thematizes the failure of idealized notions. Here, music does not lead to purification: the hero, a singer, is left without his beloved, a sympathetic ear. Inasmuch as his art is isolated, it loses the power to create meaning. *Guntram* represents another aesthetic manifesto in that it stages a critical encounter with music: its potential as well as its limitations. In contrast, *Feuersnot* (1901, with a libretto by Ernst von Wolzogen) offers a new concept. The work is a parody of Wagner, but

---

25 Letter to Hans von Bülow, August 24, 1888; Hans von Bülow and Richard Strauss, *Correspondence*, trans. Anthony Gishford (London: Boosey & Hawkes, 1953), 82.
26 "Unfehlbarkeitsdogma der Form." Richard Strauss, "Musik und Kultur," in Fred Hamel and Martin Hürlimann (eds.), *Das Atlantisbuch der Musik* (Berlin and Zurich: Atlantis, 1934), 6.

much more than this it transforms the underlying conception of music, predicated on unsuccessful human relations. Strauss's piece culminates in, and concludes with, the union of Kunrad and Diemut, signalling a new day for Munich and its inhabitants. The final sequence is not a duet, but an elaborate orchestral passage that plays while the stage remains bare. The audience sees only the pale light from Diemut's window. Thus, the opera ends by inverting Plato's allegory of the cave: characters vanish into approximate likenesses, shadows of Ideas. In this context, instrumental music has a different attraction. Full and concrete, it manifests erotic fulfillment, a new understanding of self and other (derived from Nietzsche). Music acquires a dimension beyond metaphysics: unconditional, absolute claims disappear and the prospect of communication, a world of possibility, arises. To use a phrase Hofmannsthal later coined, it embodies *das erreichte Soziale* (something like "community achieved") and extends this promise outward.

In *Feuersnot*, a distancing, parodic manner still predominated. But from this point forward, Strauss's underlying conception of music governed other works, too, including ones of a different cast. In his collaborations with Hofmannsthal, it assumed even greater dimensions. In light of the limited scope of historical circumstances for art in general, the musical theater, newly defined, should promote interaction and exchange between human—that is, social—beings. The "Unwritten Afterword" to *Der Rosenkavalier* affirms that music has the task of conferring concrete, palpable substance to whatever escapes representation in language. In other words, music does not manifest the Idea; it turns towards the conditions of shared, human existence. Instead of providing the medium for a heroic, artistic will spanning the world, it serves as a mode of interaction and sharing—in short, "created community." Art in general, and music in particular, should fulfill an eminently social function. For the composer, this meant retaining tonality. This was no easy matter, however: no longer simply a given, it was now transformed, scrambled, and encrypted—and could be regained only through immense effort. Tonality, for Strauss, was concrete and real, but also something broken and in need of repair.

When he adopted this premise, Strauss shook the foundations of music not only in Germany and Austria but throughout Europe. Stripping away all metaphysical claims and idealistic grandeur, he granted music unconditional, absolute immediacy and presence. The key scenic element is erotic—sexual—fulfillment that imparts a different sense to what the instruments play (and not just in *Feuersnot*). Such "affirmation of the flesh" also prevails in *Der Rosenkavalier* (starting with the dramatic—indeed, drastic—prelude),[27] *Ariadne, Josephs Legende,* and *Frau ohne Schatten.* Indeed, it still shapes *Liebe der Danae* and the complex self-referentiality of *Capriccio.* Music along these lines is no longer isolated and dependent on philosophical idealism or individual courage, something that stands outside of social and historical processes. Instead of amounting to flight from the world, instead of representing metaphysics, it is absolutely physical, concrete, and "plastic"; as such, it makes it possible to communicate in a manner adequate to the complexity of reality: to rediscover language and abandon silence for dialogue. Music of this sort is no longer simply aesthetic. Composition and performance yield substance: "the social."

To take up Goethe's term for embodied art, music displays "plasticity": reality and phenomenality of a different order. Accordingly—and as Hofmannsthal's "Unwritten Afterword" to *Der Rosenkavalier* makes clear—music needs no justification, aesthetic or otherwise. Its new-found plasticity makes a definitive break with idealistic notions and claims by materializing, in immediate fashion, the present with all its faults and fissures. "All kinds of valor"—which also means heroic volition, whatever its form—disappear.

In this light, we may also understand the deeper meaning held by incorporating the tonal arrangement of Wagner's *Ring* into *Ariadne.* Doing so strips away the constellation's historico-ideational content. Now, the D♭ major at the end does not herald failure, decline, or dashed hopes; instead, it announces renewal and social cohesion. It bears repeating: sexual union—Ariadne yielding to Bacchus—is a sign. The image for this new, anti-metaphysical conception of music is important: a canopy descends and veils the lovers; only their voices are heard. As in Plato's allegory of the cave, it is only possible to recognize things indirectly—in this case, through voices, not shadows. Music no longer provides a "copy of the will itself," as Schopenhauer would have it. Instead, "like the other arts," it is "a

---

27 The term "affirmation of the flesh" ("Bejahung des Leibes") was used by Schopenhauer in § 60 of *The World as Will and Representation* (by analogy to "affirmation of the will", "Bejahung des Willens").

copy of the Ideas" in a transfigured sense. Through bacchanalian "leaps" that untether it from metaphysics and epistemological ambitions, Strauss sought to release music into the world of social relations, which admit shaping—that is, he sought to bring it to bear on twentieth-century reality. This, in his eyes, was what being modern really meant.

CHAPTER ONE

Between Patriciate and Aristocracy

Munich as a Form of Mental Life

Founded in 1806 and consolidated in a modern, constitutional sense in 1818, the Kingdom of Bavaria—which finally, after lengthy debates, joined the German Empire in 1871—proved a stable entity, internal turmoil notwithstanding. It managed to stand firm even under an irresponsible monarch like Ludwig II (1845–1886), who ascended the throne in 1864. The latter's grandfather, Ludwig I, had made Munich—where life still had its medieval and baroque qualities—the royal seat. By 1900, the city was home to some half a million people and enjoyed the latest advances in sanitation and electrical services, in contrast to other capitals, such as Paris and Vienna. Maximilian II, who reigned between Ludwig I and Ludwig II, had kept abreast of technological developments. Thanks to urban planners like the historically minded architect Leo von Klenze (who died the same year that Ludwig II came to power), Munich acquired an incomparable appearance combining neoclassical style with the city's medieval and Renaissance patrimony. A unique balance was struck: many early modern aspects of the city remained untouched, while the representative structures of incipent modernity came into the orbit of the royal palace, the axis of urban expansion. The contrast with other cities was remarkable. In Vienna, for instance, the old fortification walls became a panorama from which a newly founded empire might be viewed, but the inner city's character was more or less erased. In Budapest, a mass of competing, modern buildings crowded the medieval center. Munich moved into the twentieth century by shifting expansion to areas that had once stood at the periphery. Although government offices, the palace, and court theater occupied prominent positions in the center—Ludwigstrasse, Maximilianstrasse, Wittelsbacherplatz, and Königsplatz—the surrounding neighborhoods did not suffer nearly as much as they did elsewhere. Munich became a city of vibrant and dynamic contrasts, the luminous metropolis of "festive squares, white colonnades, classicistic monuments and baroque churches, leaping fountains, palaces and parks."[1]

Here, on June 11, 1864—a few weeks after Ludwig II's coronation—the first child of Franz and Josephine Strauss was born, Richard Georg Strauss. The future composer's father played first horn in the Munich Royal Opera; in a sense, he held a position at court. Franz Strauss was already forty-two and married for the second time. Josephine Pschorr came from a brewing family that had amassed great wealth in the course of industrialization; by mid-century, the family was among the city's most prosperous residents. As such, Strauss came from a milieu that is difficult to situate, for it comprised bourgeois *parvenus* of different stripes. As a servant of the court, Franz Strauss occupied a solid position in cultural life, which orbited an eccentric young monarch obsessed with music. Not only was the Royal Opera the most important of the realm, thanks to Ludwig II the emergent avant-garde took shape here, germinating from the artistry of Richard Wagner. When the latter's project for a festival theater hall designed by Gottfried Semper fell through in Zurich, the Munich of the Wittelsbachs was slated to house the imposing structure (although these plans did not work out, either). In 1901, long after both composer and king had died, the Prinzregententheater designed by Max Littmann was constructed, in belated atonement, as it were. Here, Wagner's enduring influence may still be felt. Strauss, Littmann's junior by two years, despised this institution all his life.

In 1864, Ludwig II also summoned to Munich the man who would be Strauss's most important mentor, Hans von Bülow (1830–1894). Bülow enjoyed all manner of privileges at court, including direct access to the king. He rose to the position of Hofkapellmeister; in this capacity, he

---

1 Thomas Mann, "Gladius Dei" [1903], in *Death in Venice and Other Stories,* trans. David Luke (New York: Bantam, 2008), 93.

founded the city's Wagner tradition, properly speaking. The romance experienced an early interruption at the premiere of *Tristan* (1865), when Cosima von Bülow joined the composer at Tribschen, thereby making an adulterous liaison public knowledge. All the same, enthusiasm for Wagner thrived and amicable relations between the king and Bülow persisted. On the one hand, Ludwig favored musical projects with a historical flair comparable to contemporary architectural trends, such as the ballets he commissioned. On the other, the king gave Wagner, always a controversial figure, his most prominent platform to date, as well as political influence that was greeted with suspicion on all sides. Franz Strauss could hardly avoid entanglement in such affairs, and he made no secret of his dislike for the composer. (This dislike was so strong that Cosima, in 1882, continued to associate him with "the most distressing memories of our life in Munich"[2]). Nevertheless, he was a member of court, earned a regular income, and benefited from certain privileges. The position of soloist drew relatively high pay and commanded respect, but it held obligations, too. Thus, the year after Richard's birth, Franz Strauss performed at the premiere of *Tristan und Isolde*, which Bülow conducted. In 1868—when the younger Strauss received his first piano lesson—his father participated in the first production of *Meistersinger von Nürnberg*, also conducted by Bülow. In due course, the elder Strauss played at the premieres of *Rheingold* and *Die Walküre* (which the king, against Wagner's express will, arranged for Franz Wüllner to conduct).

Music defined life in the family, where a patrician atmosphere prevailed. Although his father recognized him Franz Strauss bore a social stigma because he had been born out of wedlock, but his marriage to Josephine Pschorr improved his standing. Technically, the Pschorrs were recent arrivals to the upper echelons of Munich society, but the wealth and influence they had amassed granted them a status comparable to that of the city's established burghers (whose means were more limited as a rule). This was Franz Strauss's second marriage, the first having ended tragically: following the death of his one-year-old son (Johann), both his wife (Elise Marie) and daughter (Klara) had fallen victim to cholera. Marrying into the Pschorr family represented a significant step up, to a position

---

2 Cosima Wagner, *Diaries: Volume II, 1878–1883*, trans. Geoffrey Skelton (New York: Harcourt Brace Jovanovich, 1980), 879 (entry of June 24, 1882).

of civic prominence that demanded commensurate outward bearing. In this regard, Richard Strauss's biography resembles that of another exemplary, late nineteenth-century figure. Thomas Mann (1875–1955)—who quit school and went to Munich in 1893—came from comparable circumstances, albeit in reverse: his father's side was patrician, and his mother's artistic. In different ways, but at more or less the same time, the novelist and the composer explored the biographical circumstances they shared: the former in *Buddenbrooks* (1901), then *Unordnung und frühes Leid* (1925), the latter in *Symphonia domestica* (1903), then *Intermezzo* (1924).

Needless to say, Richard's musical gifts were evident at any early age. The boy started piano lessons at the age of four, and violin lessons at eight. At six, he had already authored his first compositions. Clearly, then, it would have been only logical to school him formally in music. But despite a general fondness for sensation during the industrial age, no steps were taken to present a child prodigy. The young Strauss was sent to the Royal Ludwigs-Gymnasium to receive a humanist education, as fitted the scion of a respected Munich family. More remarkably, he actually finished school and received his *Abitur* in 1882; indeed, Strauss enrolled for university studies, even if he did not pursue them for long.

The sheer number of compositions at this early stage is striking. Between 1870, when the first extant piano Lied (to a text by Friedrich Christian Daniel Schubart) was written, and 1883—the year after his *Abitur*—Strauss wrote a positively intimidating array of works: eleven compositions bearing an opus number, a host of pieces for piano, six short sonatas, three long ones, and several orchestral compositions; the latter included two sizeable solo concerts, a symphony, two piano trios, and a string quartet. Nor were the pieces performed in Munich alone. A chorus that Strauss composed as a kind of warm-up for Sophocles' *Electra* was played at the Gymnasium he attended. When he was just sixteen, his String Quartet Op. 2 (written the previous year) was premiered. Two days later, on March 16, 1881, a soirée hosted by the court singer Cornelie Meysenheim (1853–1923) featured the performance of three Lieder. Strauss's Symphony in D minor (which he later repudiated) debuted on March 26, 1881; it was conducted by Hofkapellmeister Hermann Levi (1839–1900). Even if this performance left no enduring impression, it was clear that the composer would prove more than a fleeting presence in the public eye.

During this period, attention to, and mechanisms for, recruiting new talent were so elaborate that even a young composer without contacts at court or a wealthy family had plenty of opportunities to make a name for himself. Thus, in 1882, Franz Wüllner conducted the premiere of the Serenade for Wind Instruments, Op. 7, in Dresden; Strauss's Violin Concerto, adapted for piano, debuted in Vienna. In 1883, Levi conducted the Concert Ouverture in C-minor in Munich; that same year, in December, Hans von Bülow directed the premiere of the Suite in B♭ major, Op. 4. Only a few months later, the Symphony in F minor, Op. 12, premiered at the New York Philharmonic Society, under the baton of Theodor Thomas. At a mere nineteen years of age, then, Strauss already held a major position in the world of music. No other nineteenth-century composer—and certainly no one of his generation—experienced such a meteoric rise. All the same, he was careful to avoid sensation, now and later. The tension between an *oeuvre* that commanded notice (and, indeed, sparked controversy) and a restrained artistic persona ultimately—from the 1920s on—gave rise to inner and outer conflicts of greater and greater intensity.

Naturally, Strauss's first teachers were members of the Hofkapelle. He received piano lessons from August Tombo (1842–1878), harpist in the Court Orchestra, then horn player Carl Niest (who was born before 1826 and died after 1870). Benno Walter (1847–1901) taught Strauss violin and later premiered his Violin Concerto. At the age of eleven—that is, from 1875 on—Strauss received lessons in composition from Kapellmeister Friedrich Wilhelm Meyer (1818–1893). Munich's musical dynamism shaped Strauss through and through. In contrast to his father, who was drawn to Brahms, the young man fell under the spell of Wagner. In particular, he was captivated by the latter's "Munich" compositions that followed the *Ring* cycle: *Tristan* and *Meistersinger*. These works would prove important for Strauss all his life: the former for its tonal language, and the latter for its vision of communal life liberated from hierarchy through music. (Indeed, the "closing address" delivered by Sir Morosus in *Die Schweigsame Frau* [1935] may be viewed as an inversion of the finale of *Meistersinger*: Hans Sachs addressing the modern condition.)

Artists, musicians, writers, and intellectuals flocked to Munich because of the patronage of the arts under Ludwig II and his de facto successor, Prince Regent Luitpold (the brother of Maximilian II). The city exercised an all but magical pull on those born between 1865 and 1890. Sure that its unique atmosphere would foster creativity and provide an appropriate setting for their works, they came in droves to the old town and the burgeoning periphery (Schwabing, for example). The unconditional and commanding Wagnerian project, overflowing with productive tension, defined this milieu; its echoes could be heard time and again—for instance, in 1885, when Levi conducted Anton Bruckner's Symphony No. 7 (a work dedicated to Ludwig II). Unlike Vienna, Paris, and, especially, the emergent metropolis of Berlin, Munich incorporated artists into "official" hierarchies, which still cultivated airs of leisure and luxury. Thomas Mann, who belonged to the new elite, poured the climate of political representation, robust formalism, and sophisticated detachment into the figure of Gustav von Aschenbach; later, his *Doctor Faustus* would come to stand as a monument to the city's atmosphere at the turn of the century. The influence of Nietzsche and Wagner encouraged the symbiosis of life and art, for good and for ill. In 1913, that influence drew an aspiring painter from Vienna who had failed to gain admission to the academy there: Adolf Hitler.

Munich's intellectual and artistic life combined local flair and sophistication from elsewhere. In this setting, aspects of the big city and industrialization that were readily felt, one way or another, in Vienna and Berlin were not so pronounced. As such, culture "belonged" to the likes of Ludwig Thoma and Otto Julius Bierbaum, Ludwig Ganghofer and Thomas Mann, Karl Valentin and Johannes R. Becher, Hermann Levi and Bruno Walter, Wilhelm Kienzl and Hans Pfitzner, Max Liebermann and Wassily Kandinsky, Franz von Stuck and *Der Blaue Reiter*. Urban planning followed a neoclassical design; whatever form a given aspect assumed, it ultimately adhered to the sensibility that had emerged during the reign of Otto I, founder of the Wittelsbach dynasty. Richard Strauss, who enjoyed the rare distinction of being a native son of Munich, took in his surroundings with a watchful eye, in keeping with the discernment of his friends in literary circles and the visual arts. Munich's historical depth and aura of antiquity amidst modern amenities surely impressed him at an early age. At any rate, as much is suggested by the bold and improbable plan, in 1926, to construct a Festival Hall in Athens (which ultimately came to naught). Strauss never concealed just how much Munich had shaped him, even though he also retained a certain reserve (a further point in common with Mann, resembling the latter's relationship to his hometown of Lübeck). The villa the composer finally built in Garmisch represents this combination of proximity and distance—like the ambivalence that pervades *Feuersnot*. "Munich and mental life" may be defined as a mixture of devotion and aversion; that, at any rate, would account for the weight—or lack thereof—that Strauss later attached to where the *Singspiel* premiered.

Family and Milieu

It is difficult to exaggerate the significance of the convergence of different social spheres in the Strauss household—on the one hand, a father bearing the stigma of illegitimacy but ennobled by a courtly appointment and professorship (at the Munich *Akademie der Tonkunst*); and, on the other, a mother who issued from the front ranks of the dynamic and wealthy bourgeoisie. Both sides of the family embodied possibilities for social advancement during the industrial age—especially in Munich.

Joseph Pschorr (1770–1841) had still belonged to the eighteenth century. He was of peasant origins, but marriage to Maria Theresia Hacker enabled him to found the Hacker-Pschorr brewing empire in 1793. The company owed its success to storing its products in an enormous cellar arrangement that kept them cool and fresh year round. In due course, the city became a center for the production and consumption of beer (which Oskar Panizza dubbed the "opium of Munich" in 1897).[3] Indeed, in 1850 Joseph Pschorr received the posthumous honor of having his marble bust featured in the "Bavaria," a hall of fame designed by Leo von Klenze. His son Georg Pschorr (1798–1867)—who, together with his brother Matthias, took over the brewery and advanced to the position of *Kommerzienrat*—was Franz Strauss's father-in-law. Josephine (in fact, Josepha) Pschorr played a key role in the family, as did her brother Georg (1830–1894), who was also musically inclined.[4] A further sign that the family had made good is the career of Georg's youngest son Robert

---

3 "Opium von München." Oskar Panizza, *Dialoge im Geiste Huttens: Dritter Dialog* (Zurich: Verlag der Diskussionen, 1897), 87.

4 It is interesting that one of Josephine's sisters had a connection with the Hoftheater: Marie married Jakob Moralt, the chief cashier, who came from a family of musicians; their grandson was the famous conductor Rudolf Moralt (1902–1958).

(1868–1930), who became a professor of organic chemistry in Berlin. His brother August (1862–1935) took the reins of the brewery, which, following the First World War and the ensuing economic crisis, became a publicly traded company.

Franz Strauss was sixteen years older than his wife. Not only did he embody the family's musical side, he was also caught up in the spectacular politics of art during Ludwig II's reign (even if he took a critical view of proceedings). It is impossible to say whether the marriage—which also produced a daughter, Berta Johanna (1867–1966)—was a happy one. Late in life (around 1940), Strauss described his father as "embittered" and "very vehement, short-tempered, tyrannical."[5] His mother's increasingly frequent hospital stays suggest that relations came to be difficult—if they were not so from the outset. Objections to the First Vatican Council were widespread in Bavaria and at court. With other members of the Pschorr family, Franz Strauss joined the Old Catholic Church. This step, which fitted a larger pattern, may be seen in terms of the desire to assert social status, and it would hold lasting significance for Richard Strauss, too. The will shown by such decisions is best understood in light of the fact that industrialization—which was proceeding at a breakneck pace elsewhere (for instance, Berlin)—occurred more slowly in Munich, where a certain social inertia prevailed.

The Pschorrs (who held imperial sympathies that were quite obvious during the First World War) always supported the composer and financed printing costs for his scores, stays at Georg Pschorr's villa at Feldafing, and travel—notably, the lengthy trip he took to Greece and Egypt for health reasons. Despite a willful nature, Strauss never broke with his family or, for that matter, with his extremely strict father; nor, apart from his first sojourn in Berlin, did he ever pursue a bohemian lifestyle. His first opera, *Guntram*, which appeared in a lavish edition, was dedicated to his parents, and a number of early works to assorted members of the extended family. Occasionally, the choice was surprising. For instance, *Der Rosenkavalier* is a comedy about adultery, complicated social anxieties, and painful efforts at decorum. Even though the work hardly corresponds to seemly, bourgeois

---

5 Willi Schuh, *Richard Strauss: A Chronicle of the Early Years 1864–1898*, trans. Mary Whittall (Cambridge: Cambridge University Press, 1982), 83.

schemes of self-representation, Strauss made a point of dedicating it to the Pschorrs.

At the same time—and like many painters of his generation (such as Franz von Stuck [1863–1928], who was almost the same age)—Strauss always sought to cultivate upper-class (*großbürgerlich*) propriety. Such airs did not contradict his positions at court (which he held until his mid-fifties) so much as complement them. The composer's roots in the economic bourgeoisie on his mother's side surely contributed to his commercial savvy when negotiating contracts as a conductor and a composer. Indeed, his business interests went so far that he eventually organized efforts to change copyright law. Strauss's financial independence was fundamentally threatened twice; the outcome of both World Wars seems to have represented a kind of personal defeat in his eyes. That said, Strauss wanted to secure his livelihood and social status actively. Personal achievement was meant to be the opposite of the bland comforts of a conservatory professorship. The villas he had built in Garmisch and Vienna—which both amounted to an outward display of resources invested in an independent existence—represent this bearing in direct manner. Significantly, the structures stood at a remove (Garmisch) or entertained a certain tension (Vienna) with the urban center.

This active artistic bearing may have had class origins, but it did not qualify as "bourgeois." Rather, it formed the outward aspect of a new understanding of self and human existence—what Hofmannstahl would later call "the social." Strauss cultivated this habitus early, and more and more from the 1890s on. While working on *Guntram*, he fell out with his friend, the composer Alexander Ritter (1833–1896) because the opera concludes with the complete opposite of artistic redemption exemplified by *Tannhäuser*, that is, the transfiguration Wagner's epigones embraced. Guntram, who belongs to a guild of singers, kills the tyrant Robert. This means that he has broken his vow to promote human improvement only through song. But that is not all. Guntram acknowledges that he is not motivated by general concern for others' welfare (or doubt about his calling), but by love for Freihild, the tyrant's wife. The regicide has betrayed the free and autonomous art he once swore to uphold. In consequence, he must renounce his calling. Guntram entreats the widow to govern benevolently, but the couple has no further prospects. The singer breaks his lyre, the symbol of his art and its bond; then he withdraws into isolation, without an instrument or anyone to hear him. The plot of the opera (whose premiere Strauss conducted) mirrors a step the composer took in his own life, if in refracted form. The same day the work was staged in Weimar, he announced his betrothal to Pauline de Ahna, who was playing Freihild. The artist must be actively engaged and acknowledge the institutions that anchor his life and work.

Education and Readings

Strauss's intellectual curiosity and restlessness, which his teachers had no trouble recognizing, was hardly limited to music. Although we cannot know the works he read in early years, his humanist schooling was clearly formative. It is unlikely that Strauss selected the first texts he set to music; the evident preference for poems by Ludwig Uhland fits within the canon of the educated classes. But when preparing for the *Abitur,* Strauss took up literature in a more systematic and personal manner. Besides music and reading, his most important intellectual activity was visiting museums and galleries, a practice he observed until the end of his life. For diversion from more purely intellectual pursuits, Strauss was fond of playing Skat (which he seems to have learned while in Berlin, in 1883). Around the turn of the century, this card game was remarkably well-regarded socially; indeed, Klabund (Alfred Henschke, 1890–1928) made an ironic monument (the "Skat Sonnet") to the pastime a section of his *Harfenjule.*

Strauss briefly attended university in Munich, where he pursued a philosophical course of study. His teachers were distinguished; some of them were among the scholars consulted by Maximilian II. Carl von Prantl, known for his *Geschichte der Logik im Abendlande* (History of Logic in the West), was the advocate of objective idealism—a perspective Strauss would soon take to task vigorously. In all likelihood, Moriz Carrière gave the young composer his first systematic exposure to philosophical aesthetics; needless to say, the interrelationship between form and expression in beauty would prove an abiding concern. In lectures on Shakespeare, Franz Muncker (who had published a book on Wagner in 1891) acquainted him with positivist literary historiography and source criticism; just a few years later, Strauss's *Macbeth* would turn this "objective" perspective on its head. Perhaps the most lasting effect came from Carrière's colleague and friend, the cultural historian Wilhelm Heinrich von Riehl (1823–1897). Contrary to the tenets of national liberalism (an increasingly influential school of thought), Riehl set out a model of human relations that stressed the role of ethics, not economics, in bridging social gaps: institutions that bear the mark of individual initiative are more important than the abstract, legal mechanisms of the state. The utopian vision of reconciled estates in *Der Rosenkavalier* would seem to attest to Riehl's influence.

During his studies, Strauss probably gave serious thought for the first time to the relationship between individual and society and the significance this holds for art. His later turn to "the social" in his works with Hofmannsthal may be viewed in this light. At university, the composer read Schopenhauer intensively and at length. The philosopher's focus on the connection between art and the Idea, writ large, informed Strauss's projects for years to come. Strauss came to doubt, more and more, that the substance of music belongs to the order of thinking and intellection. In particular, the diary he kept on his journey to Greece reflects sustained engagement and, ultimately, disagreement with the philosopher.[6] Reading Nietzsche, in turn, confirmed his rejection of Schopenhauer's claim that music is an art of ideas. In due course, Strauss became the radically atheistic proponent of a music that seeks to help human beings find a place in the world while avoiding abstraction and metaphysics. Both early and late in life, the composer denied that religion provides insight or existential reassurance; if anything, it strips human beings of responsibility for their deeds, and it does so to their detriment. This outlook affected Strauss's early friendships. For a few years from 1885 on, Alexander Ritter, the son of the Wagner patron Julie Ritter and a Wagner enthusiast himself, was an important interlocutor. (That said, Ritter does not have the distinction of prompting Strauss to engage with the master's music: in 1882, father and son had attended *Parsifal* rehearsals in Bayreuth.) Eventually, the dealings of the two men induced Strauss to distance himself from Wagner. Rejecting Schopenhauer's notion of absolute music meant not continuing the Wagnerian project. Instead, Strauss sought to make a productive break (and, as such, he acknowledged Wagner's importance for his own works for the rest of his life). This decision soon took form in

---

6 Willi Schuh (ed.), "Richard Strauss. Das Tagebuch der Griechenland- und Ägyptenreise (1882)," in *Richard Strauss-Jahrbuch* (1954), 89–96. Unfortunately the edition is incomplete.

Guntram—which is pointedly *not* the work of a Wagner acolyte—then in the composer's renunciation of instrumental music and his turn to opera.

The other major friendship struck in this period was with Ludwig (Louis) Thuille (1861–1907). Thuille hailed from Bolzano, studied under Joseph Rheinberger, and also succumbed to the Wagner craze in Munich (where, ultimately, he came to fill his teacher's position as professor of composition). With him, Strauss discussed technical aspects of musical craft. Relations eventually cooled, but not until the turn of the century. Their exchanges inform key aspects of Strauss's treatment of Berlioz's *Treatise on Orchestration*. In this context, Strauss also gave Wagner's writings a systematic reading. Even as Strauss came to lead a more socially visible life, he continued to show reserve in matters of genuine amity. (Exceptions include his association with Engelbert Humperdinck, which began in Cologne in 1885.) It is unclear whether the composer formed any lasting friendships after 1900; the acquaintances he made in Thuille's circle (for example, Max von Schillings and Siegmund von Hausegger) stayed in the realm of formality. Indeed, Strauss and Hofmannsthal observed a respectful distance to the last—perhaps because they both realized that it benefited their collaboration. It has become commonplace to declare that the composer cultivated a willful aloofness. Yet reports to the contrary also exist. Thus, the memoirs of Lily Braun (1865–1916), an early advocate of women's rights, recounts a *soirée* hosted by her aunt in Weimar:

> A few friends from out of town, writers and theater impresarios who had come for the meeting of the Goethe Society, were gathered here; off in the corner, Richard Strauss—the pale, young Kapellmeister most of the others laughed at—stood shyly, like one of the house's children, at the home of the kindly woman who had just nursed him in his grievous illness.[7]

Here, one gets a very different picture of the composer.

All his life, Strauss held to a pragmatic understanding of education and culture. Learning may lay the foundation for identity, but it does not

---

7 "Ein paar auswärtige Freunde, Schriftsteller und Theaterdirektoren, die zum bevorstehenden Goethe-Gesellschaftstag schon angekommen waren, fanden sich ein; Richard Strauß stand schüchtern in einer Ecke, der blasse junge Kapellmeister, den die meisten verlachten, und der hier bei der gütigen Frau, die ihn eben in schwerer Krankheit gepflegt hatte, wie ein Kind im Hause war." Lily Braun, *Memoiren einer Sozialistin: Lehrjahre* (Munich: Albert Langen, 1909), 405. Braun recalled a young singer, daughter of a Bavarian colonel (406).

necessarily signify anything more. He avidly read young authors, often making personal acquaintance and setting their works to music. Around the turn of the century, the composer had contact with almost all the major writers of the day: Frank Wedekind, Otto Julius Bierbaum, Gerhart Hauptmann, Richard Dehmel, and others. Strauss's library contained a broad array of works—many of them inscribed—and he consulted them with musical adaptation in mind. As a rule, he showed a preference for lyric poetry, but he did not neglect drama. There is no knowing whether Strauss took a particular interest in modern novels (from Fontane on), but he demonstrated a certain fondness for Dostoevsky and Turgenev. Until about 1920, Strauss's appetite for new works was positively rabid, and his literary diet was constantly changing, thanks especially to his discussions with Hofmannsthal. Afterward, his hunger appears to have let off; it seems the canon he consulted in his time at the Vienna Opera was small. It is also impossible to determine whether Strauss read the major novels of the 1920s—or how familiar he was with the works of Thomas Mann (who had been on close terms with the Pringsheim family during his time in Munich). Leaving aside Strauss's age at this point— his sixtieth birthday was fast approaching—it is not idle to ask whether the composer changed his habits in response to a mounting sense of estrangement. Even though he took careful note of musical developments, Strauss felt out of step with the times. In this light, his turn to incontestable "classics"—especially Goethe—during the 1930s amounted to the taking of a pessimistic position with respect to contemporary events. Earlier in life, too, Strauss did not read with an eye to "maturation" in the Enlightenment sense of culture and education. Instead, he did so to secure his own bearings in an ongoing process of metamorphosis and change. The outlook he learned from Goethe—which knows no real vanishing point—may have prompted him to become more and more focused in his life and work, lest it prove aimless.

CHAPTER TWO

The End of the Nineteenth Century

LEAVING TRADITIONAL GENRES BEHIND

Strauss and Tradition

Strauss was born the same year as Eugen d'Albert, and the same year that Leo von Kienze died. In Paris, Giacomo Meyerbeer passed away; even as Europe fell under Wagner's spell, his grand operas continued to fascinate the continent. Gustav Mahler had been born four years earlier, in 1860. Like Strauss, he would achieve renown as a composer, conductor, and impresario. Even if the two men were opposites in terms of musical sensibility, Strauss acknowleged his contemporary's merits and directed performances of his works. In 1868, when Strauss was about four, the musicologist Moritz Hauptmann died in Leipzig, and Gioacchino Rossini died in Paris; the latter had not written an opera for some four decades. That same year, the musical embodiment of the Wilhelmine age, Max von Schillings, was born in Düren; Strauss had at least some contact with him during the middle period of his career. Also in 1868, Franz Lachner, Hofkapellmeister in Munich, retired; he had known Beethoven and Schubert personally, and he regaled the young Strauss with tales of them. When Strauss was about ten, Georges Bizet departed this world, and Maurice Ravel and Thomas Mann entered it. The previous year—1874, when Hugo von Hofmannsthal and Arnold Schoenberg were born—Johann Strauss premiered *Die Fledermaus,* which would come to stand as his greatest success. The work's combination of mannered pretense and social criticism is the very essence of of the Viennese operetta.

Along with the works of Jacques Offenbach, it held a singular attraction for Hofmannsthal and Strauss, who viewed operetta as a fitting response to the challenges of the twentieth century. In the mid-1870s, Johannes Brahms and Anton Bruckner took the stage with their major orchestral works, whom overheated critics styled as the antagonists of the age of the symphony.

Shortly before Strauss completed his *Abitur*, a serious fire—at a production of Offenbach's *Contes d'Hoffmann*—destroyed the Vienna Ringtheater. (Anton Bruckner had been on the verge of attending that evening.) The catastrophe, which claimed hundreds of victims, may be viewed as a sign of the state of opera in the final part of the nineteenth century: an institution sinking and reemerging from the flames as a professionalized enterprise. Construction of the Vienna Hofoper was completed in 1869 as part of the vast Ringstrasse project, and it provided a striking monument to the same will for renewal. Eduard Hanslick—who had no idea what to make of Strauss's orchestral works and ultimately rejected them—saw to it that a bust of Wagner (by August Sommer) adorned the foyer. Shortly after Strauss finished *Gymnasium*, Friedrich von Flotow died. He embodied a bourgeois opera tradition that existed in parallel to Wagnerism, as it were. His *Martha oder Der Markt von Richmond*, which premiered in Vienna, enjoyed vast success; the work proclaims a utopian social harmony (with aristocratic coloration) that spans all estates. After the turn of the century it again achieved a certain prominence as an example of the *Spieloper*, along with an array of comparable works of varied provenance and against the backdrop of *Der Rosenkavalier*.

In a sense, then, competing claims, if not realities, that centered on Wagner's *oeuvre* framed the final third of the nineteenth century. As far as it occurred largely (but by no means exclusively) in reference to German works, Strauss's musical development took up this conflict between compositional schemes that stressed historical awareness and approaches that emphasized discontinuity: Brahms and Wagner, tradition and rupture. Because he never trained at a conservatory, Strauss avoided the pitfalls of technical formalism and ideological battles, managing to preserve relative independence. For the most part, the emergent "German canon," which purposefully eschewed depth, determined his relationship to tradition.

Nietzsche, the unsparing critic of the age's historicizing tendencies, deemed "sacred German music"[1]—whose "vast solar orbit" stretched "from Bach to Beethoven, from Beethoven to Wagner"[2]—to be a late bloomer. For him, this was a point of merit, which to some extent freed it from the entanglements of contingency. Strauss made Nietzsche's view his own, and it shaped his relationship to tradition more and more over time. Unlike Brahms, Strauss remained unmoved by the idea that objectivity admitted generalization in the form of "the historical"; for him, the canon that opened onto modernity and modernism remained fixed and narrow.

Strauss's upbringing and the circumstances attending his entry into the musical world, which did not follow a regular course, may be deemed responsible for this outlook. All the same, it is remarkable that the composer, in spite of his education and reading habits, showed such reserve with regard to musical history—that is, proved so skeptical about making inherited forms his own (even the sonata). On a few occasions, he did reach back to works of the past; examples include Jean-Baptiste Lully (1632–1687) in the context of *Ariadne*, François Couperin (1668–1733) for his *Little Suite*, and a small number of forebears when composing *Die Schweigsame Frau* and *Capriccio*. In each case, however, Strauss did so for the purpose of securing his own position. Nor is it altogether surprising that these instances involved French music (with the exception of Monteverdi in *Die Schweigsame Frau*). Moreover, Strauss's adaptations—most strikingly of Mozart (*Idomeneo*), Beethoven (*Die Ruinen von Athen*), and Gluck (*Iphigènie en Tauride*)—belong to the more general turn towards antiquity that he made as a composer. In other words, they do not attest to a historical interest, much less a historicizing effort to revive the music of the past. The same attitude is evident in Strauss's concert programming. If he was conservative when picking operas to direct, he showed himself to be flexible, and even bold, in his choice of music to conduct.

---

1 Friedrich Nietzsche, *Untimely Meditations,* ed. Daniel Breazeale, trans. Reginald J. Hollingdale, (Cambridge: Cambridge University Press, 2014), 192.
2 Friedrich Nietzsche, *The Birth of Tragedy or Hellenism and Pessimism,* trans. William A. Haussman (Edinburgh, London: Foulis, 1910), 151.

During his final season as imperial Hofkapellmeister (1917–1918) at the end of the First World War,[3] selections ranged from Haydn, Mozart, Beethoven, and sometimes Bach, up to Schubert, Brahms, and Liszt. At the same time, Strauss made a point of including newer works (for instance, Mahler's Symphony No. 1), and he also conducted premieres (for example, Waldemar von Bausznern's Symphony No. 4).

"I can think only in terms of music history; here, the standpoint is starkly Wagnerian: the classics from Bach to *Beethoven, and from there* just a single line: Liszt, Berlioz, Wagner, and my own, modest self,"[4] Strauss declared late in life, summing up his resolute, and somewhat narrow-minded outlook. His view of tradition was teleological through and through. Like Nietzsche, Strauss had a fundamentally skeptical attitude from the outset, which became more and more pronounced as time went on. In 1944, he affirmed that "the *melody* introduced by *Mozart*, Beethoven, and Schubert and the *language* perfected by the Wagnerian and Straussian orchestra stand as the conclusion and apogee of mankind's cultural development to date."[5] In other words, Strauss considered himself the heir to, and ambassador of, a tradition culminating in Wagner, who had redeemed "the Christian-Germanic *mythos* in his sublime musical and dramatic creations." Thus he declared the following year, while working on *Metamorphosen*, "three thousand years of cultural evolution became fulfilled."[6]

This pronouncement, while exaggerated, is wholly in line with Nietzsche: the story of music follows a dynamic course; whatever

---

3 Strauss rested until 1920, but the institutional conditions after the end of monarchy are not comparable.

4 "Ich kann nur in Musik*geschichte* denken und da gibt es nur einen ganz schroffen Wagnerschen Standpunkt: die Klassiker von Bach ab bis *Beethoven, von da* nur die eine Linie: Liszt, Berlioz, Wagner und meine bescheidene Wenigkeit." Richard Strauss, *Briefwechsel mit Willi Schuh*, ed. Willi Schuh (Zurich and Freiburg: Atlantis, 1969), 49; letter of October 8, 1943.

5 "Daß das Erscheinen der *Melodie Mozarts*, Beethovens, Schuberts und die Vollendung der *Sprache* des Wagnerschen und Strausschen Orchesters der Abschluß und Gipfel der bisherigen Culturentwicklung der Menschheit ist." *Briefwechsel mit Willi Schuh*, 66; letter of May 1, 1944.

6 "Den christlich-germanischen Mythos in vollendeten musikalischen und dramatischen Schöpfungen; eine 3000-jährige Kulturentwicklung abgeschlossen." Franz Grasberger (ed.), *Der Strom der Töne trug mich fort: Die Welt um Richard Strauss in Briefen* (Tutzing: Schneider, 1967), 440; letter of summer 1945 to Ernst Reisinger.

historicists might affirm, it does not amount to a succession of discrete episodes and styles now to be used at will. Each and every time that Strauss wrote a composition with an eye on history—say, in making reference to Mozart in the Suite in B♭ for 13 Wind Instruments, Op. 4, or to Beethoven in *Ein Heldenleben*—he did so both to show reverence and to stake out his own ground. Thus, he dedicated Sonatina No. 2 (1945) "To the guardian spirits of the divine Mozart at the end of a grateful life" (*Den Manen des göttlichen Mozart am Ende eines dankerfüllten Lebens*). Such a stance was already evident in *Ein Heldenleben*, the first work to offer an array of quotations from the composer's own *oeuvre*. Tellingly, Strauss wrote it when his artistic path was at the crossroads between instrumental and operatic composition.

Early on, Strauss made a point of laying claim to key traditions of the nineteenth century (for instance, the work of Felix Mendelssohn Bartholdy in the Cello Sonata, Op. 6). He did not do so in order to continue them, but because he wanted, ultimately, to be able to cast them aside. At the same time, however, this bearing was not meant to offer a promise, much less herald a prophecy. Strauss's skeptical outlook sought definition and limits; his compositions in the 1920s made this abundantly clear, but this attitude had shaped his work from the very beginning.

Inspiration and Compositional Craft

In 1897, Friedrich von Hausegger (1837–1899), a private tutor in musical aesthetics and history at the University in Graz—and father of the conductor and composer Siegmund von Hausegger—published excerpts from his book, *Die künstlerische Persönlichkeit* (The Artistic Personality).[7] He had sent questionnaires to artists he knew one way or another, including Hans Thoma, Max Liebermann, Otto Julius Bierbaum, Peter Rosegger, Engelbert Humperdinck, Wilhelm Kienzl, and Richard Strauss.[8] The fact that the latter answered at all might have been prompted by his esteem for the scholar, whose *Musik als Ausdruck* (Music as Expression, 1885) had,

---

7 Friedrich von Hausegger, *Die künstlerische Persönlichkeit* (Vienna: Carl Konegen, 1897).
8 See Siegmund von Hausegger (ed.), *Gesammelte Aufsätze* (Munich: Bruckmann, 1903), 372 ff. Some of the answers are here published verbatim, with the exception of Strauss, whose text is condensed in indirect speech (394 ff.).

in his eyes, definitively refuted Hanslick's *Vom Musikalisch-Schönen* (On the Musically Beautiful).⁹ But the circuitous path to the publication of Strauss's full response says something, too. Hausegger only published some of the replies he received, and he put most of them in reported speech. Consequently, what Strauss shared was not available in complete, authorized form during his lifetime. Only after the composer's death could the public know all that he had said.¹⁰ This text affords a rare—indeed, unique—look at Strauss's understanding of his life and art. The key lies in the connection between "inspiration" and "technique":

> It is difficult to say how much what is usually called *technique* may be separated from what is called *inspiration—for what often seems to be inspiration is also just the product of a fantasy, which* (on the basis of assorted physiological conditions, of course) *works with elements that many years of education* [Bildung] *and a wealth of experience* [reich erfahrene Anschauung] *have provided in the way of material*. After all, "technique," in artistic production, is the name for the "ability to take all of the sensibility a[nd] artistic fantasy that one harbors *within* and bring it to light." In other words, consummate technique = optimally developed *fluency* [Sprachvermögen].¹¹

In affirming that technique and inspiration work together, the composer rejected the doctrine that inspiration is somehow an autonomous event. This is the same view that Hanslick had set forth in *Vom Musikalisch-Schönen*. However, Strauss went a step further and appealed to

---

9 "Es ist eigentlich unrichtig, in der Musik von Form zu sprechen." Friedrich von Hausegger, *Die Musik als Ausdruck* (Vienna: Carl Konegen, 1885), 66.

10 The first full and critical edition appeared in 1996, 100 years after the event; Richard Strauss, ["Schaffen"], in Walter Werbeck, *Die Tondichtungen von Richard Strauss* (Tutzing: Schneider, 1996; Dokumente und Studien zu Richard Strauss, 2), 534–539. All citations here follow this edition.

11 "Wie weit nun das, was man gemeinhin *Technik* nennt, von dem was man *Inspiration* nennt, zu trennen ist, ist schwer zu sagen—*denn was oft Inspiration erscheint, ist auch nur Product einer Phantasie, die* (natürlich auf Grund einer Reihe von physiologischen Voraussetzungen) *mit den Artikeln arbeitet, die ihr langjährige Bildung, reich erfahrene Anschauung als Material zugebracht haben*. Man nennt Technik bei künstlerischer Production doch wohl die 'Fähigkeit, Alles, was man Empfindung u. künstlerischer Fantasie *in* sich birgt, auch so an's *Tageslicht* zu bringen'—also höchste Technik = das reichste, am höchsten ausgebildete *Sprachvermögen*." Strauss, "Schaffen," *Die Tondichtungen von Richard Strauss*, 35. The citation mentioned by Strauss could not be verified, but it is close to Oskar Panizza (*Genie und Wahnsinn*, published in 1891).

Schopenhauer and Nietzsche. Specifically, he invoked the latter's polemic in the first volume of *Human, All Too Human* (1878):

> Artists have an interest in the existence of a belief in the sudden occurrence of ideas, in so-called inspirations; as though the idea of a work of art, a poem, the basic proposition of a philosophy flashed down from heaven like a ray of divine grace. In reality, the imagination of a good artist or thinker is productive continually, of good, mediocre, and bad things, but his *power of judgement*, sharpened and practised to the highest degree, rejects, selects, knots together; as we can now see from Beethoven's notebooks how the most glorious melodies were put together gradually and as it were culled out of many beginnings. He who selects less rigorously and likes to give himself up to his imitative memory can, under the right circumstances, become a great improviser; but artistic improvisation is something very inferior in relation to the serious and carefully fashioned artistic idea. All the great artists have been great workers, inexhaustible not only in invention but also in rejecting, sifting, transforming, ordering.[12]

Like Hanslick, Strauss did not believe that musical forms owe their existence to external stimuli or sources; the connection between a musical idea and attendant circumstances is arbitrary. Yet he also held that invention does not occur spiritually so much as "physiologically," and that "technique" grants it viable form. This view stands much closer to that of Nietzsche, who had declared much the same when valorizing the artist's "judgment" (*Urteilskraft*). "Fluency" prevails so far as inspiration—conceived along Schopenhauerian lines as melody—matches up with technique and content ("expression"):

> such "optimally developed fluency" is also the result of an "extraordinary *need for expression.*" Writing a good fugue in five voices is no sign of great "technique"; it is just a matter of craftsmanship, unless the fugue "expresses" something—which means going beyond "simply arranging five voices well." Academic critics often fault me . . . for offering colossally elaborate orchestral technique, rich polyphony, and artful formal innovation in my works,

---

12 Friedrich Nietzsche, *Human, All Too Human*, trans. R. J. Hollingdale (Cambridge: Cambridge University Press, 1996), 83.

but being lazy about musical *invention* (a favorite term among Hanslick's followers).[13]

All his life, Strauss insisted that inspiration cannot be separated from technique; invention and labor necessarily occur in tandem. A brief sequence in the prelude to *Ariadne* makes this point through parody: amidst the confusion attending preparations for the evening's opera, the hapless composer experiences a sudden flash of inspiration. Alas, circumstances demand that he remain focused on the work he has already completed (*das "Gearbeitete"*) and let the idea pass.

By the same token, Strauss held that music seeking to compensate for inadequate inspiration through technical virtuosity is inauthentic. Thus, in response to Hausegger's questions, he defended himself against charges that his scores were too complicated by declaring that he employed technique in order to achieve "the greatest simplicity possible"; "there's no struggle for originality in a real artist."[14] In other words, it is necessary to cultivate and constantly train one's musical "fluency" to hone and refine one's art. In appealing to the synthesis of "inspiration" and "technique," Strauss flattened the dominant principle of the nineteenth-century (and, for that matter, twentieth-century) academic tradition. Indeed, he stood the principle on its head: mastering "technique" means nothing if it is not combined, from the outset, with "expressive will" (*Ausdruckswille*). Hereby, inspiration does not represent a metaphysical, revelatory, or para-religious event. It boils down to a physiological phenomenon, which is justified only insofar as it realizes the potential for communication. The manual, purely craftsmanlike, aspect of the process occupies a central position because new forms can be brought forth only by shaping

---

13 "Ein solch 'höchst ausgebildetes Sprachvermögen' ist aber doch auch nur das Resultat eines 'außerordentlichen *Ausdrucksbedürfnisses*' (eine gute 5stimmige Fuge zu schreiben, ist doch kein Zeichen großer 'Technik,' das gehört erst unter die Rubrik der Handwerkergeschicklichkeit). (Wenn die Fuge nicht etwas 'ausdrückt,', was über die 'gute Führung der 5 Stimmen an sich' hinaus ist.) Man wirft mir (da ich nun doch von mir reden soll) in Zunftkritiken des öfteren vor, daß ich eine kolossal entwickelte Orchestertechnik, reiche Polyphonie, kunstvolle neue Formgestaltungen in meinen Arbeiten biete, daß es aber mit der musikalischen '*Erfindung*' (so ein beliebtes Wort bei den Hanslickianern) faul sei." Strauss, "Schaffen," *Die Tondichtungen von Richard Strauss*, 535.

14 "*nach möglichster Einfachheit*," "ein *Streben* nach Originalität gibt's bei einem wirklichen Künstler nicht." Ibid., 536.

and reshaping. Stefan Zweig noted, in 1931, that for Strauss matters of inspiration stood subordinate to concrete concerns. The correspondence with Hofmannsthal contains many instances where the composer bids his collaborator to view "technical" aspects of projects along mechanical lines. Strauss only seems glib when he makes comments such as "My work is flowing along like the Loisach."[15] In fact, such offhand remarks indicate that the workmanlike aspects of composition are what make it possible for inspiration to keep coming. The process involves constant fine-tuning and revision. If the final copies of his scores are flawless, Strauss's notebooks meticulously record details and points to be reworked. Indeed, the composer demonstrated the same attitude late in life when he decided to remedy the financial hardship he was experiencing in Switzerland by making new, manuscript copies of scores in order to sell them. The fact that he referred to his late works as *Handgelenksübungen*, or "wrist-exercises," suggests much the same.

"Technique," then, involves achieving more and more finely tuned control over the ability to "speak" in composition. At all stages of his career, Strauss made sure to keep conducting. On the one hand, he did so in order to master the music of others. But this is also what enabled him to realize his vision for his own works. The score Strauss used when conducting *Tristan* in Weimar has been preserved; the many notes on dynamics (always opting for understatement) seek to grant greater plasticity to connections between words and music—that is, to augment "comprehensibility." The same ambition is evident in the prologues to *Intermezzo* (1923–1924) and, even more, *Capriccio* (1941–1942): technique should not be an end unto itself, but should enhance clarity, and this bears on performance, too. In other words, the "expression" Strauss envisioned did not mean heightening foreground effects; in this regard, he followed Bülow's recommendations all his life. Rather, he aimed to make musical parameters as flexible as possible by means of orchestration. The constellation of instruments produces what Hofmannsthal called "coloration" and, at the same time, yields constitutive lines of polyphony, whereby each instrument receives marked, structural significance. Such an arrangement not

---

15 "Meine Arbeit fließt wie die Loisach." Willi Schuh (ed.), *Richard Strauss. Hugo von Hofmannsthal. Briefwechsel*, 5th edition (Zurich and Freiburg: Atlantis, 1978, originally 1926), 61; letter of May 16, 1909.

only combines melody and harmony into a new, consolidated unity but also unfolds as "psychic polyphony"[16]: musical components as a whole constitute a kind of vocabulary. "Technique" ceases to provide a norm or value in itself as it fades into elaborate, artful detail.

In 1907, Klaus Pringsheim (Katia Mann's twin brother) observed that Strauss was abandoning, "more and more, the paths of 'correct,' analytical polyphony" and, "with the grandiose recklessness of one supremely possessed of himself, forcing his way to a wholly new style."[17] The possibilities Strauss opened in this way were most evident in harmonic terms. Much earlier, his *Macbeth* (1888) had exploded the putative autonomy of formal logic that Hanslick had celebrated and brought forth a processual tonal idiom. The same approach to harmonics—that is, replacing cadence and major-minor shifts with sweeping gestures that do not proceed in linear fashion—is still evident in *Liebe der Danae* (1938–1940, premiered in 1952) and *Metamorphosen* (1945–1946).

In this light, the diagnosis Adorno would later offer is clearly mistaken. Strauss's works do not herald the triumph of autonomous "technique" in the industrial age. Instead, technical aspects of composition provide the means for making all elements of musical syntax available; as they combine with inspiration, a new perspective (that is, the creation of new, associative relations) is disclosed. This vision no longer lays claim to universal validity; rather, it arises from individual, expressive will. Even tonality is affected—already in *Der Rosenkavalier*, it has lost its status as an independent function. Two principles prevail from start to finish in Strauss's works: the connection between the work of art and "expression"—in other words, the view that music is communication—and the idea that music must be immanently comprehensible (at least for those who are prepared and willing to "face" it).

---

16 "psychische Polyphonie." Richard Strauss, "Erinnerungen an die ersten Aufführungen meiner Werke", in *Betrachtungen und Erinnerungen*, ed. Willi Schuh, 2nd edition (Zurich: Atlantis, 1957), 230.

17 "immer mehr die Wege der 'korrekten' analytischen Polyphonie," "sich mit der selbstherrlichen Rücksichtslosigkeit Dessen, der sich seiner bewußt ist, zu einem gänzlich neuen Stile durchrang." Klaus Pringsheim, "Für Strauß," in *Die Zukunft* 15 (1907), 246–249; reprint in *Die Konfusion in der Musik*, 225.

Against Sonata Form: The End of Symphonic and Chamber Music

In a 1943 letter to music critic Willi Schuh (1900–1986)—whom he eventually declared his authorized biographer, the Eckermann to his Goethe—Richard Strauss summed up the aim of his compositional craft laconically, omitting his own Symphony in D minor: "At nineteen, I wrote my sole, and final, symphony; at twenty, *the* Piano Quartet; at twenty, *the* Violin Sonata—then it was over, and my symphonic works were just preparations for *Salome*."[18] Needless to say, one cannot take this self-assessment, projected backward onto youthful efforts, at face value. All the same, it is striking that during his first ten years of composing, Strauss covered almost all the instrumental genres (and, at the same time, wrote Lieder) yet had no intention of turning his efforts into a series of works. Given the enormous weight nearly all composers attached to the sonata and symphony in the second half of the nineteenth century, it is astonishing how nonchalantly Strauss brushed these forms aside—and at the beginning of his career, at that. He completed his first symphony at sixteen and his second—which would also be his last—at nineteen. His grand concertos for solo violin, piano, and horn were done by the time he was about twenty. Strauss finished his major chamber works—cello sonata, violin sonata, piano quartet, and piano trios— not long after his twenty-third birthday. He had completed his piano sonatas (which at one point seemed would prove the exception) by the time of his first publication, Op. 5; he was then sixteen. Comparison with his contemporaries underscores Strauss's determination. Arnold Schoenberg wrote his first published string quartet when he was already over thirty (and he had made a previous effort just a few years earlier before); his solo concerts for piano and violin are late compositions, as is *Fantasie für Violine und Klavier*. Claude Debussy did not dare compose a string quartet or sonata for cello or violin until he had reached maturity.

The extraordinary density and ambition of Strauss's engagement with traditional genres—which then broke off abruptly when he started working on *Macbeth* and *Don Juan*—is impressive, as shown in Table 2.1.

---

18 "Mit 19 Jahren schrieb ich meine einzige, letzte Sinfonie, mit 20 *das* Klavierquartett, mit 20 *die* Violinsonate—dann Schluß und meine sinf. Dichtungen waren nur Vorbereitungen zur Salome." *Briefwechsel mit Willi Schuh*, 49–51, here 49; letter of October 8, 1943.

Table 2.1 Early Works in "Major" Genres

Works are ordered (omitting extremely early pieces) by date of composition, with fair copy in brackets. When known, dates of premieres are also indicated.

Sonata [No. 1] in E major for Piano (November 1877)

Piano Trio [No. 1] in A major (December 20, 1877)

Piano Trio [No. 2] in D major (1878)

Grosse Sonate [Piano Sonata No. 2] in C minor (June 10, 1879)

Symphony [No. 1] in D minor (October 17, 1880) – Premiere: Munich 1881

String Quartet in A major, Op. 2 (November 14, 1880) – Premiere: Munich 1881

Piano Sonata [No. 3] in B minor, Op. 5 (Spring 1881)

Sonata in F major for Cello and Piano, Op. 6 (May 5, 1881, revised 1882–1883) – Premiere: Nuremberg 1883

Serenade in E♭ for 13 Wind Instruments, Op. 7 (November 11, 1881) – Premiere: Dresden 1882

Concerto for Violin and Orchestra in D minor, Op. 8 (March 22, 1882) – Premiere: Vienna 1882/Cologne 1890

Concerto for Horn and Orchestra in E♭ major [No. 1], Op. 11 (1883) – Premiere: Munich 1883/Meiningen 1885

Concert Ouverture in C minor (1883) – Premiere: Munich 1883

Symphony [No. 2] in F minor, Op. 12 (January 25, 1884) – Premiere: New York 1884

Suite in B♭ for 13 Wind Instruments, Op. 4 (September 29, 1884) – Premiere: Munich 1884

Piano Quartet in C minor, Op. 13 (January 1, 1885) – Premiere: Weimar 1885

Burlesque in D minor for Piano and Orchestra (February 24, 1886) – Premiere: Meiningen 1890

Sonata in E♭ for Violin and Piano, Op. 18 (November 1, 1887) – Premiere: Elberfeld 1888

It is difficult to say at what point Strauss really decided to leave traditional instrumental forms behind, but clearly he had done so by the time he was twenty-four, at the latest. In the letter to his mentor Hans von Bülow already quoted, which he wrote just a few weeks after his twentieth birthday, Strauss declared his intention with remarkable bluntness:

> From the F minor symphony onward I have found myself in a gradually ever increasing contradiction between the musical-poetic content that I want to convey a[nd] the ternary sonata form that has come down to us from the

classical composers. In the case of Beethoven the musical-poetic content was for the most part completely covered by this very "*Sonata form*," which he raised to its highest point, wholly expressing in it what he felt and wanted to say. Yet already there are to be found works of his (the last movement of the A♭ major sonata, Adagio of the A minor quartet, etc.), where for a new content he had to devise a new form.[19] Now, what was for Beethoven a "form" absolutely in congruity with the highest, most glorious content, is now, after 60 years, used as a formula inseparable from our instrumental music (which I strongly dispute), simply to accommodate and enclose a 'pure musical' (in the strictest and narrowest meaning of the word) content, or worse, to stuff and expand a content with which it does not correspond.[20]

Bülow was puzzled and recorded his reaction, in red ink, below (see Figure 2.1): "Theory can be grey or green, but practice is making beautiful, melodious music."[21] In coming years, Strauss would not only continue to shy away from inherited notions of aesthetic form; he also made a point of forging greater and greater distance from them. In the 1903 introduction to a book series he edited (*Die Musik*), he made an apodictic pronouncement: "At any rate, the error of those who deem the real essence of music more or less playful formalism may now be declared over and done with, once and for all."[22]

This process of irreverently cycling through inherited genres—only the two pieces for wind ensemble count as major works—connects with Strauss's first public appearances as a conductor. (Needless to say, the sites where early works premiered—Munich, Dresden, Vienna, and New York—were important musical centers of the day.) The Symphony No. 1 in D minor (1880), even while realizing key elements of the form, already departs from convention. As the piece's final turn shifts to the major

19 Here Piano Sonata, Op. 110 and String Quartet, Op. 132.
20 Hans von Bülow and Richard Strauss, *Correspondence*, trans. Anthony Gishford (London: Boosey & Hawkes, 1953), 82.
21 "Theorie grau u[nd] grün—aber Praxis heißt: schöne melodiöse Musik machen." Manuscript in Meiningen, Sammlung Musikgeschichte—Max-Reger-Archiv der Meininger Museen.
22 "Jedenfalls darf schon heute der Irrtum derer, die als das eigentliche Wesen der Musik nur einen mehr oder weniger spielerischen Formalismus bezeichnen, als überwunden erklärt werden." Richard Strauss, "Einleitung," in August Goöllerich, *Beethoven* (Berlin: Bard, Marquardt & Co, 1904), iii.

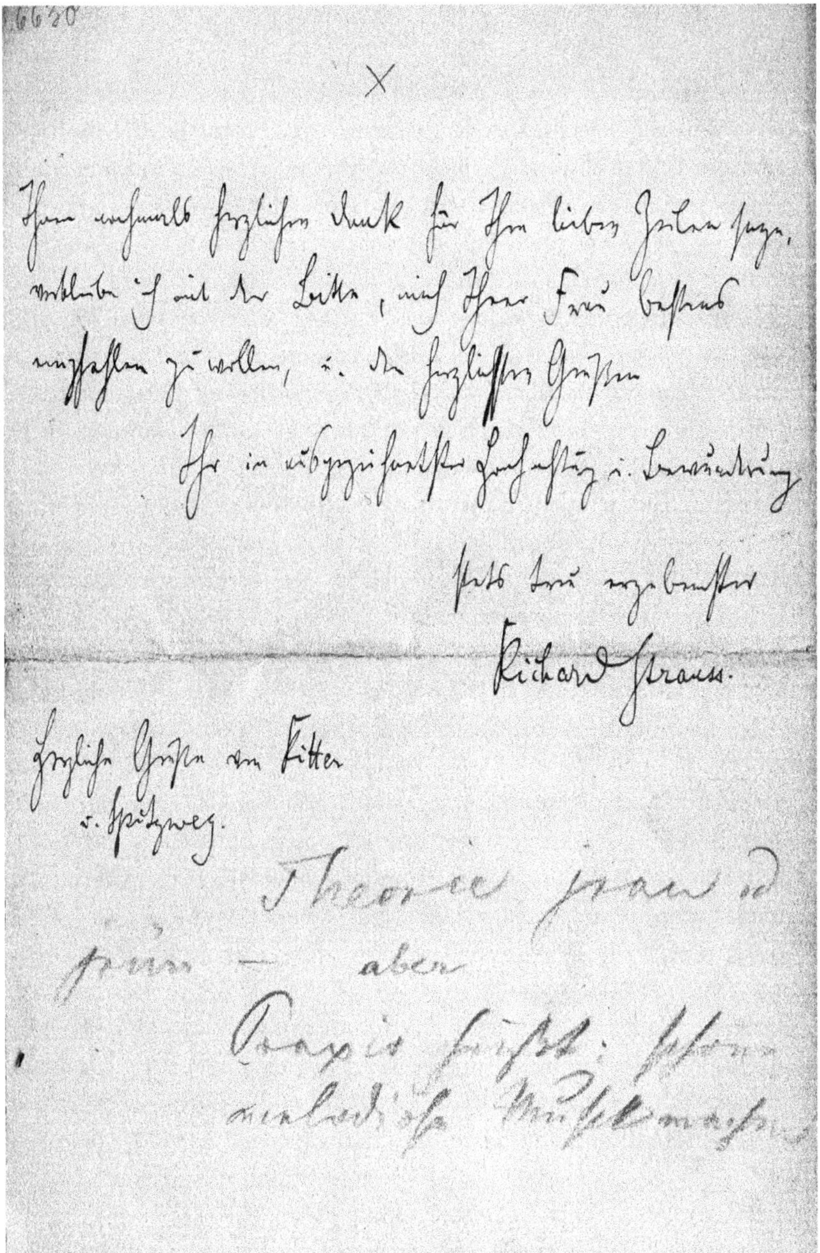
6630

X

Ihnen nochmals herzlichsten Dank für Ihren lieben Zeilen sagend, verbleibe ich mit der Bitte, mich Ihrer Frau bestens empfehlen zu wollen, u. den herzlichsten Grüssen

Ihr in aufrichtigster Hochachtung u. Bewunderung

stets treu ergebenster

Richard Strauss.

Herzliche Grüsse an Ritter u. Spitzweg.

Theorie grau ist grün — aber Praxis fehlt:

Figure 2.1 Richard Strauss to Hans von Bülow, August 24, 1888. Autograph letter with notes in red by Bülow.

This rather lengthy letter resembles a profession of faith — as always, with Strauss, a matter reserved for intimates and never shared with the public. That said, why the composer revealed so much to his mentor remains an enigma, since he could hardly count on the latter's sympathy. At the end of the letter, Bülow records his incomprehesion in red, describing Strauss's account as "gray theory" unsuited to the sphere of music.

Meiningen, Meinigner Museen, Schloss Elisabethenburg – Sammlung Musikgeschichte/ Max Reger-Archiv.

key, as in Beethoven's Ninth, it would be only natural to include a vocal allusion Yet Strauss declines to do so. Likewise, the composer's Symphony in F minor (1884) observes generic conventions while also calling them into question. Indeed, the choice of key is unusual: Tchaikovsky's Fourth Symphony (1877) provided the only major precedent, and Brahms had used it only in his chamber music and compositions for piano.[23] The overall structure deserves notice, too, as far as the order between slow and scherzo passages is "switched." The elegaic theme of the first movement is taken up again in the finale; significantly, the concluding move to a major key does not occur as an eruption of pathos (as in the Symphony in D minor) but as a festive transition to a hymnal theme that builds into a veritable frenzy. Bülow deemed the formally idiosyncratic work "altogether quite important."[24] Following its New York premiere, performances were held in the major German cities and in Switzerland. No one in the audience would have suspected that this was Strauss's way of leaving symphonic composition behind. In this light, the allusions, at beginning and end, of *Alpensinfonie* (1915) to the opening sequence of the Symphony in F minor likely amount to a declaration of the composer's overall artistic program.

Strauss's concertos for solo instruments point in the same direction. The Horn Concerto (1883), written in homage to his father, stands alone in formal terms. If the featured instrument accounts for this quality, such an explanation cannot explain the design of the Violin Concerto (1881–1883), in which a hymnal major key rings out as early as the first movement (which is as long as the two that follow). The last of the early concertos, for piano (1885–1886), bears an unusual title, *Burleske*; this name, which is traditionally reserved for an unaccompanied instrument, underscores the vast distance between Strauss and convention, eccentric virtuosity notwithstanding. The same kind of theme had been featured in the Cello Sonata (1883), but here—turned around and riddled with metrical shifts—it displays a broken, ironic form.

Finding models for Strauss's great orchestral works is no easy matter. Doing so for the chamber compositions proves more straightforward.

---

23 Bruckner's F minor symphony was surely unknown to Strauss.
24 Hans von Bülow, *Briefe*, vol. 6: *Meiningen 1880–1886*, ed. Marie von Bülow (Leipzig: Breitkopf & Härtel, 1907), 383; "recht sehr bedeutend," letter to Hermann Wolff, October 17, 1885.

The String Quartet gestures toward Beethoven in mediated fashion, by way of Felix Mendelssohn Bartholdy. One can readily imagine that the latter's works played a significant role in the Strauss home, as well as in the composer's discussions with Bülow. (Indeed, traces may be discerned in the finale of the Violin Concerto.) The Cello Sonata, especially the opening Allegro con brio, conspicuously incorporates Mendelssohn. Starting with three emphatic chords in F major (two on solo instrument, the third on piano alone), a principal theme unfolds in two parts before fading out in punctuated manner: a far-flung cantilena accompanied by broken chords. In a sense, the second theme inverts the first, building on the dominant chord in conventional fashion (albeit in C minor instead of C major); then, as the major key is taken up again, as if in reprise, both themes develop along traditional lines and blend into a harmonious continuum. At this juncture, Strauss enlists one of Mendelssohn's characteristic devices. The music calmly runs out and ends with an F major tonic. Instead of inaugurating a reprise, the lull gives way to a fugato derived from the principal theme, which eventually leads, through a complicated series of harmonics, to the dominant; only now, in a series of festive cadences, does it inaugurate the reprise—which culminates in an elaborate stretto. In contrast, the finale—allegro vivo—is a complex and layered sonata rondo. The key signals Mendelssohn, as does the elegant blending of formal elements —especially the free-standing coda with its exultant melody echoing the principal theme.

In contrast to the symphonies, a work like this (and other pieces with unusual properties, for instance the second Piano Trio in D major, whose finale starts with a passage in lento assai in an unconventional key) does not attest to the composer's awareness of a crisis. Chamber music seems to have been less "fraught" for Strauss; here, as in both his early piano trios, he demonstrates thoroughgoing effortlessness. Yet for this very reason it is all the more striking that, in the mid-1880s, he decided not to continue down this path. The woodwind compositions Op. 4 (1884) and Op. 7 (1881) occupy a threshold position. In terms of instrumentation and gesture, Strauss adopts an uncommon reference point: Mozart, in particular the *Gran Partita* K 361 (which counted as a true "Munich" piece). Such a commitment—Mozart would not provide a compositional model until about 1900, when an array of comparable works appeared—thus represents a historical standpoint. The Suite in B major, Op. 4, illustrates just how idiosyncratically Strauss viewed the musical past. The work comprises four movements. In fact, there is no reason to call it a suite, were it not that sequence of heterogeneous movements indicates as much: "Praeludium," "Romanze," "Gavotte," as well as "Introduction and Fugue." One feature unites them: the composer's avoidance of sonata form—that is, cyclical composition—until the fugue of the finale, which is not "heroic" but "cheerful." The curious historical perspective in evidence negates all the traditions that counted as obligatory during the nineteenth century. While an isolated case, this composition was entirely in character: at the very end of his life, Strauss took it up again in his sonatinas for woodwinds.

The decision no longer to observe standard practice is also remarkable because Strauss, who was just twenty, could clearly have done so without any difficulty at all. His mastery of the craft is plain, down to the finest points of instrumentation. Yet the decision only seems paradoxical: in fact, his virtuosity is what prompted him to dismiss inherited genres as formulaic. As a faithful reader of Nietzsche, Strauss always affirmed that music had but recently reached a point of technical refinement granting it a genuine connection to the other arts—indeed, assuring its preeminent status. Perfecting this standard represented the precondition for casting off all the traditions and rules that, in his eyes, no longer suited modern music—that is, the music of his own life and times.

CHAPTER THREE

The Poetry of Imagination

LIEDER

The Lied as a Form of Musical Thought

Strauss always—or at least from the mid-1880s on—stressed the significance Wagner held for his own compositional work. That said, major differences between them faded into the background over time. His father's influence may have prompted him to take conscious distance from his forebear, even though he felt his direct effect. Strauss approached Wagner's works and thinking with a certain diffidence—that is, he did not embrace them without reserve. On this score, he differed from his friend Alexander Ritter; indeed, it is why the two men ultimately parted ways (and Strauss abandoned Wagnerism as a whole). In contrast to Wagner, who basically neglected the poetic-musical genre of the Lied all his life (with the significant exception of the *Wesendonck-Lieder*), Strauss continually set lyric poetry to music. Such persistence also set him apart from his other major influences—Mozart, Beethoven, and Liszt—for whom the Lied had played no major role. At the same time, this attitude represents a point of connection with the very composers with whom Strauss increasingly felt he had little in common, for instance Schumann and Brahms. Indeed, it ties the composer to his contemporary Mahler, even though the latter asserted the relationship, however complex and tense, between song and symphony (that is, a genre Strauss considered largely obsolete).

Strauss's continuous production of Lieder is notable for bridging the divide between tone poems and operas, connecting his early and late works. For this self-appointed musical arbiter of modernity, the Lied played a singular role, which was not incidental either in quantitative or qualitative terms. A look at the chronology (Table 3.1) makes as much plain.

It is striking how regular the production of Lieder was until about the turn of the century: 203 in all, 176 for piano and twenty-seven for orchestra; these figures do not include later orchestral versions or works that are lost or remain fragmentary (apart from the exceptions specified).[1] After this point, more time passed between new efforts, especially from 1907 until 1917, a period that saw artistic fertility otherwise. What is more, the collections of Lieder published subsequently, with the exception of a flurry right at the end of the First World War, are insignificant. All the same, neither Strauss's unconditional turn to works for the stage nor his wife Pauline's retirement from professional singing in 1906 marked an important break. He still wrote another sixty-five Lieder. Even if one subtracts the orchestral cycles based on songs for piano, they number fifty-four—in other words, a good quarter of Strauss's overall production. Although the intensity of composition may have diminished, it is impossible to speak of increasing reserve with respect to this musical form.

The intimate and personal quality of the Lied genre is often reflected by dedications. However, Strauss demonstrated restraint; genuinely private qualities are evident in just a few, isolated cases. The four songs constituting Op. 27 are explicitly for "My dear Pauline, September 10, 1894"—that is, the day of the couple's wedding at the castle church of Marquartstein. Three years later, Strauss had plans for an orchestral adaptation, but he only completed the second and fourth songs (which Pauline also performed at the premiere). In 1948, in Montreux, he took up the idea of adapting the first Lied for orchestra, but by now his wife's ability to sing was a distant memory. Some late orchestral adaptations (such as Op. 32, No. 3, or Op. 36, No. 1) represent comparable undertakings.

---

1 The total number of Lieder depends on the boundaries used; the edition of all texts by Reinhold Schlötterer (*Die Texte der Lieder von Richard Strauss: Kritische Ausgabe*, Pfaffenhofen: Ludwig, 1988) lists 195 titles, including songs for stage and ensembles, but neglects the two later orchestrated cycles.

Table 3.1 Chronology of the Lieder

Dates indicate completion or, alternately, publication. "(O)" means "orchestral song"; songs arranged for orchestra at a later date have not been included, with the exception of the collection Strauss himself made in 1918 and the Brentano Cycle (Op. 68). The list also does not include two Lieder for larger ensembles (Der weisse Hirsch, TrV 6, for three voices and piano, and Alphorn, TrV 64).

Year	Number of Songs	Collections
1870	1	
1871	2	
1873	1	
1876	1	
1877	4	
1878	7, 1 (O)	
1879	3^1	
1880	3	
1883	1	
1885	9	1 (Op. 10)
1886	5	1 (Op. 15)
1887	6	1 (Op. 17)
1888	10	2 (Op. 19, Op. 22)
1890	5	1 (Op. 21)
1891	2	1 (Op. 26)
1894	4	1 (Op. 27)
1895	3	1 (Op. 29)
1896	9	2 (Op. 31, Op. 32)
1897	4 (O)	1 (Op. 33)
1898	15	3 (Op. 36, Op. 37, Op. 39)
1899	9, 2 (O)	3 (Op. 41, Op. 43, Op. 44)
1900	15	3 (Op. 46, Op. 47, Op. 48)
1901	8	1 (Op. 49)
1906	6, 2 (O)	2 (Op. 51^2, Op. 56)
1918	5 (O), 29	1^3, 4 (Op. 66, Op. 67, Op. 68, Op. 69)
1919	1	
1921	3 (O)	1 (Op. 71)

(continued)

Table 3.1 Continued

Year	Number of Songs	Collections
1922	1	
1925	1	
1928	5	1 (Op. 77)
1929	2	
1930	1	
1933	1	
1935	2	
1940	6 (O)	1 (Op. 68)[4]
1942	3	
1948	1, 4 (O)	

[1] Just the first of the three Lieder (TrV 75) survived entirely, from the second only the incipit; the third is lost.
[2] The first half of Op. 51 was printed in 1903.
[3] Without opus number; a collection of five Lieder from different operas, orchestrated later.
[4] Op. 68 was orchestrated later, and not as a coherent project (the first orchestration dates from 1933).

The six songs of Op. 37 are also dedicated "To my beloved wife, on 12 April"—in other words, the date the couple's first son, Franz, was born. All in all, Strauss shared very little private sentiment in composing the Lieder. Although he dedicated the Goethe poem *Gefunden* (No. 1 in the collection that would later become Op. 56) to his wife, the date recorded—August 8, 1903—refers to when he was awarded an honorary doctorate at Heidelberg; that is, it marks an external occasion. Strauss's final song, "Malven," which he composed almost in passing and completed in November 1948 in Montreux, is dedicated to Maria Jeritza; its riddling inscription reads, "To dear Maria, this final rose."[2] Most dedications were occasioned by friendly relations or kinship (for instance, *Krämerspiegel*, to Friedrich Rösch); however, it is difficult to establish a connection to lyrical "content." Only in isolated instances did dedications have a political significance—such as the earnest thanks Strauss expressed to

---

2 This Lied ("Der geliebten Maria diese letzte Rose") was first published after the death of the singer (1887–1982).

Joseph Goebbels in November 1933 for naming him president of the Reichsmusikkammer (*Das Bächlein*).

Initially, Strauss adhered to tradition; the first Lied given a number, *Zueignung* (Op. 10, No. 1), is an exemplary strophic song in C major. However, he soon came to treat convention with greater liberty. Early on, the composer became convinced that instrumental music had a limited scope. In this context, Lieder performed a corrective role: only by forging a connection between words and music could Strauss achieve the "plasticity" he desired. The intensity with which he composed songs during the 1890s—more than seventy works in the course of a decade—indicates that the genre provided a field of experimentation ahead of the composer's turn to opera. Efforts to devise a new array of motifs with a distinct character (following Schubert's lead, perhaps) moved to the fore. As much is evident in the fact that he conceived three collections of Lieder at the same time, in 1898. The third set, *Fünf Lieder*, Op. 39 (all but one of which were based on poems by Richard Dehmel), represent as many novel approaches to the form. *Leises Lied* abandons the underlying, declamatory mode at key points in order to find a new kind of cantability; *Befreit* observes models of melody and accompaniment as formal possibilities among others; *Junghexenlied* (a poem by Bierbaum) stages a miniature drama and, in so doing, dispenses with tonal unity (beginning in G major and ending in E major).

The Lieder of Op. 39 are no exception. The broad array of approaches that Strauss took to composing songs—up to *Vier letzte Lieder*—demonstrate that he wanted to avoid following a system. Their common feature is the unification of word and music, whereby—in contrast to Mahler, as well as to Schoenberg in his early years—poetic "tone" is not at issue. Strauss did not seek to "poeticize" the paradigm of instrumental music. Instead, he wanted to enlist lyric poetry to lend musical figures the physical, embodied quality he needed to compose operas. Accordingly, the Lieder do not "interpret" by means of music in the usual sense so much as they represent experiments for emancipating musical invention from its self-generated "autonomy." Strauss described how he would avoid anchoring composition in a poetic "tone":

> I take up a book of poems, flip through it in desultory fashion, and a poem pops up for which—often before I've even read it properly—a musical

thought occurs. . . . Obviously, music has been gathering inside, and music with a very specific content—now, when the vessel is full, so to speak, I strike upon a poem with a suitable content, and the *opus* is there in a blink of the eye [*im Handumdrehen*].³

When musical and poetic thoughts meet up, their convergence is not readily steered; yet it does give rise to a sonic figure with the desired plasticity. Once such concreteness has been achieved, the rest of the composition unfolds straightforwardly: "in a blink of the eye" (literally, "with a turn of the hand"). However little, the Lied offers leeway, or room for spontaneity—which is precisely what Strauss sought to achieve by giving up the formalist logic of instrumental music.

In his Symphony No. 1 (1888), Gustav Mahler had already combined song and orchestral music, taking the major theme of the first movement from *Lieder eines fahrenden Gesellen* (1883–1885). In contrast to "poeticization" of this kind, Strauss wanted musical reality to emerge from the interaction, indeed the collision, of words and notes. Musical effect should not be produced through the "tone" (nor, for that matter, is it ultimately "poetic"). Much later, *Capriccio* (1941–1942) would heighten this bearing even more: the concluding monologue of the Countess, by invoking the Lied, also signals the fleeting nature of this artistic form. Ultimately—and as her dialogue with her image in the mirror indicates— the "work" comprises reflections that in fact precede it: the planned festival, which provides the focus of the entire opera, does not occur on stage. In this light, the Lied represents the musical mode of thinking in which Strauss could see his conception of music and composition unfold most directly, unburdened by the demands entailed by "more important" forms. This is also why he avoided song cycles as a rule—in contrast to contemporaries (for instance, Mahler's *Lied von der Erde* [1908–1909] and Zemlinsky's *Lyrische Symphonie* [1922–1923]). Strauss sought to ensure that open space remain preserved; when he grouped songs, they were

---

3 "Ich nehme ein Gedichtbuch zur Hand, blättere es oberflächlich durch, es stößt mir ein Gedicht auf, zu dem sich, oft bevor ich es nur ordentlich durchgelesen habe, ein musikalischer Gedanke findet. . . . Offenbar hatte sich da innerlich Musik angesammelt u. zwar Musik ganz bestimmten Inhaltes—treffe ich nun da, wenn sozusagen das Gefäß bis oben voll ist, auf ein nur ungefähr im Inhalt correspondirendes Gedicht, so ist das opus im Handumdrehen da . . . ." Strauss, "Schaffen," *Die Tondichtungen von Richard Strauss*, 537.

held together by superficial traits—if at all. This understanding of form marked his distance from other German-language composers of the day, and he held to it all the more as the younger generation's abandonment of tonality threatened *melos*, its defining parameter.

Strauss as Reader and the Poetic Canon

Leaving aside 203 compositions later arranged for instruments—which constitute a cycle in their own right—there are 191 songs. They directly reflect Strauss's readings. Although they span almost eighty years of active composition, very little change in overall bearing can be seen. A look at the poets whose works Strauss set to music is instructive; see Table 3.2.

Not including the compositions of extreme youth—which adapt the established canon of the 1870s (for instance, Hoffmann von Fallersleben and Emanuel Geibel)—a significant pattern emerges from about 1880 on: Strauss mainly—indeed, almost exclusively—treats the lyric poetry of nascent modernism, that is, works by contemporary authors. In particular, this means the poets of his native Munich and surroundings, and to a lesser extent writers active in Berlin; the absence of modernists associated with Vienna, particularly Stefan George (1868–1933) and his circle, is plain. The same is evident, in reverse, in Strauss's preference for Richard Dehmel (1863–1920), George's opposite in many ways. On the whole, the composer stood close to the circle of bohemian poets grouped around Bruno Wille at Friedrichshagen (Müggelsee) in 1890; this group had its origins in Naturalism. Strauss was an avid reader all his life, although the details of his literary diet are unclear. But if determining the novels and dramas he read involves guesswork based on letters and books found in his library, the poetry he consulted may be identified with some certainty on the basis of his musical adaptations.[4] What is more, some copies of the anthologies he owned have been preserved, marginal notes and all. Strauss's own remarks, as we have seen above, also shed light on his habits. He did not set out looking for texts to set music so much as he read in order to alight upon correspondences with what he was already

---

4 One detail may be significant in illustrating the complexity of the context. Strauss's edition of the works of Goethe is preserved in Garmisch, extensively annotated. One can see, in this instance, that the composer knew the entire context of the poems he finally chose to set to music.

Table 3.2 Poets Set to Music

Author	Number of Poems	Cycles	Year(s) of Composition
Arnim	3		1918
Bethge	5	1	1928
Bierbaum	6	1	1895, 1896, 1898, 1900
Bodmann	2		1896, 1898
Brentano	6	1	1918
Bürger	1		1899
Burns/Freiligrath	1		1880
Busse	3	1	1896
Chamisso	1		1877
Dahn	9	2	1889–1890
Dehmel	11		1895, 1898, 1899, 1901
Des Knaben Wunderhorn	4		1896, 1898, 1901
Eichendorff	1		1948
Falke	1		1897
Geibel	2		1878, 1879
Gilm	9	1	1885
Goethe	15	1	1877, 1897, 1903, 1918, 1919, 1922, 1925, 1930, 1933, 1935, 1942
Greif	1		1899
Gruppe	1		1880
Hart	1		1894
Heine	7		1879, 1906, 1918
Henckell	9		1894, 1896, 1900, 1901, 1906
Hesse	3		1948
Hölderlin	3		1921
Hoffmann v. Fallersleben	7		1873, 1876, 1878
Kerr	12	1	1918
Klopstock	2		1897, 1899
Knobel	1		1948

Table 3.2 Continued

Author	Number of Poems	Cycles	Year(s) of Composition
Körner	1		1878
Lenau	3	1	1878, 1891
Liliencron	4		1896, 1898, 1899
Lindner	1		1898
Mackay	4		1894, 1896, 1899
C.F. Meyer	1		1906
Michelangelo	1		1896
Morgenstern	1		1899
Mündel	2		1901
Panizza	1		1901
Remer	1		1901
Rückert	10	1	1898, 1899, 1900, 1922, 1929, 1935
Sallet	1		1880
Schack	16	2	1886, 1887, 1888
Schubart	1		1870
Shakespeare	3	1	1918
Stieler	1		1883
Sturm	1		1879
Uhland	10	1	1871, 1877, 1899, 1900, 1902
Weinheber	2		1942

picturing in musical terms. If we take him at his word—and there is no reason not to do so—he viewed poetry as an auxiliary element for lending shape and form to music. Given the role he assigned poetry, there is nothing surprising about the prominence of current works or the temporal proximity between a poem's publication and a given musical adaptation. Examples abound: John Henry Mackay's (1864–1933) *Verführung* appeared in 1896, and Strauss set it to orchestral music almost right away; Bierbaum's *Wir beide wollen springen* was published and set to music the very same year—and the whole was promptly printed in *Jugend*; Paul Remer's (1867–1943) *In goldener Fälle* came out in 1899, and the composition appeared a mere two years later.

The up-to-date aspect of the poetry Strauss chose from the 1880s on has another feature: as a rule, the works of no single author are granted preference. Only a few authors received his sustained attention. Strauss acknowledged "genuine sympathy [*Verhältniß so aufrichtiger Teilnahme*]"[5] for the writings of Karl Henckell (1864–1929), who had fled to Zurich in the wake of the Anti-Socialist Laws, and he likewise esteemed the works of Otto Bierbaum, who edited *Pan*. Of course, he appreciated Dehmel and stuck to him despite (or perhaps because of) his *Venus consolatrix*, which had been banned as blasphemous. These three figures were the same age as the composer (and all died much earlier than he did). If Strauss adapted sixteen poems by Adolf Friedrich-Schack (1815–1894)—who was considerably older—he probably did so because the poet counted as a forerunner of the modernist sensibility in Munich. Otherwise, Strauss did not engage at length with many authors of the past apart from Goethe, whose works he consulted to the end. Exceptions include Friedrich Rückert (1788–1866) and Heinrich Heine (1797–1856)—in addition to Ludwig Uhland (1787–1862), for a brief period around the turn of the century. Often, Strauss knew writers personally and would send them the music to their poems with a dedication. Anton Lindner (1874–1929)—who drew the composer's attention to Oscar Wilde's *Salome*—received a copy of his own *Hochzeitlich Lied*, which remains preserved to this day (see Figure 3.1); he was "quite pleased"[6] and returned the favor by sending manuscript copies of poems Strauss had requested. Bierbaum dedicated *Traum durch die Dämmerung* to Strauss, who set it to music and published it with the author's inscription. When collecting songs for publication, the composer rarely grouped works by a single author together; where contemporaries were concerned, he did not do so at all (Bierbaum excepted).[7] Strauss followed the same practice even for the large-scale melodrama (about an hour in length) *Enoch Arden,* based on the work of

---

5 Schlötterer, *Die Texte*, 215; letter from Strauss to Karl Henckell, January 5, 1896; Schlötterer gives a facsimile of the entire letter.

6 "sehr gefreut." The print with the dedication is today part of a private collection in Munich, the letter from Lindner (January 1900) is published by Schlötterer, *Die Texte*, 242. In spite of this dialogue Strauss set no more poems by Lindner.

7 Three Lieder on texts by Carl Busse (Op. 31) were completed by a Lied after Dehmel. Although Schack, important for two collections (Op. 17 and Op. 19), was still alive when the prints were published, he wasn't seen as a member of Strauss's own generation.

Figure 3.1   Richard Strauss, Hochzeitlich Lied, op. 37/6, text by Anton Lindine
Dedicatory exemplar for Anton Lindner

Anton Lindner (1874–1929) was born in Lviv, but his family relocated to Vienna when he was a child. From Vienna Lindner drew Strauss' attention to Wilde's *Salome*. In 1898 Strauss published a collection of six songs as op. 37, the last one is Hochzeitlich Lied on a text of Lindner. The collection was published after the birth of his son Franz and dedicated to his wife Pauline, in the same year, when he moved to Berlin. From Berlin Strauss sent a copy of the separate print of No. 6 to Lindner with the dedication: "Dem Dichter—verehrungsvollst—der Componist". This is a good illustration of the close relationships Strauss had to many poets around 1900.

Munich, Private collection.

Alfred Tennyson (1809–1892). The piece was composed in 1897 for Ernst von Possart (1841–1921), the director of the Munich Court Theater. Even if Strauss dismissed the music as "occasional trash [*Gelegenheitsschund*], in the worst sense of the word,"[8] he still saw fit to number it among his *opera*.

After 1906, matters changed fundamentally: Strauss interrupted his composition of Lieder when he took up opera and began collaborating with Hofmannsthal. That said—and as numerous publications in 1918 make clear—he eventually returned to the genre (in contrast to, say, Schoenberg, who wrote only a smattering of songs after 1914). Now, however, Strauss observed a different principle for selecting texts. Once he had teamed up with a single poet—a venture that effectively persisted long after Hofmannsthal had died—the composer basically gave up on contemporary authors. The work that is the only major exception, *Krämerspiegel*, adapts poems by Alfred Kerr (1867–1948), who displayed a literary sensibility quite different from his peers. Moreover, this piece stands alone in transferring the ironic and parodic tone of the stage to the Lied. In brief, working with Hofmannsthal ended Strauss's engagement with contemporary lyric poetry, at least in practical terms. The composer's understanding of genre also changed. This shift did not bear on the process of composition (which Strauss never again addressed) so much as the way he sought out texts in order to lend concreteness to musical visions he already had. Two new factors entered the equation. First—as evidenced by the Brentano Cycle, Op. 68 (1918)—Strauss took up the form of the Lied to secure *melos*, which the menace of atonality now made him value more and more. Second, he granted the Lied an increasingly prominent role in the process of musical reflection and self-reflection. Goethe already occupied a position of key importance in Strauss and Hofmannsthal's joint efforts, helping the composer achieve the "plasticity" he desired. The great poet continued to prove important, too, especially because of his morphological writings (*Die Metamorphose der Pflanzen* [1817] and two poems on the transformation of animals and plants). It is hardly by chance that Strauss developed an interest in

---

8 Strauss in his "Schreibkalender" on February 26, 1897; Schuh, *Richard Strauss*, 298. The second melodrama (*Das Schloß am Meer*), composed 1899 (after Uhland), did not receive an opus number.

Joseph von Eichendorff (1788–1857), whom he had neglected until this point. *Tageszeiten* (completed in 1927) transfers the thought-form of the Lied to a choral work. This self-reflective quality might have been what fascinated Strauss in his very last songs, based on poems by Hermann Hesse (1877–1962); here, the composer took up a contemporary author again (hardly guessing that the poet had no particular fondness for his music and preferred the works of Othmar Schoeck).

Border-crossings: Lyric and Chorus

In addition to the Lieder, Strauss's choral compositions reveal how he engaged with the lyric. All his life, Strauss took on large-scale choral projects; the year he died, he still had plans for an elaborate adaptation of Hesse for chorus and orchestra (*Besinnung*). In contrast to the Lieder, however, the composer's choral works mark major shifts and occupy threshold positions in his creative activity. An overview (Table 3.3) shows not just the extent, but also the intensity, of Strauss's work in this regard.

Table 3.3   Chronology of Choral Works

Purely occasional compositions are not included.

Year	Opus	Genre/Title	Instrumentation	Poet(s)
1876		2 Lieder	Quartet, 4-voice choir	Eichendorff
1877		Mass (3 movements)	Quartet, 4-voice choir	
1880		7 Lieder	Quartet, 4-voice choir	Eichendorff, Gensichen, Reinick, Böttger
1881		Chorus	Unison male chorus, orchestra	Sophocles [*Electra*]
1884		Lied	4-voice male choir	Löwe
1885		14 *Wandrers Sturmlied*	6-voice choir, large orchestra	Goethe
1897		2 Chants	16-voice choir	Schiller/ Rückert

(*continued*)

Table 3.3 Continued

Purely occasional compositions are not included.

1897		Hymn	4-voice female choir, wind instruments, large orchestra	Schiller
1899		Soldatenlied	4-voice male choir	Kopisch
1899	45	Drei Männerchöre	4-voice male choir	Herder
1899	42	Zwei Männerchöre	4-voice male choir	Herder
1903	52	Taillefer	3 soloists, 8-voice choir, orchestra	Uhland
1905		6 Volkslied-bearbeitungen	4-voice male choir	[folk songs]
1906	55	Bardengesang	3 4-voice male choirs, large orchestra	Klopstock
1913	62	Deutsche Motette	4 soloists, 16-voice male choir	Rückert
1927	76	Die Tageszeiten	8-voice male choir, orchestra	Eichendorff
1929	78	Austria	Unison male chorus, large orchestra	Wildgans
1935		Die Göttin im Putzzimmer	8-voice choir	Rückert
1934		Olympische Hymne	8-voice choir, large orchestra	Lubahn
1935		Drei Männerchöre	4-voice male choir	Rückert
1938		Durch Einsamkeiten	4-voice male choir	Wildgans
1943		An den Baum Daphne	9-voice choir	[Gregor]

Leaving out early works for choir and the *Electra* chorus written while still at school, this panorama puts important milestones into relief. Strauss started *Wandrers Sturmlied* in the spring of 1885. Although he did not give the piece a generic designation, it stands in the choral ballad tradition and, at the same time, is expressly modeled on Brahms (specifically, the latter's *Nänie* and *Alt-Rhapsodie*); as such, it belongs to Strauss's effort to cycle through "traditional," nineteenth-century genres.

Example 3.1 Taillefer Op. 52, first occurrence of the Taillefer-motif.

Das ist der Tail - le - fer

Of course, as Strauss told Engelbert Humperdinck, music should "become as deep a[nd] philosophical as possible in form and content."[9] *Taillefer*, a monumental composition for choir, would seem to represent a final encounter with the form, even though certain breaks are already in evidence. Strauss first conceived the work after completing *Feuersnot* and while working on *Symphonia domestica*. It premiered in 1903 at opening ceremonies for the *Stadthalle* in Heidelberg, expressing thanks for the honorary doctorate the university had awarded him (at the instigation of Philipp Wolfrum). Even though relatively brief (some fifteen minutes), the work boasts titanic orchestration (twenty-four woodwinds, twenty brass instruments, ninety strings, and nine percussionists) approaching Schoenberg's *Gurre-Lieder* in scale and employing more instruments than *Alpensinfonie*. At the same time, however, Uhland's ballad is straightforward and even monotonous, lacking the multidimensionality that otherwise distinguishes the lyric poetry Strauss set to music. It seems that here (much more than in *Bardengesang*, completed only a little later), the genre of choral ballad is being used, for one last time, in hypertrophic form stripped of all artistic-religious pretensions (in other words, "philosophy"). Moreover, the work is extraordinarily difficult to play and combines meter and motifs in a way comparable to the operas: the first time "Tail-le-fer" is uttered (Example 3.1), it reveals the theme that unifies the work as a whole.

In 1906, Strauss also stopped composing choral works—before returning to the form in striking fashion on the eve of the First World War. His *Deutsche Motette* would prove his most demanding a capella composition—indeed, one of the most difficult choral works of the twentieth century. Moreover, it represented a vast change of

---

[9] "in Form und Inhalt auch so tief u. philosofisch als möglich werden." *Lieber Collega!: Richard Strauss im Briefwechsel mit zeitgenössischen Komponisten und Dirigenten*, ed. Gabriele Strauss (Berlin: Henschel, 1996), 203; letter of March 27, 1885.

program. Strauss was singularly stimulated by the virtuosic language of Friedrich Rückert's *Ghasel* (a kind of poetry comprising two-line stanzas), which he understood as a corrective to lyric based on personal sentiment and experience [*Erlebnis*]. *Deutsche Motette* stands at the heart of his engagement with the poet, which continued until late in life. In the context of Strauss's radically anti-metaphysical conception of music, the work exemplifies the self-definition of the modern artist: the uncompromising composer standing firm and resolute in the present day. Even if Strauss himself never made a public pronouncement about the piece, its title clearly points in two directions. In a Nietzschean sense, the first word, "German," signifies an authentically daimonic force—in other words, a cultural element corresponding to the "Dionysian" (and, as such, worlds apart from the nationalism on which a later generation would base its hegemonic claims). By staging a confrontation with the motet—a genre with a religious air, if not aura—in an a capella arrangement, Strauss offers a historico-philosophical (self-)portrait. Although he performed analogous gestures on other occasions, this is the only time he did so with an eye on the tradition of religious music before Bach. Hereby, the motet-genre receives a secular meaning in keeping with compositional technique alone: the application of orchestral polyphony to vocal material (that is, what Strauss would call "nervous counterpoint" in 1935).

The third work indicative of Strauss's artistic course is the Eichendorff cycle *Tageszeiten*, which he completed for the Vienna *Schubertbund* in 1927 (clearly after many years of reflection). The composer sticks to the original arrangement of poems but adds his own "cock's crow" to *Morgen*. On the one hand, *Tageszeiten* provides a further instance combining choral music and Lied. On the other, the choice of Eichendorff is surprising inasmuch as Strauss otherwise demonstrated no interest for overarching religious sentiment (much less piety). Here, the modern individual's self-reliant constitution—that is, what Hofmannsthal called "the social"—plays a different role than in *Die ägyptische Helena* and *Arabella*. This aspect appears in the singability (achieved through the composition of operas) that unfolds as choral movement and, in conjunction with the polyphony and practically "classical" configuration of the orchestra, attains a new degree of plasticity and concreteness. Tonality—which remains unaltered

Figure 3.2 Rehearsals for the *Olympic Hymn*, by Richard Strauss. Berlin, Olympic Stadium, 1936.

Richard Strauss was enlisted to compose the Olympic hymn in 1932, and he continued the project under National Socialist rule. This is especially remarkable in light of the fact — and as correspondence documents — that the composer viewed the task with skepticism, indeed with distaste. When Strauss was removed as the president of the newly founded Reichsmusikkammer, Goebbels wanted to cancel the commission. This did not occur, however, and Strauss presented the score to Hitler personally, while still in office. The piece displays a singularly "inauthentic" tone, which remains puzzling; the Olympic Committee had requested an "official" work for posterity. Strauss conducted the premiere himself.

Richard Strauss Institute, Garmisch-Partenkirchen.

on a basic level while at the same time occurring developmentally—gives rise to a "lyrical" genre. From now on, this form would be Strauss's main concern. (The composer's *Daphne,* composed for nine voices in 1943 and likewise a paradigmatic work, shows just how closely opera, Lied, and choral polyphony were tied together for him.)

Much later, and in a wholly unexpected context, Strauss thematized this departure from conventional choral music. In 1932, he was commissioned to compose a hymn for the 1936 Olympic Games (see Figure 3.2). After some difficulties—in particular, finding a poet to write the text (Gerhart Hauptmann declined the offer)—he finished the work. Although no longer president of the Reichsmusikkammer, Strauss conducted the premiere. That said, he did not view his vast choral work as a welcome challenge so much as something "for the proles,"[10] which he had simply "cobbled together [*getonsetzert*]."[11] The assessment is especially remarkable as the the key of D major intones a hymnal gesture (like the finale of *Friedenstag*) with such vigor that it is difficult not to see it as programmatic (and, as such, an intentional departure from "real" composition).

First and Last Lieder

One of Strauss's earliest compositions to have been preserved is a song. The first pieces with which he took the public stage, properly speaking, were Lieder (performed by Cornelie Meysenheim in March 1881). The first vocal compositions to be printed were eight Lieder, Op. 10, in 1887 (the texts were by Hermann von Gilm [1812–1864], an Austrian official who wrote in the vein of Heine). In 1940, when he was almost seventy-six, Strauss came back to these compositions and arranged orchestral versions to be performed by the soprano Viorica Ursuleac (1894–1985). Indeed, during the 1930s and 1940s, he reworked a number of older Lieder for orchestra. The new versions did not adhere strictly to the originals; in particular, preludes and postludes were added. However, this return to the Lied in what Strauss pointedly declared to be his "late work" (which dispensed with *opus* numbers), did not continue right away. Surprisingly, and after decades of abstention, the composer again turned to instrumental music (while steering clear of genres he deemed obsolete). As such, the key works of the late period stand alone in terms of genre. *Metamorphosen*, for twenty-three solo strings, premiered in Zurich under the direction of Paul Sacher in 1946. That same year, Hermann Scherchen directed the Second Sonatina for sixteen woodwinds (*Fröhliche Werkstatt*, dedicated to Werner Reinhart). Only in this context did Strauss finally return to the Lied, composing four orchestral pieces with an air of finality in 1948. Even if the title is apocryphal, they were indeed "four last songs."

---

10 "für die Proleten." Willi Schuh (ed.), *Richard Strauss—Stefan Zweig: Briefwechsel* (Frankfurt: S. Fischer, 1957), 90; letter of December 21, 1934.

11 Letter to Werner Reinhart (undated), in Peter Sulzer, *Zehn Komponisten um Werner Reinhart: Ein Ausschnitt aus dem Wirkungskreis des Musikkollegiums*, vol. 2, Winterthur: 1920–1950 (Winterthur: Stadtbibliothek, 1980), 167 (a facsimile in Schuh, *Richard Strauss—Stefan Zweig*, ill. 32).

Metamorphosen is the first work to lend concrete expression to the self-interpretation that defines Strauss's late work: an effort to encompass the whole of musical history, which is also meant as universal history. For Strauss, the key figures of the former were Mozart, Beethoven, and Wagner; in turn, Goethe stood front and center in the latter. The composer sets the stage for his late work in a way that, while derived from the nineteenth century, fundamentally differs from its guiding assumptions insofar as it recognizes no utopian promise. Hereby, his return to the Lied—now connected with the works of a contemporary poet (in contrast to his practice during the preceding decades)—amounts to a "purification" of vocal music. It remains uncertain whether and how the four last songs constitute a cycle. They premiered—and were published—under this title only after the composer's death. The chosen texts are surprising in that they do not stem from Goethe (or Nietzsche). Finally, the sequence in which the compositions were written, in Montreux and Pontresina, does not correspond to the order that they were subsequently given.

The later arrangement connects parts of the day with the stages of life (*Frühling—September—Beim Schlafengehen—Im Abendrot*). The orchestration changes from song to song, and only *September* and *Im Abendrot* are in the same key. Nevertheless, this is the first time that Strauss's Lieder are organized in a way that goes beyond loose association: the songs form a cycle. An autobiographical element is particularly evident in the Eichendorff piece: this is the sole instance, in all of Strauss's work, where a Lied is framed (by an extended, 21-measure orchestral cantilena and a postlude of equal length). For one last time, the composer employs E♭ major, the signature key of the nineteenth century extending from Beethoven's *Eroica* up to his own *Heldenleben*. A final act of self-quotation,

Table 3.4 *Four Last Songs*

Im Abendrot (Montreux, May 6, 1948; Eichendorff, 1837; dedicated to Ernst Roth) – 4.

Frühling (Pontresina, July 18, 1948; Hesse, April 1899; dedicated to Willi Schuh and his wife) – 1.

Beim Schlafengehen (Pontresina, August 4, 1948; Hesse, July 1911; dedicated to Adolf Jöhr and his wife) – 3.

September (Montreux, September 20, 1948; Hesse, September 23, 1927; dedicated to Maria Jeritza and her husband) – 2.

from *Tod und Verklärung*, reveals the Nietzsche-reader again; now, instead of fusing artistic biography and *oeuvre* as a metaphysically vaulted destiny, it signifies the temporally and ideationally bound perspective of musical modernity. Yet the gesture that defines *Abendrot*—setting off into uncertainty—does not mean the abandonment of all prospects. Instead, the last songs thematize the process of metamorphosis that defines artistic existence—even if it does not assign a direction or make any promises. Hesse, who avoided a meeting with Strauss in Baden in 1946, had no sympathy for this quasi-"autobiographical" dimension. He considered the compromises Strauss had made with the National Socialists to be unforgiveable—and even associated them with his music itself. ("We have no right to level accusations, yet we do have the right to distance ourselves from him."[12])

Reflection on self and metamorphosis is precisely what Strauss's late works foreground. This feature underscores the importance of the Lied. *Daphne* culminates in the heroine singing a kind of song; here, the shape and form of the language that Strauss had worked to achieve with Hofmannsthal start to dissolve again. Likewise, *Capriccio* culminates in the heroine's songlike exchange with her own reflection. Even Jupiter's departure in *Liebe der Danae* resembles a song. Thus, Strauss's return to the Lied not only capped some eighty years of creative activity—ultimately, it also proclaimed a striking sense of disorientation, if not of being lost entirely. For Strauss—his late, instrumental compositions notwithstanding—lyrical song represented the only way that music could still communicate at the end of a cultural-historical period he still understood. For all that, his profound skepticism did without metaphysical claims, proclamations, or sentimentality. To the end, he remained convinced that human beings, especially in light of modern catastrophes, needed art—music—to reflect on themselves and their times.

---

12 "Wir haben kein Recht, ihm große Vorwürfe zu machen. Aber ich glaube, wir haben doch das Recht, uns von ihm zu distanzieren." Hermann Hesse, *Gesammelte Briefe: 1936–1948* (Frankfurt: Suhrkamp, 1982), 325; letter to Ernst Morgenthaler, February 1, 1946.

CHAPTER FOUR

Music and Life

THE KAPELLMEISTER AND HIS DUTIES

Beginnings: Meiningen, Weimar, Munich

In 1850, deeply moved by *Lohengrin*—in Weimar, Franz Liszt had directed the premiere in the composer's absence—Hans von Bülow sought out Richard Wagner in Zurich. Their meeting inaugurated a remarkable process of change. As Bülow began conducting, thereby laying the foundation for his career as Kapellmeister, his patron increasingly withdrew from the day-to-day business of conducting. For Mendelssohn and Schumann, the connection between composing and musical direction was still a matter of course. Now, in German-speaking lands, it fell apart. The princely role cultivated by Rossini or Meyerbeer in Paris played no role for composers here—including for Brahms, who essentially organized a kind of commercial enterprise and lived from the interest his honoraria earned. From now on, composers (such as Reger or Schoenberg) chiefly held conservatory positions, whereas conductors and musical directors composed only on occasion—or, at any rate, not primarily in an official capacity (for instance, Furtwängler and Klemperer). In contrast, Strauss stuck to his true mentor, Bülow, for all his life and continued to compose and conduct simultaneously (unlike Schillings, for example, who all but abandoned composition when he took over the Berlin Opera in 1919). This bearing is another point of similarity between Strauss and Mahler ("really quite my opposite"[1]),

---

[1] "meinem reichlich gegensätzlichen Antipoden." Personal note of July 1935, in Schuh, *Richard Strauss—Stefan Zweig*, 173.

even though the latter sought to hold the different spheres apart by focusing on writing during the break between seasons and limiting himself to two genres: symphonies and Lieder. Strauss, of course, wanted to "cycle through" inherited musical forms and viewed the different aspects of his professional life as interconnected.

Although such a bearing entailed considerable vexation and difficulty, Strauss persevered. In a letter to Karl Henckell in 1896, he expressed his irritation in unambiguous terms:

> How good Bierbaum's got it: a whole castle at Bolzano, up on St. Eppan; I paid him a visit there at the end of November [1895]. Complete freedom, living for his work alone—to die for; but I have to pursue art as a "civil servant" [*Beamter*] and choke down the fog of the Isar Valley, condemned to Germany's nine-month-long winter.[2]

Strauss never took a step to set things right, even when his earnings would have permitted him to do so—at the latest, after *Salome*. He went on conducting all his life, although he made significant changes to his repertory and focused on a narrower range of works. This fact is especially remarkable given that he—the son of an orchestral musician who had grown up in the milieu of the Hofkapelle—never received systematic instruction. Strauss did not learn how to conduct or compose in the manner typical of the late-nineteenth century, by attending a conservatory. It is difficult to determine exactly how he acquired technical expertise; keen observation and hands-on experience clearly played a decisive role. By the time Strauss was twenty years old, his skills were so readily apparent that he counted as a "natural." In 1885, Bülow told the concert agent Hermann Wolff that his pupil succeeded at everything "right away"; a "born conductor," he could be his "immediate successor" at Meiningen.[3]

---

2 "Wie schön hat es Bierbaum; der bewohnt ein ganzes Schloß bei Bozen, auf der Höhe von St. Eppan; ich besuchte ihn Ende November [1895] daselbst. So absolute Freiheit; nur seinen Arbeiten leben—wer das könnte; statt dessen muß man die Kunst als 'Beamter' treiben, u. die Nebel des Isarthales schlucken, zum 9monatlichen Winter Deutschlands verdammt . . . ." Schlötterer, *Die Texte*, 215; Letter to Karl Henckell.

3 "gleich auf's erste Mal", "ein geborener Dirigent", "sofortiger Nachfolger." Bülow, *Briefe*, 383; Letter to Hermann Wolff, October 17, 1885.

With that, Strauss's career began, and it continued on a remarkable course. At 21, he was musical director at the Meiningen court, which Duke Georg II had put on the map of musical life in Europe. The following year, Strauss held the position of third Kapellmeister at the Munich Court Opera. In 1889, he was Saxon-Grand Ducal Hofkapellmeister in Weimar. In 1894, he became Royal Kapellmeister in Munich—and, before long, succeeded Bülow as conductor of the Berlin Philharmonic. Between the ages of 20 and 30, Strauss's ascent was positively meteoric. From the beginning, his appointments were prominent; he bore sole— or principal—responsibility in all the positions he held, apart from his first three years in Munich. He also distinguished himself as a pianist at Meiningen, performing Mozart's Concerto in C minor K 491 as soon as he took office; afterwards, he also played as a chamber musician. Here, he met Brahms, too, and even appeared in concert with him. Yet despite such renown at a young age, Strauss does not seem to have exhibited the gruff self-assurance he displayed later on. Lily Braun's recollection (already quoted) of a shy and pale young man may be considered symptomatic of how success and self-consciousness combined with the desire to hold his public persona and private life apart—which spoke of a deep insecurity. That said, appointment in the Weimar of Goethe and Liszt struck Strauss as a portentous matter; in later years, he would attach greater and greater significance to this circumstance. Needless to say, other parties noticed the same. As Rudolf Steiner subsequently observed:

> In Weimar at that time, Richard Strauss was taking the first steps in his career, and working as deputy directory of music alongside [Eduard] Lassen. Strauss's first compositions were performed in Weimar. This composer's musical endeavours struck one as intrinsic to the cultural life of Weimar itself.[4]

A defining feature of Strauss's early career is that he avoided civic [*bürgerlich*] positions and sought only courtly appointments. This preference—a further point of similarity with Mahler, who gave up the practice only when engaged in New York—fits with his upbringing in a courtly milieu. Of course, it also entailed social privileges and comforts. Relatively good working conditions and a high degree of personal

---

4 Rudolf Steiner, *Music: Mystery, Art and the Human Being*, trans. Matthew Barton (Forest Row: Rudolf Steiner Press, 2016), 182.

freedom were associated with such offices, given the high salary and tenure that was, in principle, secure. (In his letter to Henckell, Strauss does not use the word "civil servant" in only a pejorative sense.) In Berlin, the composer would systematically take advantage of such liberty and seek to expand it, notwithstanding the Kaiser's disapproval of some of his Hofkapellmeister's activities. Almost all the major premieres until 1918 occurred in this setting: the tone poems (up to *Till Eulenspiegel*), as well as all operas up to *Frau ohne Schatten*, which premiered shortly after the Vienna Opera ceased to be under courtly supervision. Even a piece like *Salome* was first staged at a court opera, which did much to cushion ensuing scandals.

Clearly, Strauss felt that he belonged to this world (which *Intermezzo* still invokes), even if he did not want to be absorbed by it, or depend on it. Perhaps—in contrast to, say, Schillings—it is no coincidence that he did not pursue ennoblement, which was a real prospect. Strauss also broke with standard practice by actively combining positions at court and composition. His conception of writing music was inseparable from making the orchestra into a polyphonous "instrument" with numerous articulations; only by actively engaging with it in this way is composition permissible—indeed, possible in the first place. Strauss's encounter with Brahms at Meiningen and the latter's performance there made as much plain. When Brahms conducted his Fourth Symphony on October 25, 1885, he was clearly turning toward the courtly sphere—where he was met with acceptance. His Fourth manifests a singular understanding of the symphonic art: historicizing refraction is meant to realize objective form on the basis of logical musical syntax and motivic "labor." It creates a structure that develops from two central (as it were "bourgeois") aspects of symphonic composition: catchy passages and appeals to the broader public—a feature also evident in the "classical" orchestration. This effort may point to a deeper connection between Brahms and the exclusive court at Meiningen than has long been assumed. However, Strauss had no understanding of the work (just as Brahms failed to appreciate his counterpart's Symphony in F minor); he wished to retain the "broad" cast of orchestral music. This attitude surely underpins his resolve to distance himself from prevailing musical notions within the courtly world—that is, to use the standing institution to find a vantage point that would call its very framework into question. As such, it is not by chance that the court rarely plays a role in Strauss's operas—and when it does, it appears in a state of decline (for instance, in *Der Rosenkavalier, Arabella,* and *Capriccio*). By the same token, it is no coincidence that the prelude to *Ariadne* thematizes the fundamental conflict pervading this milieu.

Berlin and Modernism

Undoubtedly Strauss's most important musical appointment was as First Prussian Kapellmeister at the Court Opera in Berlin, from 1898 on. This was also the only position at which he did the programming for a significant span of time. The physiognomy of Wilhelmine Berlin proved contradictory as the city, defined by military armament and imperial ambitions, also flourished in terms of high culture. Systematic efforts (and with remarkable foresight and a broad perspective) were made to recruit elites to Prussian institutions: theaters, academies, and universities; accordingly, Berlin attracted outsiders in great number. The metropolis never fused into a whole; instead, it was constantly expanding outward. It thrived artistically—and musically—under the patronage of the imperial house and officialdom, notwithstanding the reserve the monarch displayed with regard to certain forms assumed by cultural life. Between 1895 and 1900, Alfred Kerr's *Berliner Briefe* (initially published in Breslau) described the "ascendant imperial city" as an international metropolis of modernism; although the theater critic occasionally let an ironic distance be felt, he characterized "the Kaiser's interest in art" as "rather comprehensive."[5] Later on, Max Reinhardt's dramaturg Arthur Kahane (1872–1932) would write that Berlin displayed "a more general, almost supranational" quality; it had become "center of culture, a world market, a megalopolis" and was "driven by unprecedented vitality."[6] Although content with his position in Munich at first, Strauss initiated the move to Berlin—where, indeed, his new employers were simply waiting for a sign. The composer had grown disenchanted (as sarcastic comments reveal) when efforts were

---

5 "emporkommende Kaiserstadt," "das kaiserliche Kunstinteresse," "ziemlich umfassend." Alfred Kerr, *Wo liegt Berlin? Briefe aus der Reichshauptstadt, 1895–1900*, ed. Günther Rühle (Berlin: Aufbau, 1999), 158; 22.

6 "etwas Allgemeingültigeres, fast Überstaatliches," "ein Kulturzentrum, ein Weltmarkt, ein Stadtriese," "von beispielloser Vitalität." Arthur Kahane, "Die Jahre 1905–1924," in Hans Rothe (ed.), *Max Reinhardt: 25 Jahre Deutsches Theater: Ein Tafelwerk* (Munich: Piper, 1930), 15.

made to poach Felix von Mottl from Karlsruhe to be Kapellmeister in Munich. Strauss expected great things of Berlin, and the city expected great things of him:

> If my demands are met, then Berlin is more practical for making my name better known in Europe for a while and not falling by the wayside too soon—as I'm somewhat afraid might occur in America.[7]

Hermann Wolff, a professional agent, had passed along the offer to replace Anton Seidl as the conductor of the New York Philharmonic. Strauss declined, but he likely improved his negotiating position in the process.

Strauss shared the position with Carl Muck (1859–1940), who was the same age and considered an important interpreter of Wagner. In 1908—again in tandem with Muck—he was appointed General Musical Director and Conductor of the Royal Court Orchestra. The financial benefits and administrative conditions were luxurious, drawing comparison with what Mahler enjoyed as director of the Vienna Court Opera. Strauss eventually earned twice as much as he had made in Munich. He also held all the privileges of a court official (with a corresponding pension) and did not have to work for three months a year. In 1905, this leave time was expanded to five months; finally, in 1908, he had a whole year free from professional duties. As a conductor and composer in Berlin, Strauss occupied the musical center of a cultural metropolis, and he took full advantage of the benefits it entailed: a broad network of contacts in the artistic world extending far beyond the courtly milieu, deep into the ranks of the Berlin Secession. Strauss kept up with literature, theater, and art, and became a cardinal figure in the city's cultural life. The portraits that Max Liebermann painted in 1918 (see Figure 4.1), which are certainly the most important likenesses to have been made of the composer, illustrate the privilege and authority he enjoyed.

Meeting Max Reinhardt and Hugo von Hofmannsthal shaped Strauss's Berlin years. It is telling that the artists encountered each other here, and

---

7 "Wenn man in Berlin meine Forderungen erfüllt, ist Berlin jetzt noch praktischer für mich, um meinen Namen in Europa noch eine Zeitlang mehr auszubreiten und nicht zu früh aus der Reihe zu kommen, was doch in Amerika etwas zu fürchten ist." Franz Grasberger (ed.), *Die Welt um Richard Strauss in Briefen* (Tutzing: Schneider, 1967), 115, letter to his wife Pauline of April 8, 1889.

Figure 4.1 Max Liebermann: *Richard Strauss*. Oil on canvas, 1918.

Max Liebermann (1847–1935)—one of the founders, in 1892, of the Berlin Secession (which made a great impact on Strauss)—painted two portraits of the city's General Music Director; although the end of the courtly milieu was imminent, both the artist and the composer stood at the height of their fame. One portrait was meant for public display, and the other for private use. Pauline Strauss did not like either picture. Liebermann portrays Strauss as unapproachable and aloof; no signs of his profession are included. The artist clearly seeks to foreground his subject's personal demeanor. Its uncompromising nature makes it the most significant portrait of the composer.

Richard Strauss Institute, Garmisch-Partenkirchen.

that the city remained the geographical center for their collaborative efforts until 1918. The fact that the Hofkapellmeister was able to hold premieres in Dresden (despite some difficulties with censors)—and not at his site of employment—speaks for, and not against, the privileges he held. The only major composition to premiere in Berlin (although it was performed by the Dresden Hofkapelle) was *Eine Alpensinfonie*. As a matter of course, the position involved official commissions. Strauss happily acquitted himself of such duties. The most striking instance involved two marches he composed in 1906 and proudly designated Op. 57; these have entered the Prussian military music in a broad array of adaptations. This is also a defining trait of Berlin culture at the turn of the century: official duties and productive independence existed side by side, with remarkably little conflict. Both general intendants overseeing Strauss's work, Hans Heinrich XIV Bolko von Hochberg and (from 1903 on) Georg von Hülsen-Haeseler, had very different priorities, yet they did not interfere with the liberties that institutional frameworks granted the composer.

Archival work on Strauss's Berlin period has only just started, and many questions remain unanswered. They include how he collaborated with other musical directors in the city (for instance, Bruno Walter) in terms of programming, engaging performers, and expanding the repertoire. Under Hochberg's supervision, German works predominated, but with an eye to a broader, European context. Strauss produced an astonishing array of works including Auber's *Fra Diavolo* and *La Muette de Portici*, Meyerbeer's *Robert le Diable*, Bizet's *Carmen*, Chabrier's *Briséïs*, Saint-Saëns' *Samson et Dalila*, Verdi's *Falstaff* and *Aida*, Mascagni's *Cavalleria rusticana*, and Leoncavallo's *I Pagliacci*.[8] Puccini is notably absent from the picture, and this omission was never rectified. Among German-language operas, Wagner's works stood at the fore (practically everything from *Rienzi* on, with the exception of *Parsifal*, which still could not be performed outside Bayreuth). When Strauss started composing operas, his own works assumed more and more prominence, even though he remained mindful of the bigger picture. The operatic compositions developed in the context of leeway afforded by concerts with the Königliche Kapelle and, especially, the Tonkünstler-Orchester (which he directed for two seasons [1901–1903]). In this setting, Strauss directed d'Indy's symphonic poem after Uhland, *La forêt enchantée* (1901), Elgar's *Cockaigne* overture (1901), and Stanford's *Irish Rhapsody No. 2* (1903). Other pieces included works by Tchaikovsky—among them, his Violin Concerto and Second Piano Concerto (but not the symphonies, apart from the *Pathétique*)—Bach's Brandenburg Concertos; Bruckner's Fourth and Ninth; Mahler's Third and Fourth Symphonies, as well as *Lied von der Erde*; Saint-Saëns's Second;

---

8 All information follows the lists in Raymond Holden, *Richard Strauss: A Musical Life* (New Haven and London: Yale University Press, 2011), 179 ff. Holden's lists (the first ones concerning Strauss as a conductor) refer only to fixed positions, not guest appearances.

Figure 4.2 Photos of the last apartment of Strauss in Berlin.

(a) Outside (the apartment in the upper floor on the left)

(b) Workroom

During his time in Berlin Strauss had three different apartments, two of them are still existing. The first one was in Knesebeckstrasse 30 in Charlottenburg; the facade of the house was rebuilt during the 1920s, but inside it relieved nearly untouched. In 1904 he moved to Joachimsthaler Strasse 17, this house was destroyed in World War II. Both apartments have been in the heart of Charlottenburg and close to 'Café des Westens', the meeting point for the intellectual elite. In 1912 he moved to a newly erected house in Kaiserdamm 39 (today Heerstrasse 2) in the noble western end of Charlottenburg. He influenced the structure of his apartment in the upper floor, reachable with an electric elevator. The apartment was extremely large (more then 470 square yards) and houses today several offices. The second photo shows his former work room where was working on *Alpensinfonie, Ariadne auf Naxos* and *Die Frau ohne Schatten.*

Private collection.

and compositions by Strauss's friend Humperdinck. Pieces that did not belong to the repertory also received consideration—for instance, the overture to Schubert's *Fierabras* and Mozart's *Gran Partita*. That said, two features are apparent. Even though composers acknowledged Strauss as the most important figure in contemporary German music, testimony from some of his contemporaries is missing. Both Debussy and Ravel sent him scores with a dedication—*La mer* and *La valse,* respectively.[9] Strauss would have known these works quite well, then, and he actively sought further scores from Debussy. However, with the exception of *Prélude* (1907, in Vienna), he never conducted any of them. Indeed, tonality defined the strict borders of his repertory. Even though his correspondence, as well as engagements during the 1920s (in Donaueschingen, for instance), reveal that Strauss kept abreast of developments in tonal language much more than scholars have long assumed, this aspect of music remained non-negotiable to the very end.

As a musical director, Strauss was considered a modernist at the turn of the century. It is odd, however, that new compositions were rarely dedicated to him, despite his institutional power and profile. Besides a few literary works—the German edition of George Bernard Shaw's *Perfect Wagnerite* (1908), Otto Julius Bierbaum's *Traum durch die Dämmerung,* and Hermann Bahr's 1909 comedy *Das Konzert* (which would prove important for Strauss's own compositions)—relatively few musical pieces honored him: Max von Schilling's *Ingwelde* (1894), Hermann Bischoff's Symphony in E major Op. 16 (1904), Josef Suk's *Symphonie Asrael* Op. 27 (1906), Heinz Tiessen's Symphony in C minor Op. 15 (1911), Max Reger's Fantasia and Fugue in C minor Op. 29 (1898) and Fantasia and Fugue in D minor Op. 135b (1915), Erich Wolfgang Korngold's "symphonic overture" *Sursum corda* Op. 13 (1919), and Hans Huber's Symphony No. 3, *Heroische* (1902), which directly references *Ein Heldenleben*. Not only is the number slight; these are works of limited significance. Dedications decreased even more following the First World War; rare exceptions include Havergal Brian's eccentric First Symphony, *Gothic* (1927), which took eight years to complete and called for an enormous orchestra. Works by the composer's own friends were dedicated to him only rarely—for instance, Ludwig Thuille's String Quartet in A major

---

9 Both scores are preserved in the Richard Strauss-Archiv, Garmisch-Partenkirchen.

(1878) and Alexander Ritter's opera *Wem die Krone* (1890), the premiere of which Strauss conducted. Occasionally, but rarely, theoretical writings were dedicated to him (for example, Artur Seidl's *Moderner Geist in der deutschen Tonkunst* [1901], Fritz Rögely's *Harmonielehre* [1910], and Gemma Bellincioni's *Scuola di canto* [1912]). It seems that a certain unapproachability surrounded Strauss's position in Berlin, then—both at court and in the milieu of nascent modernism. In terms of artistic creation, only Hofmannsthal would overcome this distance.

Vienna and the Republican Task

Like many of his generation, Strauss was caught off-guard when the aristocratic world ended in the wake of the First World War. Its collapse imperiled the livelihood of all who had constructed their plans largely—or exclusively—in terms of appointments at court. Strauss's difficulties worsened when the fortune he had invested in England was impounded and then, in the context of reparations, seized altogether. Initially, the composer—who conducted his final concert for the Kaiser on the eve of the latter's resignation (see Figure 4.3)—remained loyal to the Berlin Opera, which no longer had a patron, by serving as interim director and conducting performances while the orchestra regrouped. The programming of the last season that Strauss oversaw was particularly ambitious and sophisticated; it demonstrates a clear will to face events confidently and with elan. That said, Strauss had been cultivating closer and closer ties to Vienna—beginning in 1912, when he accepted the commission of composing festival music for the opening of the Konzerthaus. In 1916, the "new version" of *Ariadne auf Naxos* premiered at the Vienna Court Opera; the same year, Strauss was named an honorary member of the city's *Gesellschaft der Musikfreunde*. In general—and thanks to his collaboration with Hofmannsthal, in particular—the composer's visits to Vienna became more and more frequent. The high point occurred with the founding of the Salzburg *Festspielgemeinde* in 1917, which represented Strauss's first real foothold in Austria. In the context of *Die Frau ohne Schatten*, Vienna would come to play a role of unanticipated significance in his work.

Ariadne auf Naxos and *Die Frau ohne Schatten* defined the years between 1910 and 1917, representing antiquity regained and the fairy-tale, as it were. Plans for *Die Frau ohne Schatten*, which began in 1910, took

> :: KÖNIGLICHES OPERNHAUS ::
>
> Berlin, Freitag, den 8. November 1918,
> abends 7 1/2 Uhr:
>
> ## III. SINFONIE-ABEND DER KÖNIGL. KAPELLE
>
> zum Besten ihres Witwen- und Waisenfonds.
>
> Dirigent:
> **Herr Generalmusikdirektor Dr. Richard Strauss.**
>
> PROGRAMM:
>
> 1. Ouvertüre zu Goethes Trauerspiel „Egmont"
>   L. van Beethoven
>
> 2. Holländische Sinfonie } zum ersten
>   1. Allegro. 2. Adagio.   Male in diesen } C. Dopper
>   3. Allegro. 4. Allegro   Konzerten
>   non troppo. Feestdag.
>
> 3. Siebente Sinfonie, C-dur . . . . . Schubert
>   a) Andante. Allegro ma non troppo. b) Andante con moto. c) Scherzo. Allegro vivace. d) Allegro vivace.
>
> Während der Musik bleiben die Türen geschlossen.
>
> Auf vielseitigen Wunsch findet im Vorraum des Kgl. Opernhauses ein Verkauf von Partituren statt, soweit diese im Druck erschienen sind.
>
> Programm-Bücher sind bei den Logenschliessern für 50 Pf. zu haben.
>
> Nach dem zweiten Glockenzeichen werden die Türen geschlossen und kann niemand mehr Einlass erlangen vor Beendigung des angefangenen Musikstückes.
>
> Zum **Mittags-Sinfonie-Konzert** sind Einlasskarten bei BOTE & BOCK, Leipziger Str. 37 und Tauentzien-Str. 7, am Konzerttage im Königl. Opernhause zu haben.
>
> ## IV. Sinfonie-Abend: 29. November 1918
>
> 1. Sinfonie, Es-dur (Rheinische) . . . R. Schumann
> 2. Suite (zum 1. Mal) . . . . Volkmar Andrää
> 3. Siebente Sinfonie A-dur . . . . . L. van Beethoven
>
> Verlag: **Albert Stahl**, Berlin W 35, Potsdamer Strasse 39

Figure 4.3 Program of the Royal Orchestra's Third Symphony Evening, Berlin, Royal Opera House, Friday, 8 November 1918.

During his official engagement in Berlin, Richard Strauss rehearsed a comprehensive repertory of works from the eighteenth century to the present. The latest compositions were incorporated as a matter of course — a fact evident in the many premieres that took place under his directorship. Strauss also conducted some of these works regularly (for instance, Mahler's First Symphony). On 9 November 1918—one day before Wilhelm II's public declaration that he would not take the throne, and against the backdrop of newly proclaimed republican rule—Strauss conducted Beethoven's Egmont Overture and Schubert's Symphony No. 9 ("the Great"); the same evening, he also premiered Symphony No. 6 ("Amsterdam," here called "Dutch Symphony" [Holländische Sinfonie], 1912) by Cornelis Dopper (1870-1939), second conductor of the Concertgebouw Orkest.

Private collection.

concrete form in spring 1914, when the text for Act One was completed. Strauss had already held discussions with Alfred Roller (1864–1935), the set designer at the Hofoper, about the piece's elaborate requirements, which would tax the machinery in place. Shortly before the score was ready, in 1916, the composer sought to stage the premiere in Vienna; Franz Schalk, the director of the Hofoper, had suggested that Maria Jeritza and Lotte Lehmann play the soprano leads. Hofmannsthal, on the other hand, did not like this focus on the Habsburg royal seat and recommended production at Munich, instead. However, Strauss was already engaged in negotiations and wanted the piece to be staged with all the trappings of the Court Opera. The talks met with vehement opposition within the opera house because—among other things—Strauss sought to split duties with Schalk and, accordingly, did not intend to be in Vienna for the whole course of preparations. Strauss took these objections seriously and even considered a premiere in Berlin—with Oskar Kokoschka reworking Roller's set design.

Terms were finally reached—and under a new, republican government, at that. However, the difficulties leading up to the contract overshadowed Strauss's time in office and brought his tenure to a premature end in 1924—the same year that a city festival celebrated his sixtieth birthday and he was named an honorary citizen of Vienna. Both *Intermezzo* and *Die ägyptische Helena* premiered in Dresden. All the same, Strauss felt enduring ties to Vienna—as is evident in his defiant plans to build a villa there (where he resided until he was forced to evacuate in 1944). In 1923, the composer became an honorary member of the Academy of Arts and Vienna Philharmonic. The following year, his son Franz married Alice Grab (1904–1991), the daughter of Jewish patricians. Here, Strauss also tested out new forms of confronting past and present with his Couperin Suite and *Le Bourgeois gentilhomme*. Vienna is the only city for which he would compose festival music to the end.

The composer clearly felt that Berlin offered an appropriate stage for positioning himself vis-à-vis incipient modernism. His turn to Vienna, in contrast, came from different intentions. Strauss felt estranged from certain modernist tendencies after 1918, especially in music. The rise of atonality struck him as fundamentally misguided. The distance he took from it culminated in the *Helena* project; here, he sought to affirm the rights of tonality and singability once and for all. Yet this resolute ambition foundered. Subsequently, Strauss changed his view again; increasingly, his position was shaped by a drive for historicization and canonization. Even though Vienna provided the backdrop for this realignment, the composer did not view his course as a turn backward so much as movement forward, into the twentieth century. In this context, Strauss systematically broadened his approach to antiquity—which had started in earnest with *Ariadne*—through *Die ägyptische Helena* and plans for *Liebe der Danae*. In Vienna—and still in collaboration with Hofmannsthal—he adapted material for *Prometheus*, set to the music of Beethoven, in order to create a new kind of *Festspiel*. In addition, he reworked Mozart's *Idomeneo*. Strauss sought to bring together all the figures of musical history that he deemed significant (except for Wagner) in a new outlook based on the ancient world. Vienna also provided the site where he continued the concrete musical historicization that had started with *Arabella* (and culminated in *Die Schweigsame Frau*). In other words, Strauss did not consider Vienna as just a musical metropolis; it was where he hoped his musical vision would achieve physical, "plastic" reality. This view is responsible for his remarkable decision, in the early 1940s, to undertake a large-scale instrumental composition, *Die Donau* (which, however, never got beyond the planning stage).

Strauss exercised his official duties in Vienna in parallel to the emergence of republican structures. His appointment did not represent a new beginning so much as it afforded him the opportunity to secure a place in musical history. Accordingly, the position connected with his effort to forge a new, definitive canon; hereby, opera would bid farewell to the post-revolutionary age once and for all. During the few years he was active in Vienna, Strauss concentrated more and more on Beethoven's *Fidelio*, Mozart, Wagner, and his own works. He left all the rest to Schalk, who was also in charge of coordinating day-to-day business (which, given the political circumstances, proved no easy matter). Entirely in line with the idea of Salzburg festivities, Strauss celebrated his own presence as a *Festspiel*. He therefore rarely abandoned his canon; early exceptions include Bizet's *Carmen* and Rimsky-Korsakov's *Scheherazade* (which, however, he combined with his own *Josephs Legende*). Over time, Strauss stopped doing so altogether. On just one occasion, he also directed *Fledermaus*, a work of immense importance to him and Hofmannsthal. Apart from his own compositions, he no longer took charge of premieres;

when giving concerts with other orchestras, he also cultivated an increasingly narrow repertoire. In other words, one of the twentieth century's most important conductors did not devote his time and energy to fulfilling the duties of Kapellmeister, but to securing his own place in history. When Strauss left office in 1924, he did so amidst quarrels and burned bridges—with Schalk, too—thereby abandoning connections that had provided the foundation for his professional life for some forty years. Although he still conducted, Strauss gave up everyday dealings with the opera. He made one, brief return in 1933 (and 1934), when he tactlessly filled in for Arturo Toscanini at Bayreuth. This seems to have occurred (as Strauss told Stefan Zweig) not out of respect for the institution, so much as because he wanted to crown his tenure as Kapellmeister by conducting *Parsifal* one first and last time. (In 1882, he and his father had attended rehearsals for the work's premiere.[10])

Strauss as Conductor

Strauss's activities as Kapellmeister have been examined only in part until now. Given the advanced age he reached and the length of his appointment, both indirect and direct forms of evidence exist. The former include the concert and opera series he programmed, as well as reviews. The latter comprise sound recordings and a handful of films that show him conducting (his own compositions, for the most part).[11] Strauss also published a book; he had planned to discuss matters of composition, but in fact the work reflects his experience as a conductor. The Peters publishing house wanted to put out a new edition of Hector Berlioz's *Treatise on Instrumentation*. Despite reservations, Strauss agreed. In the preface to the first volume, which appeared in 1905, he insisted on the connection between Berlioz and Wagner—a typical reading in the German-speaking world; more significantly, he stressed that "questions of mechanics" cannot be separated from "the esthetic aspects of orchestral

---

10 Strauss was, in spite of his break with Bayreuth, engaged in the question of *Parsifal*. The copyright protection of Wagner's last music-drama was part of his copyright activities in general. Nevertheless he conducted the work 1917 in Berlin and thought about a production in Vienna. In 1933 he conducted the 1882 version in Bayreuth and in 1934 the new production with Heinz Tietjen and Alfred Roller.

11 As usual, early photos were staged. They are not at all significant for the practice of conducting.

technique."[12] Against this backdrop, Strauss's work as a conductor appears in singular, and telling, light. It proves all the more remarkable, then, that Berlioz's final chapter—"On Conducting"—is left entirely untouched; Strauss offers no remarks of his own. Just as he refused to interpret his own compositions, he provided no commentary on how he conducted. As such, it is also little wonder that he never actively trained anyone else in this art.

Strauss published no important writings on conducting. His *Dirigentenerfahrungen* (Experiences of a Conductor), from 1934, has a rhapsodic form—and, moreover, went unpublished during his lifetime. It is worth noting, however, that this text affirms the connection between mechanics and aesthetics: "Conducting is, after all, a difficult matter—you have to reach the age of seventy to understand it in full."[13] A piece that appeared in 1929, *Über Komponieren und Dirigieren* (On Composition and Conducting), is altogether vague.[14] Likewise, the "Ten Golden Rules" published in 1934 are basically anecdotal; they have become famous largely for the witticism that the conductor should not break a sweat in concert, but that the audience should.[15] *Capriccio*—the only opera, besides *Intermezzo*, for which Strauss provided prefatory remarks—includes a somewhat more thorough discussion of the issue. In keeping with the views of Hans von Bülow (and also, perhaps, Ernst von Schuch), Strauss deems the conductor an advocate [*Anwalt*] of clarity. Accordingly, he defends "his" orchestration with regard to song, in particular. The differentiated orchestra amounts to an instrument in modern times; only a conductor who stands "in daily conduct with its magic powers"[16] is in the position to derive benefit for composition.

---

12 Hector Berlioz and Richard Strauss, *Treatise on Instrumentation* (New York: Edwin F. Kalmus, 1948), i.

13 "Dirigieren ist halt doch eine schwierige Angelegenheit—man muß siebzig Jahre alt werden, um dies ganz zu begreifen." Richard Strauss, "Dirigentenerfahrungen mit klassischen Meisterwerken," in *Betrachtungen und Erinnerungen*, 68.

14 Richard Strauss, "Über Komponieren und Dirigieren," in *Berliner Börsen-Courier* (June 8, 1929), reprinted in *Betrachtungen und Erinnerungen*, 47f.

15 Richard Strauss, "Zehn goldne Regeln: Einem jungen Kapellmeister ins Stammbuch geschrieben," in *Dresdner Anzeiger* (April 29, 1934); reprinted in *Betrachtungen und Erinnerungen*, 46.

16 Berlioz and Strauss, *Treatise on Instrumentation*, 1.

The few films in which Strauss appears—apart from curiosities such as the performance of the *Olympische Hymne* in Berlin—show a restrained conductor who keeps strict time and maintains alert eye contact with performers (see Figure 4.4). Strauss seems to follow scores

Figure 4.4 Richard Strauss conducting at rehearsal. Photograph from 1942, signed by the composer.

Strauss has added an ironic inscription to the picture, which shows him at some seventy years of age: "When the score isn't in your head, then your head's in the score" ["Wenn man die Partitur nicht im Kopf hat, steckt der Kopf eben in der Partitur"]. The words allude to his habit of having the notes at the ready when conducting. Significantly, however, films reveal that he almost never looked at the score, and even turned the pages intuitively. Strauss counted as a phenomenal conductor. He would beat time almost casually, holding the baton from the side. Rarely but quite emphatically — in this regard, he resembled Toscanini — he would punctuate with his left hand. Strauss retained a sovereign bearing and displayed utmost precision even when conducting repertory pieces (which occurred less frequently over time). In contrast to Mahler, who aimed to overwhelm the audience by capturing the spirit of the original, and Furtwängler, who sought to bring out psychological nuance, Strauss observed distance vis-à-vis the score, notwithstanding an intensive commitment to the work at hand. The photo was made in Munich (Deutsches Museum) in June 1941 during a planned film with *Alpensinfonie*. The film project was never finished.
Richard Strauss Institute, Garmisch-Partenkirchen.

closely—including those for his own works—even though he does not actually use them; mindfully turning the pages, he does not so much as look at the notes. Such a bearing contrasts dramatically with Mahler, of whose work we have no film or sound recordings, but whose habits were described by many observers. Unlike Mahler, Strauss did not view the conductor as a spiritual "recreator" [*Nachschöpfer*], but as the advocate of the composer and his score; as a Munich reviewer put it in 1928, "the duty of the artist of reproduction."[17] is what animated him. For all that, Strauss acknowledged the relativity of his views. At the end of his preface to *Capriccio*, he affirms that the final form of a given work depends on the institutional and individual conditions governing its performance. Evidently, the composer accepted the wide range of variation that his position entailed. One example will illustrate as much. *Ein Heldenleben* was recorded two times in 1941. Strauss directed the Bayerische Staatsorchester in Munich, and Willem Mengelberg (1871–1951, to whom the work was dedicated) conducted the Concertgebouw Orkest in Amsterdam. Strauss's rendition lasts some thirty-nine minutes, and Mengelberg's about forty-two—that is, three minutes longer. The difference is even more pronounced in the recording of Strauss conducting the Vienna Philharmonic in 1944, where the performance takes just thirty-seven minutes. His own, highly personal mode of reading relies on uniform meter; a basic tempo prevails throughout, and individual parts unfold in strict proportion to each other. The few departures from this approach—for instance, the "Reprise," which is prepared by a broad *ritardando* and therefore sets in gradually—prove all the more striking for representing conscious decisions. In contrast, Mengelberg's rendition begins with the orchestra fanning out in *rubato*, and the first section already yields a broad array of different tempos; in other words, the change of pace does not serve as a structural marker, but is what sets the whole, in organic gradations, into motion in order to "shape" it in turn. The contrast to the composer's own interpretation could hardly be greater. (The difference is also apparent in the many modifications Mengelberg makes, starting with the E♭ augmented by tuba—which the score does not call for.)

17 "Pflicht des reproduzierenden Künstlers." *Münchner Neueste Nachrichten* (August 18, 1928), quoted in Roswitha Schlötterer-Traimer, "Richard Strauss als Dirigent: Mit einer Dokumentation seiner in München dirigierten Konzerte," in Hartmut Schaefer (ed.), *Richard Strauss: Autographen, Porträts, Bühnenbilder: Ausstellung zum 50. Todestag* (Munich: Bayerische Staatsbibliothek, 1999), 61.

Strauss and Mengelberg had an amicable relationship; there is nothing to indicate that the composer did not accept his colleague's reading, even though it did not agree with his own. As such, Strauss displayed a willingness not to declare his own interpretation absolute. This attitude is apparent in recordings, which are relatively numerous. They started in 1917, while he was still employed at court in Berlin, and the last were made in 1947. Some thirty years of solid documentation thus exists (notwithstanding a high degree of technical variation). Throughout, the basic pattern is extremely consistent, despite points of difference with those conductors Strauss esteemed—Fritz Busch, Clemens Krauss, and Karl Böhm. In general, Strauss conducts his own works in recordings. Rare exceptions include Mozart's late symphonies, Beethoven's Seventh, and Wagner (Strauss's sole production with the Berlin Philharmonic, in 1928).[18] The idea of plasticity, which animated him as a composer, also shaped his work as a conductor. Inasmuch as it meant avoiding the spectacular aspects of performance and efforts to overwhelm the audience, his bearing differed from that of many contemporaries.[19]

Strauss had a vast repertoire at his disposal. His experience conducting operas and concerts—over a span of some sixty years as Kapellmeister—was more or less comprehensive. For the most part, it involved premiering his own works and those by others, although eventually, as his habits changed during his Vienna tenure, this focus faded (although without affecting his technical precepts). After 1918, Strauss only conducted premieres of his own compositions (see Table 4.1).

---

18 Strauss's recordings took place (so far we know) as follows: 1917 (Berlin); 1921 (London); 1926 (Berlin and London); 1927, 1928, 1929, 1930, and 1933 (all Berlin); 1940 and 1941 (Munich); and 1943 and 1944 (Vienna). Parts of his concerts in London (1947) have been recorded. In addition recordings exist with Strauss as pianist (1905, 1906, 1942, and 1943). The best overview is provided in Ulrich Hein, "Richard Strauss als Interpret: Die Aufnahmen auf Compact Disc: Diskographie," in Schaefer, *Richard Strauss*, 311–314.

19 This preliminary list cannot be complete. In addition it should be noted that Strauss conducted a large number of local, first performances in Meiningen, Weimar, Munich, and, especially, Berlin. Among these were some symphonies by Mahler (who was invited to conduct the premieres himself).

Table 4.1 Premieres conducted by Richard Strauss

Composer	Work	Place	Year
Ludwig Thuille	Symphony in F major	Meiningen	1886
Richard Strauss	*Burleske*	Eisenach	1886
Richard Strauss	*Aus Italien*	Munich	1887
[Richard Wagner rehearsal]	*Die Feen*	Munich	1888
Richard Strauss	*Don Juan*	Weimar	1889
Richard Strauss	*Macbeth*	Weimar	1890
Alexander Ritter	*Wem die Krone*	Weimar	1890
Richard Strauss	*Tod und Verklärung*	Eisenach	1890
Richard Metzdorf	*Hagbart und Signe*	Weimar	1893
Engelbert Humperdinck	*Hänsel und Gretel*	Weimar	1893
Felix von Mottl	*Fürst und Sänger*	Weimar	1894
Joseph Gabriel Rheinberger	Organ Concert No. 2	Munich	1894
Richard Strauss	*Guntram*	Weimar	1894
Gustav Brecher	*Rosmersholm*	Leipzig	1896
Max von Schillings	*Zwei symphonische Fantasien*	Munich	1896
Richard Strauss	*Also sprach Zarathustra*	Frankfurt	1896
Ludwig Thuille	*Theuerdank*	Munich	1897
Siegmund von Hausegger	*Zinnober*	Munich	1898
Richard Strauss	*Ein Heldenleben*	Frankfurt	1898
Leo Blech	*Das Tal*	Berlin	1903
Bernhard Scholz	*Anno 1757*	Berlin	1903
Richard Strauss	*Symphonia domestica*	New York	1904
Engelbert Humperdinck	*Die Heirat wider Willen*	Berlin	1905
Jean Sibelius	Concert for Violin and Orchestra in D major, new version	Berlin	1905
Richard Strauss	*Zwei Militärmärsche*	Berlin	1907
Heinrich XIV Bolko von Hochberg	Symphony No. 3 in F major	Berlin	1909
Ernst Boehe	*Die Klage der Nausikaa*	Berlin	1911
Franz Poenitz	*Vineta*	Berlin	1911

Table 4.1 Continued

Composer	Work	Place	Year
Philipp Rüfer	Sinfonie No. 1	Berlin	1912
Wilhelm Taubert	Suite for String Orchestra	Berlin	1912
Richard Strauss	Ariadne auf Naxos, first version	Stuttgart	1912
Georg Schumann	Variations and Fugue on a theme by Bach	Berlin	1914
Antonio Scontrino	Sinfonia romantica	Berlin	1914
Richard Strauss	Josephs Legende	Paris	1914
Richard Strauss	Eine Alpensinfonie	Berlin	1915
Siegmund von Hausegger	Barbarossa: Symphonic Poem in Three Movements	Berlin	1916
Richard Mandl	Ouvertüre zu einem gaskognischen Ritterspiel	Berlin	1916
Georg Schumann	Im Ringen um ein Ideal, Symphonic Poem	Berlin	1916
Robert Müller-Hartmann	Symphonic Overture	Berlin	1917
George Szell	Variations on an Original Theme	Berlin	1917
Ewald Strässer	Drei Frühlingsbilder	Berlin	1917
Felix von Weingartner	Symphony No. 4	Berlin	1917
Waldemar von Bausznern	Symphony No. 4	Berlin	1918
Cornelis Dopper	Symphony No. 6, "Amsterdam"	Berlin	1918
Wilhelm Taubert	Symphony in G minor	Berlin	1918
Hermann Hans Wetzler	Ouverture to Shakespeare's As You Like It	Berlin	1918
Richard Strauss	Der Bürger als Edelmann	Vienna	1921
Richard Strauss	Schlagobers	Vienna	1922
Ludwig van Beethoven	Die Ruinen von Athen, new version (Strauss)	Berlin	1924
Richard Strauss	Der Rosenkavalier—film score	Dresden	1926
Richard Strauss	Austria	Vienna	1929
Richard Strauss	Suite from Schlagobers	Mannheim	1932

(continued)

Table 4.1 Continued

Composer	Work	Place	Year
Richard Strauss	Olympische Hymne	Berlin	1936
Richard Strauss	Festmusik der Stadt Wien	Vienna	1943

Ultimately, the conductor and the composer parted ways—in keeping with Strauss's view that if his work belonged to the twentieth century, it had also put an end to the cultural context from which it arose.

CHAPTER FIVE

Poetry of the Real

THE TONE POEMS

Distance from Wagner

In 1910, at the first Congress of German Sociologists in Frankfurt am Main, Max Weber offered a lengthy response to a lecture the economist Werner Sombart had delivered on "Technology and Culture." In the course of his remarks, he also spoke about music, specifically the relationship between "artistic will" and its technical requirements. In this context, Richard Wagner's oeuvre marks a dividing line:

> As a rule, artistic will produces the technical means for solving a problem. On this point, Sombart is naturally quite right: there is no doubt that music like Wagner's and all that followed it, up to Richard Strauss, has technical requirements in terms of instrumentation and orchestration. However, at most we would speak of "conditions"—which, as given, the artist must "take into account," and especially as *limitations*. The "technique" the artist needs and *can* have, he *creates*; technique itself does not give him this.[1]

---

[1] "Die Regel ist, daß das künstlerische Wollen sich die technischen Mittel zu einer Problemlösung gebiert. Natürlich, darin hat Sombart ganz recht: es ist kein Zweifel, daß eine Musik wie die Wagnersche und alles, was ihr gefolgt ist, bis zu Richard Strauß, instrumental- und orchestraltechnische Voraussetzungen hat. Aber wir würden auch dabei wohl höchstens von 'Bedingungen' sprechen, mit denen, als gegeben, der Künstler zu 'rechnen' hatte und zwar als mit *Schranken*. Denn was er an 'Technik' braucht und haben *kann, schafft* er sich, nicht aber die Technik ihm." Max Weber, "Geschäftsbericht und Diskussionsreden auf dem ersten Deutschen Soziologentage in Frankfurt 1910," in Marianne Weber (ed.). *Gesammelte Aufsätze zur Soziologie und Sozialpolitik* (Tübingen: Mohr, 2nd ed., 1988), 454.

Richard Strauss would probably have agreed with this definition of the relationship between "technique" and "artistic will"—although he would have spoken of "expression" instead of "will." It is also likely that he would have agreed with another distinction Weber made: the question concerning instrumental technique and musical will, which admits historical delimitation, must be posed in conjunction with the sociological question concerning the "spirit" of a given kind of music and the attendant conditions of modern metropolitan life. The composer's lifelong effort to refine orchestral settings (which was especially vigorous into the 1920s) was based on his belief that the orchestra—already an urban phenomenon by nature—provides an appropriate "instrument" and that its limitations in fact offer a challenge; this view is still evident in the singular dissolution of boundaries that occurs in late works. At the same time, Strauss acknowledged that this technical aspect is not autonomous, but indebted to the conditions of the present—as such, it should serve to make art part of life once more.

In other words, Strauss found limitations not only in the orchestral apparatus itself, but also in the forms of communication connected with it. His letter to Bülow (August 1888) already makes this argument:

> But whether I can immediately reverse the direction in which I have been moving by way of development from the F minor symphony is something about which I cannot yet give an assurance. A linking up with the Beethoven of "Coriolan," "Egmont," the "Leonore" III Overture, of "Les Adieux," above all with late Beethoven, whose complete oeuvre, in my opinion, could never have been created without a poetic subject, seems to me the only course for the time being by which an *independent further* development of our instrumental music is yet possible. If I lack the artistic power and talent to achieve something worthwhile in this direction, then it is certainly better to let it rest with the big 9 and their four distinguished offshoots; I don't understand why, before we have tried our strength to see whether we are capable of independent creativity and perhaps advancing our art by a tiny step, we immediately want to talk ourselves into decadence and assume the attitude of decadence in advance; if nothing comes of it—well: I still think it is better perhaps to have taken a wrong turning and said something wrong, but in

pursuit of one's genuine artistic conviction, than to have said something superfluous on the old, well trodden high road.²

Far-reaching conclusions follow from this diagnosis:

> If you want to create a work of art that is unified in its mood and consistent in its structure, and if it is to give the listener a clear and definite impression, then what the author wants to say must have been just as clear and definite in his own mind. This is only possible through the inspiration by a poetical idea, whether or not it be introduced as a programme. I consider it a legitimate artistic method to create a correspondingly new form for every new subject, to shape which neatly and perfectly is a very difficult task, but for that very reason the more attractive. Of course, purely formalistic, Hanslickian music-making will no longer be possible.³

Hereby, Strauss committed himself to the conditions for composing associated with—indeed, created by—Wagner, especially those bearing on the orchestra. He would hold to them all his life. At the same time, however, he called into question their normative validity, as well as the paradigm of the symphony; ultimately, in 1896, this would lead him to break with the Bayreuth cult.⁴ Wagner himself considered *Musikdrama* to represent the necessary consequence of the failure of "pure" instrumental music, which, in his eyes, had reached its apogee in Beethoven's Ninth. Strauss, on the other hand, thought the paradigm of instrumental music would prove viable at least "for a while"—that is, for as long as its internal borders could be transgressed in a meaningful way. That is also why he avoided the consequence drawn by Mahler, who reached back to vocal elements (and, in so doing, to the claims of Beethoven's Ninth) in his instrumental works. When Strauss advocated individualized form—in other words, the idea that form does not bring

---

2 Hans von Bülow and Richard Strauss, *Correspondence* 81–83; Letter to Hans von Bülow, August 24, 1888.
3 Ibid.
4 Strauss reflects on the break with Bayreuth in his "Schreibkalender" (January 11, 1896), recalling a discussion with Siegfried Wagner ("zwar unausgesprochene, aber vollzogene Trennung von Wahnfried-Bayreuth"; Schuh, *Richard Strauss*, 414.

forth a work so much as it is necessary to find specific configurations for each composition and whatever is to be expressed in conjunction with it—it meant subjecting the paradigm of instrumental music as a whole to a violation of boundaries. In this context, "form" becomes a component of "technique." In shifting to operatic composition, then, Strauss was not turning to Wagnerian music-drama; instead—and already in *Guntram*—he called the latter into question by pursuing a new crossing of boundaries. In keeping with his reading of Nietzsche, Strauss took a measured step that observed limits insofar as it raised no claims to normativity.

Strauss's name for his conception of instrumental music was *Tondichtung*. Although he did not invent the term (Carl Loewe had used it from 1824 on to describe certain piano works on a grand scale), he sought to lend it a specific meaning—perhaps in contradistinction to Wagner, who occasionally used the word to refer to Beethoven's symphonies. (Nietzsche avoided the designation.[5]) Strauss wanted to preserve the aspect of communication he had learned from Liszt—in other words, "content," however one defines it. On the other hand, he wanted to dispense with symphonic aspects, which Liszt still sought to achieve with his "symphonic poetry." And so, just as much as Strauss fell under Wagner's spell (especially through Ritter), he also, as a good reader of Nietzsche, set himself apart from the Wagnerian project because he did not believe it could be continued in a productive fashion. Accordingly, his preface to Berlioz's *Treatise on Instrumentation* (1905) ties his forebear's incontestable prominence in contemporary composition precisely to this feature: Wagner "combined the *symphonic* (polyphonic) technique of composition and orchestration with the rich expressive sources of the *dramatic* (homophonic) style."[6] The formulation encapsulates the tension between "will" and "technique." Strauss considered the "polyphonic" possibilities of orchestration, not its "dramatic" components, central.

---

5 In his 1852 explanation of Beethoven's *Eroica* Wagner used the term "highly significant tone poem" ("höchst bedeutsame Tondichtung"); Richard Wagner, "Beethoven's 'heroische Symphonie'," in *Gesammelte Schriften und Dichtungen*, vol. 5 (Leipzig: Fritzsch, 2nd ed., 1888), 169.

6 Berlioz and Strauss, *Treatise on Instrumentation*, ii.

His later formulations—"psychic polyphony" and "nervous counterpoint"⁷ —mean much the same.

What Strauss wrote to Bülow in 1888 concerned *Macbeth*—a work that would endlessly vex the latter. It had been preceded by *Aus Italien*, which had been inspired by the composer's first trip to Italy (especially southern parts) in spring 1886; dedicated to Bülow, it had premiered in Munich in 1887. The subtitle announces a "symphonic fantasy." Prior to Strauss, only Tchaikovsky had employed this generic designation; subsequently, it was used only rarely—and by composers Strauss had influenced, such as Gustav Brecher, Bruno Walter, and Max Reger. Although *Aus Italien* comprises four movements and displays traditional orchestration, it stands apart from convention by unfolding in G major, a key "unburdened" by associations with the symphonies of Beethoven and Brahms (or, for that matter, Bruckner). The four movements only indirectly meet the requirements of a sonata cycle. In his sole published commentary on one of his own works, Strauss observed that *Aus Italien* switches the "correct" sequence.⁸ In fact, the piece is unusual in other ways, too. Although the first movement exhibits aspects of sonata form, the overall design is simply expository: the languorous introduction does not give way to a second movement in the full sense. *Aus Italien* is idiosyncratic and autobiographical. Taking distance from the paradigm of "absolute" music, it conveys "*sensations* felt when viewing the majestic, natural beauty of Rome and Naples, *not descriptions* of the same—I was given a musical Baedeker to read."⁹

---

7 Even in a text written in 1942 Strauss uses the term ("psychischer Polyphonie") in reference to *Elektra*, reflecting the utmost limits of harmony ("äußersten Grenzen der Harmonik"); "Erinnerung an die ersten Aufführungen meiner Opern," in *Betrachtungen und Erinnerungen*, 230; the text remained unpublished during his lifetimes. In a letter to Joseph Gegor he discusses Wagner's orchestra, the "psychological counterpoint" ("seelischer Contrapunkt") of *Tristan,* and Cosima's role in Bayreuth. In this context he mentions his own "subtle, nervous counterpoint, if this audacious expression be permitted" ('subtilen Nervencontrapunkt', wenn der gewagte Ausdruck gestattet ist"') (Roland Tenschert (ed.), *Richard Strauss und Joseph Gregor: Briefwechsel* (Salzburg: Müller 1955), 17; letter of January 8, 1935).

8 Richard Strauss, "Aus Italien (op. 16): Sinfonische Fantasie (G-Dur) für Orchester," in *Allgemeine Deutsche Musik-Zeitung* 16 (1889), 263–266.

9 "*Empfindungen* beim Anblick der herrlichen Naturschönheiten Roms und Neapels, *nicht Beschreibungen* derselben – ein musikalischer Baedeker Süditaliens bekam ich einmal zu lesen." Schuh, *Richard Strauss*, 135; undated letter to Karl Wolf. It seems that the invective refers to Joachim Raff and his *Italienische Suite* (1871).

Aus Italien does not focus on culture, but nature. Hence Strauss's observation:

> It really is ridiculous to suggest that a present-day composer, whose tutors have been the classics, especially late Beethoven, as well as Wagner and Liszt, would write a work three-quarters of an hour in length in order to show off with the kind of piquant tone painting and brilliant instrumentation that almost every advanced composition student still at the conservatory can write nowadays. *Expression* is our art, and a piece of music which has nothing truly poetic to convey to me—content that is, of course, which can be properly represented *only in music,* a content that words may be able to *suggest but only suggest*—a piece like that in my view is anything you care to call it—but not music.[10]

Such poeticization (in Strauss's parlance, "expression") acknowledges no outward frame of reference. The "images" in *Aus Italien* cannot, nor are they supposed to, claim general validity. This aspect is particularly evident in the treatments given to the encounter with antiquity: a formative experience for generations of travelers plays only a mediated role, during the second movement (*In Roms Ruinen*). The final movement starts with Luigi Denaza's song *Funiculi, Funiculà* (1880), which is matter-of-factly styled as a "popular" element. The composition bears on the present more than anything. The tone poems after *Aus Italien* display the same fundamental bearing. Like Brahms, Strauss began working on highly different, and often opposing, works simultaneously. The first instance of the approach occurred with *Macbeth* and *Don Juan*; it is also the path Strauss took for his operas, when he worked on *Daphne* and *Feuersnot*, and *Capriccio* and *Liebe der Danae*, concurrently.

In the early tone poems literary texts occupy the center for the first and last time. For *Macbeth*, Strauss used the translation that Schiller had made at Weimar in 1800; no doubt he was mindful of the prominent position the latter granted Shakespeare alongside Homer in *Über naive und sentimentalische Dichtung*. The only words accompanying the score start with Lady Macbeth's theme in measure 65. In *Daybreak* (1881), Nietzsche had discussed *Macbeth* as theater that does not exemplify moral instruction

---

10 Schuh, *Richard Strauss*, 136.

or catharsis so much as self-assertion: "He who is really possessed by raging ambition beholds this its image with *joy*; and if the hero perishes by his passion this is precisely the sharpest spice in the hot draught of this joy."[11] Strauss, it seems, endorses this interpretation of uncompromising resolve that violates standing borders.

The first part may be understood to echo the expository sonata form. (Incidentally, it is also the only section to exist in a revised version.) Two opposing themes occur in juxtaposition: "Macbeth" and "Lady Macbeth."[12] Content, not form, determines the relationship between the themes. The brief (five-bar) introduction does not only provide a portentous fanfare that acquires tectonic significance in the further course of the piece. It also evokes Beethoven's Ninth Symphony—and, more specifically, Wagner's stylization of the latter work into a turning-point in the genre. Significantly, Strauss conjures up this framework in order, first, to level it completely and then, out of the pieces (of the fanfare, in particular), to fashion a new arrangement. The introduction (in A) and main movement (in D) stand in a cadential relationship. Once the two themes have been counterposed, the formal contours begin to disappear. Episodes haunted by ambiguity create a succession of indeterminate and equal parts. This holds even for a sequence that suggests a reprise for formal and thematic reasons—as well as the fact that the score specifies *tempo primo*. It is preceded by a brief passage evoking the funeral march in the coda of the first movement to Beethoven's Ninth—although it distorts it by putting it into three-quarter time. If Strauss decided to revise *Macbeth*, he did so to make this aspect more apparent. The triumphal march originally planned for Macduff would have connoted ethical cleansing—which the composer, as a reader of Nietzsche, could not admit. The wild and stormy work—whose drastic nature represents an exception in his *oeuvre*—exemplifies an effort to perform a character study by heightening the relationship between "expression" and "technique."

In contrast, *Don Juan* steers a calmer course. Now that he had made a break with convention, Strauss no longer deemed such radical measures

---

11 Friedrich Nietzsche, *Daybreak: Thoughts on the Prejudices of Morality,* trans. R. J. Hollingdale (Cambridge: Cambridge University Press, 1997), 140 (§240).

12 In the first case one can find an explicit remark in the score ("Macbeth"), in the second a single explicit quotation from the text (I, 9); the reference here is to the third version.

necessary. His distance from Wagner also appears in the orchestration; while the bass trumpet performs a key function in *Macbeth,* here it is not featured at all. Strauss selected three passages from Nikolaus Lenau's (1802–1850) posthumously published drama in verse, of the same name, for his own *Don Juan.* Although taken from different parts of the play (the first two passages from the beginning, the third from a section closer to the end), they form a unified context, offering a portrait of the title character while omitting plot. Significantly, Lenau was considered the poetic counterpart of Nietzsche among the skeptical philosopher's younger readers. In other words, Strauss's enlistment of Lenau amounts to a corrective to literary and cultural history: since Mozart and E.T.A. Hoffmann (up to Mahler's productions at the Vienna Court Opera), *Don Giovanni* had been a work charged with metaphysical claims. Strauss changes Don Juan from a figure of metaphysical yearning into an embodiment of nihilism; erotic excesses do not elicit punishment so much as simply fade into nothingness. Formally, the work unfolds in much the same way as *Macbeth*: after a fulgurous beginning leading to the mediant, and main key, of E major, two contrasting themes emerge—which would seem to indicate movement toward sonata form. This is not the case. In contrast to *Macbeth,* the thematic figurations achieve a dense, plastic quality. For the first time, Strauss demonstrates the fondness for paratactic sequences that, from now on, will define his compositions—as well as the will to deny a final gesture of triumph to a fundamentally pessimistic work. Alternating between E minor and D minor, the composition fades away—like its protagonist—and, with it, any and every idea of formal or "technical" universality. With *Macbeth* and *Don Juan,* Strauss took leave from Wagner—albeit without casting doubt on his forebear's importance for his own work. In turn, the tone poems would establish a new foundation for "will" and "technique."

Leaving behind the Metaphysics of Music

In retrospect, the path Strauss steered in his tone poems seems extraordinarily consistent, even though there is no evidence that he was following a strict plan. Shortly before fleeing to the Netherlands in 1939, the Germanist Georg Witkowski (1863–1939) described the composer's manner as "realistic." Hereby, he understood "realism" as "everything that counts as daring, if not illicit, from the standpoint of conventional bourgeois morality." Specifically, Witkowski was referring to "the mixture of Zola, Ibsen, and Tolstoy's 'power of darkness,' combined with the theory it entails. In painting, [this attitude] emerges when Franz von Uhde turns equal attention to all parts of actual existence; in music, [it is evident] in Richard Strauss's early works."[13] (Witkowski had the composer's initial series of tone poems in mind when writing of "early works.") *Tod und Verklärung* (1888–1889) represents a surprising turn. For the first time, the composer dispensed with a literary component. Prompted by his readings of Schopenhauer, Strauss foregrounded material that did not come from an external source but, as he wrote to Cosima Wagner, had "imposed itself as inevitable necessity."[14] Alexander Ritter took Strauss's words as an affirmation of the integral connection between life and work—that is, as his friend's surrender to orthodox Wagnerism—and wrote a programmatic poem for the piece. Strauss allowed it to be published with the score, but he did so with reservations. In fact, the work was meant as the complete opposite: life should pervade the work of art and thereby acquire a wholly new charge.

Strauss had doubts about the autobiographical aspects of composition, which Ritter took for granted. On the one hand, he acknowledged that "six years ago, the idea occurred to me of depicting, in a tone poem, the final hour of a human being who, all his life, had strived for the highest ideas, that is, an artist."[15] However, Schopenhauer's conception of will had taught him to reject any personal connection:

> A real experience was not at at issue; at this point, I had not endured any serious illness myself, nor had I witnessed another human being dying; I also cannot recall a direct model in what I had been reading.[16]

13 "alles, was vom Standpunkt konventioneller bürgerlicher Moral als gewagt, als eigentlich unerlaubt galt," "jenes Gemisch aus Anregungen Zolas, Ibsens und der 'Macht der Finsternis' Tolstois mit einer daraus abgeleiteten Theorie. In der Malerei trat das freilich als gleichwertige Annäherung an die Wirklichkeit in den Bildern Fritz von Uhdes hervor, in der Musik bei Richard Strauss mit seinen Frühwerken." Georg Witkowski, *Von Menschen und Büchern: Erinnerungen 1863–1933* (Leipzig: Lehmstedt, 2003), 326.
14 "sich ihm eben mit unabwendbarer Notwendigkeit." Franz Trenner with Gabriele Strauss (ed.), *Cosima Wagner—Richard Strauss: Ein Briefwechsel* (Tutzing: Schneider, 1978), 36.
15 "Es war vor 6 Jahren, als mir der Gedanke auftauchte, die Todesstunde eines Menschen, der nach den höchsten ideellen Zielen gestrebt hatte, also wohl eines Künstlers, in einer Tondichtung darzustellen." Strauss, "Schaffen," in *Die Tondichtungen von Richard Strauss*, 538.
16 "ein wirkliches Erlebniß lag nicht vor; ich hatte bis dahin weder selbst eine schwere Krankheit durchgemacht noch der Todesstunde eines Menschen beigewohnt; auch aus meiner Lectüre ist mir eine directe Andeutung nicht erinnerlich." Ibid.

In other words, the "realistic mode of expression" was not in line with the standard conception of lyric in the late nineteenth century, whereby "experience" underlies works of art. Instead, it represents a "cerebral process": an "insignificant stimulus" is "unconsciously placed under a magnifying glass and elaborated from within, for years."[17] Strauss's physiologico-psychological terminology also points to another conclusion he drew from Schopenhauer. The appeal to free will as the parameter for creation—and here, Strauss took marked distance from Ritter—meant breaking, once and for all, with the themes of death and redemption that, ever since *Tristan,* had supposedly ensured the coherence of musical works; indeed, it meant breaking with placing any metaphysical demands on music.

The compositional core of *Tod und Verklärung* does not involve reference to Wagner. Rather, the work takes up a decisive topos of symphonic form in the nineteenth century: the breakthrough of C minor following a sequence in C major; tellingly—and as in Beethoven's Fifth—the C minor sets in as an "indeterminate," major third: E♭–G. That said, *Tod und Verklärung* does not just begin in a "blurry" manner in metrical, dynamic, and harmonic terms; it ends the same way, too. In other words, the shift amounts to an act of revision: instead of representing a structurally justified, metaphysically augmented gesture of triumph (as in the D major Mahler employed in his First Symphony, composed at about the same time), it represents a turning point based on the formative power of free will alone; then it falls silent and vanishes. This radically anti-metaphysical conception of music emerges from a compositional topos that, with its citational nature on display, undergoes devaluation. (The same occurs at the beginning of *Macbeth.*) As it solemnly takes the stage, the convention is stripped it of its historico-ideational content. At the end of his life, Strauss would renew the skepticism—if not nihilism—declared here, quoting the work again in *Vier letzte Lieder.*

Shortly after the premiere of *Tod und Verklärung,* Strauss enthusiastically read *Der Einzige und sein Eigentum* by Max Stirner (1806–1856), which advances an anti-Hegelian conception of the subject inspired by John

---

17 "realistische Ausdrucksweise," "cerebraler Prozeß," "unbedeutende Anregung," "unbewußt unter ein Vergrößerungsglas gesetzt u. Jahre lang innerlich ausgebaut wird." Ibid.

Henry Mackay's novel, *The Anarchists* (which had appeared in Zurich in 1891). In a letter to his father, the composer extolled Stirner as "the most important antagonist of Schopenhauer and Christianity" for the "absolute egoism" he propounded.[18] The literary encounter also provided the backdrop for the dialectic of the two tone poems that followed. *Also sprach Zarathustra* (1895) and *Till Eulenspiegels lustige Streiche* (1896) were conceived in parallel from the outset; both pieces bear the mark of Nietzsche and Stirner. Around the turn of the century, Till Eulenspiegel experienced a boom as the embodiment of the fool (for instance, in Dehmel's comedy *Michel Michael* [1911] and Wedekind's *Oaha* [1908]). Strauss took keen interest in the character and at one point even intended to write an opera. However, his tone poem does without literary models; for the first time, the composer set out without intending to follow a pre-established program; the subtitle simply indicates ironic distance: "in old-fashioned, roguish manner [*nach alter Schelmenweise*]." In purposeful contrast to its gigantic orchestration, the work lasts for about a quarter of an hour, developing a narrative (which is at most tangentially related to an actual "plot") with the modern artist in the guise of a fool, who experiences triumph at the same time as he encounters failure. For the first time in the tone poems, an anachronistic "rondeau form," in conjunction with the key of F major, lends a certain solidity to the proceedings. At the same time, this musical structure does not stand on its own so much as it follows from the "roguish" narrative. Accordingly, it culminates in a frenzy following the hero's death: a "punchline" that stands diametrically opposed to the very idea of the rondeau.

Zarathustra represents a complementary, if more pointed, formulation of the same approach. Cosima Wagner expressed immense confusion that Strauss did not opt for a literary but a philosophical text—and moreover by an author who had become an opponent of her husband. The circumstance warrants notice for two reasons. For one, it was now clear that Strauss's tone poems were not "narratives"—that is, his concept of poeticization had no straightforward, expository intentions. Strauss did not embrace the "expressivity" of the late nineteenth century: moods, atmospheres, or "life experiences." Second, his choice made a new demand on music with vast implications. His syntactic principle

18 Schuh, *Richard Strauss*, 258; letter to Franz Strauss, April 7, 1892.

of composition corresponds to the Nietzschean method of replacing dogmatic-axiomatic doctrine with a purposefully heterogeneous collection of aphorisms, observations, and commentaries. The bond holding such philosophy together does not rest on "logic" so much as association. The approach would hold great significance for Strauss's operas, too. In this light, the two-part structure of *Zarathustra* is not a matter of sonata form (however modified). Instead, formal expansion outward—and in keeping with the shorter tone poems Strauss already composed—involves an elaborate dramaturgy of contrasts, whose meaning does not follow from working through motifs logically. The monumental C major cadence that begins the work by hoisting a flag, as it were—a gesture as famous as it is commonly misunderstood—does not represent a goal so much as a point of departure. Over the course of the rest of the piece, it comes to stand—"always immobile, rigid, [and] unchanged," Strauss specifies in the sketches—as a constant marker of boundaries. The phrases from Nietzsche's text, rhapsodically scattered throughout the score, indicate that it obeys a coherent, but not a systematic, principle of "narration." *Zarathustra*, presenting tragic counterpole to the "fool" of *Till*, announces a musical anti-metaphysics—indeed, the complete end of organic musical thinking.

"Autobiography" and New Musical Semantics

Tod und Verklärung had already tested out a novel kind of musical semantics deriving not from absolutes but individual action. Strauss always denied the autobiographical connotations of his works: although radical subjectivization permits art to "function" in the first place, the matter does not involve personal "experience." The balancing act he struck has given rise to any number of misunderstandings—in particular, the view that his music tells the story of his own life. Although aware of the risks his position entailed, Strauss made no compromises. The resulting tensions also shaped the tone poems following *Tod und Verklärung*. These works also emerged in tandem, between the end of 1896 and late 1898. As with *Till* and *Zarathustra*, the "more ironic" work was embedded, as it were, in the "more serious" one; that is, Strauss started it later and completed it sooner. *Zarathustra* elaborated the outer, symphonic dimension of composition. The works that followed were meant to complete a concert program. That said (and in contrast to, say, Mahler), they never filled out an entire evening and required the contrast of other works—even *Eine Alpensinfonie*.

By its very title, *Ein Heldenleben* evokes Beethoven's *Eroica*—as does the key of E♭ major. Strauss himself still stressed this context in 1946, insisting that the nineteenth century "ultimately ran from *Eroica* to *Heldenleben*."[19] But *Ein Heldenleben* represents a rejoinder to *Eroica*—just as the composer's *Festliches Präludium*, written fifteen years later, responds to the Ninth Symphony with a similar gesture. Beethoven's title heralds objectivation: the heroic independence of seemingly autonomous music (with the *Marcia funebre* precisely halfway through). Strauss, in contrast, opts for a title signifying unconditional subjectivation. The indefinite article (*"Ein" Heldenleben*) makes as much plain, as does the avoidance of symphonic elements. Strauss cycled through a series of titles he later abandoned (*Der Held, Des Helden Widersacher*, and so on). The new musical semantics he sought did not need to be spelled out so directly. Scholars have often observed that *Ein Heldenleben* ultimately resembles a symphony in its merging of sonata form and sonata cycle. However—and as Mathias Hansen has stressed—this view is misleading. The piece does not amount to a restoration of form so much as it affirms the worth of independent elements functioning as discrete, "plastic" units. As the nineteenth century drew to a close, Strauss came to the conclusion that musical communication could occur only by way of characterization, not through inherited formal arrangements; this is also why the work contains numerous self-quotations.

From the outset, *Don Quixote* was conceived as a foil—a "satyr-play," as Strauss put it in his working notes.[20] Indeed, the composer wanted both pieces to premiere together, even though this did not occur. They represent "direct pendants to such an extent that *Don Q.*, in particular, can be understood in full only after *Heldenleben*."[21] The pairing is significant, and not just because the "stories" remain "unfocused" and vague in either case. The "subjectivated," symphonic form of *Heldenleben* and

---

19 "schließlich von der *Eroica* bis zum *Heldenleben* gereicht hat." *Briefwechsel mit Willi Schuh*, 92; letter to Willi Schuh, June 2, 1946.
20 Entry of April 16, 1897; Schuh, *Richard Strauss*, 465.
21 Letter to Gustav Kogel, April 20, 1897, ibid.

the "objectivated" variations that constitute *Quixote* stand in opposition, simultaneously reinforcing and calling each other into question. The "symphonic" form of *Ein Heldenleben* emerges only through its musical characterization. Conversely, the ten variations constituting *Don Quixote* (which begins with a "bipolar" theme and unfolds accordingly) gradually abandon the contours defined at the outset. In his journal, Romain Rolland remarked that the piece amounts to "sketches, scenes in miniature, rather than real descriptions."[22] The same holds for the way the composition as a whole is organized: it does not feature a functioning sequence of variations so much as a series of disjointed parts—like a collection of aphorisms.

It is not by accident that Nietzsche provides a key to understanding the works. Don Quixote and "the Hero" are two articulations of the same character, defined by modern, anti-metaphysical self-affirmation. The first volume of *Human, All Too Human* takes the Christian need for redemption and "false" heroism to task:

> The Christian who compares his nature with that of God is like Don Quixote, who under-estimated his own courage because his head was filled with the miraculous deeds of the heroes of chivalric romances: the standard of comparison applied in both cases belongs in the domain of fable.[23]

In this light, the semantics of the tone poems derives from radically concentrating on the modern subject. At most, autobiography serves as a vehicle; it does not represent a goal. This is also the context for understanding the decisive step Strauss took after completing *Ein Heldenleben*. Having composed a series of tone poems at breakneck pace, he finally returned—after a pause of several years and while working on *Feuersnot*—to the symphony. Strauss did not do so because he now acknowledged that its formal requirements were valid, after all. Instead, he went about reinterpreting the elements of symphonic composition in terms of the modern individual's confrontation with nihilism; here, the traditional

---

22 Rollo Myers (ed.), *Richard Strauss & Romain Rolland: Correspondence* (Berkeley and Los Angeles: University of California Press, 1968), 121; letter of May 20, 1899.

23 Friedrich Nietzsche, *Human, All Too Human*, trans. R. J. Hollingdale (Cambridge: Cambridge University Press, 1996), 72.

parameters of composition amount to "social" institutions for securing a place in the world. Strauss's collaboration with Hofmannsthal on a new conception of comedy would soon affirm this bond as the only way for the individual to achieve a suitably flexible ("plastic") constitution.

Symphonia domestica (1903), then, does not celebrate the bourgeois individual. Instead, the work valorizes art that stands firm under modern conditions. Surface features already indicate the rupture: the combination of Greek (*symphonia*) and Latin (*domestica*) in the title, the "pastoral" key of F major, and the "confusion" of traditional and modern names for movements, which heightens contrast. At some three-quarters of an hour in length, this monumental work stands as one of Strauss's longest tone poems. The newly achieved dimension of character forms the work's centerpiece.

Although he included few of them in the score, Strauss's programmatic remarks irritated his contemporaries, who deemed his unabashed fusion of autobiographical matters and the work of art pushy and intrusive. However, when addressing objections voiced by Rolland, the composer was quite clear:

> In my opinion, too, a poetic programme is nothing but a pretext for the purely musical expression and development of my emotions, and not a simple *musical description* of concrete everyday facts. For that would be quite contrary to the spirit of music. But so that music should not lose itself in pure abstractions and drift in limitless directions, it needs to be held within bounds which determine a certain form, and it is the programme which fixes these bounds. And an analytic program of this kind should be nothing more than a starting-point. Those who are interested in it can use it. Those who really know how to listen to music doubtless have no need for it.[24]

Symphonia domestica does not mean to transfigure the everyday through high-flung composition, but to make quotidian experience suffuse art. Ultimately, it seeks a productive relationship with the world by suspending the pretensions of symphonic form and addressing humankind as a whole.

---

24 *Richard Strauss & Romain Rolland*, 29; letter of July 5, 1905.

CHAPTER SIX

Music without Metaphysics

THE PATH TO OPERA

Künstleropern

Strauss's turn to opera followed from his view that the validity of instrumental music was limited in scope. At first, the composer made hesitant steps, but then bolder and bolder strides—until all else vanished. The process lasted for about a decade, between his thirtieth and fortieth years of life (which coincided with the shift from the nineteenth century to the twentieth). That said, the change did not occur in response to any sense of crisis. Moreover, it was not uncommon at the time for composers to try their hand at opera only upon reaching relative maturity: Debussy was about thirty when he completed *Pelléas et Mélisande*, Schoenberg about thirty-five when he finished *Erwartung*, and Humperdinck almost forty when he was done with *Hänsel und Gretel*. Strauss's case was unusual because he had been acknowledged as a European composer of the first order since his twenties. Accordingly, his shift to operatic composition occurred within a context fraught with tension and reflection about the artist's role in modernity, the task of art, and, finally, how to confront Wagner's legacy.

The sole element of crisis attending the move was circumstantial. In 1891, Strauss fell ill with serious pulmonary inflammation; he never fully recovered and, the following year, the condition became life-threatening. On the lengthy trip he took to Greece, Egypt, and southern Italy to recover his health—a voyage financed by his uncle Georg Pschorr—the composer read intensively and found a new sense of orientation. He also set out plans for an opera—*Guntram*—for the first time. None of his previous ventures along these lines (including those involving Cosima Wagner) had gone beyond the planning stage.

Strauss had started work on *Guntram* in 1887, but only set about giving it concrete form while he recovered during the second half of 1892.[1] *Guntram* records, as it were, two stages of the composer's voyage: the musical core was completed in Cairo in December 1892, Act One in Luxor two months later, Act Two in June 1893 in Sicily, and Act Three back at the de Ahna family's country house in Marquartstein, Bavaria (where Franz Strauss also came to stay on occasion). As such, the piece was written during a trip that also served as a traditional educational journey [*Bildungsreise*], even if this was not its motivation. It is also telling that Strauss based his travel journal on the model of Goethe's *Wilhelm Meisters Wanderjahre*. This diary constitutes a fairly detailed autobiographical document, even if it remained fragmentary (and went unpublished during the author's lifetime). As Strauss told Cosima Wagner, he made the voyage in an effort to approach "the primal state of artistic feeling, so to speak."[2]

The trip to Egypt via Greece and back through Sicily thus represented an exploratory venture. Strauss hoped that outer (retrospective) history and subjective (prospective) experience would come together, but he was not looking to reconcile art and life. On the contrary, he sought to determine the role of the latter in shaping the former. Strauss traveled in the company of Goethe's and Wagner's works; in addition to mending his health, he wanted to work on new projects, especially operas.

The composer also intended to create a productive distance from Schopenhauer. He had come to view the philosopher's pessimism in a critical light, above all thanks to the valorization of individual action he had learned from Nietzsche. Such a position went beyond free will to involve love: the vital link between the forms that will assumes and its point of origin, a flesh-and-blood human being.

---

1 The best chronology is found in Schuh, *Richard Strauss*, 267 ff.
2 "sich gleichsam dem Urzustande künstlerischen Gefühls anzunähern." *Cosima Wagner—Richard Strauss: Ein Briefwechsel*, 142; letter of December 9, 1892.

> Between "nature" and "art" . . . stands love, as that which is governed by the strongest drive (of human life) and belonging really, as the necessary extension of one's own ego, to "being alone with oneself."[3]

Strauss did not view love as metaphysical yearning for redemption that can never be fulfilled so much as a physical experience of selfhood. In marked contrast to Schopenhauer, its focus, he observed in his journal, is "pleasure in the act of generation"—which alone gives it tangible presence. In other words, embodied eroticism is what makes reality possible in the first place, creating "awareness of *eternal being* in eternally new, neverending becoming"; such beatitude is "truly physical, not just ideal."[4] Much later, Strauss would write to Stefan Zweig: "About Sigmund Freud we have to talk some time face to face. The notion of Eros being creative in every artist was not so entirely unknown even before him."[5]

The idea that mankind's crisis can be mitigated came to be Strauss's central concern for the rest of his life. Skepticism and pessimism did not vanish, but their effects were muted, so to speak. For Strauss, the task of art is to help the individual, now free of the strictures of Christianity and European tradition, to inhabit the world. *Guntram* makes this goal plain. In contrast to what scholars have long affirmed (and as some still do), the work does not represent an outgrowth of Wagnerism; indeed, it takes a position fundamentally removed from it. The absence of a generic designation—that is, the singular title, *Guntram: In drei Aufzügen*—already indicates as much. The work depicts a singer, the eponymous hero, who frees his land from a tyrant. Yet he does not do so through the power of song, as his confraternity demands. Instead, his actions follow from his love for the tyrant's wife, Freihild, and his own jealousy. Strauss's decision to make the protagonist follow the impulse of active, embodied eros met with objection on the part of his friend Alexander Ritter. The composer

---

[3] "zwischen 'Natur' und 'Kunst' . . . steht die Liebe, als durch den stärksten Trieb (des Menschenlebens) bestimmt und als notwendige Ergänzung des eigenen Ichs eigentlich zum 'Alleinsein mit sich selbst' gehörend." Strauss, *Tagebuch*, 95 (entry for November 29, 1892).

[4] Schuh, *Richard Strauss*, 311 (entry for January 1893).

[5] "Über S. Freud müssen wir uns einmal mündlich unterhalten! Ganz so unbekannt war vor ihm doch der im Künstler producierende Eros nicht!" *Richard Strauss—Stefan Zweig: Briefwechsel*, 42; letter of January 24, 1933.

clearly took a cue from Nietzsche. In the end, his hero must pay a stiff price for his deed, renouncing both his love and his art.

The overall setting of the work displays this underlying conflict. In external terms, it still resembles Wagner. Echoes of the orchestral prelude to *Lohengrin* are unmistakeable. (Incidentally, this is the last free-standing overture Strauss would compose until *Die Schweigsame Frau*.) However, such superficial similarity covers up fundamental points of difference, which concern not only ideas (e.g., the hero's renunciation of the need for redemption) but also the tonal language. In particular, technique is under question. For Wagner, motifs had served to establish concrete presence onstage. For Strauss, they serve the purpose of "characterization" along the lines of his tone poems. In other words, they bear on the "inner life" of figures and, as such, remain unfocused on purpose. External proximity to Wagner is paired with an equally pronounced inner distance. The arrangement of musical keys (shifting from G major to G♭ major) underscores as much: *Guntram* evokes Wagner's *Ring* (with E♭ major and then D♭ major), but not "faithfully"—the key progression is abbreviated and broken in telling fashion. Wagnerian music-drama remains a productive force, but in essence represents a distant memory.

Although Strauss provided no generic designation, *Guntram* is a *Künstleroper*. The work failed to meet with success because of the demands it placed on singers—which exceeded even the rigors of *Tristan*—as well as the widespread perception that it represented yet another Wagnerian music-drama. Ten years later, when Strauss returned to the *Künstleroper*, he did not change the basic premise, but he added an ironic tone and elements of parody. In this way, he made plain the break with Wagner. This second opera, *Feuersnot*, is indebted to the milieu of the Berlin Secession, especially as Strauss wrote it in collaboration with Ernst von Wolzogen (1855–1934). Wolzogen completed the libretto at the same time as he opened a cabaret in the Alexanderstrasse. The name of the establishment, *Überbrettl*, paid parodic homage to Nietzsche's *Übermensch*. The prominent erotic allusions of the opera (which Strauss, with equal measures of archaism and irony, dubbed a *Singgedicht*) led to a conflict with the censors. Berlin had just passed the so-called *Lex Heinze*, named after a notorious pimp, which prohibited the depiction of "immoral" activities. Indeed, the director of the Hofoper, Hans Heinrich XIV Bolko von Hochberg, was forced to resign when Kaiser Wilhelm

II took offense at Wolzogen's text. Consequently, the piece premiered in Dresden on November 21, 1901, where the censors were more liberal; a staging in Berlin had to wait. The Vienna production, directed by Mahler, also encountered difficulties with the censors (who would soon prevent *Salome* from being performed).

Feuersnot is based, on the one hand, on a Dutch legend about the loss of fire and, on the other, a tale about the chaste "Virgil in a basket" already given dramatic form by Hans Sachs. The spirit of Expressionistic distortion already marks a certain distance from Wagner. Equally—but only on a superficial level—the piece settles Strauss's accounts with Munich. At the center stands self-assured individual fate, cast in a light that is more ironic than pathos-laden. In contrast to Wagnerian music drama, the couple—Kunrad and Diemut—succeed in achieving a happy union. (This constellation recurs in Strauss's later works for the stage, with the exception of *Daphne* and *Capriccio*.) The lovers in *Feuersnot* have no need for redemption. Instead, they are "delivered" when they consummate their relationship. The finale of this *Künstleroper* proves cheerful and shockingly explicit in equal measure. In the grand orchestral passage just before the last scene, instrumental music is given the task of lending concrete, "plastic" form to the sexual congress of the characters, which takes place in the play of shadows behind a lighted window. This represents more than an ingenious allusion to Plato's cave allegory in reverse—the primacy of "deed" over "idea." As Strauss himself put it, the "pleasure of the act of generation" is what rekindles light for Munich. The meaning of art does not transcend life so much as it suffuses it. Just as the cadence in C major of *Zarathustra* already contains the gesture of a "final" cadence, the ironic distance on display in *Feuersnot* conveys the appearance of a final *Künstleroper*—that is, the end of the genre.

The New Theater: Max Reinhardt in Berlin

Strauss decided to shift to opera in the context of his duties in Berlin. The period he spent here gave rise to works for the stage from *Feuersnot* to *Die Frau ohne Schatten*. In addition, this is where he struck up a meaningful relationship with Hofmannsthal. Even though Strauss now held one of the most significant musical appointments in Europe, he entertained many contacts among members of the Berlin Secession, especially its literary exponents. These contacts bore fruit in the tone poems, above all. Strauss also considered continuing his collaboration with Wolzogen after *Feuersnot*; however, an opera after Calderón never got beyond a first draft. The parodic tone evident during this period is closely tied to the flourishing world of Berlin cabaret. The Überbrettl was soon joined by other establishments such as the "Cabaret zum hungrigen Pegasus" and "Die Bösen Buben" (which both opened in the same year). These venues appealed to ambitious composers. Überbrettl, for instance, attracted Oscar Straus (even if, in Hofmannstahl's estimation, he numbered among the "luminaries of the third order"[6]), Victor Hollaender, and Arnold Schoenberg. The cabaret-milieu also had close ties to the flourishing world of the operetta which, with Paul Lincke's *Frau Luna* (1899), had become the most important musical genre in the expanding metropolis. Even after the First World War, Berlin still had some twenty stages where operettas were performed.

The most successful cabaret, however, belonged to Max Reinhardt (1873–1943). In 1901, he opened his theater in Bellevuestrasse under the somewhat ad hoc designation of "Schall und Rauch" (Smoke and Mirrors, or Sound and Fury [literally, "sound and smoke"]); the following year, when it moved to the Viktoria Hotel (Unter den Linden), it was renamed "Kleines Theater." Born 1873 in Baden bei Wien, Reinhardt had come to Berlin in 1894, where his directorial efforts exercised a magical pull on literati, painters, and musicians. After being renamed, his stage featured only spoken works; in 1905, it found a permanent home in the "Deutsches Theater"—which the director owned and managed as a private concern. In the main Reinhardt's theater featured contemporary works: Maurice Maeterlinck's *Pelléas et Mélisande*, Oscar Wilde's *Salome*, Hugo von Hofmannsthal's *Elektra*, as well as pieces that counted as forerunners of modernism—for instance, Heinrich von Kleist's *Penthesilea* and Georg Büchner's *Dantons Tod*. Strauss regularly attended performances. Without Reinhardt and his productions, the composer's musical adaptation of *Elektra* would have been inconceivable. Mustering all the forces at his disposal, Strauss insisted on Reinhardt's participation in the premiere of *Der Rosenkavalier* at the Dresden Court Opera, notwithstanding antisemitic prejudices there. He succeeded only at the last

---

6 "Herrschaften dritten Ranges." *Richard Strauss. Hugo von Hofmannsthal. Briefwechsel*, 103; letter from Hofmannstal September 10, 1910.

minute. The closeness of the connection between the composer and the director is especially evident in the production of Molière's *Bourgeois Gentilhomme*. Strauss stressed that it was wholly indebted to Reinhardt: all four versions of the music received the designation of Op. 60; with Hofmannsthal's agreement, the piece was also dedicated to him.

Reinhardt's theater—which employed such innovations as a revolving stage, original music for each piece, a new kind of scenery (marked, in particular, by the designs of Alfred Roller), and the stylized immediacy of performances exemplified by Gertrud Eysoldt (1870–1955)—heralded aesthetic modernism in its combination of past and present. In a volume of *Deutsche Theater* dedicated to his works, Hofmannsthal declared that "there cannot be any doubt the epoch starts with [Reinhardt]."[7] The director, in his contemporary's estimation, had inaugurated nothing short of an ontological event that had left behind all "conventional contexts" and taken up the primal "elements" of theater itself. This bearing overlapped with the desire Strauss had already voiced in 1892: to approach "the primordial state of artistic sensation, as it were."[8]

Conventional theater, in Hofmannsthal's estimation, had "lost touch with both the festive and the social."[9] He credited Reinhardt with completing the reform that Otto Brahm (1856–1912), his predecessor at the Deutsches Theater, had begun when he turned to naturalism—only he took it further still. Here, "the feeling of the epoch" was conveyed because "the social and the artistic" conditioned each other.[10] Reinhardt's stage captured the world as a whole, achieving the fusion of art and life. His art possessed truthfulness—and not in a quotidian (that is, naturalistic) sense, but in terms of a state of exception. This "festive" spirit would in turn animate the Salzburger Festspiele. Reinhardt's "principal composer" Einar Nilson (1881–1964), who also wrote the first score for *Jedermann*, acknowledged the significance of music: instead of merely standing "in the service of the theater," it also has the role of making clear "final,

---

7 "ohne jeden Zweifel von ihm Epoche datieren." Hugo von Hofmannsthal, "Vorrede," in Ernst Stern, Heinz Herald (ed.), *Reinhardt und seine Bühne: Bilder von der Arbeit des Deutschen Theaters* . . . (Berlin: Eysler, 1919), 3.
8 Letter to Cosima Wagner. *Cosima Wagner—Richard Strauss: Ein Briefwechsel*,
9 "sowohl das Festliche als das Soziale abhanden gekommen." Hofmannsthal, "Vorrede," 4.
10 "das Gefühle der Epoche," "Soziale und Künstleriche." Ibid., 5.

unspeakable [matters] on the stage." In other words—as Hofmannsthal also remarked apropos of *Der Rosenkavalier*—music provides a means of "bonding."[11] Reinhardt himself stressed this connection between the "festive" with the "social." Theater's task is to "lead" human beings "beyond themselves, out of the gray beggary of the everyday." As such, its object is the "purely human"—not in the sense of outward depiction so much as in terms of a "deep and refined art of the soul."[12] This conception of the theater is not idealist but psychological and modern: the stage should not transfigure life or represent it in realistic manner so much as entertain a dialectical relationship with it. As the director put it elsewhere:

> The art of the actor [*Schauspielkunst*] frees man of life's conventional stage [*Schauspielerei*]. For the art of the actor is to unveil life, not to distort it. . . . With the light of the poet, he explores the unchartered abyss of the human soul, *of his own soul*, and mysteriously transforms himself.[13]

Strauss would certainly have agreed with this conception of the theater—which unites the "festive" and the "social" in an artistic present held together by "unveiling" and "transformation"—although he would likely have used other terminology: *Festspiel* and *das Plastische*. The "modern" quality of Reinhardt's theater, in his eyes, stemmed from striving to surpass the function the educated bourgeoisie assigns to art in order to arrive at a vision unifying disparate aspects of the world; during a "festive" interlude, its contradictions may be tolerated, at least temporarily. "Metamorphosis" should promote a sense of groundedness and certainty, however fleeting.

At the same time, Strauss affirmed an important difference. As his correspondence with Hofmannsthal makes clear (in which he often speaks quite frankly), the appropriate response to the aesthetic challenge posed

---

11 "im Dienst des Theaters," "Letztes, Unaussprechliches auf der Bühne," "Bindung." Einar Nilson, "Musik bei Reinhardt," in Stern and Herald, *Reinhardt und seine Bühne*, 186f.

12 "aus der grauen Alltagsmisère über sich selbst hinauszuführen," "rein Menschliche," "in einer tiefen und verfeinerten Seelenkunst." Max Reinhardt, "Über ein Theater, wie es mir vorschwebt [1901]," in Hugo Fetting (ed.), *Max Reinhardt: Leben für das Theater. Briefe, Reden, Aufsätze, Interviews, Gespräche, Auszüge aus Regiebüchern* (Berlin: Argon, 1989), 73.

13 Quoted in Wolf von Eckhardt and Sander L. Gilman, *Bertolt Brecht's Berlin: A Scrapbook of the Twenties* (Lincoln: University of Nebraska Press, 1993), 79 (Max Reinhardt, "Rede über den Schauspieler," 1928).

by Wagner (in other words, the "festive") and the concrete challenge of reality (the "social") does not mean drama that includes music; instead, it bears on music itself, which is where theater finds its source—that is, opera. As he specified in the context of *Ariadne,* such theater must follow a definite course: "not without Reinhardt!"[14]

Oriental Antiquity and "Nervous Counterpoint"

Salome was composed thanks to the encounter with Max Reinhardt. Its complicated course of development also points to the composer's many ties in Berlin. Oscar Wilde (1854–1900) did not write his only tragedy, a drama in one act, in English but in French, during his sojourn in Paris in 1891; the work was published two years later. Banned in London (until 1931), it premiered in Paris in 1896, with Sarah Bernhardt (1844–1923) in the title role. The English version appeared in 1894, translated by Wilde's companion Lord Alfred Douglas. From Berlin, events were followed with due attention. In 1898, the Deutsches Theater—still under the direction of Otto Brahm—witnessed the premiere of the biblical tragedy *Johannes* by the naturalist playwright Hermann Sudermann (1857–1928); the influence of Wilde's text was evident. It is likely that Strauss attended the production and became familiar with the work here. The first translation of Wilde's *Salome* into German followed the English version and appeared in the *Wiener Rundschau* in 1900. The scandal surrounding the work continued—especially as the translation had been made by Hedwig Lachmann (1865–1918), who would later be the second wife of noted anarchist Gustav Landauer. A book edition followed. Although *Salome* was censored in Berlin, a single—supposedly "private"—production occurred on November 15, 1902 at Reinhardt's Kleines Theater, with set designs by Lovis Corinth. Gertrud Eysoldt played the lead—and Richard Strauss numbered among the audience members.[15] Before this staging, the poet and critic Anton Lindner—whose verse Strauss had used for a tone poem—had suggested that the piece be adapted to music. Strauss hesitated at first: the Berlin production, which eroticized and brutalized

---

14 "nicht ohne Reinhardt!" *Richard Strauss. Hugo von Hofmannsthal. Briefwechsel,* 156; letter from Strauss of December 21, 1911.

15 The first public performance took place on February 3, 1903, in Reinhardt's "Deutsches Theater," after a lengthy public debate.

the main character, strengthened his reservations. (Reinhardt, for his part, found the "mood" of the work "forceful and unique."[16])

Also in 1902, Debussy's *Pelléas et Mélisande* premiered in Paris. Although Strauss had little sympathy for Debussy and never conducted his works, he knew them well and made a point of stepping in to advocate for his contemporary's music even as late as 1933. The score of *Pelléas et Mélisande* represented a milestone because Debussy only abridged Maeterlinck's text (which formed part of the repertoire at Reinhardt's theater). Strauss subsequently decided to set Wilde's drama to music likewise, without textual modifications apart from a few cuts and rearrangements. His piece premiered in 1905, once again at the Hofoper in Dresden. The importance Strauss attached to the libretto may be discerned from his decision—which remained an isolated experiment—also to compose a French version using Wilde's original; the resulting difficulties were surmounted only through intensive collaboration with Romain Rolland. The French *Salome* premiered in Brussels in 1907. For decades, Strauss's work remained the only musical adaptation of Wilde in the German-speaking world (apart from *Geburtstag der Infantin* [The Birthday of the Infanta] in versions by Franz Schreker and Alexander von Zemlinsky). In Lyon, Antoine Mariotte (1875–1944) composed his own version of Wilde's play at around the same time, but Strauss had secured the rights, and the rival version could not premiere until 1908; ultimately, it made little impact.

This complicated run-up indicates just how important it was for Strauss to work with language and music [*Vertonung*] together. On the one hand, his collaboration with Wolzogen had already been shaped by a desire to draw a line between librettist and composer; on the other, the objective was to make the text a literary genre in its own right. Such ambition was fueled by the dramaturgy of one-act plays featuring what August Strindberg had dubbed "the intimate." This psychologizing turn had defined the "Intimate Theater" founded by Max Halbe in 1885 in

---

16 "stark und eigenartig." Fetting, *Max Reinhardt*, 86; letter from Max Reinhardt to Berthold Held, August 1902.

Munich—which Strauss attended.[17] Reinhardt's "Little Theater" was indebted to the same idea. Strauss's interest in a subtle "inner" realm, with multidimensional connections to the world, prompted him to reassess his view of antiquity fundamentally. Now, rough, anti-classical aspects moved to the fore. Wilde had already drawn on the same perspective: for instance, Gustave Moreau's Salomé-canvas *L'Apparition* (1875, now in Paris), Henri Regnault's *Salomé* painting (1870, now in New York), and Flaubert's novella *Hérodias* (1877). Max Klinger crafted his colorful bust of "The New Salome" (1887–1888, now in Dresden) in a similar spirit, Max Slevogt painted Salome dancing (1895, whereabouts unknown), and Lovis Corinth painted her, too (1899, now in Leipzig). The broader context for such works was scholarly discussion about the striking colors of ancient statuary; major contributions included studies by the archeologist Adolf Furtwängler, father of the renowned conductor. In other words, Wilde's drama occupied a space in the "borderlands" between pagan antiquity and Christianity. If the former came across as irredeemably decadent, the latter's bearing of renunciation seemed quaint and equally doomed to fail.

Nietzsche held that "the Greek" was "very foreign" to modern sensibilities because the world had become "too labyrinthine."[18] In this context, excavating the rough and jagged aspects of antiquity did not mean uncovering polished, classical elements but grappling with what remained obscure. This had a correlate in contemporary music. Strauss's Salome is repulsed by the "old" civilization of the Greeks, Jews, Egyptians, and Romans—and fascinated by the coarseness of Christianity, which, however, denies her precisely what she seeks. Music has the task of sounding the spiritual tensions this process entails. The score juxtaposes speech and speechlessness, desire and disrupted communication. The centerpiece is Salome's mute dance, which accelerates "very quickly and violently" as she sheds the seven veils. The savagery on display amounts to the rejection of "noble" antiquity.

---

17 Shortly after this Max Halbe, Ernst von Wolzogen, Ludwig Ganghofer, and Strauss founded, in 1897, a "Literarische Gesellschaft," whose first meeting took place in the hotel Vier Jahreszeiten.

18 Nietzsche, *Daybreak*, 90 (§169).

The spectacle Herodes lustfully observes signifies the inversion of the classical nude. Salome's dance does not stylize (Reinhardt would have said "disfigure") the body so much as expose its raw carnality. The scene implies a fundamental critique of the (supposedly) Christian worldview. Decades later, in 1935, Strauss told Zweig that the "pedantic-Philistine air on four horns" accompanying Jochanaan follows "the commandments of contrast"; essentially, "this kind of preacher in the desert, living from locusts, to boot," has "something indescribably comical about it."[19] Accordingly, when Salome's monologue "detonates" in a shift of key (F♯ major to A major, resolved onto C♯ major), the technique that the composer called "psychic polyphony" reaches a climax, affecting tonality itself: the depths of modern humanity are sounded, without regard for neo-classical norms.

Before steering a more radical path, the theater critic Ludwig Rubiner (1881–1920) frequented the same Berlin milieu as Reinhardt and Strauss. In his introduction to Tolstoy's journals, he described the tensions at play:

> With Socrates and the Sophists, the Occident began to ask whether action is possible at all. Everything we call Western reason and sentiment means: what is not self-evident. "Eastern" means: self-evident, a matter of course. In the Orient, carrying out action was a holy matter; in Europe, it became a question of power.[20]

"Orientalism" defined in this way does not amount to exotic "local color." Instead—and as Strauss himself contended, it should manifest a "truly Eastern color and a glowing sun."[21] In this light, orchestral polyphony does not serve as a means of technical virtuosity or dignified

---

19 "4 Hörner-Schulmeister-Philisterton," "Geboten des Gegensatzes," "so ein Prediger in der Wüste, der sich noch dazu von Heuschrecken ernährt, etwas unbeschreiblich komisches." *Richard Strauss—Stefan Zweig: Briefwechsel*, 128; letter from Strauss of May 5, 1935.

20 "Das Abendland beginnt mit Sokrates und den Sophisten zu fragen, ob man denn überhaupt handeln könne. Und alles, was wir klar abendländisches Denken und Fühlen nennen, heißt: Unselbstverständlichkeit. Das Orientalische heißt: Selbstverständlichkeit. Die Vollendung des Handelns ist im Orient eine Frage der Heiligkeit; in Europa wird sie eine Frage der Macht." Ludwig Rubiner, "Vorwort," in *Lew Tolstois Tagebuch 1895–1899* (Zurich: Max Rascher, 1918); here quoted from the abridged first edition in *Die Aktion* 8 (1918), 1–7, at 6.

21 "wirklich östliches Kolorit und glühende Sonne." Strauss, "Erinnerungen an die ersten Aufführungen meiner Opern," in *Betrachtungen und Erinnerungen*, 224.

expression so much as it permits and animates "nervous counterpoint."[22] Needless to say, the striking decision not to follow tonal language as it stood, but to lay a new foundation for it—from the inside-out, as it were—demanded an existential ontology in lieu of a "classical" one. Such a vision may have had a counterpart in Franz von Stuck's painting of Salome (1906, now in Munich).

From here to *Elektra*—for which Reinhardt's theater again provided a point of reference—was not far. However, Hofmannsthal observed that the differences between the two dramas are more significant than their outer similarities: they exhibit wholly different "blend[s] of color"; moreover, *Elektra* features the (Nietzschean) "deed" peformed by Orestes, which culminates in "victory and cleansing."[23] For his part, Strauss sought to to oppose "daimonic, ecstatic Greek culture of the sixth century to Winckelmann's Roman copies and Goethe's humanism."[24] He had come to a new understanding by traveling to Greece and Egypt, where people viewed their inheritance in quite different terms. To achieve this newfound plasticity, composition should bring out the psychological substance of "daimonism" in opera marked as "tragedy"—and not assigned a musical genre.

In contrast to *Salome, Elektra* evolved in collaboration with the work's librettist. Tonal language was reworked and built on new foundations. The astonishing results of Strauss's orchestral polyphony include motifs that arise from the words that hold the score together: they prove melodic and harmonic in equal measure—for instance, "A-ga-mem-non" at the beginning. In this way, the question brewing since the late seventeenth century about the relative primacy of melody or harmony is resolved and stripped of potential conflict. In addition, the simultaneity of harmonic and melodic elements entailed another change: it is purposefully unclear whether motifs really emerge from the text or vice-versa. Strauss would observe this practice up until *Capriccio*. The simultaneity of harmony and

---

22 With respect to the terminology cf. Chapter 5, fn. 7.

23 "Farbenmischung," "auf Sieg und Reinigung hinauslaufende Tat." *Richard Strauss. Hugo von Hofmannsthal. Briefwechsel*, 19; letter from Hofmannsthal of April 27, 1907.

24 "dieses dämonische, ekstatische Griechentum des 6. Jahrhunderts Winckelmannschen Römerkopien und Goethescher Humanität." Strauss, "Erinnerungen an die ersten Aufführungen meiner Opern," in *Betrachtungen und Erinnerungen*, 230.

melody corresponds to the relationship between words and notes, and therefore semantics and syntax, as well.

In keeping with the Aristotelian doctrine of unities and by fitting the time of narration to events onstage, *Elektra* is structured by the protagonist's extensive monologues; notwithstanding latent divisions, the tragedy culminates in a maenadic dance. Instead of representing a "number," in the manner of *Salome,* the sequence marks the protagonist's entry into social interaction once the deed is done. However, there are no words for what has occurred, and so the ability to speak goes missing again. This loss does not signify the loss of meaning in general so much as the overwhelming advent of something new, something so powerful that it induces muteness. The "silence" with which *Elektra* concludes

FIGURE 6.1   Richard Strauss: *Elektra*. Sketch for set design by Emil Rieck, Dresden premiere, 1909. Gouache on paper

From 1879 to 1919, Emil Rieck (1852-1939) held the position of set designer (*Hoftheatermaler*) in Dresden; during his tenure, he resided at Moritzburg. Rieck designed the décor for *Feuersnot, Salome,* and *Elektra*. Strauss took a keen interest in the artist's precise scenography. In preparations for *Elektra*, detailed reflection was devoted to shaping the space Hofmannsthal had imagined. Rieck's design (here, Clytemnestra's scene) is based on an exact translation of the poet's vision, enhanced by lighting effects introduced to the Meiningen Royal Theater by the brothers Brückner.

Dresden, Sächsische Staatsoper.

is full—terrifying, tumultuous, and loud—and pours out in C major darkened with E♭ minor. Regaining Oriental, anti-classical antiquity not only assures the ultimate meaning of the tragedy; it also opens up a new, but also archaic, sense for the composer's music, which rejects all metaphysical claims.

Elektra led to charges of plagiarism. In 1905, the Milanese composer Vittorio Gnecchi (1876–1954) had premiered his opera *Cassandra* in Bologna.[25] But whether or not Strauss was familiar with Gnecchi's score, the works differ in terms of the underlying conception of antiquity—and all that it entails. The differences are so basic that one might speak of "suggestion," at most. Comparison only puts into relief the singular course that Strauss had set for himself and his work.

The End of Instrumental Music

Strauss was convinced that theater represented the exemplary modern form of art; only in this context can opera satisfy the demands placed on it. In the 1880s, he already deemed it self-evident that instrumental music had limited prospects. *Ein Heldenleben* expressed as much, but further emphasis—indeed, a kind of definitive declaration—came with *Symphonia domestica* and *Eine Alpensinfonie*. Preceded by a series of works in pairs (*Salome* and *Elektra, Der Rosenkavalier*, and *Josephs Legende*), these two compositions also represent a stark, "bipolar" juxtaposition. Especially when compared to the brisk pace at which Strauss crafted each of his tone poems, work on *Eine Alpensinfonie* proceeded slowly—ultimately extending to one-and-a-half decades (and more). In relation to *Symphonia domestica*, the composition stands for nothing short of the author's wish to be done, once and for all, with the logic of instrumental music. Up until his late period, when he looked back at the idiosyncratic course he had steered, Strauss remained true to a single impulse: the only exceptions—both compositions for (left-hand) piano and orchestra—are explicitly situated in the context of other works, and the composer's spectacular attempt to return to the tone-poem genre in *Die Donau* (1941–1942, TrV 284) ultimately remained a fragment (notwithstanding his completion of

---

25 Giovanni Tebaldini, "Telepatia musicale: A proposito dell' Elektra di Strauss," in *Rivista Musicale Italiana* 16 (1909), 400–412, 632–659. In 1909 the first part of the article was published separately in Milan.

more than 400 bars). *Symphonia domestica* and *Eine Alpensinfonie* are also related because their very titles—for the first time since the Symphony in F minor—feature the word "symphony"; this designation would not recur again.[26] After combining Greek and Latin for the title of *Symphonia domestica,* Strauss returned to an Italianate name for *Eine Alpensinfonie,* albeit in a compound word qualified by an indefinite article.

Clearly, public controversies—especially those occasioned by *Salome*—did not impede the composer's self-assurance. The extended process through which *Eine Alpensinfonie* came to be written involved an array of influences; some of them made their way into the final version, and others were discarded, but the work's overall, monumental design was never subject to doubt. The piece's heterogeneous aspects are united in the theme of the artist, a key feature of Strauss's works at least from *Tod und Verklärung* on. The earliest "layer" of *Eine Alpensinfonie* gave this aspect concrete form. In the years around the turn of the century, the life of the painter Karl Stauffer (1857–1891) and his relationship to his patron Lydia Welti (1858–1891) were a *cause célèbre*: running away to Italy (first Florence, then Rome), arrest, and incarceration in psychiatric clinics led to the former's death and the latter's suicide. Welti had sent her literary testament and private correspondence to Otto Brahm, who published them in 1892.[27] The public interpreted Stauffer's fate as the tragedy of an artist committed to his work to the exclusion of all religious, metaphysical, social, and institutional ties. For Strauss, a personal element entered the equation, too: he had met Stauffer, who lived in Berlin from 1881 to 1888, when he first spent time in the city (1883–1884).

Initially, *Eine Alpensinfonie* was supposed to be dedicated "To the memory of Karl Stauffer"; the composer's working notes speak of an "artistic tragedy" (*Künstlertragödie*).[28] Gradually, Strauss came to view Stauffer, an avid alpinist, as exemplary of the modern artist in general, foundering on the demands of the world. In this light, his fate pointed beyond the

26 Only in *Panathenäenzug, Intermezzo,* and the late excerpts of *Frau ohne Schatten* and *Josephs Legende* did Strauss return to the notion of "symphonic," but then in a very limited form (etude, interlude, fantasy, fragment).

27 Otto Brahm, *Karl Stauffer-Bern: Sein Leben—seine Briefe—seine Gedichte* (Stuttgart: Göschen 1892).

28 "Schreibkalender" 1900, quoted in Rainer Bayreuther, *Richard Strauss' "Alpensinfonie": Entstehung, Analyse und Interpretation* (Hildesheim: Olms, 1997), 18.

particular, towards an autonomous state of mind—and being—that casts off the strictures of Christian Europe once and for all. Here again, Nietzsche played a key role—especially his call, at the end of *Der Antichrist* (1888), for the "transvaluation of all values" (*Umwertung aller Werte*). Once more, Strauss made the philosopher's words a "program." His notes from 1902 include plans to call the piece *Der Antichrist: Eine Alpensymphonie* (see Figure 6.2). Gustav Mahler's death in 1911 renewed this intention. In his writing calendar, the composer declared: "I intend to call my alpine symphony *The Antichrist*, since it concerns moral cleansing through one's own power, liberation through work, [and] worship of eternal, majestic nature."[29] Initially, Strauss foresaw multiple movements—four units or "segments." But after 1913, as work proceeded, they faded more and more, vanishing entirely in the completed score (1915).

Eine Alpensinfonie comprises twenty-one passages that evoke a journey through the mountains on foot. Notwithstanding the backstory, the work does not evoke a para-religious experience of nature so much as the stages of an artist's destiny, fused with figures signifying the natural world. The "bareness" of the metaphors pointing only to themselves, as it were, heralds Strauss's definitive abandonment of an idealist—indeed, symbolic—role for instrumental music. *Eine Alpensinfonie* features lonesome, self-referential metaphors of artistic existence: the counterpart to the social images constituting *Symphonia domestica*. (Viewed in this light, the latter are revealed as nothing more than metaphors, too.) The polarity of artistic existence—active experience prompting borders to vanish, on the one hand, and the search for security within the social order, on the other—is a theme Thomas Mann also addressed in his writings. Here, however, it is not represented so much as shared: the listener is initiated into projective participation—a foreshadowing of what Hofmannsthal (in reference to Reinhardt) would call "the festive" and "the social."

Accordingly, and also along figural lines, Strauss oriented *Eine Alpensinfonie* on his own biography—not, as in *Symphonia domestica*, its social aspects, but artistic ones (albeit without seeking to dissolve art into life). The piece begins a strange B minor scale that condenses into a diffuse

---

29 "Ich will meine Alpensinfonie: den Antichrist nennen, als da ist: sittliche Reinigung aus eigener Kraft, Befreiung durch Arbeit, Anbetung der ewigen herrlichen Natur." "Schreibkalender" May 1911, quoted in ibid., 208.

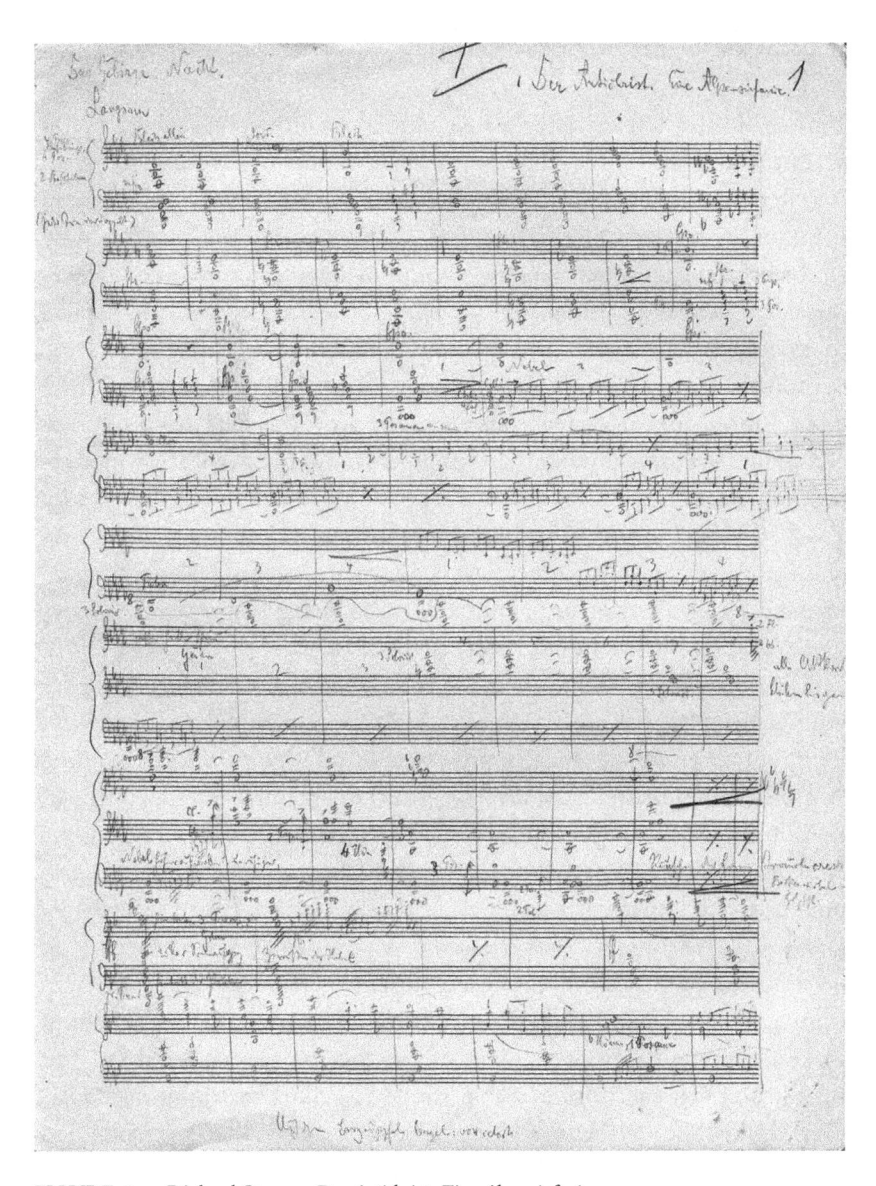

FIGURE 6.2 Richard Strauss: *Der Antichrist: Eine Alpensinfonie.*

Wherever he went, Strauss brought a pencil to take notes (as a rule, in small memo books). He even made light of the habit in *Ariadne auf Naxos*. Various jottings would yield a rough outline for a composition, which in turn transformed into a score. Strauss stressed this "mechanical" aspect of composition: the idea that the act of writing constitutes an integral part of artistic creation. The process ended with the fair copy—a stage the composer perceived as arduous. Strauss did not attach any particular significance to his sketches; he parted with loose pages and notebooks easily and deemed it unnecessary to catalog them. For all that, however, his notes reveal essential aspects of how he developed scores and blended works together. The page pictured here, recording preparations for *Alpensinfonie*, makes its convoluted genesis plain; the piece's original title—*Der Antichrist*—still sets the tone. This preliminary sketch traces the progression to the first "breakthrough," which the final version retained (albeit with significant modifications).

Richard Strauss Archive/Richard Strauss Institute, Garmisch-Partenkirchen.

constellation of layered chords that ultimately proves bitonal (B minor against A♭ major). This arrangement, which frames the work as a whole, is a literal quotation from the beginning of Strauss's own Symphony in F minor. In this way, the dramaturgy of *Eine Alpensinfonie*, abandoning all formal logic, ties the objective aspects of the piece to the composer's own experiences and subjectivity. This point represents the real parallel to *Symphonie domestica*—a juxtaposition with effects as complex as those occasioned by pairing *Ein Heldenleben* and *Don Quixote*. Once again, the composition does not create an evening's worth of playing time. *Eine Alpensinfonie* admits performance only in conjunction with (or in contrast to) other works. The orchestra takes on gigantic dimensions: ideally, 22 woodwinds, 34 brass instruments, percussion (including a thunder machine and cowbells) for three players, four harps, organ, celesta, timpani manned by two performers, and at least 64 string instruments. Such a work may follow others, but hardly precede them.

The objective of "moral cleansing from within" holds together a score whose metaphorical aspects do not seek to gesture beyond the work itself, but to ensure the reality present at hand. The cowbells sounding "on the alpine pasture" (*auf der Alm*—in the "sublime" key of E♭ major) do not signify something metaphysical—as Mahler sought to do by the same means in his Sixth Symphony—but simply the generation of a stark presence. The festive turn to C major that occurs with "at the summit" (*auf dem Gipfel*) underscores the same with ostentatious flair—only to be followed by a "vision" that leads nowhere. Self-confidence emerges from diffuse elements and then dissolves back into them: it cannot make enduring claims to validity. Strauss thereby also declared the end of instrumental music as a viable mode for thinking about composition: the dichotomy between "social" and "festive" aspects, exemplified by *Symphonia domestica* and *Eine Alpensinfonie*, no longer admit resolution without the stage—that is, opera. This assessment was simultaneously affirmed in another, unexpected context. As he worked on *Eine Alpensinfonie*, the composer was asked whether he would contribute a piece for the opening of the Konzerthaus in Vienna, to introduce Beethoven's Ninth Symphony. Somewhat surprisingly, Strauss agreed. *Festliches Präludium* is only ten minutes long, but its dimensions approach those of *Eine Alpensinfonie*: 20 woodwinds, 29 brass instruments, double timpani, percussion, organ, and 96(!) strings. Ultimately, the piece does not represent a prelude to Beethoven so much as it offers a corrective to the idealistic claims underlying the latter's work. The main theme, which alludes to the finales of both Beethoven's Ninth and Brahms's First Symphony,[30] does not offer a new conceptual framework. Instead, the piece strips its historical forerunners of pretense. Without elaborating a new, free-standing context, *Festliches Präludium* proudly steers its course toward the present. The ostentatious key of C major admits comparison to the passage "Auf dem Gipfel" in *Eine Alpensinfonie*: it is "festive" and paves the way for a new experience of music, one that does not observe the religion of art but is "social" through and through. Mahler, in his own Ninth Symphony, had sought to break apart Beethoven's work and piece together new relations from the shards. In contrast, Strauss wrote *Festliches Präludium*—and, soon thereafter, *Eine Alpensinfonie*—in order to consign to history the thought that animated instrumental music as a whole; in this, he was pursuing the same objective as Adrian Leverkühn in Thomas Mann's *Doktor Faustus*.

---

30 Strauss had quoted the Finale of the Ninth Symphony much earlier, in the *Fanfare* he composed in 1891 for a performance of Ifflands's play *Die Jäger* in Meiningen (TrV 165).

CHAPTER SEVEN

"The Social Achieved"

STRAUSS AND HOFMANNSTHAL

Language-crises and the "Way to the Social"

The most important event in Richard Strauss's artistic life, perhaps, was meeting Hugo von Hofmannsthal—just as, conversely, the latter's career took a decisive turn when he began working with Strauss. The poet and composer first encountered each other in 1899 in Berlin, and then the following year in Paris; plans for a ballet, *Der Triumph der Zeit*, did not come to fruition. But when Strauss attended Max Reinhardt's production of *Elektra* (with a stage design by Lovis Corinth and with Gertrud Eysoldt playing the title role), the relationship changed fundamentally and, it would seem, immediately. This hardly means that the two artists had an easy time with each other. Their correspondence (which also sheds light on the frequency and nature of meetings in person) abounds in irritation, crises, reproaches, and admonitions. Strauss always stressed the significance of opera and its incomparable advantages with respect to theater, and he faulted Hofmannsthal for lacking dramaturgical vision, producing at an inconsistent rate, and seeking distance from embodied performance. Hofmannsthal, on the other hand, found his counterpart's pragmatism importunate and pedantic, and he took issue with Strauss's over-hasty reliance on stage effects, his never-ending tide of plans and projects, and his self-centeredness. On June 12, 1909, on the way back from their sole meeting in Garmisch, Hofmannsthal wrote to Strauss that the music of Act One of *Der Rosenkavelier* had turned out to be "truly beautiful"; it gave him "great and lasting pleasure,"[1] he affirmed. But the same evening, he sent a letter with an entirely different cast to his real confidant, Count Harry Kessler (1868–1937): "If only I had a more artistically refined composer. Everything he says and desires, all his inclinations, are quite unappetizing to me. I envision such lovely things for the opera." In a word, Strauss is a "fantastically unrefined person."[2] Comments of this kind were not the exception, either. In June 1914, Hofmannsthal told his patron Eduard von Bodenhausen (1868–1918) bluntly: "If only I had a composer who were less famous but closer to my own heart and sensibility, I'd be much happier."[3] For a time, the playwright considered collaborating with Bruno Walter instead of Strauss.[4] In turn, the composer (who was deeply disappointed by Hofmannsthal's lack of interest in *Intermezzo*) tried to enlist Hermann Bahr for the project; when Bahr refused, he even ventured to write the libretto himself.

In other words, the relationship was fraught, and it held only in spite of great resistance on both sides. Strauss and Hofmannsthal (see Figure 7.1) never interacted on a first-name basis. What underwrote their association—like the relationship between Kurt Weill and Bertolt Brecht, in many ways—and made it last for almost a quarter-century was profound agreement on basic matters, paired with a shared ambition to lay the foundations for art that would be truly modern. One of the cornerstones may be discerned in a piece by Hofmannsthal published in the Berlin newspaper *Der Tag* (October 18 and 19, 1902), shortly before the writer and the composer met again. Here, Hofmannsthal diagnoses an incapacity to communicate linguistically or intellectually. Crafted as a

1 "wirklich wunderschön," "große, bleibende Freude." *Richard Strauss. Hugo von Hofmannsthal. Briefwechsel*, 63; letter from Hofmannsthal of June 12, 1909.
2 "Wenn ich einen raffinierteren künstlerischeren Componisten hätte. Alles was er sagt, was er sich wünscht, wonach er tendiert, degoutiert mich ziemlich stark. Mir schweben so schöne Dinge für Opern vor," "so fabelhaft unraffinierter Mensch." Hilde Burger (ed.), *Hugo von Hofmannsthal—Harry Graf Kessler: Briefwechsel 1898–1929* (Frankfurt: Fischer, 1968); letter from Hofmannsthal to Kessler, June 12, 1909, 244 and 242.
3 ". . . hätt ich einen Componisten, der minder berühmt aber meinem Herzen näher, meiner Geistesart verwandter wäre, da wärs mir freilich wohler." Dora Freifrau von Bodenhausen (ed.), *Hugo von Hofmannsthal—Eberhard von Bodenhausen: Briefe der Freundschaft* (Düsseldorf: Diederichs, 1953), 167.
4 Lotte Walter-Lindt (ed.), *Bruno Walter: Briefe 1894–1962* (Frankfurt: S. Fischer, 1969), 108; letter from Walter to Hofmannsthal of April 23, 1910.

Figure 7.1   Hugo von Hofmannsthal and Richard Strauss. Silhouette (*Scherenschnitt*) by Willi Bithorn.

This paper-cut silhouette, made in 1914 by the illustrator and caricaturist Willi Bithorn, depicts the labors shared by Strauss and Hofmannsthal in an ironic light. Whether or not Bithorn ever really managed to peer into their "workshop," he captured the sensational novelty of their collaborative endeavors.

Vienna, Österreichische Nationalbibliothek, Pf 691:C (3).

letter from Philipp Lord Chandos to Francis Bacon, this celebrated work of fiction—unassumingly entitled "A Letter"—projects the author's own, autobiographical crisis back to the year 1603. It heralds the beginning of modernity as a grave loss:

> I lived at that time in a kind of continuous inebriation and saw all of existence as one great unity. The mental world did not seem to me to be opposed to the physical; likewise the courtly and the bestial, art and barbarism, solitude and society.[5]

---

5 Hugo von Hofmannsthal, *The Lord Chandos Letter: And Other Writings*, trans. Joel Rotenberg (New York: New York Review Books, 2005), 120.

When such unity fell apart, the possibility of securing order by means of language and orienting oneself in the world went missing, too. One passage in particular, where juridical and medical discourses intersect, has become famous:

> In brief, this is my case: I have completely lost the ability to think or speak coherently about anything at all.
>
> First I gradually lost the ability, when discussing relatively elevated or general topics, to utter words normally used by everyone with unhesitating fluency. I felt an inexplicable uneasiness in even pronouncing the words "spirit," "soul," or "body." I found myself profoundly unable to produce an opinion on affairs of court, events in Parliament, what have you. And not out of any kind of scruples—you know my candor, which borders on thoughtlessness. Rather, the abstract words which the tongue must enlist as a matter of course in order to bring out an opinion disintegrated in my mouth like rotten mushrooms.[6]

To escape this crisis of "rottenness" and decay, the fictive author dreams of a new language not yet at hand, which might at least offset the loss:

> the language in which I might have been granted the opportunity not only to write but also to think is not Latin or English, or Italian, or Spanish, but a language of which I know not one word, a language in which mute things speak to me and in which I will perhaps have something to say for myself someday when I am dead and standing before an unknown judge.[7]

What has gone missing for Lord Chandos—"Everything came to pieces, the pieces broke into more pieces, and nothing could be encompassed by one idea"[8]—points beyond speech. His words amount to a critique of the arts, their self-contentment within the supposedly autonomous sphere of the *Gesamtkunstwerk*—and, as such, their failure to interact with the social realm.

Strauss shared this assessment. Writing to Bülow in 1888, he already lamented not only the crisis of instrumental music, but also its failure to communicate. The composer's term for such capacity was (and remained)

---

6 Ibid., 121.
7 Ibid., 128.
8 Ibid., 122.

"expression." Strauss was dissatisfied with the artistic formalism exemplified by the sonata form in composition, and by the aesthetic theory elaborated by Eduard Hanslick in his influential book, *Vom Musikalisch-Schönen*. Fifteen years later—and now with the "Chandos Letter" in mind—Strauss, in his introduction to *Die Musik*, indicted contemporary music for being restricted, "more or less," to "ludic formalism."[9] Over-concentration on formal aspects (what Hofmannsthal called "the abstract") had estranged art from life, which alone can justify it. For Hofmannsthal, the answer to the problem involved trying "to think with our hearts" in order to achieve "a new, momentous relationship with all of existence [*ein neues, ahnungsvolles Verhältnis zum Dasein*]."[10] Likewise, Strauss demanded "an immediate connection with life";[11] indeed, he affirmed that art "is subject to the same laws as life, which is always shaping itself anew."[12] Significantly, the path that came into view represented the opposite of what Wagner had called for in radicalizing Romantic notions along political lines. Instead of art pervading life, life should suffuse art, and in ways that surpass realist and naturalist poetics. The results would necessarily be ambiguous. This point is key: art should remain inexact, multilayered, and momentous—that is, "framed" by a historical perspective that also lacks clear definition.

To lend some clarity to his new understanding of art based on "intentional communicability"[13] Hofmannsthal appealed to "the social," which corresponded to what Strauss understood as "plasticity." In *Der Dichter und seine Zeit* (1907), Hofmannsthal enjoined poets to observe the world actively and participate in its affairs in order to produce works that incorporate their life and times in dialectical suspension, as it were. Doing so meant taking a step beyond the social criticism of Naturalism and related schools of literature. To counter the dissolution of institutional

---

9 "auf einen mehr oder weniger spielerischen Formalismus." Strauss, "Einleitung," in Göllerich, *Beethoven*, iii.

10 "ein neues, ahnungsvolles Verhältnis zum Dasein." Hofmannsthal, *The Lord Chandos Letter*, 125.

11 "den unmittelbaren Zusammenhang mit dem Leben." Strauss, "Einleitung," in Göllerich, *Beethoven*, iii.

12 "denselben Gesetzen unterliegt, wie das immer neu sich gestaltende Leben." Richard Strauss, "Gibt es für die Musik eine Fortschrittspartei?" in *Morgen: Wochenschrift für deutsche Kultur* 1 (1907), 15. Hofmannsthal was one of the editors of *Morgen*.

13 "absichtliche Mitteilbarkeit." Hugo von Hofmannsthal, "Ad me ipsum," in *Aufzeichnungen* (Frankfurt: S. Fischer, 1973), 239, entry of November 5, 1926.

and communal bonds, the "social" aspect of art should help people find a new bearing and orientation in the world—albeit in ways that are plural, polyvalent, and temporary, not absolute. This view held implications for the work of art itself. Whether in a piece of music or a poem, "communication" [*Mitteilingsform*] could not stand alone or simply vanish into a superficial "whole." It involved separating composition and libretto (an unheard-of act in the German-speaking world of the day), paying careful heed to events onstage, as well as dialogical collaboration, personal difficulties notwithstanding. Strauss and Hofmannsthal envisioned a work of art that would not represent the "deed" of a heroic individual so much as emerge from participation in "the social." In this light, a given work would not amount to the decree of a single party; its manifold connections to the world would disclose something greater. In concrete terms, works paired in dynamic manner opened onto a new—and deeper—dimension: *Elektra* versus *Rosenkavalier* and *Josephs Legende*, *Ariadne auf Naxos* versus *Die Frau ohne Schatten*, *Die ägyptische Helena* versus *Arabella*. Tension transformed into dialogue between elements in fruitful opposition.

Strauss stressed that Hofmannsthal helped him discover "operatic terrain" that was "un-Wagnerian": "the opera of play, sentiment, and human being."[14] Later, he would describe the process as "circumnavigating" Wagner.[15] This kind of opera did not traffic in abstract words or clear-cut language so much as what Hofmannsthal first called "coloration" in "The Lord Chandos Letter" and simply "color" in *Der Dichter und seine Zeit*.[16] The task of music is to produce such hues—which later came to life in the figure of Barak the Dyer in *Die Frau ohne Schatten*. The "Unwritten Afterword" to *Der Rosenkavalier* (1911) declares that the role of music is to lay bare what lies hidden between words. Only music can convey the ambivalent, opaque qualities of language. In the foreword to *Intermezzo* (a project in which Hofmannsthal declined to participate because of its autobiographical cast), Strauss himself said as much, too. The second

---

14 "Gebiet der unwagnerschen Spiel-, Gemüts- und Menschenoper." *Richard Strauss. Hugo von Hofmannsthal. Briefwechsel*, 358; letter from Strauss of August 16, (?)1916.

15 "Umweg." Stefan Zweig, *Die Welt von gestern: Erinnerungen eines Europäers* (Frankfurt: Suhrkamp 1949, originally 1944), 408.

16 Hofmannsthal, *The Lord Chandos Letter*, 122.

(published) version is even clearer than the first draft: this "bourgeois comedy" involves "reaching, perhaps too boldly, 'into the full of human life'"; the score offers a spectrum extending "from sober, everyday prose, over an array of chromatic dialogues, up to expressive song."[17] Comedy is the genre for "the social achieved."[18]

Silence and Dance

The search for "intentional communicability" did not proceed without difficulty, however, for it involved replacing "abstract," univocal meaning with "momentous" pluralities. The "quest for a possible—necessary deed" did not seek an emancipatory coup so much as a process in stages. The actions performed by Elektra in Strauss and Hofmannsthal's first collaboration still followed from "a kind of obsession"; in fact, it would have been better had her deed emerged "out of innermost essence, from fate."[19] The desired connection between "deed" and "innermost essence" was struck in the comedies. Here, action amounts to more than a liberatory event simultaneously condemning the one who carries it out to silence; instead, it takes place as human beings turn toward each other in an open-ended process without conclusion. The comedies feature couples who find the way back to each other, even though much remains unresolved. Although erotic union crowns this process, it is only suggested—and does not provide the object of representation onstage, as in *Feuersnot*. The first example of this perspective is the finale of *Der Rosenkavelier,* and the last occurs in *Arabella*. Music performs a key function in the context of such "intentional communicability." For Strauss, inherited musical forms correspond to the abstractions that, as Hofmannsthal's Lord Chandos puts it, have fallen apart like "rotten mushrooms." In other words, to achieve the new communicability, it is necessary to sound the depths of possible connections between music and language, but without resorting to notions of an autonomous work of art. The extraordinary nature of this

---

17 "vielleicht allzu kühnen Griff 'ins volle Menschenleben'," "nüchternster Alltagsprosa durch mancherlei Dialogfarbenskalen bis zum gefühlvollen Gesang." Richard Strauss, "Vorwort," in *Intermezzo: Eine bürgerliche Komödie mit sinfonischen Zwischenspielen in zwei Aufzügen,* op. 72 (Vienna: Strauss-Verlag, 1996), [ix].

18 "das erreichte Soziale." Hofmannsthal, "Ad me ipsum," 226.

19 "Suche nach einer möglichen—notwendigen Tat," "aus seiner Art Besessenheit," "aus dem Wesensgrund, aus dem Geschick." Ibid., 237.

approach is especially clear in light of contemporary efforts that head in precisely the opposite direction—that is, attempts to enlist "autonomous" musical forms for dramaturgical purposes. Examples range from Paul Dukas' *Ariane et Barbe-Bleue* (1907) (which Strauss conducted in Vichy to commemorate the composer in 1935) to Alban Berg's *Wozzeck* (which premiered in 1925 and which begins with a programmatic "suite").

For Strauss (and, it stands to reason, for Hofmannsthal, too) the performance genre best suited to this end was dance. *Salome* represents the first work in which dance comes to the fore as non-linguistic and gestic communication. That said, Salome's dance remains sealed-off—a "number"—even though it is performed in a double sense, as it were. In contrast, the heroine's enjoinder in *Elektra* ("be silent and dance") calls for a new kind of "communicability"—yet it also remains incomplete since the deed prompting it arises from her "obsession," not her "innermost essence." The tension between the final stage direction ("silence") and the rage of the final chords results from this contradiction—indeed, the concluding juxtaposition of E♭ minor and C major heightens it. All the same, the sequence makes it clear what the role of dance should be: to mediate between language and music.

In this respect, the pieces participated in the widespread "gestic" turn in contemporary performance. Dance's potential to generate meaning beyond language led to a renewed appreciation of ballet, for which Serge Diaghilev and the *Ballets Russes* provide the most important point of reference (although hardly the only one). Nevertheless, Strauss and Hofmannsthal's efforts stand out. In contrast to early works by Franz Schreker, for instance, the point was not to use dance to compensate for what had gone missing in language. Nor was it a matter of finding a distinct, elemental language in rhythmic gestures—as Stravinsky sought to do. Instead, dance was given the task of bridging disparate realms. Significantly, Strauss harbored many plans for ballets (in particular, a *Semiramis* to be written with Hofmannsthal, but also, later on, a project with Zweig), even though he only completed two independent works.[20] The second, *Schlagobers* (1922), was conceived as a "mute," satirical response along Viennese lines to postwar conditions. The first, *Josephs Legende* had a spectacular premiere as a "German" work performed

---

20 The dance piece *Verklungene Feste* (1940/41) was a form of historical reminiscence.

by Diaghilev's company just a few months before the First World War erupted; as such, it exemplified the composer's new aesthetic orientation directly. Unlike *Schlagobers*, for which Strauss himself wrote the book, *Josephs Legende* follows the design of Hofmannsthal and Count Harry Kessler; like Wagner's *Tristan*, it bears the title of *Handlung*—a generic designation that points to "successful" redemption. Here, dance is a means for achieving characterization through embodied action.

Taking up the subject of Joseph in Egypt—that is, turning to "Oriental" antiquity—was meant to continue the process initiated by *Elektra*: sifting through the past and reclaiming it for the present. As such, *Josephs Legende* represents an important step on the way to the conception of antiquity featured in *Ariadne auf Naxos*. However, in contrast to *Elektra*, *Josephs Legende* presents a fragmented view of antiquity since its events are set in sixteenth-century Venice. This setting, Hofmannsthal wrote in his preface to the work, is meant to ensure "more free room for fantasy."[21] Decades later, in 1941, Strauss still stressed that the ballet was not a matter of rhythmical autonomy (a reference to Stravinsky) or telling a story through movement (as for Ravel); instead, it attempted to "rejuvenate" dance dedicated to "proper, purely inspirational motion and absolute beauty."[22]

In light of Hofmannsthal's view that music represents what lies hidden "between" words—that is, all that defies formulation, writing, and articulation—*Josephs Legende* may be understood as the effort to elaborate a narrative without using language at all. It is hardly surprising, then, that the poet suggested that Strauss, inspired by his "vision," should compose a "tragic symphony" entitled *Orest und die Furien*.[23] The seed for the ballet lies here. Although he hesitated at first, Strauss came to attach great significance to the work, as is evident in the dimensions it assumed: running for an hour, it goes well beyond the standard length of productions

---

21 "in ein noch freieres Gebiet der Phantasie." [Hugo von] Hofmannsthal, "[Vorwort]," in *Josephslegende: Handlung von Harry Graf Kessler und Hugo von Hofmannsthal. Musik von Richard Strauss* (Berlin and Paris: Fürstner, 1914), 11.

22 "richtigen, rein inspirativen, der Bewegung und der absoluten Schönheit," "verjüngen." Richard Strauss, "Meine Josephslegende," in *Dramaturgische Blätter der Bayerischen Staatsoper* 11 (1940/41), 117f.; reprinted in *Betrachtungen und Erinnerungen*, 135.

23 "Vision", "tragische Symphonie." *Richard Strauss. Hugo von Hofmannsthal. Briefwechsel*, 171; letter from Hofmannsthal of March 8, 1912. Since both met immediately after this letter in Vienna, Strauss's reaction is unknown.

performed by the *Ballets Russes* and features a vast orchestra of 112 musicians. The piece takes "form" in a series of fourteen scenes arranged to heighten contrast within a musical framework that begins in D major and ends in G major, constituting a kind of vast, narrative cadence. In kaleidoscopic fashion, all the possibilities of musical "storytelling" are featured, from gently pouring sand in the first scene to the angelic epiphany of the finale. No quotations from musical history occur, nor—in contrast to *Ariadne*—are there ironic interruptions. Scenes unfold in succession, in a kind of cinematic dramaturgy (a method to which Strauss would return ten years later, in the film version of *Der Rosenkavalier*).

Josephs Legende represents an experiment, then, exploring how dance condenses gestic action within a field of tension anchored by words and music. The idea had first taken shape the previous year in *Der Rosenkavalier*, specifically the much-criticized and "misunderstood" waltz scenes.[24] Waltzes pervade the entire score. Starting with Octavian and the Marschallin's breakfast, they recur with varying levels of significance: in the princely bedchamber (the site of outwardly displayed intimacy), in the reception hall (where privacy is willingly set aside), and in the "extra room at an inn" ("Extrazimmer in einem Gasthaus," an impersonal place for erotic escapades and thus of feigned intimacy). Of course, no waltz is likely ever to have occurred in any of these spaces. To this fragmented picture of reality corresponds the fact that, although there is waltz music in all three acts, no actual dancing occurs. All the characters in this "comedy for music" constantly seek a language and a means by which to communicate: dialogue. The musical sign of their struggle is the waltz, which lends concrete expression to their efforts to interact (and failure to do so). A dance for couples, the waltz is authentically gestic. But in Strauss's opera—in contrast to, say, Act One of Gounod's *Faust*—it is never carried out. Two people intertwined in dance signifies erotic desire, but this reality is never borne out in *Der Rosenkavalier*. The waltz possesses a deep semantic charge, yet this never materializes fully; even the "little song" (*Liedl*) that Ochs tries to sing to the music in Act Two yields nothing more than incoherent stammering.

In condensed form, the waltz signifies the task assigned to music in a new kind of comedy. It lends concreteness—"plasticity"—to faltering

---

24 "mißverstandenen." Ibid., May 3, 1928, letter from Strauss of May 3, 1928.

communication; ideally, it would enable characters to understand each other when words fail. In the "Unwritten Afterword," Hofmannsthal observed:

> Thus one group stands opposed to the other; those who are connected are also separated, and those separated are connected, too. They all belong together, but the best lies in-between: momentary and eternal, it provides space for music.[25]

This momentary and eternal space lends the waltz its meaning. A form of dance with specific historical contours, it does not belong to the period in which the comedy is set, the mid-eighteenth century. Accordingly, its presence is what inaugurates history—and, at the same time, negates it. Its whirling movement calls space and time into question, but the orderly arrangement to which it is supposed to provide a point of contrast no longer exists.

In this light, the waltz in *Der Rosenkavalier* represents a "cipher" marked by incomprehension but filled with music. The beginning of the opera evokes, without words but in ironic fashion (the orchestra strikes E major, alluding to Wotan's departure in Wagner) the erotic encounter between Octavian and the Marschallin the night before (see Figure 7.2). At the end of Act Three, the little Moor—a mute, Orientalizing figure—picks up the lost handkerchief while performing a mincing dance set to orchestral music in G major.

Plastic Antiquity

Antiquity takes shape in a different way in *Ariadne auf Naxos*. Following the "Orientalist" experiments of *Salome, Elektra,* and *Josephs Legende,* the ancient world no longer stands on its own; here, its meaning derives from the fragmented, ironic form it assumes. The prelude to the opera proper—the elaboration of a theater within the theater—transforms it into an imaginary, eighteenth-century universe, which in turn is

---

25 "So stehen Gruppen gegen Gruppen, die Verbundenen sind getrennt, die Getrennten verbunden. Sie gehören alle zueinander, und was das Beste ist, liegt zwischen ihnen: es ist augenblicklich und ewig, und hier ist Raum für Musik." Hugo von Hofmannsthal, "Ungeschriebenes Nachwort zum Rosenkavalier," in *Der Merker* 2 (1911), 488f; cited in Hugo von Hofmannsthal, *Operndichtungen* 1 [Der Rosenkavalier], ed. Dirk O. Hoffmann and Willi Schuh (Frankfurt: S. Fischer, 1986), 547.

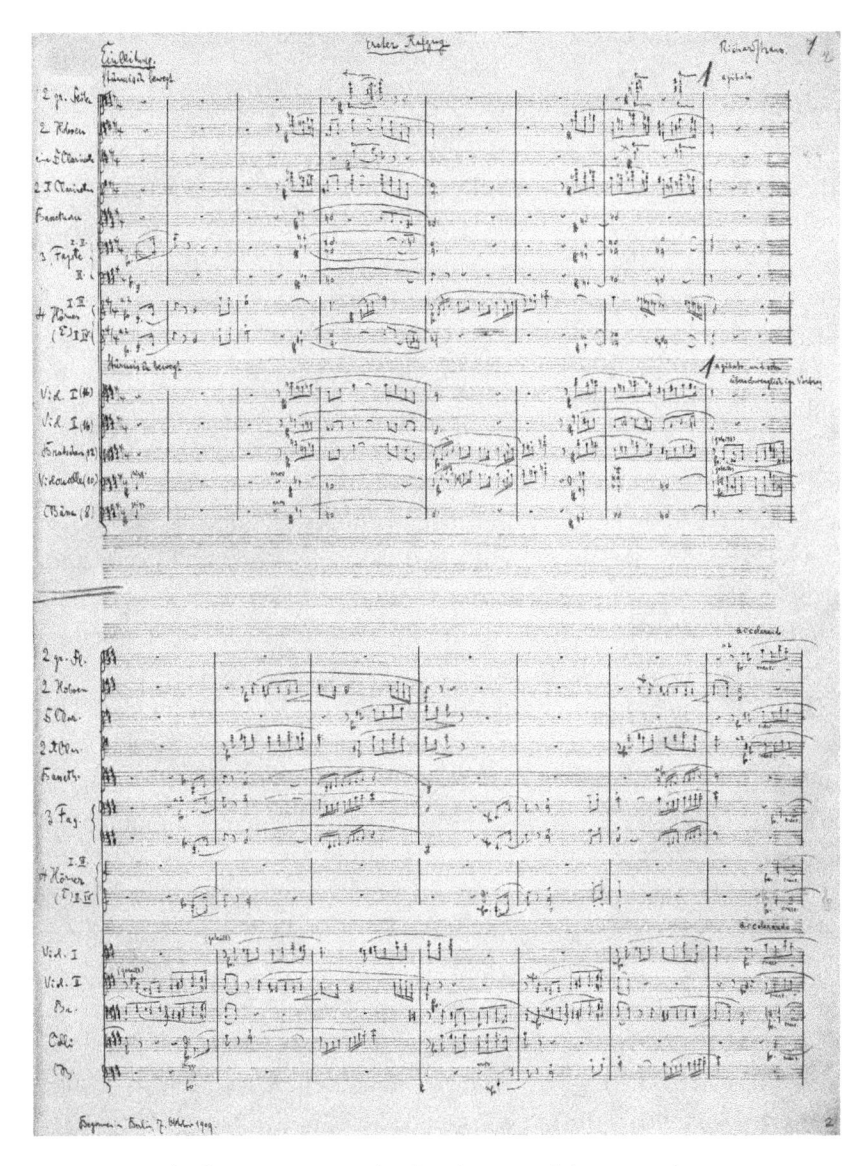

Figure 7.2 Richard Strauss: *Der Rosenkavalier*. First page of the autograph score.

When he took office in Vienna, Strauss wanted a villa representing his status — in a sense, a counterpart to his residence in Garmisch. In exchange for the parcel of land, he gave the Austrian state the three-volume fair copy, written in his own hand, of *Rosenkavalier* (among other things). The inscription dated 13 May 1924 declares that it is "Dedicated to the Vienna National Library, as the property of the Austrian Federal Treasury." This document provides an excellent example of the painstaking care the composer showed when completing his complicated scores. The house at Garmisch still bears witness to the concentrated energy at work: the desk is marked by many arcs and flourishes that flew from the composer's hand when making final copies.

Vienna, Österreichische Nationalbibliothek, Mus. Hs. 2123.

presented to a twentieth-century audience. As Nietzsche described it in *The Birth of Tragedy,* Greek art was "plastic" because it fused Dionysian and Apollonian elements into a whole; the crises of modernity have broken apart this unity—and with it, the possibility for substantive communication. In this light, the "raw" and anti-classical qualities featured in *Salome* and *Elektra* represent first steps toward recovering antiquity in purified form, so to speak. Strauss does not seek to renew the ancient world, as Nietzsche did. At most, antiquity can claim validity as a momentous and ambiguous memory that persists in the present day. In other words, it takes concrete form as a mnemonic space that—ramified, subdivided, and three dimensional—offers different perspectives from different standpoints. Where plasticity and memory meet, transformation occurs. *Der Rosenkavalier* had already suggested as much. When Ochs celebrates his insatiable sexual appetite in Act One, it is hardly surprising that he winds up professing allegiance to the ancient world: "If only I could be blessed like Jupiter with a thousand shapes! I'd take every woman." At precisely this juncture, an abrupt shift occurs from D♭ major (preceded by A♭ major) to G major (the dominant of C major), thereby signaling the motif of metamorphosis. The sequence illustrates a central premise of the composer's craft: it takes comedy—not tragedy—to renew antiquity in a credible manner.[26]

The plasticity Strauss sought—the momentous recollection of Dionysian and Apollonian elements working in concert—is already in evidence, on a conceptual level, in the tone poems, especially through the parallels between *Don Quixote* and *Ein Heldenleben, Symphonia domestica* and *Eine Alpensinfonie. Ariadne auf Naxos,* where the tragic dimension is embodied only by the young composer who rejects change in every form, shows the same through the opposite pairing of Ariadne and Zerbinetta, each of whom is unthinkable without the other. In other words, the desired concreteness does not involve vague reflection on the past so much as a sounding out of all its contrasts. The latter are already given in vocal registers (dramatic soprano versus the soubrette's coloratura), and they culminate in the *habitus* that extends from the

---

26 "Wollt' ich könnt' sein wie Jupiter selig in tausend Gestalten! Wär' Verwendung für jede." Richard Strauss, *Der Rosenkavalier: Komödie für Musik in drei Aufzügen von Hugo von Hofmannsthal,* op. 59 (Vienna: Strauss-Verlag, 1996), 80f.

innovative *parlando* in the prelude to the grand, symphonic gesture of Bacchus's epiphany. At the same time, however, this final scene has the effect of a recollection, too, in that the orchestra has been reduced to thirty-seven musicians and therefore performs the music on a smaller scale. In other words, the elements of tradition that Strauss musters no longer stand for themselves; they achieve reality (and meaning) only by way of contrast. This feature makes them plastic, like a sculpture: they admit multiple perspectives.

The encryption of music already evident in *Der Rosenkavalier* shows a new side in *Ariadne*. Here, the prelude begins in C major and ends in C minor: a central topos of instrumental music from Beethoven on that Strauss had already employed in *Tod und Verklärung*—*per aspera ad astra*, the shift from C minor to C major—is inverted and thereby stripped of its idealist implications. Likewise, the opera's conclusion, which depicts the union of the lovers following their metamorphosis, occurs in the key with which *Götterdämmerung* ends. D♭ major receives a new, vital charge: in Wagner, the lovers are not joined; now the Dionysian and Apollonian merge through the figures of Ariadne and Zerbinetta. Instead of being framed by mythological drama, the work presents a humanized, if fragmented, picture of antiquity.

The final version of *Ariadne* displays a novel structure: instead of two acts, a *prelude* and *opera* are presented. This arrangement proves dialogical—a quality Strauss would call into question only in his late work (*Capriccio* is just a prelude, and no opera follows; it remains in the realm of mere possibility). Dialogue opens onto a dimension that also extends beyond particular works: *Ariadne auf Naxos* and *Die Frau ohne Schatten* form a pair (as do other works that followed). In contrast, *Die ägyptische Helena* strikes a balance between newly achieved, plastic antiquity and its Orientalist counterpart; eventually, taking up a plan by Hofmannsthal, Strauss would give it form as a kind of last will and testament in *Die Liebe der Danae*. However, comedy was not simply a genre in which to make this kind of antiquity present in the modern world. Strauss also deemed it the only way to react to conditions he perceived as oppressive. In 1916—that is, at a point when no end to the war, which was only getting more and more brutal, was in sight—the composer observed that "tragedy [*Tragik*] on the stage" struck him as "pretty stupid and childish." "Indeed, I feel I have been called to be the twentieth-century Offenbach, and you will, and must, be my poet."²⁷ Ultimately, he decided that the combination of "classical" and "parodic" elements featured in Jacques Offenbach's Paris operettas, especially *Orphée aux enfers* (1858), would provide the basis for the plasticity he sought—and in terms of music, not just stagecraft. Accordingly, Strauss and Hofmannsthal understood *Die ägyptische Helena* as an effort to provide a sense of direction to the modern world. In a rare exception, both parties issued programmatic statements about the work: Hofmannsthal wrote a study of the text, and Strauss discussed the piece in an interview. In the former's eyes, a new version of antiquity represented the sole possibility for responding to the distortions of the present day, which could not be addressed directly (say, along the lines of social criticism or revolutionary pronouncements). Although he acknowledged that the work contained elements of "human tragedy [*Tragik*]," Strauss emphasized that comedic traits serve to negate them. He observed that his Helen is different from Goethe's, in *Faust*, where she "symbolizes antiquity itself."²⁸ His own work, in contrast, makes sure not to violate certain borders: the music is "melodious, euphonious, and presents no problems to ears that have matured beyond the nineteenth century."²⁹

In brief: Strauss hoped to counter the betrayal of tonality that had only grown more pronounced in the course of the 1920s. His score enlists a "noble Greek bearing"—which does not mean neoclassical clarity so much as ready comprehensibility. The new mythology it represents does not content itself with symbolism detached from human existence. Instead, it is meant to be anchored in life. Much earlier, when writing to Count Harry Kessler (who, incidentally, was mystified by *Helena*) about the role of actors, Hofmannsthal had declared: "They are gods, and I believe in them."³⁰

---

27 "nach diesem Kriege Tragik auf dem Theater vorläufig ziemlich blöde und kindlich," "ja, ich fühle mich geradezu berufen zum Offenbach des 20. Jahrhunderts, und Sie werden und müssen mein Dichter sein." *Richard Strauss. Hugo von Hofmannsthal. Briefwechsel*, 344; letter from Strauss of June 5, 1916.

28 "menschlichen Tragik," "mehr ein Symbol für die Antike selbst." Richard Straus, "Interview über 'Die ägyptische Helena' [with Ludwig Karpath]," in *Neue freie Presse*, May 27, 1928; reprinted in *Betrachtungen und Erinnerungen*, 152f.

29 "melodiös, wohlklingend, und bietet für Ohren, die über das neunzehnte Jahrhundert hinausgewachsen sind, keinerlei Probleme." Ibid., 150.

30 "Denn es sind Götter, und ich glaube an sie." *Hugo von Hofmannsthal—Harry Graf Kessler: Briefwechsel*, 244; letter from Hofmannsthal to Kessler of June 12, 1909.

Strauss revisited this concept on two occasions after Hofmannsthal's death, in *Daphne* and *Liebe der Danae*. The motif of reconciliation between the Apollonian and Dionysian in *Ariadne* changes in *Daphne*, where the heroine ultimately refuses Apollo. Here, the music's "noble, Greek bearing" displays an unwonted quality in that the tragedy, brought back to a "bucolic" setting, seems to emerge from a single thought in an endless process of transformation: the theme at the beginning, which, played on the oboe, evokes the *aulos* of Dionysos. When Daphne completes her final metamorphosis and becomes a part of nature, language, definition, and meaning vanish again. In this light, it is hardly surprising that the ancient world presented in *Liebe der Danae* is corrupt beyond redemption: the couple's "Oriental" quality heralds the composer's final break with it.

Strauss also sought a historical pedigree for his conception of plastic antiquity. His treatment of Beethoven's *Ruinen von Athen*, undertaken in 1924, as well as the new version of Mozart's *Idomeneo* from 1930 heralds the will to find such a world in the works of predecessors he deemed particularly important. It is not by chance that Mozart and Beethoven represent antagonists in this dramaturgy, respectively corresponding to the Apollonian and the Dionysian. Indeed—and as we will see at greater length below—the Salzburg Festival may be viewed as a political response (in the realm of theater, of course) to the catastrophe of 1918, that is, as an effort to make plasticity serve the reality of the stage: the union of the Dionysian and the Apollonian, the festive and the social. In a text he authored on June 19, 1949 (which was published two years later as "Letzte Aufzeichnung" ["final note," or "final record"]), Strauss underscored this aspect of contrast, declaring that he had composed "music of the twentieth century. The Greek Teuton!"[31]

A New Reality: Fairytale and Operetta

The years between 1910 and 1917 witnessed numerous projects, at the center of which stood *Ariadne auf Naxos* and *Die Frau ohne Schatten*—that is, antiquity regained and a fairytale outside of time. Initally, Strauss's plans for *Frau ohne Schatten* centered on material following *Das kalte*

---

[31] "Musik des 20. Jahrhunderts. Der griechische Germane!" Richard Strauss, "Letzte Aufzeichnung," in *Betrachtungen und Erinnerungen*, 182.

Herz by Wilhelm Hauff. The composer envisioned lavish natural settings in the forest—which Hofmannsthal categorically rejected. Although this element was discarded, the central idea persisted: petrification. The same motif also plays a key role in *Ariadne*: the composer declares that he would like to turn the world "to stone"; in contrast, Ariadne and Bacchus affirm the power of metamorphosis at the opera's end.[32] The tale that ultimately emerged seeks to combine the divergent aspects of modernity. It displays multiple points of connection with works both Strauss and Hofmannsthal appreciated: Gozzi's comedies, Dostoevsky's *Idiot*, Hugo's *Ruy Blas*, Mozart's *Magic Flute, A Thousand and One Nights*, Wagner's *Fliegender Holländer*, and Goethe's *Faust*, among others. The title was fixed as early as 1911, but the process went ahead slowly—framed, as it were, by the premiere of *Der Rosenkavalier*, all three versions of *Ariadne, Josephs Legende*, and *Eine Alpensinfonie*. The first production, which the First World War had delayed, coincided with Strauss taking the helm of the Vienna Opera, now no longer under courtly patronage. For the first time in Strauss and Hofmannsthal's joint endeavors, the piece is called an "opera" without further qualification. The composer and poet make a point of stressing this exceptional status. As much is also evident not just in the demands placed on singers—there are five main dramatic roles—but also in the elaborate stage design and the massive orchestration. The requirement of 120 musicians (including parts on stage) has no parallel, even in Strauss's vast body of work.

As opposed to the ancient world summoned forth in the comedies, *Die Frau ohne Schatten* seeks to offer a synthesis of nineteenth-century operatic traditions and, in so doing, to surpass them in order to derive new perspectives on the present day. "Let us resolve to make *Die Frau ohne Schatten* the final Romantic opera,"[33] Strauss told Hofmannsthal. Here, "Romantic" means the lavish world of symbols in fairytales, the array of non-linear points of reference. Three works of theater history in particular provide the backdrop for the work. The "high-" and "lowborn" couples (Emperor and Empress—the Dyer and his wife) correspond to

---

32 Hofmannsthal, *Ariadne auf Naxos*, 25; Ariadne even calls Bacchus a "transmuter" ("Verwandler").

33 "Wir wollen den Entschluß fassen, die 'Frau ohne Schatten' sei die letzte romantische Oper." *Richard Strauss. Hugo von Hofmannsthal. Briefwechsel*, 354; letter from Strauss, June 28, 1916.

the characters in Mozart's *Magic Flute* (Tamino/Pamina—Papageno/Papagena); the motif of interconnected insight, trial, and temptation points to Goethe's *Faust*; and the overall setting of a mythological world-theater evokes Wagner's *Ring*. It is not by chance that the overarching concept behind *Die Frau ohne Schatten* arose in close proximity to the idea of the Salzburg Festival. The work represents a sketch for a world-theater in the twentieth century. In this way—and in marked contrast to Wagner—the role of visual symbols stands in the background: even the key scene, when the Empress's shadow falls, does not amount to a spectacle. Instead, an array of varying perspectives occupies the foreground; the abundant contrasts that result represent the main stage event; staging them successfully remains one of the greatest challenges facing operatic stagecraft (see Figure 7.3).

The fairytale world of symbols can only achieve plausibility insofar as it stands apart from antiquity, and so admits no clear-cut resolutions. Accordingly, *Die Frau ohne Schatten* exemplifies the new "social" quality of art; the jubilant proclamation of unconditional, mutual human devotion at the piece's end requires no external justification. Barak's manifest sexual vigor, to which the concluding chorus of the unborn lends further emphasis, belongs to the timeless present. In this manner (and in contrast to the prelude to *Ariadne*), *Die Frau ohne Schatten* moves from C minor to C major. That said, the final key arises through a lengthy process: it does not represent "pure" so much as "purified" clarity. Its symbolism and tonality are regained in a complex manner. Accordingly, the work's vast orchestration assumes its full import only in contrast to the stripped-down instrumentation of *Ariadne*. At the same time, the fairytale gives the orchestra a new task: to stand on its own during the interludes. Although these orchestral passages are necessitated by the many elaborate scene changes, they also communicate in their own right, without words and beyond dance and "gestic" action (thereby calling to mind in a sense the finale of *Feuersnot*).

Die Frau ohne Schatten attempts to sum up a theatrical tradition one last time, in order to reveal a new perspective for the twentieth century—and then to leave this same tradition behind. In the process of its composition, the parodic element—that is, the operetta—increasingly came to the fore. In his initial work on *Der Rosenkavalier* Strauss had already toyed with the *Spieloper*, as exemplified by Albert Lortzing's comic operas, pieces by

Figure 7.3 Richard Strauss: *Die Frau ohne Schatten*. Schlafgem[ach] d[er] Kaiserin [Bedchamber of the Empress], Act 2, Scene 4 Set design by Alfred Roller (1864-1935), Gouache and drawing ink on card, 33 x 49, 8 cm. Vienna premiere 1919.

Strauss's joint endeavors with Hofmannsthal are unthinkable without Max Reinhardt. Reinhardt's conception of the theater included set designs that did not aim for realism. To achieve this ideal, he enlisted Alfred Roller, who hailed from Brno and was one of the founders of the Vienna Secession. In 1903, Roller was engaged at the Vienna Court Opera by Gustav Mahler, whose program of reform is inextricably tied to the artist's name. In 1909, Roller began working closely with Reinhardt. His set designs played a key role in Strauss and Hofmannsthal's *Rosenkavalier* and, especially, *Frau ohne Schatten* (to which he contributed from the earliest stages on). At the invitation of Adolf Hitler, who had hoped to be apprenticed to the artist in 1908, Roller designed the décor for the new staging of *Parsifal* in Bayreuth; Strauss conducted the production.

Vienna, Österreichisches Theatermuseum, HÜ 15635.

French composers such as Daniel Auber, and "mixed" works like Friedrich von Flotow's *Martha*; in other words, compositions that contrasted with Wagnerian music-drama. More and more, the operetta provided the map for the course that Strauss came to steer. Eventually, Hofmannsthal acknowledged that *Der Rosenkavalier* and *Ariadne* amounted to "operettas" in this vein. A host of factors account for the fascination the genre exerted: a marked distance from tragedy, purposeful ambiguity, parodic orientation, and the role of change produce a kind of theater based on a new mode of interaction between words and music. On July 13, 1928 Hofmannsthal wrote to Strauss:

For me, the actual poetic creation lies in what figures say. How they speak, how the tone changes, how their diction rises and falls—this provides the means for me to make characters come alive, to make palpable all the social differences, including much that remains *in-between* them, which can scarcely be voiced.[34]

Music lends color to hidden "speech" and gives it concrete, embodied form. That is, it affords a space of representation, (especially) when words fail or are missing.

When he embraced the operetta and Offenbach in 1916, then, Strauss was being entirely serious. And Hofmannsthal accepted the challenge. In 1919, he wrote to fellow poet Rudolf Pannwitz (1881–1969) that his plans for *Danae* involved "a kind of operetta" that would be "more of an operetta than *Ariadne,* with a mythological core, all of it outside of space, swaying back and forth between the mythically eternal and the social, indeed the instantaneous, as in Offenbach's texts."[35] From *Die Frau ohne Schatten* on, all of Strauss's works were conceived under the sign of the operetta—including *Intermezzo,* while Hofmannsthal was still alive, and *Die Liebe der Danae,* after his death; indeed, *Die ägyptische Helena* combines the idea of the operetta and the composer's vision of the ancient world. More than any other work, however, *Arabella* belongs to the world of this genre. Not only does the setting, 1860s Vienna, directly border on modernity, modernism, and their attendant crises, but this period was the operetta's heyday. Discussion of *Arabella* is difficult since Hofmannsthal's sudden death interrupted its completion. Only the delicate balance achieved in Act One represents, at least in terms of composition, the fruit of shared labors; for the remaining two acts Strauss

---

34 "Im Reden der Figuren sehe ich die eigentliche dichterische Kreation. Wie sie reden, wie ihr Ton wechselt, wie ihre Diktion steigt und sinkt—darin ist mir das Mittel gegeben, die Charakteristik wahrhaft lebendig zu machen, alle sozialen Unterschiede, auch vieles kaum direkt Aussprechbare *zwischen* den Figuren fühlen zu machen." *Richard Strauss. Hugo von Hofmannsthal. Briefwechsel,* 638f; letter from Hofmannsthal, July 13, 1928.

35 "Art Operette," "noch mehr Operette als Ariadne, der Kern mythisch, das Ganze raumlos, hin- und wieder wehend zwischen dem Mythisch-ewigen und dem Socialen, ja dem Augenblicklichen wie die Offenbach-texte." Gerhard Schuster (ed.), *Hugo von Hofmannsthal—Rudolf Pannwitz: Briefwechsel 1907–1926, mit einem Essay von Erwin Jaeckle* (Frankfurt: S. Fischer, 1993), 459; letter from Hofmannsthal to Pannwitz of December 8, 1919.

basically set Hofmannsthal's first draft to music. For all that, however, *Arabella* reaches new heights in terms of conception. This much is evident in the fact that—in contrast to *Der Rosenkavalier*—a waltz really is performed. Like *Danae, Arabella* features a debauched and degenerate world. Vienna is rife with pleasure-seeking and hypocritical decorum; the characters are given to gambling, debt, occultism, and indifference. Only through "the exotic," in the form of Mandryka, might any change occur. Yet the title figure ultimately rejects anything of the kind, declaring in a tempestuous cadence in F major, "Take me as I am." In a final, terrible rub, the reality of the times overshadows the prospect of new social identification. Dedicated to "My Friends Alfred Reucker and Fritz Busch," *Arabella* premiered in Dresden on July 1, 1933, a few months after the National Socialists came to power. Reucker (1868–1958), who managed the theater and would eventually be removed, was facing pressure from the new authorities. Busch (1890–1951), the musical director, had already been driven from town. Strauss stuck to the production plan, but he insisted that Hofmannsthal be credited, too. The premiere of *Arabella* inaugurated the meteoric rise of conductor Clemens Krauss (1893–1954) in Nazi Germany.

CHAPTER EIGHT

New Mythology and the Plasticity of Music

Mozart's Melody and Wagner's Orchestra: Tonality and the New Musical Communicability

Writing to Willi Schuh in March 1945, Strauss articulated his teleological view of music history as the history of mankind—a theme that runs throughout his late correspondence—in a pithy fomula: "Mozartian melody, Beethovenian symphony, and the Wagnerian orchestra are the end and culmination of world culture."[1] Hyperbole notwithstanding, these words express a concern that had shaped Strauss's compositions as a young man, too: the dissolution of melody and harmony. It is only surprising at first glance that Strauss assessed Wagner's significance in terms of the "orchestra" alone—that is, sound. Even though he professed undying admiration for his forebear all his life, these words make it clear that he understood music and the theater in a new and different way. The "plasticity" Strauss sought is based on purposefully blurring the parameters of "melody" and harmony" by reworking music's fundamental syntactic unit, the motif. In works devised in collaboration with Hofmannsthal, words give rise to motifs, as if the latter had been struck from the coin of metrical language: "A-ga-mem-non," "Ma-rie Theres (Wie—du—warst)," "Cir-ce," or "Kei-ko-bad." (See Example 8.1.)

---

[1] "Die Mozartsche Melodie, die Beethovensche Sinfonie und das Wagnersche Orchester sind Ende und Höhepunkt der Weltkultur." *Briefwechsel mit Willi Schuh*, 78; letter from Strauss of March 8, 1945.

Example 8.1 Language-generated motifs.

A - ga - mem - non

Ma - rie   The - res!

Cir - ce   Cir - ce

[Kei - ko - bad   Kei - ko - bad]

Even though Strauss moved away from this technique from *Intermezzo* on, it clearly served the important purpose of lending solidity—and therefore reality—to his motifs. Insofar as it arose from the fusion of music and language, such reality was melodic and harmonic at one and the same time. In other words, it united "Mozartian melody" and the "Wagnerian orchestra." This stance is still preserved in the aporetic conclusion to *Capriccio*—a context in which it is uncertain whether a "work" has resulted at all.

A new kind of semantics follows from such concision. On the surface, Strauss's motifs are Wagnerian, but his technique differs from what since Hans von Wolzogen's *Thematischer Leitfaden* (published in 1876 for the *Ring* cycle in Bayreuth) had been known as *Leitmotivik*. Wagner, who preferred the term *Hauptmotive* ("principal motifs"), used this technique to produce quasi-material evidence and presence. The "sword-motif" is exemplary in this regard. At the end of *Rheingold*, it seems that "a great thought has seized" Wotan: in a single blow, as it were, the pace and key of the music change. Then, in the course of Act One of *Walküre*, the motif is "set free" step by step: Siegmund remembers the sword, catches sight of its gleam, then draws it from the trunk and displays it to Sieglinde, who marvels in awe. Only now does the motif in C major, based on a triad, sound in full: its meaning is made manifest. Motifs display a fundamentally different character in Strauss's works. As he observed in the foreword to *Intermezzo*, their purpose is the "representation of spiritual experience when characters act."[2] In other words, motifs do not make manifest or present so much as they encrypt psychological events—providing the "coloration" Hofmannsthal deemed the task of music (after working on *Der Rosenkavalier*). These complex semantic fields do not stand on their own, however; they acquire full meaning—"expression"—in the context of the contrapuntal, multi-perspectival arrangement of the orchestra. Such simultaneity, which Strauss called "psychic polyphony," gives rise to a reality that no longer follows a linear scheme, as in Wagner; that is, motifs do not correspond to objects. Strauss's motifs point in multiple directions and therefore admit change. By the same token, they cannot really be compartmentalized in syntactic fashion. The first bars of the introduction to *Der Rosenkavalier* are exemplary: the Octavian-motif played on horns is checked only in contrast to the Marschallin-motif of the strings and woodwinds—which the sharp shift from E to E♭ underscores from the second measure on. As such, the motifs no longer contain their own syntactic borders.

The contours of this conception of the motif remained more or less stable over the course of Strauss's later operas, but internal transformations and change did take place. *Der Rosenkavalier* and *Ariadne* explore possible relations between language and music in a psychological light. The "psychic polyphony" of motifs that resulted assures the "symphonic unity" of the scores.[3] At the same time, such unity also represents, on a basic level, the continuation of the paratactic forms that shaped the composer's tone poems. As a rule, the orchestra provides accompaniment in the operas. Only occasionally does it achieve independence—most clearly, in Act Three of *Der Rosenkavalier*, with its "pantomimes" (which are explicitly designated as such). *Josephs Legende* takes orchestral autonomy as far as

---

2 "Darstellung der seelischen Erlebnisse der handelnden Personen." Strauss, "Vorwort," in *Intermezzo* [x].

3 "symphonischen Einheit." *Richard Strauss. Hugo von Hofmannsthal. Briefwechsel*, 58; letter from Strauss of May 4, 1909.

possible, but this feature is also responsible for separating vocal passages and grand-scale orchestral interludes in *Die Frau ohne Schatten*. *Intermezzo*, which did not employ metrically generated motifs, also observed this separation, which was taken up again in *Die ägyptische Helena* and *Arabella*. Evidently, the idea of "symphonic unity" was now fixed in Strauss's eyes. From this point on, no real changes of syntax occurred, although Zweig (perhaps in keeping with plans Hofmannsthal had devised) saw to it that its symbolic dimension faded more and more, in keeping with the view, already evident in *Intermezzo*, that music could have an external referent.

Holding fast to tonality represents a key aspect of the "intentional communicability" that Strauss sought. The broadened tonality of *Salome* and *Elektra* enabled the composer to sound out the possibilities his new approach to music and drama entailed, without calling the overall framework into question. The so-called break between *Elektra* and *Der Rosenkavalier* that scholars are fond of pointing to is not really there. Strauss himself never spoke of any such thing, nor did he arrive at a different view of these works, even late in life. In other words, expansion and experimentation did not explode tonality so much as they helped the composer find his way back to it. Now, however, Strauss no longer viewed tonality as a given, a framework to be accepted without questioning. Just as Hofmannsthal's linguistic crisis led him to re-evaluate language itself, the crisis of tonality prompted Strauss to identify a new sphere of validity for it, circumscribed temporally and functionally, in the interest of communication. From *Der Rosenkavalier* on, tonality connects with the concept of "the social" (which, in turn, connects with the genre of comedy). Regained and revalorized, tonality proves as rich in reference as the language onstage, as dramatic events themselves, for it unfolds in multiple directions and dimensions. Strauss never saw fit to question tonality on a fundamental level: doing so would have cast doubt on what he deemed the essence of the work of art: communication. (This conviction accounts for his reserved attitude toward atonality, which, at least until the end of the 1920s, he made a point of following—with remarkable thoroughness—in others' scores.)

At the same time, tonality—the "social" at the heart of music, as it were—did undergo changes in the course of Strauss's work. Multiply inflected motifs meant abandoning goals in favor of process—which could purposefully prove aimless. Over time, Strauss refined this approach more and more, until it took a singular turn in his late period. Thus, in *Daphne*, the title figure's sympathy for Leukippos's fate does not culminate in a concrete, "plastic" relation. The couple is not united; instead, Daphne's sentiments dissolve into a fractal array of organic forms.

The Present and Presence of the Theater

At first, it seems paradoxical that Strauss would affirm that the theater and music could found life in the present and enable human beings to lay full claim to it, given the way he positioned himself in his own day. At the turn of the century, Strauss was viewed as an *agent provocateur*, yet from 1920 on, he was considered the complete opposite. When they premiered, both *Salome* and *Elektra* attracted shock and scandal, and there is every indication that the composer enjoyed the ensuing controversies. These works made Strauss a prominent exponent of "modernism"—as many caricatures in the contemporary press attest (even if they subsequently vanished as quickly as they had appeared; see Figure 8.1).[4] At the age of forty, Strauss stood at the center of heated debates. By the time he was sixty, no one would contest his prominence, yet he hardly qualified as a representative of the latest musical trends in the German world. Although the composer offered no commentary on this state of affairs, he was irritated by how public perceptions had shifted: all his life, he acknowledged that his career was constantly changing course, but he did not see any points of rupture in the overall trajectory. At the very end, Strauss continued to insist on the coherence of his artistic creations from the tone poems up to the operas—leaving out the compositions up to the Symphony in F minor (which he had set apart early on). But by the time he wrote his final works, Strauss had come to be viewed as part of the past. Writing to Willi Schuh at the premiere of *Metamorphosen,* he grumbled: "I was somewhat piqued by the thought of featuring in a novelty concert, since I have not written any 'novelties' since *Capriccio*."[5]

---

4 A good overview of caricatures may be found in Roswitha Schötterer-Traimer, *Richard Strauss: Sein Leben und Werk im Spiegel der zeitgenössischen Karikatur* (Mainz: Schott, 2009).

5 "Mich hatte nur der Gedanke etwas froissiert, in einem Novitätenkonzert zu figurieren, da ich seit Capriccio keine 'Novitäten' mehr schreibe . . . ." *Briefwechsel mit Willi Schuh*, 87; letter from Strauss of November 6, 1945.

Figure 8.1 "Anonymous, *Salome auf Reisen* ("Salome Abroad"). Caricature, Berlin 1910 (*Der zerpflückte Richard Strauss: Richard-Strauss-Karikaturen in Bild und Wort* (Berlin 1910), 32)

More than any other composer, Strauss became the object of caricature and satire around the turn of the century; after 1920, this was no longer the case. All in all, the composer seems to have enjoyed the attention. In this anonymous work from 1910, the touring production of *Salome* is cast in an absurd, parodistic light. In addition to Strauss, one clearly recognizes Ernst von Schuch (1846–1914), who conducted the premiere, and Marie Wittich (1868–1931), who performed in the title role.

Private collection.

A wealth of material documents how Strauss understood contemporary music at the turn of the century. Evidence includes the pieces he conducted, his interventions on behalf of Mahler and the young Schoenberg, and the scores that Debussy and Ravel dedicated to him. Stravinsky, who was in Berlin in 1912 for a production of *Petrushka*, recalled that Strauss—whose "triumphant banality" he would come to despise[6]—demonstrated "great interest" in his composition.[7] Even

---

6 Igor Stravinsky and Robert Craft, *Conversations with Igor Stravinsky* (New York: Doubleday, 1959), 83.
7 Igor Stravinsky, *An Autobiography* (New York: Norton, 1962), 43.

though Strauss took strong positions (e.g., declaring Schoenberg "mad"[8]) and held a dim view of developments after the First World War, such interest did not fade. In summer 1921, the Society of Friends of Music organized the first Donaueschingen Chamber Music Festival. As a matter of course, Strauss—the leading German composer of the day—was asked to head the Honorary Committee, which included Ferruccio Busoni, Franz Schreker, and Arthur Nikisch; he took part in performances, too. "Back from Donaueschingen," he wrote to Franz Schalk about Paul Hindemith's String Quartet No. 2: "a very insolent, mad, but quite talented" work.[9] In 1922, he assumed the directorship of the Internationale Kammermusikaufführung in Salzburg, which soon led to the founding of the International Society for New Music; his first encounter with his Winterthur patron Werner Reinhart may date to this time. As the director of the city's opera, he was a member of the jury for the Vienna Music Prize, which went to Alban Berg and Anton von Webern in 1924, and to Hanns Eisler the following year.

Unlike twenty years earlier, now Strauss faced the present as though it were a foreign world. More and more, he endeavored to launch his own works for the stage, especially during his time in Vienna. In addition, he still exercised significant influence on the Berlin Opera, which he sought to exploit in similar fashion. All the same, there were consequences to his estrangement. Strauss's works of the 1920s include two key efforts to take a position vis-à-vis the present through his art: *Intermezzo* and *Die ägyptische Helena*. The latter was intended to take a stand against the "eccentrics of contemporary modernism."[10] Hofmannsthal ends the essay he wrote to accompany the work with a fictional conversation with the composer; here, Strauss declares that only historical ambiguity, the "influx of Orient and Occident into our self," represents the true "signature of our life" in the present. This truth cannot be "captured in bourgeois dialogues." The essay concludes: "Let us make mythological operas, this

---

8 "der wahnsinnige Schönberg." Günter Brosche (ed.), *Richard Strauss—Franz Schalk: Ein Briefwechsel* (Tutzing: Schneider, 1983), 164; letter from Strauss to Schalk of June 8, 1920.

9 "ein sehr freches, verrücktes, aber recht talentvolles [Werk]." Ibid., 225; letter from Strauss of August 3, 1921.

10 "Exzentrics der heutigen Moderne." *Richard Strauss. Hugo von Hofmannsthal. Briefwechsel, Briefwechsel*, 541; letter from Strauss of June 1, 1925.

is the truest of all forms."[11] That said, Strauss did not think it possible for the mythological opera to stand alone. Evidently, it required "bourgeois dialogues" for contrast. Accordingly, in May 1916—in the middle of the First World War and during work on *Die Frau ohne Schatten*—he shared his plan with Hofmannsthal:

> Apropos of a new opera, I have the following two things in mind: either an *entirely modern* one, an absolute comedy of character and nerves of the kind I already mentioned when you referred me to Bahr, or a pretty piece of love and intrigue—somewhere between Schnitzler's *Liebelei*, which is naturally too cloying and vapid, and Hackländer's *Geheimer Agent* or Scribe's *Verre d'eau*, which is the kind of piece for which I have always had a special fondness.[12]

Strauss had no literary ancestors in mind for this initial project—in contrast to the genealogy he devised for the second (including Eugène Scribe [1791–1861], Friedrich Wilhelm von Hackländer [1816–1877], and Arthur Schnitzler [1862–1931]). Clearly, he hoped that Hofmannsthal would fill in the blanks. However, the poet hesitated to do so. Instead, he suggested Hermann Bahr (1863–1934) and, finally, provided an unambiguous response:

> As I perceive it, what you are proposing there are truly abhorrent things to me, and they could deter me from ever becoming a librettist—not anyone at all, but me in particular. But, you know, let's not agonize about it: what you envision, I will never be able to do, even with the best will in the world.[13]

---

11 "Hereinfluten von Orient und Okzident in unser Ich," "Signatur unseres Lebens," "in bürgerlichen Dialogen aufzufangen,""machen wir mythologische Opern, es ist die wahrste aller Formen." Hugo von Hofmannsthal, *Die ägyptische Helena*, in *Prosa IV* (Frankfurt: S. Fischer, 1966, originally 1928), 460.

12 "Bezüglich einer neuen Oper schweben mir folgende zwei Sachen vor: entweder eine *ganz moderne*, absolut realistische Charakter- und Nervenkomödie in der Art, wie ich Sie Ihnen schon angedeutet habe, wo Sie mich auf Bahr verwiesen—oder so ein hübsches Liebes- und Intrigenstück, etwa in der Mitte zwischen Schnitzlers 'Liebelei', die natürlich zu süß und fad ist—und Hackländers 'Geheimer Agent' oder Scribes 'Glas Wasser', für welche Art von Intrigenstück ich immer besondere Vorliebe gehabt habe." *Richard Strauss. Hugo von Hofmannsthal. Briefwechsel*, 342; letter from Strauss of May 25, 1916.

13 "Das sind ja für mein Gefühl wahrhaft scheußliche Dinge, die Sie mir da proponieren, und könnten einen für lebenslang abschrecken, Librettist zu werden, d.h. nicht irgendeinen, sondern gerade mich. Aber wissen Sie, wir wollen uns darüber nicht den Kopf zerbrechen, das,

For help with *Intermezzo,* Strauss did, in fact, turn to Bahr—who drew up a plan that failed to satisfy him. The composer specified what he wanted: the "whole" was to be "broken up into separate pictures of character"—"practically cinematic images in which the music says everything and the poet provides only key phrases in gradual progression."[14] In other words, nothing that otherwise constitutes poetry should provide a theme. Strauss was interested in the private dimension of everyday life, its "composability" (and not in the sense of social criticism). Bahr gave up: "it's just that I *can't* ((write)) this dialogue of *yours,* and presumably no one can do so but you. Therefore I suggest: this time, *you* have to write the text on your own."[15] Finally, Strauss did just that. The result was a forerunner to the so-called *Alltagsoper* or *Zeitoper* of the 1920s (for instance, Hindemith's *Hin und Zurück* [1927] and *Neues vom Tage* [1929], or Schoenberg's *Von heute auf morgen* [also 1929]).

Intermezzo is, in fact, based on an autobiographical event. The similarity between the fictive composer's name, Storch, and that of the real composer makes as much plain. Indeed, Julius Kapp (1883–1962), the dramaturg for the piece's production at the Berliner Staatsoper in 1925, informed the audience:

> Strauss based *Intermezzo* on an actual incident in his life, which had threatened to destroy marital peace in 1905. One day, the tenor [Emilio] de Marchi [1861–1917], his manager, and the Prague Kapellmeister Josef Stranski [1872–1936] were at a bar in Berlin. At the time, de Marchi was singing at the Kroll Opera House during an Italian *stagione;* Stranski shared conducting duties with [Arturo] Vigna. As the three gentlemen discussed all and sundry, a lady, on her own and in need of company, joined them. She accepted a cocktail and, knowing what they had in mind, naturally requested a complimentary

was Ihnen vorschwebt, werde ich—mit bestem Willen nie machen können . . . ." *Richard Strauss. Hugo von Hofmannsthal. Briefwechsel,* 342; letter from Hofmannsthal of May 30, 1916.

14 "in einzelne Charakterbilder aufzulösen," "fast nur Kinobilder, in denen die Musik Alles sagt, der Dichter nur ein Paar allmählich vorwärts schreitende Schlagworte." Joseph Gregor (ed.), *Meister und Meisterbriefe um Hermann Bahr: Aus seinen Entwürfen, Tagebüchern und seinem Briefwechsel* . . . (Vienna: Bauer, 1947), 97, 100; letters from Strauss to Bahr of October 21, 1916 and January 1, 1917.

15 "nur *kann* ich diesen *Ihren* Dialog nicht ((abfassen)), und vermutlich kann ihn überhaupt niemand als Sie, weshalb mein Vorschlag ist: *Sie* müssen sich diesmal Ihren Text selber schreiben." Ibid., 102; letter from Bahr to Strauss of July 5, 1917.

ticket. In broken German, the tenor assured her that it would be taken care of by "Kapellmeister Strausky"—which what he always called Stranski—but he forgot just as soon as he was no longer in the young lady's presence. But she did not forget, and looked him up in the directory; instead of finding a Kapellmeister Strausky, she found the Hofkapellmeister Richard Strauss, residing at Joachimsthaler Strasse 17. In no time at all, she dispatched a missive: "My precious sweetheart, don't forget to bring me the ticket. Your faithful Lovey-dovey, Lüneburger Strasse 5." Since the Hofkappelmeister was away, the note was opened in the presence of his wife, Pauline. A grave matrimonial storm ensued, with threats of divorce, and only with great effort was the misunderstanding finally resolved.[16]

The scenery for the Dresden premiere, which was modeled on the composer's villa in Garmisch (much to his displeasure), underscored the connection between autobiography and work. However, like Strauss's other creations, *Intermezzo* achieves full meaning only in relational terms. As with *Symphonia domestica* and *Eine Alpensinfonie*, there is an important contrast to note. The opera makes a "social" dimension present that stands in opposition to mythological flights of fancy. At its core, it acknowledges existing social institutions, not out of veneration or awe, but on the basis of the insight that they alone can secure claims to reality—if only in passing. Since such meaning only comes to light in view of mythological aspects, this reality

---

16 "Strauß hat dem 'Intermezzo' eine wahre Begebenheit aus seinem Leben zugrunde gelegt, die im Jahre 1905 den Frieden seiner Ehe zu zerstören gedroht hatte. Eines Tages saßen der Tenor de Marchi, sein Manager und der Prager Kapellmeister Josef Stranski in einer Berliner Bar. De Marchi sang damals bei Kroll inmitten einer italienischen Stagione, und Stranski dirigierte abwechselnd mit Vigna. Während die drei Herren von allem Möglichen, nur nicht vom Theater sprachen, gesellte sich eine alleinstehende und anschlußbedürftige Dame zu ihnen, ließ sich einen Cocktail kredenzen und verlangte natürlich eine Freikarte, als sie heraus hatte, wes Geistes sie waren. Der Tenor versprach es in seinem gebrochenen Deutsch: 'Das werden die Kapellmeister Strausky—er nannte Stranski nie anders—besorgen', vergaß es aber in dem Augenblick, in dem er die junge Dame nicht mehr vor sich hatte. Sie ließ es aber nicht dabei, sondern schlug im Adreßbuch nach, wo sie zwar keinen Kapellmeister Strausky, dafür aber den Hofkapellmeister Richard Strauß, Joachimsthaler Straße 17, fand. Und flugs ging ein Briefchen an ihn ab: 'Lieber Schatz, bring mir doch die Billette. Deine getreue Mitze Mücke, Lüneburger Straße 5.' Das Briefchen wurde in Abwesenheit des Herrn Hofkapellmeisters von dessen Gattin Pauline geöffnet. Es gab ein heftiges Ehegewitter, Drohung mit Scheidungsklage, und erst allmählich löste sich das Mißverständnis." Julius Kapp, "Einführung in das Werk," in *Blätter der Staatsoper [Berlin]* 5 (1925), 7f.

also amounts to a cipher. For Strauss, the present held together only within a field of tension. Depicting this state of affairs was the only viable way to react to the destruction wrought by the First World War. His approach also represented a means of making the work of art self-reflective: encrypting tonal language down to its smallest elements. The composer always denied that commentary or elucidation from without would serve the same purpose. It never occurred to Strauss that art—music—could respond to the present through new forms of compositional syntax, for in his eyes this would mean abandoning "communicability." From *Die ägyptische Helena* on, he clung to this belief more and more.

Music as Festival: Salzburg

As the First World War raged, the Salzburger Festspielgemeinde was founded in Vienna, nominally by the jurist and Bruckner-disciple Friedrich Gehmacher (1866–1942) and the journalist Heinrich Damisch (1872–1961). Plans for such an organization had existed since 1890, but to move things forward an "artistic advisory board" was now set up; its members included Max Reinhardt, Franz Schalk, Alfred Roller, Hugo von Hofmannsthal, and Richard Strauss. The first Salzburg Festival took place after the war, in 1920; a production of Hofmannsthal's *Jedermann* directed by Reinhardt on the city's Cathedral Square made clear the undertaking's vast dimensions. The following year, concerts were added. In 1922, the Vienna Opera made a guest appearance and performed Mozart's operas in the Stadttheater (now the Landestheater), with Schalk and Strauss directing. There were plans to build a festival hall in honor of the latter in Heilbrunn, based on designs by Hans Poelzig (1869–1936). Strauss himself laid the foundation stone, but the structure was never erected; instead, the royal mews underwent renovation, and the stage was officially opened in 1926. This project represents further collaboration between Strauss, Hofmannsthal, and Reinhardt—who may be deemed its actual instigator. In a short piece from 1917, Reinhardt had described the underlying motivation: the theater, as "the most popular and mightiest art, at least in terms of immediate effect" should found one of "the first works of peace" in the dawning epoch.[17] To this end, the director enlisted

---

17 "populärsten und in der augenblicklichen Wirkung jedenfalls mächtigsten Kunst, dem Theater"; eines "der ersten Friedenswerke." Max Reinhardt, "Denkschrift zur Errichtung eines Festspielhauses in Hellbrunn," in Fetting, *Max Reinhardt*, 216.

"a dramatic censor in the noblest sense of the word" (Hofmannsthal) and a composer "who will fill this venerable, musical city, where Mozart was born, with the music of our day" (Strauss).[18] Thereby, he hoped, Salzburg would represent the starting point for general renewal.

Reinhardt sought to fit the theater to the demands of the present— to free it from the constraints of business and repertory and, as per Hofmannsthal's words, make it a site where "the festive" and "the social" could meet. The theater should both suspend everyday life and secure it at one and the same time. For his part, Hofmannsthal composed a short text outlining the objectives, a dialogue that reworked Reinhardt's programmatic declarations as questions and answers. Events would be held in "a festival hall built especially for this purpose": to respond to warped aspects of contemporary life by suspending distinctions between opera and drama, elites and the masses, one nation and the other, and past and present. As "the heart of the heart of Europe," Salzburg embodied the artistic ideal exemplified by its native son, Mozart.[19] Despite their grandiose ambitions, the three principal organizers did not want to set forth a manifesto. From the outset, their bearing was pragmatic. The "real" idea of the Salzburg Festival, then, was the actually carrying out of the festival itself.

Strauss embraced this program, for it overlapped with his own understanding of, and approach to, operatic composition. He viewed the Salzburg plans as a challenge; at the same time, they influenced practical steps he took (including "political" negotiations of the Vienna repertoire). The new theater should not just modify borders inwardly, but should also do so outwardly, by dissolving the oft-lamented, business-like aspects of the craft. The new endeavor would provide an example for others to follow. In addition, the Salzburg plans represented an attempt to update the Wagnerian festival idea for the twentieth century—with equal measures of distancing and appreciative appropriation, needless to say. It is

---

18 "dramatischen Zensor im feinsten Sinne des Wortes," "der diese alte musikalische Stadt, Mozarts Geburtsort, mit der Musik unserer Zeit erfüllen könnte." Max Reinhardt, "Auf der Suche nach dem lebendigen Theater," in ibid., 229.

19 "eigens dafür gebauten Festspielhaus," "das Herz vom Herzen Europas." Hugo von Hofmannsthal, "Die Salzburger Festspiele," in *Prosa IV*, 88–94.

impossible to tell just how much Strauss himself determined the shape of things, but the programming of works surely fell within his remit. Because the festival involved close collaboration with the Vienna Opera, a viable financial structure was also necessary. Internally, the Salzburg Festival sought to remedy the ills inflicted by the First World War. The importance Strauss attached to the project is evident in the lofty and thoroughgoing effort not only to combine "the festive" and "the social," but also to reconcile antiquity and modernity. This is the context for his adaptations of *Ruinen von Athen* and *Idomeneo*. (The same holds for plans conceived in 1926—which went as far as concrete designs—for a festival hall designed by the architect Rosenauer in honor of the composer, which would have been built in Athens.)

Ultimately, the Nazi seizure of power overshadowed activities in Salzburg. In 1934, Strauss directed *Parsifal* in Bayreuth. At Goebbels' behest, he had been obliged not to participate, but this was not a problem now that the Festival was up and running. The Reinhardt era ended in dreadful fashion when Damisch—an early party member—welcomed an NSDAP directorship in 1938. In the coming years, Strauss remained loyal to the Festival, however compromised it had become. Indeed, the concert hall rebuilt under Nazi oversight opened in 1939 with *Der Rosenkavalier*, directed by Karl Böhm. In 1944, Strauss deemed the public dress rehearsal for *Danae*—which Goebbels permitted in honor of the composer's eightieth birthday, even though performance of his works was forbidden—as the institutional end of the Salzburg Festival.

CHAPTER NINE

Music and Reality

Life-Worlds: Social Praxis and the Villas in Garmisch and Vienna

The notion of a "social" fusion of art and life, that is, of a new reality animated by art *in* life, affected how Strauss organized his own existence. Even though, by the age of thirty, he was quite a public figure by late nineteenth-century standards, the composer did not make a show of private moods or circumstances; indeed, he concealed them. However, the personal sphere he cultivated contrasted with a certain pleasure in scandal that is revealed by his correspondence (which ultimately became known to outsiders, too). Strauss's sole affair to have become common knowledge was with Dora Weis (1860–1913), a native of Bremen residing in Dresden who was a bit older and married, for four years, to the cellist Hans Wihan.[1] Real affection seems to have existed, but circumstances made the liaison difficult. All the same, it was several years (starting in 1884), before relations broke off for unknown reasons. (In the final phase, both partners addressed each other formally.) Marriage, in 1894, to Pauline de Ahna (1863–1950), a general's daughter and aristocrat, granted Strauss an institutional anchor in his "private life" that corresponded to his conception of art. It seems that Pauline de Ahna was a difficult person, however. Contemporaries described her as quite direct, sometimes to

---

1 Dvořák's Cello Concerto and Strauss's Sonata Op. 6 were dedicated to Wihan.

the point of being crude and tactless. Count Harry Kessler, for instance, deemed her "a pretty grotesque woman, common beyond measure and with a sentimental heart"—"all in all, a cook."[2] This, evidently, was why Hofmannsthal visited the couple at Garmisch only once and avoided further encounters with Pauline. Everyone agreed that man and wife had altogether different characters, especially since Pauline Strauss made a show of her aristocratic pretensions and Catholicism in direct proportion to the lack of interest she showed for intellectual matters. There is no way of knowing what, exactly, sustained the marriage or how stable it was.[3]

At any rate, Strauss always respected wedlock because it signaled his rootedness in the standing order, and he made sure to cultivate domestic life, especially after the birth of his son Franz (1897–1980)—which proved sufficiently difficult to make the prospect of more children unthinkable. As the site of social decorum and a means of striking a balance with the world, the family played a greater and greater role in the composer's existence. After 1933, it disclosed an unanticipated dimension. Strauss initially sought close ties to the National Socialist dictatorship, even though his daughter-in-law Alice Grab was Jewish; the situation was dangerous and, before long, life-threatening—as it was also for his two grandchildren, who, according to the Nuremberg Laws, counted as "half-Jewish." One can only speculate about which of the arrangements Strauss made with the Nazis were a matter of calculation, rashness, or the result of extortionate measures; the welter of conflicting factors makes a clear picture impossible to discern.

Strauss conducted his life in a singular manner analogous to his understanding of tonal language: instead of being "set" in terms of traditions secured by civil society or religion, it was conceived as a conscious process of finding stability. As such, the composer did without external sources of legitimation—anything beyond the present at hand. In this light, the "bourgeois" qualities that Strauss's contemporaries frequently noted did not derive from endorsement of the social code—a class-conscious

---

2 "ein ziemlich groteskes Weib; maßlos ordinär mit einem sentimentalen Herzen," "alles in allem eine Köchin." Harry Graf Kessler, *Tagebücher: 1918–1937* [selection], ed. Wolfgang Pfeiffer-Belli (Frankfurt: S. Fischer, 1961, 450; entry of January 19, 1926.

3 There is no public access to their correspondance, part of the Richard Strauss-Archiv in Garmisch-Partenkirchen.

attitude founded in the quest for success—so much as a desire to strike a balance with, and against, circumstances marked by deterioration and decay at every turn, and which offered no normative points of reference. However "bourgeois" it seemed, this life was wrested from and defied contemporary reality. Here, too, a similarity to Thomas Mann may be observed: distance both from inherited convention and from an "artistic" existence in active opposition to the rest of society. Strauss's vanity may have made him obsessed with honors, awards, and distinction, but on a deeper level, such an attitude was due to his view that "the social" entailed reciprocity: society should esteem those devoted to it.

This social praxis—the composer's "bourgeois mask," as Stefan Zweig called it[4]—was also in evidence in the two building projects Strauss conceived. During the 1920s, his attitude almost included a public dimension, in addition to a "private" one. There was something programmatic about his plans: the summer house (see Figure 9.1) was in Garmisch, far away from official duties in Berlin (where Strauss had recently rented an ultra-modern apartment with twenty rooms on the Kaiserdamm), and the villa in Vienna (see Figure 9.2) sought to translate a vision of music history into a domestic setting, to erect a kind of living monument. After his marriage, Strauss had already used summer stays at his inlaws' residence in Marquartstein for reflection and concentrated work. When *Salome* met with success, he decided to build a villa of his own and looked at options south of Munich before choosing an undeveloped plot in Garmisch. The commission went to the architect Emanuel von Seidel (1856–1919), who, at the time, was also overseeing the construction of the Deutsches Museum in Munich. Strauss clearly sought to make a representative statement, but also to express, in concrete terms, the present as he perceived it. Consequently, he took an active role: the centerpiece of the house, into which he moved in 1908, was the *Herrenzimmer* (which Seidl originally conceived as a study). The room was equipped with a large, round desk, an Ibach grand piano (rarely used for composition, however), an elaborate filing system for scores, and part of the library. In this setting, composition was not supposed to occur in a tide of inspired genius so much as result from carefully regulated "labor." It is only surprising at first glance that the first large-scale work to be developed here was *Elektra*.

---

4 "bürgerlichen Maske." Stefan Zweig, *Die Welt von gestern*, 410.

Figure 9.1   Emanuel von Seidl (1856–1919), Villa Strauss, Garmisch-Partenkirchen
Photograph, 1908.

Built in 1908, the villa in Garmisch—which, apart from a few additions, stands unchanged today—was designed in an ambitious, modernist spirit by the Munich architect Emanuel von Seidl (1856–1919). In Berlin, Strauss had already made a point of living in the "modern," western part of the city, not the area of the Court Opera; each of his three apartments exhibited increasingly "representative" flair. The elegant Garmisch villa, with its many amenities, continued in the same vein, serving both as a retreat for the family and as a place for composition. This picture shows the married couple in front of the building, the domestic staff behind them.
Richard Strauss Institute, Garmisch-Partenkirchen.

The sober environment (of which contemporaries remained largely unaware) fits with Strauss's understanding of his craft, which dispensed with metaphysical claims. In a kind of counterpoint to his down-to-earth sensibility, the composer displayed a passion for religious art: votive tablets

Figure 9.2   Michael Rosenauer (1884–1971), Villa Strauss, Vienna

The Vienna villa, where Strauss took up residence in 1924, was designed by Michael Rosenauer (1884–1971)—one of the most influential young architects of the city until he left Austria in 1928. It was constructed when Rosenauer stood at the height of his fame, even though he still had few residential buildings to his name. Strauss's plans were complicated by the fact that neighbors and surroundings had to be considered. In terms of ambition and scale, the villa should be viewed as a counterpart to the house in Garmisch.
Private collection.

and assorted objects of popular piety, which cannot have held more than a certain "ethnological" interest for the collector. The same outlook was evident in his fondness for playing cards.

Accepting the Vienna position meant remaining true to the city even if the appointment did not last for long—as it seemed would be the case. Some ten years after building the house in Garmisch, Strauss decided on another construction project. In 1919, the year after Max Liebermann had painted his portrait, he inspected several potential sites suggested by the city (or governmental offices of the new republic), rejecting two parcels in Schönbrunn. Finally, agreement was reached: part of the so-called chamber garden (*Kammergarten*) in the Belvedere. Initially, the plot was to be a gift, but then a ninety-year lease was arranged, following which the land and structures would revert to the city. Strauss had lost his fortune during the First World War, so an unusual price was negotiated: the autograph scores of *Der Rosenkavalier* and *Schlagobers* (today held in the Österreichische Nationalbibliothek). Ultimately, the composer managed to secure ownership, after all, by forfeiting payment for 100 scores he had directed and surrendering the fair copy of *Die ägyptische Helena*.

Plans in Vienna were ambitious—and expensive. Strauss obtained loans for construction through his daughter-in-law. This time, he engaged another renowned architect, Michael Rosenauer (1884–1971). No guidelines were issued, apart from the governmental specification that the surrounding Belvedere be taken into account. Unlike the Garmisch villa, which was meant to foster composition, this structure—situated close to the house where Hofmannsthal was born—focused on outward representation and was designed to showcase Strauss's collection of furniture and art. Here, a matter that had already been realized in a creative work, *Josephs Legende*, was repeated: the architect and composer traveled to Venice to come up with building plans inspired by the city and its surroundings. In the ballet, the Venetian complexion had translated into "Oriental" antiquity; in real life, it was supposed to provide a design fitted to social life. The result contrasted sharply with the villa in Garmisch, and not just because of the emphasis on appearances. Instead, Venetian elements introduced a modern element outside of time (even though this aspect is only visible from the inside).

In the coming years, Strauss conducted his public and private life between these two sites, Vienna and Garmisch—until the shadow of National Socialist dictatorship fell, once again, after 1938. The family settled in Vienna in 1941, where Baldur von Schirach had held the post of Gauleiter since the beginning of the year. Although a fanatical anti-Semite and the official responsible for deporting the city's Jews, Schirach protected the composer's relatives and even sought to moderate threats facing Alice Strauss and her children. When, in 1944, Strauss finally came to be considered *persona non grata* throughout the Reich, Schirach saw to it that festivities were held in honor of his eightieth birthday (in June). Following the celebration, the composer left the city and never saw the house again, which was damaged as soon as air raids began. Schirach managed to save the furnishings and "archive," which was held under state protection. The various parties (the SS, the Serbian government-in-exile, and, finally, the Red Army) occupying the structure from late 1955 on disfigured it to such an extent that nothing was preserved. (In contrast, the Garmisch villa remains much as it was.) Strauss's home in Vienna was then used as the mess hall for officers in the British Sector; since 1949, it has served as the ambassadorial residence of the Netherlands.

Copyright and Musical Materiality

Until 1918, Strauss was employed by European royal courts; as the General Music Director in Berlin, he numbered among the best-paid conductors on the continent. To date, no detailed study exists on the material circumstances of such positions in the late-nineteenth and early-twentieth centuries. All the same, it is clear that they afforded intendants a great deal of leeway—as exemplified by Mahler's appointment in Vienna, where the earnings of the office were only part of the benefits. But unlike Mahler, who used his exorbitant salary to indulge in compositions that did not bring great monetary returns, Strauss wrote works that proved materially successful. Even though lacking data makes it impossible to know his financial circumstances in detail, or even in comparison to other composers, a significant shift is evident. To take one example, he asked a new publisher, Adolph Fürstner (1833–1908), for 60,000 marks in exchange for the *Salome* score (to the horror of his aged father)—in other words, about one-third of his yearly pay in Berlin. What is more, the considerable flexibility of the contract—which the Berlin theater manager Georg von Hülsen-Haeseler deemed unprecedented—still left room for sizeable earnings from guest appearances. Strauss's self-confidence in business was no secret to his contemporaries. After the end of the First World War, when he lost his fortune and pension, it only became more pronounced. At the same time, Strauss's dealings make it plain that he viewed compositions as central, and conducting works as secondary (albeit extremely well-paid).

Unlike Wagner, who, as a matter of course (and in anticipation of his ensuing dramas), laid claim to the capital he initially had set out to destroy, Strauss viewed his works as achievements that commanded commensurate honor in financial terms. The sums entailed represented a way of measuring the work performed. Although precedents existed for such a view, Strauss took this approach to a new level. His musical turn to human life and the abandonment of otherworldly—spiritual or idealist—claims matched his view of composition as a business. To be sure, such an enterprise did not concern everyone—only those parties in the know were relevant—yet it was subject to contractual negotiation. As such, together with two friends, the jurist and musician Friedrich Rösch (1862–1925) and the mathematician Hans Sommer (1837–1922), Strauss sent a letter in 1898 to his fellow composers, calling for greater rights and the founding of a "Cooperative of German Composers" (Genossenschaft deutscher Komponisten); that same year, the organization set to work.

Although he had been its chairmain since 1901 (following a host of disputes at the Heidelberg Tonkünstlerfest), Strauss claimed that the Allgemeiner Deutscher Musikverein, founded in 1861, was not fulfilling its mission. Accordingly, on January 14, 1903, he established the Genossenschaft Deutscher Tonsetzer (GDT—a somewhat more archaic sounding version of the Genossenschaft Deutscher Komponisten); by ministerial decree, the organization was granted legal capacity on April 7 that same year. The association's charter set out a clear mission: "The preservation and promotion of members' inherited and professional interests" (§3.1) as well as the "establishment of measures for using musical copyrights" (§3.2).[5] The governing body, over which Strauss presided, included Philipp Rüfer, Engelbert Humperdinck, Friedrich Rösch, and Georg Schumann; among others, Eugen d'Albert, Felix Draeseke, Friedrich Hegar, Joseph Joachim, Gustav Mahler, and Philipp Wolfrum served in an advisory capacity. Since the foundation of the German Empire, authorial rights had received increased attention, especially with regard to music. The term of protection was one matter of concern; a span of thirty years was set for German lands, which conflicted with the period foreseen by the Berne Convention. The other item up for debate was publishers' exclusive rights to material. For instance: Strauss had sold his *Don Juan* and the three Lieder comprising Op. 29 to the Aibl publishing house; the standard form of contract granted the press "for all time and therefore for all editions,

---

5 "Die Wahrung und Förderung der Standes- und Berufsinteressen der Mitglieder," "Einrichtung von Anstalten zur Verwertung musikalischer Urheberrechte." Erich Schulze, *Geschätzte und geschützte Noten: Zur Geschichte der Verwertungsgesellschaften* (Weinheim: VCH, 1995), 31.

without restriction of the number and volume of the same, as well as for all printings, the right of exclusive and unlimited use of these works."[6] The copyright law passed in 1901, which went into effect the following year, represented a partial victory in Strauss's eyes. The GDT would advocate for composers' interests in this framework. Its charter (§3.2) stipulated the founding of a collecting society designed on the French model: the Anstalt für musikalisches Aufführungsrecht (AFMA). Practical legal arrangements lay in the hands of Rösch—to whom Strauss had dedicated *Feuersnot* in 1901.

What subsequently happened ran counter to plans, however. As early as 1915, there was competition when some members left the organization and founded the Genossenschaft zur Verwertung musikalischer Aufführungsrechte (GEMA). In 1929, badly hit by the economic crisis—to say nothing of the recent media revolution (in particular, the cinema)—the GDT ceased to be an independent entity and folded into the partnership already formed by GEMA and the Austrian Collecting Society (Österreichische Verwertungsgesellschaft). In the wake of these events, Strauss resigned his position. In 1933, the Staatlich genehmigte Gesellschaft zur Verwertung musikalischer Aufführungsrechte (STAGMA) was founded, which swallowed up the GDT once and for all in 1934. Within a few years, copyright holders could no longer collect on their own. In the spirit of National Socialist *Gleichschaltung*, the business director would be appointed by the government, in keeping with recommendations made by the president of the Reichsmusikkammer (§16). With that, what had been a collecting society became a state agency.

Although clearly motivated by self-interest, Strauss's engagement also followed from a broader outlook: compositions represent a "value" with a material equivalent, which may be used at their creator's discretion. As he put it laconically: "Authorial rights for the author, publishing rights

---

6 "für alle Zeiten und demgemäss für alle Auflagen, ohne alle Beschränkung in Betreff der Zahl und der Grösse derselben, sowie auch für alle Veröffentlichungen, überhaupt das Recht der ausschliesslichen und unbeschränkten Verfügung über diese Werke." Facsimile in *Bassenge Auktion* 99, April 2012, 200 (lot 2109).

for the publisher[.] There's no other way."[7] Such a view also represents a sign of the modern (and modernist) sensibility: authorial rights are equal to—or even surpass—other instances. It might seem surprising that this notion developed in what was still largely a courtly milieu. However, it attests to the real freedom that such a setting could provide around the turn of the century. Moreover, it illustrates that Strauss viewed his activity at court in terms of musical direction, not composition. The interest Strauss took in protecting his authorial rights also relates to restrictions on staging *Parsifal* at the time. Wagner had insisted to Ludwig II that performance of his "sacred festival drama" (*Bühnenweihfestspiel*) be reserved for his Festival Hall in Bayreuth. Now that the term had expired, this restriction no longer applied. The ensuing uncertainty gave the GDT an opportunity to expand the copyright period and bring it into line with the fifty years foreseen by the Berne Convention—especially in view of the fact that no *Lex Parsifal* was enacted (as some parties had hoped). Strauss may have been prompted by concerns of a more general nature, but ultimately the "*Parsifal* question" connected with the composer's own desire for artistic sovereignty. Strauss's pragmatic bearing exemplifies as much: although he strongly advocated that *Parsifal* continue to be protected, he directed the work at the Berlin Hofoper and (as his correspondence with Schalk reveals) even considered doing so in Vienna.

Tying works—and performances—to material equivalents protected by copyright did not just represent a change in legal status; it also reflected Strauss's conception of music itself. Scholarship has viewed the matter largely in terms of the law, but its consequences for compositions and the conceptions underlying them has never received systematic evaluation. In this light, it is remarkable—although ultimately hardly surprising—that Strauss also called this very perspective into question in *Capriccio*. The bitter rub is that the expanded copyright protection sought by so many, especially from 1927 on, finally became the law under National Socialism, on December 13, 1934.

7 "Urheberrechte dem Urheber, Verlagsrechte dem Verleger[.] Anderen Modus gibt's nicht." Manuela Maria Schmidt, *Die Anfänge der musikalischen Tantiemenbewegung in Deutschland: Eine Studie über den langen Weg bis zur Errichtung der Genossenschaft Deutscher Tonsetzer (GDT) im Jahre 1903 und zum Wirken des Komponisten Richard Strauss (1864–1949) für Verbesserungen des Urheberrechts* (Berlin: Duncker & Humboldt, 2005), 678; letter from Richard Strauss to Eugen Spitzweg of November 22, 1898.

Figure 9.3   Richard Strauss as car driver. Photograph 1932.

Strauss was passionate car driver. On this photo of 1932 one can see him just arrived or starting; sometimes he used car excursions with Hofmannsthal to discuss projects. This photo was taken on July 10th 1932 in Bocken, a manor of the 17th century near Zurich. Since 1912 this manor was in the possession of Alfred Schwarzenbach, a prominent silk manufacturer. His wife Renée Schwazenbach-Wille made the house to a meeting point for artists, musicians and intellectuals.

Zurich, Zentralbibliothek (legacy Schwarzenbach).

The Reichsmusikkammer

The National Socialists' seizure of power shook and shaped Strauss's life. On the one hand, he was prepared for this event, yet at the same time—at least in the early years of the dictatorship, but probably to the very end—he fundamentally misjudged its scope and implications. For a long time, but especially in the late twentieth century, the controversy sparked by Strauss heading the Reichsmusikkammer alternated between condemnation and resolute defense of the composer. A host of studies has established the basic facts; indeed, the years from 1933 to 1935 represent the most thoroughly researched period of Strauss's life. For all that, it remains difficult to determine how, exactly, Strauss comported himself during the first few months of this time. Almost sixty-nine years old, he no longer held any appointment; he stood in no need of institutional or material security, nor was there reason for him to intervene in public affairs. Notwithstanding these circumstances, Strauss traveled to Berlin in March, where he participated in the opening of the Reichstag. Moreover, he met with the new functionaries presiding over cultural life, including Hitler and Göring. That such meetings were possible at all confirms the profile and prestige he enjoyed. On March 20, 1933, Strauss stood in for Bruno Walter and conducted a Philharmonic concert. Although the latter had been barred from performing in Dresden, this was not the case in Berlin. Still, the SA had threatened violence, and governmental officials in the Ministry of Propaganda refused to provide security. Walter left the city and asked his wife to enlist the agency Wolff & Sachs to get Strauss to conduct in his stead. Initially, the composer declined, and Ernst Wendel (1876–1938), from Bremen, received the commission. Through intervention on the part of composer Julius Kopsch (1887–1970) and the music critic at the *Völkischer Beobachter*, Hugo Rasch (1873–1947)—who both avidly supported the regime—Strauss was persuaded to change his mind and conduct, after all. He stipulated, however, that he be announced as Walter's replacement, and he turned down payment for his services.[8]

The signal Strauss sent in accepting this role proved catastrophic. The National Socialist press celebrated it as a triumph of the regime's cultural politics. Abroad, it was considered a grave misstep on the part of the composer, who was judged to have acted opportunistically. Strauss himself does not seem to have been aware of the political implications; initially, the new government commanded his respect. What he observed in Berlin "impressed [him] greatly" and inspired "hope for the future of German art, once the initial revolutionary storms had passed," he told the publisher Anton Kippenberg.[9] Indeed, in April he added his signature

---

8 Bruno Walter, *Thema und Variationen: Erinnerungen und Gedanken* (Zurich: Atlantis 1947); Edith Stargardt-Wolff, *Wegbereiter großer Musiker: Unter Verwendung von Tagebuchblättern, Briefen und vielen persönlichen Erinnerungen von Hermann und Louise Wolff, den Gründern der ersten Konzertdirektion 1880–1935* (Berlin, Wiesbaden: Bote & Bock 1954), 275ff.

9 "große Eindrücke mitgebracht und gute Hoffnung für die Zukunft der deutschen Kunst, wenn sich erst die ersten Revolutionsstürme ausgetobt haben." Willi Schuh (ed.), "Richard

to a letter of protest on behalf of the "Richard-Wagner-Stadt Munich" initiated by the director of the opera, Hans Knappertsbusch (1888–1965), decrying a lecture by Thomas Mann about the illustrious composer.[10] Evidently, it did not occur to Strauss that the petition would put Mann's life at risk; he never bothered to read the document before it was printed and he did not know what the lecture actually said (in fact, the position articulated was not so different from his own). Mann never forgave him.

From spring 1933, Strauss's actions began to display a strange mixture of misjudgment, confused gestures, and self-interest—prompted, in all likelihood, by the hope that at least the cultural politics of the Weimar Republic, which he despised, would be whipped into shape (as his remarks to Count Harry Kessler in 1928 make especially clear[11]). The same attitude was in evidence, albeit in different terms, when *Arabella* premiered in Dresden on July 1, 1933. Now, for the first time, the composer came into real conflict with the regime, although he resolved matters in pragmatic fashion. Göring and Hitler had wooed the conductor Fritz Busch (1890–1951), but he was unwilling to compromise; exposed to livid attack by the NSDAP, he opted to go into exile. Initially, Strauss insisted that Busch conduct and Alfred Reucker (1868–1958) direct the piece. But soon he relented and agreed to the regime's decisions for the Dresden premiere—with Clemens Krauss conducting. Although this solution might still have avoided conflict, difficulties ensued when Strauss insisted that Hugo von Hofmannsthal receive due credit for the libretto—which indicated that he did not fully agree with the political machinations. That same summer, Strauss returned, for the first time in almost forty years, to Bayreuth; the town had become a focal point for National Socialist musical propaganda, since the Wagner family unconditionally hailed Hitler's love for the composer. Here, too, Strauss played the part of a substitute, replacing Toscanini, who stayed away because of the regime's persecution

---

Strauss und Anton Kippenberg: Briefwechsel," in *Richard-Strauss-Jahrbuch* 1959/60, 120; letter from Strauss to Kippenberg of March 29, 1933.

10 Facsimile of *Münchner Neueste Nachrichten* in Jürgen Kolbe (ed.), *Wagners Welten* (München, Wolfratshausen: Edition Minerva 2003), 241.

11 Kessler remembered a breakfast where Strauss reflected "unter andrem seine drolligen politischen Ansichten, Notwendigkeit einer Diktatur usw., die niemand ernst nimmt" (Kessler, *Tagebücher*, 563; entry of June 14, 1928).

of Jewish musicians. (Indeed, he also filled in for Busch, who was Heinz Tietjen's first choice as Toscanini's replacement.) In the public eye, this was perceived along conflicting lines, too: the National Socialist press welcomed the news, while opponents of the regime at home and abroad reacted with horror.

Strauss stubbornly displayed these contradictory qualities of accommodation and insistence over the coming years. Deeply hurt by his friend's behavior, Busch attempted to make sense of it all. Later, he described Strauss as a "riddle." The composer was one of the "most astonishing talents, yet not penetrated [or] obsessed" by his gift—which he "wore like a suit that could be taken on and off again" (thereby revealing his "pronounced material inclinations"). At the same time, "in quiet, intimate company," when speaking of "his favorite composer, Mozart," Strauss could hold forth at length about the Quintet in G minor as the "crowning achievement of all music." "On the inside," Strauss "could only stand in manifest opposition to National Socialist ideology," yet "in practice he observed one of its guiding principles decades in advance: 'If it benefits me, it's right.'"[12] Mere seeking of personal advantage cannot account for the composer's actions after 1933. Surely the actual reasons lie on another level. As Hofkapellmeister, Strauss had always been met halfway by the authorities; likewise, he enjoyed extraordinary liberties, and almost all his conflicts with censors ultimately resolved in his favor. His Genossenschaft Deutscher Tonsetzer—a special interest group with concrete objectives—was not only granted legal recognition; it was spared political wrangling, too. As such, success is what prompted Strauss to misjudge cultural politics under National Socialism. Evidently, he was unable—or unwilling—to admit that the complete fusion of ideology and art was no accident, but a defining feature of the dictatorship.

The legislation establishing the Reichskulturkammer on September 22, 1933 completed the organizational *Gleichschaltung* of cultural life. All

12 "erstaunlichsten Begabungen, dennoch nicht von ihr durchdrungen und besessen," "wie einen Anzug, den man ablegen kann," "starken materiellen Neigungen," "in stillem, intimem Zusammensein," "seinen Lieblingskomponisten Mozart zu sprechen," "Gipfelpunkt aller Musik"; Strauss, "der innerlich nur in krassem Widerspruch zur nationalsozialistischen Ideologie stehen konnte," has "in der Praxis einen ihrer Leitsätze um Jahrzehnte vorausgenommen: 'Recht ist, was mir nutzt'." Fritz Busch, *Aus dem Leben eines Musikers* (Frankfurt: S. Fischer, 1982, originally 1948).

realms of artistic and journalistic activity were arranged in six bodies: the "chambers" of literature (*Schrifttum*), press, radio, theater, music, and fine arts. Prior to this legislation, officials at the highest level—that is, Goebbels and Hitler—had decided how to fill executive positions, including the chairmanship of the Reichsmusikkammer. It seems that Hitler initially wanted Max von Schillings, a strictly observant party-member who already controlled the Berlin Academy. When Schillings fell gravely ill in May—he soon died, in July—another dutiful loyalist, Gustave Havemann (1882–1960), was weighed as an option. It appears that Strauss came into consideration only gradually, perhaps on the basis of discussions he held with Goebbels and Hitler in Bayreuth during the summer. Strauss is likely to have viewed it as a matter of course that when such an office was being filled, he would be the first in line. After all, he deemed himself the most significant representative of German music. In November, he received the appointment and promptly dedicated a Lied to Goebbels. This gesture is difficult to interpret in that it was based on an apocryphal text by Goethe, and it seems that Strauss exercised his functions half-heartedly. In essence, the composer viewed the position of chairmanship of the Reichsmusikkammer as a matter of secondary importance and focused instead on the new musical prospects opened by his incipient collaboration with Stefan Zweig. He made no meaningful statements about politics, apart from isolated polemics bearing on musical matters (for instance, his remarks at a public assembly at the Berlin Philharmonic on February 17, 1934).[13]

Expectations on both sides led to the opposite of the expected. Strauss superintended the "Standing Council for the International Cooperation of Composers" (*Ständiger Rat für die Internationale Zusammenarbeit der Komponisten*)—an organization the Nazis now set up to counter the IGNM—from mid-1934 on. His refusal to stop working with Zweig led to greater and greater tensions, which resulted in disadvantageous directives from higher up. In 1934, Strauss was forbidden to make an appearance at Salzburg, and the following year he was not allowed to conduct at Bayreuth. In June 1935, the Gestapo intercepted a letter to Zweig that included dismissive remarks about the Reichsmusikkammer. Strauss

---

13 Text in Gerhard Splitt, *Richard Strauss 1933–1935: Ästhetik und Musikpolitik zu Beginn der nationalsozialistischen Herrschaft* (Pfaffenweiler: Centaurius 1987), 102–105.

claimed he was only "pretending" to direct the organization in order "to do good and avoid greater ill."[14] He was forced to resign and replaced with Peter Raabe without delay. The first run of Die Schweigsame Frau was stopped after four performances, and the work banned. Strauss no longer enjoyed any favor, and Goebbels entertained the idea of revoking the commission for the Olympic hymn that had been extended in 1932. Finally, the situation facing the composer's daughter-in-law and grandchildren was becoming more and more perilous.

It is not easy to determine the extent to which Strauss was capable of assessing matters realistically. In 1943, he attempted to obtain the release of one of his daughter-in-law's relatives from Theresienstadt simply by showing up at the camp's gates. The same year, in September, Strauss appealed to Göring to secure leave for his gardener, who was on the front, with a letter omitting the customary salutation of Hitler—and he failed again.[15] The regime avoided the composer more and more; the only reason his works were not banned altogether was the embarrassment it would entail. Festivities marking his eightieth birthday in Vienna, overshadowed not just by the war but also by the material threat facing his daughter-in-law and grandchildren, occurred at Schirach's initiative.

From the outset, Nazi potentates had harbored reservations about the composer. Hitler never wooed Strauss the way he courted Busch (who had, of course, responded in disgust). The strange shifts of attitude over the long term are most evident in Goebbels's diaries, which feature, with remarkable regularity, assorted remarks of disapprobation (even if the self-satisfied tone in the welter of observations suggests that the writer did not lend the matter as much thought as the genre otherwise implies). Unqualified appreciation is expressed only for *Till Eulenspiegel, Der Rosenkavalier*, and (especially) *Festliches Präludium*. Thus, in 1933, Goebbels noted: "He must remain at our disposal."[16] Just a few days later, however, he declared *Arabella* a "senile" work, with "flashes of inspiration only here

14 "Gutes zu tun und größeres Unglück zu verhindern." *Richard Strauss—Stefan Zweig: Briefwechsel*, 142; letter from Strauss of June 17, 1935.
15 Letter from Richard Strauss to Hermann Göring, September 3, 1943; Vienna, Österreichische Nationalbibliothek, Mus. Hs. 41704.
16 "Er muß uns erhalten bleiben." Angela Hermann (ed.), *Die Tagebücher von Joseph Goebbels Teil I: Aufzeichnungen 1923–1941*, vol. 2/III, *Oktober 1932–März 1934* (Munich: Saur, 2006), 283; entry of October 3, 1933.

and there."[17] (In general, the Minister of Propaganda viewed the verbal component of operas with vague dislike or outright incomprehension.) The first plans for replacing Strauss in the Reichsmusikkammer occurred in autumn 1934; in this light, the Zweig affair does not seem to have triggered events so much as it afforded a timely excuse. Goebbels did not approach the composer again with an offer of patronage until the latter's seventy-fifth birthday was drawing near. He attended the premiere of *Friedenstag* with high hopes, but was disappointed to find it "more of a work of old age."[18] Although he was enthusiastic about the insistent, if "inauthentic," jubilation of the final scene, his journal entry from the following day laments: "If only [Strauss] had a better character."[19] Ultimately, Goebbels deemed the composer "senile and stubborn beyond measure."[20] The final exchange between the two men in February 1941 (which Werner Egk recorded) concluded with Goebbels humiliating Strauss by launching into a tirade about how he was obsolete and a relic. In 1944, when the composer was heard making disrespectful remarks about the war at his home in Garmisch, local party officials campaigned to have him declared *persona non grata*, and all further communications ceased.

The experience of dictatorship had fundamentally shaken Strauss's belief that art and life might be combined in a new way in the twentieth century. The works he now composed seemed to react to this shock. For the first time since *Elektra*, Strauss wrote a tragedy, *Daphne*, which revisits—and revises—the "discovery of language" in the comedies. *Die Liebe der Danae* returns to purified, Oriental antiquity only to declare it gone forever. Finally, *Capriccio* casts doubt on the very possibility of finding a suitable form of art at all. From the 1930s on, Strauss made increasingly pessimistic observations about the course of history; ultimately, he decided that an insuperable caesura had occurred and relegated late compositions to an inferior position, separate from his works to date.

---

17 "senil und nur hier und da noch Glanz und Flimmer." Ibid., 291; entry of October 13, 1933.
18 "mehr ein Alterswerk." Jana Richter (ed.), *Die Tagebücher von Joseph Goebbels Teil I: Aufzeichnungen 1923–1941*, Vol. 6, *August 1938–Juni 1939* (Munich: Saur, 1998), 374; entry of June 11, 1939.
19 "Wenn er doch nur einen besseren Charakter hätte." Ibid., 375; entry of June 12, 1939.
20 "maßlos senil und eigensinnig." Elke Fröhlich (ed.), *Die Tagebücher von Joseph Goebbels Teil I: Aufzeichnungen 1923–1941*, Vol. 9, *Dezember 1940–Juli 1941* (Munich: Saur, 1997), 65; entry of March 1941.

CHAPTER TEN

After Hofmannsthal's Death

Intermezzo with Stefan Zweig

Strauss's collaboration with Hofmannsthal filled more than two decades. While hardly free from tension and difficult at times, mutual respect and shared convictions sustained their work together. But even though agreement prevailed on fundamental matters, the resulting body of work does not represent a monolithic totality. Between *Elektra* and *Arabella*, a wide range of possibilities unfolded, always with an eye to the stage, the signature genre of modernity. An orientalizing view of antiquity and comedy (bearing strong traits of the operetta) provided the cornerstones, but the framework allowed for internal transformation, changes, and shifts. What is more, the conception the artists shared did not develop in a linear fashion. As their correspondence reveals, it emerged over the course of many projects that were carefully weighed, carried out, rejected, or postponed to a later date. An early example is the *Vision der Semiramis*,[1] a spectacular proposal that was entertained for a remarkably long time. In 1935, Strauss returned to it again and doggedly sought Stefan Zweig's assistance to make the vision reality. (Eventually, Joseph Gregor even worked out a plan at his behest.)

The composer and poet came to work together exclusively as the result of this same process. They were not initially wedded to the idea of

---

1 *Richard Strauss. Hugo von Hofmannsthal. Briefwechsel*, 19; letter from Hofmannsthal of April 27, 1906.

partnership. Hofmannstahl considered working with other composers, and Strauss at least thought about collaborating with Gabriele d'Annunzio, Hermann Bahr, and Gerhart Hauptmann. Many documents make it plain that they judged the price of working together steep. Count Harry Kessler's journal contains an instructive example, recording his last encounter with his friend: at a "gloomy, joyless breakfast in June [1928] . . ., Strauss babbled such nonsense that Hofmannstahl subsequently wrote me a letter of apology."[2] The poet's abrupt death put an end to confidence laboriously won, which both parties thought would last for quite some time yet. The "terrible blow" it represented for Strauss held implications reaching far beyond the self-centeredness he displayed in his condolence letter to Hofmannsthal's widow: "No one will take his place for me or the world of music!"[3] These words attest, above all, to the composer's belief that collaboration on *Arabella* signaled a new stage of shared endeavor.

Hofmannsthal's death shook Strauss to the core, and he deemed it a caesura in his work. Paradoxically, he did not attend the funeral (or that of Max Reinhardt, for that matter), but sent his son and daughter-in-law instead. The composer was forced to "acknowledge, with regret, that [his] creation of operas had come to an end."[4] He finished *Arabella* as a kind of debt of honor; without the poet's assistance, he knew how difficult this would prove. Indeed, as Strauss confided to Zweig in October 1932, he hesitated to share the score with the public.[5] As if to underscore the work's status as a legacy, he simultaneously undertook the project of reworking Mozart's *Idomeneo* together with Lothar Wallenstein (1882–1949), the senior director at the Vienna State Opera (until he emigrated in 1938). The work represented a pendant to the reworking of *Ruinen von Athen* made with Hofmannsthal, conceived in light of the *Festspiel*.

---

2 "stimmungslosen, unerfreulichen Frühstück im Juni vor einem Jahr, wo Richard Strauß solchen Unsinn redete, daß Hofmannsthal sich nachher bei mir schriftlich entschuldigte." Kessler, *Tagebücher*, 589; entry of July 18, 1929. Kessler is obviously referring to Strauss's harsh critique of the republic.

3 "furchtbaren Schlag," "niemand wird ihn mir und der Musikwelt ersetzen!" *Richard Strauss. Hugo von Hofmannsthal. Briefwechsel*, 698; letter from Strauss to Gerty von Hofmannsthal of July 16, 1929.

4 "resigniert bekennen, mein Opernschaffen sei beendet." Richard Strauss, "Geschichte der Schweigsamen Frau," in *Richard Strauss—Stefan Zweig: Briefwechsel*, 155.

5 *Richard Strauss—Stefan Zweig: Briefwechsel*, 25f; letter from Strauss of October 7, 1932.

The lack of orientation that seems to have struck Strauss in the years before his seventieth birthday was basically resolved by chance, through a conversation with Anton Kippenberg (1874–1950). The latter directed the Insel publishing house and drew his attention to the fact that Stefan Zweig (1881–1942) was his ardent admirer. In turn, the writer contacted the composer and proposed two projects: a large-scale pantomime and a comedy. Strauss opted for the second, deeming the story of Morosus a "natural-born comic opera—. . . better suited to music than even *Figaro* and *The Barber of Seville*."[6] Zweig stressed the material's proximity to the cinema and affirmed that comedy should not go beyond the scope of contemporary events. This position fundamentally differed from Hofmannsthal's: "To be frank, I see the last Hofmannsthal libretti as too heavily burdened with the search for style and symbolism, both beyond the normal vision of an unsophisticated audience not equipped with special glasses for reading libretti." In his eyes, "this desire to reach what one might call a higher dimension was attainable only at the expense of its effective communication."[7] There is no telling whether Strauss shared this view or simply saw it as a necessary consequence of the material underlying of *Die ägyptische Helena* and *Arabella*; conceivably, his conversations with Hofmannsthal had gone in a similar direction.

Zweig had emerged from the First World War a convinced pacifist. His view of cultural history suited the attitude Strauss sought from the 1920s on. The composer read Zweig's work with great enthusiasm—including his treatment of Ben Jonson's *Volpone* (1926). In Strauss's eyes, the broad perspective of comedy offered the only possibility for reacting to the present and the challenges it afforded. In addition to his avowed admiration for Strauss, Zweig noted fundamental agreement with the composer in his correspondence—which was based on his own musical knowledge. Accordingly, the *Sprechgesang* he wrote for *Die Schweigsame Frau* aimed to present "something modern in the best sense of the word,

6 "die geborne komische Oper – . . . für Musik geeignet wie weder der Figaro noch der Barbier von Sevilla." Ibid., 18; letter from Strauss of 24, June 1932.

7 "Darf ich offen sprechen, so finde ich die letzten Hofmannsthaltexte zu sehr mit der Suche nach einem Stil belastet, zu sehr in eine Symbolik gedrängt, für die die normale Sehschärfe eines unbefangenen, nicht mit Textbuchbrille ausgerüsteten Zuschauers nicht mehr ausreicht," der "Auftrieb zu einer gleichsam andern Dimension" habe die "transportable Wirksamkeit geschädigt." Ibid., 11; letter from Zweig of November 3, 1931.

and at the same time something light and ironical."[8] *Die Schweigsame Frau* incorporates two temporal breaks, shifting its model from the seventeenth century to the eighteenth, but it is meant as a comedy of the present day. For the first time, Strauss used the term "comic opera" to label a work. The opening sequence, "Potpourri," gestures toward the operetta genre and represents his first independent overture since *Guntram*. The fugue that introduces the third act—and culminates in an almost grotesquely distorted C♯ major—ironically references the prelude to Act Three of Wagner's *Meistersinger*; in addition, it provides a comic rejoinder to Strauss's "psychic polyphony," or "nervous counterpoint." *Die Schweigsame Frau* also includes historical quotations from a range of contexts, for instance the *Rheingold*-motif shortly before Morosus's final monologue and the excerpt from Monteverdi's *Incoronazione di Poppea* during the third act. Finally, this is Strauss's first opera with large-scale, varied ensembles displaying unbridled vocality. (The chorus at the end of Act One was especially dear to both collaborators.)

However, modernity made an appearance in the work in a wholly unexpected way. Shortly after the National Socialists seized power, Zweig was listed among the most ostracized writers, and his works were publicly burned. If his correspondence with Strauss demonstrated a strange reserve with regard to political events, the circumstances under which he lived looked very different. Zweig soon left for England. When his first marriage failed, he then went to New York and finally, via Paraguay, to Brazil. There he and his second wife, Lotte, committed suicide (a decision that sparked vigorous discussion in the emigrant community). Strauss had enlisted all the means at his disposal to prevent the failure of his work with Zweig, which had hardly even begun. Assessing events in altogether unrealistic fashion, he sought to reassure his collaborator and went so far as to suggest not publishing libretti and scores; at this juncture, he was convinced that the National Socialists would stay in power for only a few years. Zweig sought a way out by suggesting a number of other writers: first Rudolf Binding (1867–1938), who belonged to the party, then Alexander Lernet-Holenia (1897–1976), and, finally, Joseph Gregor. Strauss summarily rejected the lot: "Once and for all, please

---

8 "etwas Modernes im edelsten Sinne und zugleich ironisch Leichtes." Ibid., 37; letter from Zweig of December 19, 1932.

stop thrusting new poets on me!"[9] Matters changed when the Gestapo intercepted a letter from Strauss dated June 18, 1935. Now, he had to acknowledge the bitter reality of the dictatorship. The composer was forced to step down as President of the Reichsmusikkammer, and he was merely tolerated by the regime until 1938, when careful overtures were made again. Strauss's notes from July 1935 express regret that he "did not keep [his] distance from the whole National Socialist movement"; the "Jew-baiting of Streicher and Goebbels" struck him "as a disgrace to German honor, a sign of weakness, and the lowest weapon of talentless, lazy mediocrity."[10]

For a brief spell, Strauss and Zweig still communicated under pseudonyms; then their correspondence broke off. In his autobiographical reflections, *The World of Yesterday*, Zweig included a concise study expressing his admiration and respect for Strauss—as well as his surprise and displeasure at the compromises the composer had made with the Nazi regime. (Events after 1935 are left out.) At the latest, Strauss learned of Zweig's suicide when Willi Schuh told him. There is no record of his reaction. The two men had discussed an array of projects, including an operatic version of Kleist's *Amphitryon*. Strauss continued to pursue *Friedenstag* and *Capriccio*; the former premiered when Zweig was still alive, and the second after his death.

Joseph Gregor and Final Plans

Stefan Zweig, although possessed of a friendly and non-confrontational temperament, never harbored any illusions about the National Socialist regime. Politely but firmly, he refused to continue writing texts for Strauss. To be sure, he derived a certain satisfaction from the fact that the *Die Schweigsame Frau* (and the matter of obtaining authorization for the piece's performance) had made its way to the top of the party—that is, Hitler himself had been forced to read it. However, his contribution amounted to a way of severing ties with Germany—a final statement.

---

9 "Bitte, geben Sie es definitiv auf, mir einen neuen Dichter anzuempfehlen!" Ibid., 130; letter from Strauss of May 17, 1935.

10 "sich von vornherein nicht von der ganzen nationalsozialistischen Bewegung fern gehalten," die "Streicher-Goebbelsche Judenhetze für eine Schmach für die deutsche Ehre, für ein Armutszeugnis, für das niedrigste Kampfmittel der talentlosen, faulen Mittelmäßigkeit." The passage cited by Willi Schuh in documentation accompanying the correspondence, ibid., 175.

Ultimately, Strauss accepted Zweig's recommendation that he collaborate with Joseph Gregor (1888–1960), a native of Czernowitz and the founder of the theater collection at the Österreichische Nationalbibliothek. (His actions under National Socialism remain a matter of controversy.) Strauss had read Gregor's *Weltgeschichte des Theaters* (1933) appreciatively, but the decision to work with him did not mean he wanted a partnership on equal footing. Clearly, the composer felt that his seventieth birthday marked a milestone. With characteristic unsparingness towards himself—a feature Zweig had remarked—Strauss wanted to "round out" his *oeuvre* in a way that Hofmannsthal's death had prevented. This ambition might look like overblown egoism, but it derived from self-discipline and self-censure— and it led to increasingly fraught political entanglements. Strauss viewed concepts developed with Zweig as the continuation of his work with Hofmannstahl, and he sought to bring it to an appropriate, if ambivalent, conclusion—just as he had done, for instrumental music, with his *Eine Alpensinfonie*.

Strauss no longer had a partner; at best, Gregor was an agent, or accomplice. In contrast to Wolzogen, Hofmannsthal, and Zweig, Gregor never enjoyed equal rights. In fact, Strauss did not even accept him on personal terms, and he terminated the relationship while working on *Capriccio* (which had been developed in conjunction with Zweig). If the composer had sometimes adopted a gruff tone in his dealings with Hofmannsthal, the latter had decorously stood his ground. And notwithstanding unfavorable circumstances, remarkable agreement prevailed between Strauss and Zweig, largely owing to the latter's refined musical knowledge.

But with Gregor, things were entirely different. The correspondence— which essentially amounts to a series of commands and expressions of compliance—abounds in irascible outbursts, gestures of rejection, and outright humiliation. "The most brutal vehemence"[11] is in evidence throughout. Thus, *Semiramis* (which was begun with Zweig, following Hofmannsthal's notes) is declared "no real theater" in Gregor's hands— not "a serviceable opera."[12] *Daphne* amounts to "a complete mess," "often

---

11 "brutalster Drastigkeit." *Richard Strauss und Joseph Gregor: Briefwechsel*, 134; letter from Straus of October 12, 1938.
12 "kein wirkliches Theater," keine "brauchbare Oper." Ibid., 28; letter from Strauss of May 24, 1935.

[written] in pale imitation of Homer";[13] "many of the formulations require improvement if [the text] is to be set to music."[14] *Friedenstag* offers "a kind of 'poetry' utterly unsuited to the theater."[15] Indeed, Strauss found Hofmannsthal's rough sketch for *Danae* "subtler, gentler, and more graceful" than Gregor's final version.[16] He deemed the poet's first scenario for *Capriccio* a "grave misstep";[17] the revised version "unfortunately corresponds to my wishes in no way at all."[18] And so on and so forth—including statements that are simply rude ("No, that won't do at all!"[19]). For the most part, Gregor adopted a submissive bearing; only at the very end, when it was clear that the relationship would not continue, did he even try to defend himself with any measure of self-confidence.

The projects that Strauss engaged Gregor to complete after repeated efforts to secure Zweig's assistance had failed were *Semiramis, Friedenstag*, and *Capriccio*. *Semiramis* never went beyond the planning stage. In a sense, the project was replaced by another work started with Hofmannsthal, *Die Liebe der Danae*. It is impossible to say when Strauss decided to make the switch. Willi Schuh's recollections suggest that he simply forgot about *Semiramis*, but this seems highly unlikely; instead, Strauss probably returned to a project comparable in scope. *Daphne* appears to take up new subject matter. In fact, the opera connects with standing interests and previous efforts. In the "Chandos Letter," the fictive author whose voice Hofmannsthal adopts has written a work entitled *Der Traum der Daphne* (before the linguistic crisis, of course), and Strauss was a great admirer of Bernini's Roman sculptures. The figure of Daphne occupies a cental position in the tradition of picturing metamorphosis. The composer's contribution to this tradition is to make her lose not only her

---

13 "ein völliges Nacheinander," "in nicht immer glücklich imitiertem Homerjargon." Ibid., 34.

14 "vieles in der sprachlichen Formulierung noch verbesserungsbedürftig, soll es componierbar sein." Ibid., 60; letter from Strauss of March 29, 1936.

15 "eine Art von 'Poesie', die auf dem Theater völlig versagt." Ibid., 35; letter from Strauss of October 6, 1935.

16 "feiner, harmloser, graziöser." Ibid., 72; letter from Strauss of July 27, 1936.

17 "schwere Entgleisung." Ibid., 183; letter from Strauss of May 25, 1939.

18 "entspricht leider in keiner Weise meinen Wünschen." Ibid., 191; letter from Strauss of August 16, 1939.

19 "Nein, so geht es nicht!" Ibid., 30; letter from Strauss of July 16, 1935.

physical form but also the power of speech. The four works following *Die Schweigsame Frau* display close, inward connections that were sufficiently important to Strauss for him to accept working with Gregor, even though he found the collaboration agonizing. There is no telling whether the outlines went back to Hofmannsthal, but it is not unlikely. From the start, the ideas the composer developed in conjunction with the poet had a provisional nature—only now, in the late operas, did doubt fall on their underlying conception, and their possible obsolescence come into view. It seems that Strauss's self-reflective attitude stood in a tense dialectical relation to contemporary events; increasingly, he showed a pessimistic outlook when elaborating the material along cultural-historical lines.

The systematic nature of the four works after *Die Schweigsame Frau* is remarkable. In the words of Zweig, the resolute pacifist, *Friedenstag* means to bring together "the tragic, the heroic, and the humane" as a response to the ruinous present. Accordingly, events occur in an abstract framework: "Everybody is thought to be gestalt, symbol, and not a specific individual."[20] (This is also why Strauss returned to plays in a single act.) At the same time, such abstraction entailed difficulties; these were compounded when the dictatorship cast a shadow over Zweig's vision, which was quite clear. In one of his rare admissions of writer's block, Strauss confessed: "For several weeks I have been busy composing, but I have not found the music that I expect of myself."[21] The end result proved ambivalent in that the basic plot was translated into a linear sequence, up to the exultant finale in C major. *Friedenstag* is the only one of Strauss's works to conclude without any points of rupture being introduced—that is, it ends with an imposing gesture of grandeur. This feature makes the overall tone "inauthentic": the objectives conceived in conjunction with Zweig did not admit realization under the circumstances. The grotesque heading given to the three central musical figures ("Despair," "Love," and "Rejoicing") makes the piece seem unreal, a matter of deception.

---

20 "das Tragische, das Heroische und das Humane," "es soll alles nur Gestalt sein, Symbol und nicht einmaliges Individuum." *Richard Strauss—Stefan Zweig: Briefwechsel*, 74 and 76; letter from Zweig of August 21, 1934.

21 "Ich beschäftige mich nun schon einige Wochen mit der Composition, aber es will keine Musik werden, wie ich sie von mir verlangen muß." Ibid., 147; letter from Strauss of October 31, 1935.

Against this background, one can see why Strauss deemed it so important to pair *Friedenstag* and *Daphne*, and why he was unhappy that the works were first performed independently. *Daphne*—for the first (and only) time, apart from *Elektra*—is a tragedy that, as it takes a bucolic turn, gives up on the possibility of thoroughgoing catharsis. For the first time since *Der Rosenkavalier*, the two works, taken together, raise a claim to "the festive" and "the social" (even if the happy resolution promised by comedy is absent). Until this point, all of the operas had foregrounded how the modern individual achieves bearing and language by turning to fellow human beings—as in the love-scene in *Friedenstag*. *Daphne* indicates that such reassurance might not (or no longer) be possible. The heroine takes flight into renunciation and, indeed, ultimately succumbs to a linguistic crisis: only with difficullty does her song finally resolve in F# major (see Example 10.1).

That said, the Daphne drama —in contrast to the "Chandos Letter"— does not represent conditions before the language crisis, but afterward. As such, its tragic aspects bear on the historical circumstances that frame what Strauss and Hofmannstahl understood as "the social achieved," especially in light of contemporary events. Language loses its fullness and concreteness once more. Heinrich von Kleist, the embodiment of embattled linguistic encounters, provided the barometer for the work's tragic dimension. Strauss had first engaged with the writer's work in an 1886 composition (*Bardengesang,* now lost) and devoted considerable reflection

Example 10.1 *Daphne*-motifs: oboe solo at the beginning; final sequence with text and vocalization.

to adapting Kleist's *Amphitryon* before concluding that the work was, in fact, "uncomposable."[22] This same writer was to provide a standard for the work at hand: "Daphne . . ., Apollo, and Leukippos would have to clash in a Kleistian scene."[23]

The connections between *Daphne* and *Friedenstag* persist in the last two operas, which also go back directly to plans elaborated in conjunction with Hofmannsthal. In both cases, *Ariadne auf Naxos* provides the backdrop. *Die Liebe der Danae* and *Capriccio* separate aspects that had been fused earlier on: the genesis of the work of art under the sign of modernity and antiquity regained. It is as if the canopy descending on Ariadne and Bacchus now was lifted. Although the setting is the ancient world, *Die Liebe der Danae* presents this universe as decayed and decadent. The Orientalist aspect no longer possesses a tragic or exotic quality so much as a general air of questionability; as such, it signals an unbridgeable gulf. At the end of *Ariadne,* the epiphany of Bacchus (and therefore the Dionysian) occurs as a break with the key of *Götterdämmerung*, D♭ major, signaling the renewal of antiquity as social reality. In contrast, *Danae* ends with Jupiter (and the Apollonian dimension he embodies) disappearing from the human world altogether. The final key is soft, B major, and wholly un-Wagnerian; it represents the melancholy departure of the divine and thus a last reminder that human beings may preserve what they have only in turning to one another. As such, *Die Liebe der Danae* not only stands opposed to the violent conditions attending its genesis; it also calls into question the validity of the work of art in general, at least as Strauss had understood it to date. This is the matter addressed in the final sequence of *Capriccio*, for which the composer finally retained the services of Hans Swarowsky and Clemens Krauss. (Apart from *Guntram* and *Intermezzo*, this was also the only time he took credit for the libretto.) A self-reflective work, the piece makes a point of connecting with the prelude of *Ariadne*—except that now the intended opera does not follow. The juxtaposition of words and music (and, implicitly, the question of which one governs the other) does not represent a sentimental return to an aesthetic debate of the eighteenth century; instead, it leads to a wholly unexpected conclusion: the work of art's own impossibility.

---

22 "unkomponierbar." Ibid., 134; letter from Strauss of May 22, 1935.

23 "Daphne . . ., Apollo und Leukippos müßten in einer Kleistschen Scene aufeinanderplatzen." Ibid., 148; letter from Strauss of October 31, 1935.

In a letter to Joseph Gregor, Strauss called the end of *Capriccio* "one big question-mark."[24] The question follows from the composer's belief that considerations factoring into the work of art do not co-determine its substance (as is the case in *Ariadne*); instead, they have the potential to replace the work itself. Once more, the opera features D♭ major in the final sequence; now, however, it does not signal a break with Wagnerian connotations so much as it marks their definitive resolution. In dialogue with her own likeness in the mirror, the Countess—whom the composer pictured as a young woman not yet thirty with a liberal attitude towards erotic matters—comes to the conclusion that a work of art has no need for clarity either in form or content. The mirror is a metaphor. When taking her dinner (alone) —thereby affirming the rights of life over art—she summons the majordomo. He has no idea what to make of her declarations, which are gently punctuated by a cadence played on the horn (an instrument with marked "autobiographical" connotations for Strauss).

The pair formed by Strauss's last two works also puts the "festive" aspect of art into question: in one, the divine dimension vanishes; in the other, a celebratory opera is announced, which then does not take place. While working on the pieces, Strauss made frequent reference to the limitations that historical circumstances imposed. Unexpectedly—and surprisingly—he combined this new form of artistic and musical self-reflection with a wholly "modern" understanding of his craft pointing far into the second half of the twentieth century (as scholars came to realize only long after the fact). This is why Strauss persisted in his tedious collaboration with Gregor: to round off his own creative activity, not in the sense of reaching a conclusion so much as to open it up again (as exemplified by the vocalization in *Daphne*). At the same time, he wanted this opening to integrate his work into the historical present, which surely could not go on as it was. Yet again—even if fundamental differences prevail in terms of day-to-day existence—the parallel between Strauss's understanding of composition and his life-world calls to mind the story of Adrian Leverkühn in Thomas Mann's *Doctor Faustus*: a life chronicled in light of the destruction of the Europe of old during the Second World War.

---

24 "großes Fragezeichen." *Richard Strauss und Joseph Gregor: Briefwechsel*, 1996; letter from Strauss of September 20, 1939.

CHAPTER ELEVEN

Metamorphosen and the End of History

Final Works

Richard Strauss deemed his life's work complete in 1941, with the "big question-mark" of *Capriccio*. In contrast to twelve years earlier, the step he now took was not a matter of chance but a conscious decision prompted by the circumstances. The score was finished in August; the composer, who otherwise would already have been busy with other projects, now seemed to fall silent. It was more than a year before he completed a new work: the Horn Concerto No. 2 in E♭ major, which was performed for the first—and, as Strauss conceived it—last time in Salzburg the following year. It occupied a kind of no-man's-land: after the premiere of *Capriccio*, but still before *Liebe der Danae* had reached the public in any form. Even for Strauss, it was becoming increasingly clear that the Second World War was taking a turn for the worse; eventually, his remarks—that no soldier need fight on his behalf—made him a *persona non grata* to the National Socialist leadership. In this context, it is surprising (if only at first glance) that the composer's second Horn Concerto, which seemed to distance itself from current events, inaugurated his late works. Consisting of ten compositions (if one takes the four orchestral Lieder as a unit), the late works are marked by nine instances where Strauss reaches back to earlier works, grouped in two "blocks." The series began with free-standing excerpts from *Capriccio* and led to treatments that were broader and broader in scope.

Table 11.1 The Late Work

Treatments of older works are indented

Horn Concerto No. 2 in E♭ major for horn and orchestra (1942)
Festmusik der Stadt Wien for brass instruments and timpani (1943)
    Sextet from *Capriccio* (1943)
    Dances from *Capriccio* for violin, cello, and harpsichord (1943)
Sonatine in F major, *Aus der Werkstatt eines Invaliden*, for 16 wind instruments (1943)
An den Baum Daphne ("Geliebter Baum") for nine-part chorus (1943)
    Suite from *Capriccio* for harpsichord (1944)
    Der Rosenkavalier. Waltz sequence [from Acts I and II] (1944)
    Daphne-etude for solo violin (1945)
Metamorphosen. Study for 23 solo strings (1945)
    Sonatina No. 2 in E♭ major, *Fröhliche Werkstatt. Den Manen des göttlichen Mozart am Ende eines dankerfüllten Lebens*, for 16 wind instruments (1945)
Oboe Concerto in D major (1945)
    Symphonic Fantasy from *Die Frau ohne Schatten* (1946)
    Symphonic Fragment from *Josephs Legende* (1947)
Duet-Concertino in F major for clarinet, bassoon, harp, and orchestra (1947)
    Allegretto in E major for violin and piano (1948)
    [Last Songs] for soprano and orchestra (1948)
    Malven [song for voice and piano] (1948)

Strauss's own assessment was unambiguous:

> With *Capriccio* my life's work is at an end, and the notes I'm still throwing together as wrist exercises (as Hermann Bahr called the dictations he made daily) for posterity have no significance for musical history at all.[1]

Strauss meant these words in earnest. Previously, he had always sought out performance opportunities—even if it meant making questionable compromises. Now, he did not even wish to have the pieces published. The compositions existed, but they were not distributed with an eye to forming part of the repertory. Indeed, Strauss did not even assign them

---

1 "Mit Capriccio ist mein Lebenswerk beendet und die Noten, die ich als Handgelenksübung (wie Hermann Bahr sein tägliches diktieren nannte) jetzt noch für den Nachlaß zusammenschmiere, haben keinerlei musikgeschichtliche Bedeutung." *Briefwechsel mit Willi Schuh*, 50f; letter from Strauss of October 8, 1943.

opus numbers. Writing to Willi Schuh, he declared, "Perforce, I am busying my wrist with unnecessary finger-exercises in composition—one can't read all day long."[2] Strauss told Karl Böhm (1894–1981), his conductor of choice during the late period, much the same about *Metamorphosen*: "For some time now, to keep my wrist . . . trained, I have been working on an adagio for about 11 solo strings."[3] Finally, he informed the Argentine music critic Johannes Franze (1889–1968):

> My life's work is done with *Liebe der Danae* and *Capriccio*. Two sonatinas for 16 wind instruments, *Metamorphosen* for 16 solo string instruments, an oboe concerto, and the Second Horn Concerto, an epilogue to *Daphne* for nine a capella voices (text by Gregor)—recently called to life by the Vienna State Opera Chorus—are all workshop projects so that my right hand, now free of the baton, does not fall asleep prematurely.[4]

All the same, the wording of such declarations deserves attention. In speaking of "wrist exercises," Strauss was referring to Hermann Bahr's habit of dictation, which did not concern the wrist at all. The mechanical aspect, also evident in the phrase "finger exercises," evokes the way piano and violin are taught, that is, the manual component of playing music. In this light, composition appears as a kind of rote activity. Strauss always deemed this feature important, but only insofar as it connected with "inspiration"—which is precisely what his choice of words conceals. The compositions that now emerged display ambivalence, then: on the one hand, they were denied the status of being a "work"; on the other hand,

---

2 "Mein Handgelenk beschäftige ich notgedrungen mit unnötigen compositorischen Fingerübungen, da man doch nicht den ganzen Tag lesen kann." Ibid., 53 f., here 53; letter from Strauss of November 30, 1943.

3 "Ich arbeite schon seit einiger Zeit, um das Handgelenk . . . in Übung zu erhalten, an einem Adagio für etwa 11 Solostreicher." Martina Steiger (ed.), *Richard Strauss—Karl Böhm: Briefwechsel 1921–1949* (Mainz: Schott, 1999), 171; letter from Strauss to Böhm, September 30, 1944.

4 "Mein Lebenswerk ist mit 'Liebe der Danae' und 'Capriccio' beendet. Zwei Sonatinen für 16 Bläser, die 'Metamorphosen' für 23 Solostreicher, ein Oboenkonzert und das zweite Hornkonzert, ein Epilog zu 'Daphne' für neunstimmigen a cappella-Chor (Text von Gregor)—unlängst vom Wiener Staatsopernchor aus der Taufe gehoben—sind Werkstattarbeiten, damit das vom Taktstock befreite rechte Handgelenk nicht vorzeitig einschläft." Grasberger, *Der Strom der Töne*, 460f; letter from Strauss to Franze of April 1, 1947.

Strauss did record them. Although they were not *opera,* they were meant for public performance. The composer did not have them printed, and their effect was not intended to last; nevertheless, he did not destroy them and instead consigned them to his *Nachlass*. In brief, the pieces are both complete and, at the same time, exercises. Time and again, Strauss stressed their connection to *Capriccio*. As such, they represent the consequence of the opera's finale: compositions that lay no claim to general validity. They are music that—like the conversation the Countess has with her likeness—takes place in a mirror of the present at hand. Inasmuch as they possess no "musical-historical significance," they are "superfluous."[5]

The pieces were part of the world, but no longer stood on their own so much as they commented it in a diffuse and amorphous process. This late, nihilistic turn did not occur in a gesture of heroic downfall—as performed by, say, Oswald Spengler's adherents, or, in its most cynical and soulless form, by Hitler and those loyal to him. Rather, in keeping with the understanding he had achieved in conjunction with Hofmannsthal and Zweig, Strauss found a cheerful, "social" dimension, even if it lacked future prospects. This circumstance accounts for further features, too: beginning with the Second Horn Concerto, dedicated to his father's memory, the composer incorporated autobiographical elements—references to a long life in music, with their author the protagonist of a now-finished culture. For those who are able to decipher it (and the reception history proves that many are not), this music is highly intimate. All the pieces connect with previous works. The Second Horn Concerto relates to the First, and the Sonatinas to the Suite in B♭ major, Op. 4, and the Serenade in E♭ major, Op. 7; *Metamorphosen* connects with *Ein Heldenleben,* and the Duet-Concertino with the fairytale world of *Die Frau ohne Schatten*; the Oboe Concerto has points of contact with *Daphne,* and *Festmusik* with *Feierlicher Einzug*. Finally, the orchestral songs take up the early Lieder, on the one hand, and *Tod und Verklärung,* on the other. Such autobiographical elements, in turn, are expanded through reference to musical history—especially Beethoven and, most of all, Mozart.

The late "exercises" also represented a surprising return to instrumental music. However, they did not take up the conventions of old so

---

5 "überflüssige Musik." *Briefwechsel mit Willi Schuh,* 84; letter from Strauss of July 6, 1945.

much as they reinvented the underlying "language." A remarkable circumstance preceded this step. In 1941, Strauss was asked to contribute a piece for the centenary of the Vienna Philharmonic, and he set about composing a large-scale orchestral work, *Die Donau*. There is no telling why he accepted the commission, which was never completed, but he did write more than 400 bars. This is enough to discern the overall design: a flowing narrative, starting at the river's source, with unmistakeable allusions to Smetana's *Vltava* (*Die Moldau*). Strauss broke off work either because he was never really convinced about the project, or because it struck him as impossible to return to the genre of the tone poem at this stage. Now, instrumental language did not "precede" composition—as had been the case for the tone poems—so much as it resulted from operatic works, especially *Daphne* and *Capriccio*. Even when performed, then, the pieces defied inherited contexts of validity—and they purposefully charted aberrant (and therefore new) paths, which no longer had anything to do with the program underlying the tone poems. The core gesture unleashed a polyphonic movement connecting with the unbridled vocality that had been evident since *Die Schweigsame Frau*. By retracting the psychologizing quality of "nervous counterpoint"—a process begun in the latter work— they created another, overflowing form of contrapuntal composition. The two sonatinas make this aspect especially plain. The keys employed—F major and E♭ major—provide the framework for a musical event with a contrapuntal basis and development; hereby, form proves secondary. Moreover, the backdrop for both pieces is Mozart's *Gran Partita*, whose orchestration—two flutes and a clarinet—is expanded, with a bass clarinet taking the place of the second basset horn. In either case, a workman-like character is plain.

The first sonatina's title, *Aus der Werkstatt eines Invaliden*, points to the fact that Strauss now felt that the basis for his understanding of music had been destroyed. The second sonatina affirms the same. Strauss crafted the piece by starting with the finale, *Einleitung und Allegro*, then composed the opening movement; the middle sequence emerged last. The gigantic dimensions of his design—especially the outside movements—did not follow from formal considerations; instead, it represented the studied exploration of all the polyphonic possibilities available—and thus a reworking of what the nineteenth century called "organic" form. The workman-like aspects of the pieces have a bearing on technique, above all. If the first sonatina was written when the Europe of old collapsed, the second represented the composer's reaction to the inevitability of such a loss. *Die Fröhliche Werkstatt* does not herald good cheer borrowed from antiquity; that is—and in contrast to works from twenty years beforehand—it does not amount to a refusal of the tragic in the face of boundless disaster. Rather, the piece incorporates Nietzsche's *Gay Science* (*Fröhliche Wissenschaft*) into the process of composition. This is the only time that Strauss saw fit to make two dedications, one of them historical and the other rooted in his own time. The latter was to his patron in Winterthur, Werner Reinhart (1884–1951), one of the most important advocates of contemporary music. The former extended "To the guardian spirits of the divine Mozart at the end of a grateful life." By invoking the ancient spirits of the dead [*Manen*] when concluding his own work, Strauss sought to present the now-gone legacy of Europe and Germany.

Here, one last aspect of Strauss's late work is evident: after the operas—"the social achieved"—and indications that this unity had dissolved, the composer deliberately offered no future prospects. Ultimately, his late instrumental music amounts to a remarkable, and disconcerting, response to the horrors of war, which Strauss understood as the destruction of both European music and humanity. In turn, the dialectical connection between pessimistic cheer and contemporary disaster led him, in his four final songs, to round off his own biography and face death without any metaphysical framework at all. Initially, Strauss deemed the matter definitive—a closed book. Zweig recalled his first meeting with the composer: "He cannot see how music can continue and believes a certain pause has set in. In not quite 250 years, music really developed—which was extremely quick—and so now there is this stifled lull."[6] But at the very end of life, evidence exists that Strauss became convinced that a new culture might develop, albeit one that had nothing more to do with the one he knew. Statements he made about humanist education—as well as his late idea to compose a school opera, *Des Esels Schatten*, based on Christoph Martin Wieland's fable adapted from an ancient source (a

---

6 "Er sieht überhaupt nicht wie die Musik noch weitergehen könne und glaubt an eine gewisse Pause. In knapp 250 Jahren habe sich eigentlich die Musik entfaltet, das sei rasend rasch gewesen, daher jetzt diese Stockung [. . .]." Stefan Zweig, *Tagebücher*, ed. Knut Beck (Frankfurt: S. Fischer, 1984), 353; entry of November 1931.

project that did not go beyond a rough sketch)—would seem to point to such a legacy.

Self-Interpretations: *Metamorphosen*

Metamorphosen represents the key work for understanding the connection between self-reflective musicality and the position Strauss ultimately sought in history; it is the only late score that does not have a technical, generic designation (such as concerto or sonatine) but a programmatic title. Through the mediation of Willi Schuh, the composer relocated to Switzerland immediately after the war's end. The project was conceived in response to Paul Sacher, Willi Schuh, and Karl Böhm's request for a work to inaugurate Sacher's newly established Collegium Musicum in Zurich. However, Strauss completed the score in 1945, while still in Garmisch. Initially, the composer planned an "adagio for about eleven solo string instruments, which will likely develop into an allegro—I can't really stand Brucknerian silence for too long."[7] The draft that was finished in March, while already given the title it would take in its final form, still imagined a string septet. It is impossible to determine when Strauss changed this arrangement—if he ever meant it seriously. At any rate, the finished version, for twenty-three solo string instruments, defies classification. At just under half an hour in length, the composition comprises a single movement divided into three passages that flow into each other (slow—fast—slow); it is structured by two opposing thematic constellations exhibiting the florid style characteristic of the late work, with counterpoint that seems to unfold "on its own." Likewise the amorphous quality characteristic of the sonatinas: an articulated yet seamless continuum.

This composition, which enlists models from the past at most indirectly, culminates in a clearly demarcated coda. It is preceded by an extended general pause—the only one in the piece, which otherwise moves forward without interruption. In turn, the coda concludes with a "very slow" passage that starts out *ritardando* and elaborately resolves the two main themes into the basic key of C minor. Now, the beginning of

---

7 "Adagio für etwa 11 Solostreicher, das sich wahrscheinlich zu einem Allegro entwickeln wird, da ich es in Brucknerscher Orgelruhe nicht allzu lange aushalte." *Richard Strauss—Karl Böhm: Briefwechsel*, 171; letter from Strauss of September 30, 1944.

Example 11.1 Beethoven-theme in *Metamorphosen* and its original articulation.

Beethoven's *Marcia funebre* from *Eroica* (1804) is quoted. Its first four bars are repeated note-for-note, but the sequence is placed at a remove, as it were: instead of violins, three cellos and basses play, *legato* and doubling the length of notes (see Example 11.1). The contrasting main themes fade in on top. Since Beethoven's music is connected to the core motifs of Strauss's own composition, the arrangement serves as a parenthesis: ultimately, all of the work's figures depend on the funeral march; at the same time the deeper connection between the two central themes is affirmed after the event.

At the point the quotation arrives, Strauss wrote on the score the pathos-laden words, *"In memoriam!"*—a clear parallel to his dedication of the second sonatina to Mozart's *Manen*. The passage from Beethoven points back to *Ein Heldenleben*, which Strauss understood as a response to his forebear's symphony. After all, as he interpreted his own *oeuvre* late in life, the nineteenth century "ultimately" extended "from *Eroica* up to *Heldenleben*."[8] In this light, the reference in *Metamorphosen* is negative: just as the latter piece is not an orchestral composition or chamber music, its gesture to Beethoven represents a mere memory. In *Ein Heldenleben*, *Eroica* also did not represent a new starting point; likewise, before the final strains of *Metamorphosen*, the piece signifies both its driving force and an open ending. E♭ major and C minor—the two keys Beethoven employed to such great effect as a kind of cipher—are draped over a

---

8 "schließlich von der Eroica bis zum Heldenleben." *Briefwechsel mit Willi Schuh*, 92f; letter from Strauss of June 2, 1946.

whole life's work. Just as the beginning of *Ein Heldenleben*, in E♭ major, is impossible to understand without familiarity with *Eroica,* the quotation of the *Marcia funebre,* in C minor, occurs after a compositional framework almost a half hour in length has been introduced.

In offering this fragmented recollection of Beethoven, Strauss sought to draw a circle, marking out an intermediate position between music and *oeuvre* that is characteristic of not just *Metamorphosen,* but the late work as a whole. The title indicates that the key point of reference is Goethe. Strauss had already sought to do the same in the tone poems, especially *Tod und Verklärung.* Even if he stuck to allusions, it struck him as significant that he served as Kapellmeister in Weimar, where Goethe and Liszt had played such important roles. From *Die Frau ohne Schatten* and *Die ägyptische Helena* on, Strauss increasingly made reference to Goethe, and with *Metamorphosen* the poet came to represent his view of his life and work as a whole. Curiously disregarding the crimes perpetrated by the Nazis, Strauss understood the war as the extinction of human culture—symbolized, in "plastic" form, by the bombed-out opera houses. Such destruction was tied to the physical existence of Goethe's legacy: at the end of the conflict, "Goethe's sacred house and the opera halls of Dresden and Vienna, which are so dear to me, sank into ruins and ashes."[9] Strauss was an atheist, but this sacralizing perspective was hardly a figure of speech: "The *Goethehaus,* the world's holiest shrine, destroyed! My beautiful Dresden—Weimar—Munich, all gone!"[10] At the same time, the composer became increasingly convinced that his own life made sense in parallel to Goethe's. In this context, reading the newly republished biography by Herman Grimm (1828–1901), a pupil of Leopold von Ranke, proved significant. Here, wholly in line with Strauss's own view, Goethe was presented as the pioneer of a new, Germanic cultural hegemony that reconciled antiquity and modernity. "It positively inspired [*begeistert*] me that I could flatter my vanity by observing a few remarkable parallels between the life-course and working methods of this greatest of men

---

9 "das heilige Haus Goethes und die mir besonders teuren Opernhäuser von Dresden und Wien in Schutt und Asche sinken." Ibid., 78f; letter from Strauss of May 10, 1945.

10 "Das Göthehaus, der Welt größtes Heiligtum, zerstört! Mein schönes Dresden—Weimar—München, Alles dahin!" *Richard Strauss und Joseph Gregor: Briefwechsel,* 285; letter from Strauss of March 2, 1945.

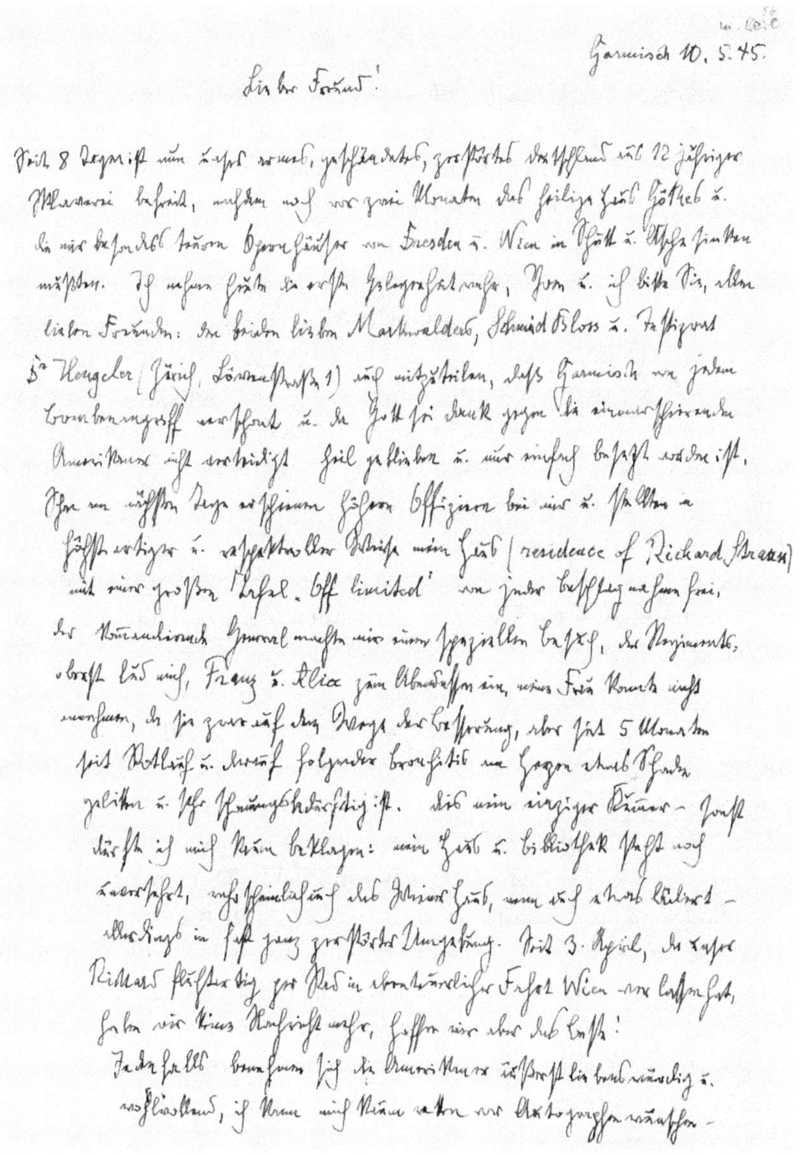
Garmisch 10. 5. 45.

Lieber Freund!

Figure 11.1 Richard Strauss, letter to Willi Schuh, 10 May 1945. Autograph.

In this late letter, Richard Strauss announces the end of the Second World War to the Swiss music critic: “For eight days now, our poor, disgraced, and devastated Germany has been freed from twelve years of bondage” [“Seit 8 Tagen ist unser armes, geschändetes, zerstörtes Deutschland aus 12jähriger Sklaverei befreit”]. Garmisch stands occupied by American forces, but has been spared destruction. Strauss also shares that his work on *Metamorphosen* is complete. To date, Strauss’s letters have been available only in separate editions; a complete register of his correspondence does not exist. Strauss wrote a great deal of letters, and they tend to be rather long.

Munich, Bayerische Staatsbibliothek, Ana 330. I. Schuh, Nr. 56.

with my own development (at a humble remove)."¹¹ In early 1944, Strauss wrote to Schuh: "I am quietly working along just for myself (following Goethe's sublime example)."¹² These words illuminate the late compositions, especially *Metamorphosen*. The composer's first mention of the work, in correspondence with Karl Böhm, had already quoted the melancholy and alienated *Chorus mysticus* in *Faust*. Strauss's notes also include two short poems from Goethe's posthumous *Zahme Xenien*—which popular literature on the author at the turn of the century had presented as paradigms of purifying self-knowledge and transformation.

Accordingly, Strauss sought to connect Goethe's conception of metamorphosis with his own soul-searching in a kind of music he purposefully denied the status of a work of art. Such a view was not unprecedented. During the Weimar Republic, Goethe had already been understood in terms of civilizational critique, whereby the poet offered a corrective to the overly technological worldview of the natural sciences. The issue did not involve actually understanding nature so much as expanding the anthropological import of the idea of metamorphosis. In this context, the notion of persistence in a world of change was itself transformed: existence does not represent the precondition for, or result of, transformation so much as it forms part of the continuum of incessant physio-biological change. Strauss would have already encountered initial formulations of such a view when he attended Wilhelm Heinrich von Riehl's Munich lectures. Now, he extended its implications to include music, which came to represent human history as a whole. "Goethe himself acknowledges that the realm of music begins where the incommensurable is inaccessible to the understanding."¹³ The apex of the process, in Strauss's eyes, was Wagner, whose completely Germanic body of work amounted to a physiological limit of sorts. In the historical process of cultural evolution governing the idea of

---

11 "Geradezu begeistert hat mich, daß meine Eitelkeit ein Paar sehr merkwürdige Parallelen im Lebenslauf und der Arbeitsart dieses Allergrößten mit meiner eigenen Entwicklung (in bescheidenem Abstand) zu constatieren mir schmeichle." *Briefwechsel mit Willi Schuh*, 106; letter from Strauss of November 15, 1946.

12 "Ich arbeite so still für mich hin (nach Goethes erhabenem Vorbild) . . . ." Ibid., 61; letter from Strauss of January 23, 1943.

13 "Und Göthe selbst bekennt, daß das Reich der Musik beginnt, wo das Incommensurable dem Verstande unerreichbar ist." *Richard Strauss und Joseph Gregor: Briefwechsel*, 270; letter from Strauss of February 4, 1945.

metamorphosis music has the final word: "Since 1 September [1944, the day theaters were closed], the flower of German music, flourishing for two centuries, has begun to wither; its spirit has been caught in the machine, and its crowning achievement, the German opera, is now bent forever."[14]

In this light, *Metamorphosen* stands as the final musical cipher that Strauss created. Once more, there is a parallel, both puzzling and insistent, between the real-life composer and the fictional Adrian Leverkühn. It is not by chance, perhaps, that Thomas Mann has the protagonist of his novel (already infected with syphilis) travel from Leipzig to the Austrian premiere of *Salome,* in Graz. Here, Leverkühn—whose own symphonic poem *Meerleuchten* amounts to a parody of Strauss's lush orchestration— witnesses the performance in a mixture of awe and reserve. The event really did occur, in 1906. Many of the luminaries of European music made the journey, too—as did the young Adolf Hitler, still hoping to gain admission to the Vienna Academy and to become an artist himself. Strauss, the signatory of the Munich letter protesting Thomas Mann, did not leave the author unmoved. In 1952—a few years after his son, Klaus, had interviewed the composer in Garmisch and been left troubled and confused—he wrote to Theodor W. Adorno:

> The revolutionary as a child of the sun—truly a unique case and entertaining in the best sense. I have always had a considerable amount of time for him, probably because of his great commercial sense. His nonchalance was attractive and with his own enormous talent he was capable of great openness and affection. "That Mozart! Can he write! It's beyond me!"[15]

Earlier, upon learning of Strauss's death—"serious news" in his eyes— Mann had written in his diary that Adrian Leverkühn "should have been the first post-Straussian composer."[16]

---

14 "Seit dem ersten September fängt die seit 2 Jahrhunderten gedeihende Blume der deutschen Musik zu verdorren an, ihr Geist ist in die Maschine gefangen gesetzt und ihre Hochblüte, die deutsche Oper, für immer geknickt." Grasberger, *Der Strom der Töne*, 432; letter from Strauss to Heinz Tietjen of November 25, 1944.

15 *Theodor W. Adorno and Thomas Mann: Correspondence, 1943–1955,* ed. Christoph Gödde and Thomas Sprecher (Cambridge: Polity, 2006), 73; letter from Mann of February 9, 1952.

16 "mit Ernst aufgenommen," "der nach-Straußische Komponist, den es hätte geben müssen." Thomas Mann, *Tagebücher: 1949—1950,* ed. Inge Jens (Frankfurt: Fischer, 1991), 95 and 102; entries of September 8, 1949 and September 23, 1949.

The New Presence of History?

Richard Strauss's death, on September 8, 1949 in Garmisch, seemed like the coda to an epoch that belonged to the past, extinguished by world war and the new order that emerged in its wake. The pianist and journalist Ludwig Kusche (1901–1982) left a record of the cremation ceremony, which took place at the Munich Ostfriedhof on September 11, 1949. The weather was beautiful, but attendance was sparse. By Kusche's account, one-third of the 150 spaces reserved for dignitaries remained unfilled. As Georg Solti, the young director of the Bavarian State Opera, conducted Beethoven's *Marcia funebre*, noise from American military aircraft drowned out the music.[17]

The previous year, Strauss had written to Willi Schuh: "I have really outlived myself."[18] Indeed, he had already hinted at the same during the 1920s:

> Perhaps it is in the nature of our time that our heirs, the "new generation," today's "young people," are no longer able to view my dramatic and symphonic works as an adequate expression of what made it possible for me to live in them in musical and human terms—works representing a musical and artistic problem that is over for me, but just beginning for the "new generation." We are all children of our time and can never jump over its shadow.[19]

When composing his tone poems, Strauss had willfully consigned himself to history. In his late compositions, he stepped back into it still more. Stefan Zweig, in his memoirs, notes his contemporary's singular habit of somehow standing outside himself: his ability to view his artistic life unsparingly and at a paradoxical distance. Strauss had asked him (especially in reference to the terzet from *Der Rosenkavalier*), "Must one become

---

17 Ludwig Kusche, "Der Rosenkavalier auf dem Friedhof," in *Auf musikalischen Schleichwegen* (Munich: Süddeutscher Verlag, 1968, originally 1959), 56–61; there are some film excerpts of the ceremony.

18 "ich mich tatsächlich überlebt habe." *Briefwechsel mit Willi Schuh*, 170; letter from Strauss of December 26, 1948.

19 "Es liegt vielleicht im Wesen der Zeit, daß unser Nachwuchs, unsere 'junge Generation', unsere 'Heutigen' meine dramatischen und sinfonischen Arbeiten nicht mehr als einen vollwertigen Ausdruck dessen ansehen können, was mich musikalisch und menschlich in ihnen leben ließ, die aber im musikalischen und künstlerischen Problem schon für mich erledigt sind, wenn sie für die 'junge Generation' erst beginnen. Wir sind alle Kinder unserer

seventy years old to recognize that one's greatest strength lies in creating kitsch?"[20]

More and more, the composer came to situate his own work at the end of a period of cultural history. Evidence abounds—for instance, clipped remarks on the essence of opera that he offered in 1944: "The revelation of the human soul in the melody of Mozart, Beethoven, Schubert, Wagner and the speaking opera of Haydn, Weber, Berlioz, Wagner, and Rich. Strauss!"[21] This assessment followed from his conviction that European culture, which started in antiquity, had reached its high point in music, and in German music, in particular. This heritage should be preserved for posterity in an "opera museum." During the final years of his life, such notions solidified more and more. "Mozartian melody, Beethovenian symphony, and the Wagnerian orchestra are the end and culmination of world culture."[22] As such, "the *melody* of Mozart, Beethoven, and Schubert and . . . the *language* of the Wagnerian and Straussian orchestra" amount to the "conclusion and summit of mankind's cultural evolution to date."[23] At the same time, the composer assigned his own *oeuvre* a secondary, supplementary, status in this scheme. When the process of "cultural evolution" ended, his own work lost its historical significance, which is why he attached no particular importance to his late, instrumental compositions.

In 1946, Strauss wrote to Wieland Wagner:

> Now that the Vienna Opera has closed its gates with *Götterdämmerung* and Hans Sachs has issued his final warning call from the Bayreuth Festspielhaus,

---

Zeit und können niemals über ihren Schatten springen." Strauss, "Über Komponieren und Dirigieren," in *Betrachtungen und Erinnerungen*, 48.

20 "Muß man 70 Jahre alt werden, um zu erkennen, daß man eigentlich zum Kitsch die meiste Begabung hat?" *Briefwechsel mit Willi Schuh*, 55; letter from Strauss of January 21, 1934.

21 "Die Offenbarung der menschlichen Seele in der Melodie Mozarts, Beethovens, Schuberts, Wagners und im sprechenden Orchester Haydns, Webers, Berlioz's, Wagners und Rich. Strauss's!" *Briefwechsel mit Willi Schuh*, 64; letter from Strauss of March 9, 1944. Strauss is referring to a text sent as a letter to Karl Böhm later (April 27, 1945) that he himself called "Vermächtnis."

22 *Briefwechsel mit Willi Schuh*, 49; letter from Strauss to Schuh of March 8, 1945.

23 "das Erscheinen der *Melodie Mozarts*, Beethovens, Schuberts und die Vollendung der *Sprache* des Wagnerschen und Strausschen Orchesters der Abschluß und Gipfel der bisherigen Culturentwicklung der Menschheit." *Briefwechsel mit Willi Schuh*, 66; letter from Strauss of May 1, 1944.

chaos has finally invaded the world of culture. It is not chance, but fate, that Germany's world mission ended once German music had finished its course from the *Matthäuspassion* to *Parsifal*. The parallel to Greece after Sulla destroyed Athens is distressing.[24]

Accordingly, after the dress-rehearsal for *Liebe der Danae* he noted: "At any rate, my artistic life is done after September 1; I feel I have been buried alive."[25]

Strauss also made an outward display of this feeling of confinement. When Joseph Gregor introduced him to Erich Hermann Müller von Asow (1892–1964), a composer working on a catalog of his works, he unapologetically declared:

> I understand nothing of the librarian's duties; it seems to me that the thematic index has too much useless material: worthless sketches and uninteresting juvenilia. Trivial matters like that are a waste of paper![26]

In other words, Strauss deemed that "half" of his *oeuvre* amounted to "worthless philological dust":

> Two-thirds of the unpublished works from youth listed are not worth mentioning, and the sketches in particular simply belong in the wastepaper

---

24 "Nachdem die Wiener Oper mit der *Götterdämmerung* ihre Pforten geschlossen hatte und Hans Sachs vom Bayreuther Festspielhaus seinen letzten Mahnruf gesprochen, ist nun tatsächlich das Chaos in die Kulturwelt hereingebrochen – aber es ist kein Zufall – sondern Schicksal, daß Deutschlands Weltmission beendet war, nachdem es die deutsche Musik von der Matthäuspassion bis zum *Parsifal* geschaffen hatte. Die Parallele mit Griechenland nach der Zerstörung Athens durch Sulla ist erschütternd [. . .]." Ernst Krause (ed.), *Richard Strauss: Dokumente, Aufsätze, Aufzeichnungen, Vorworte, Reden, Briefe* (Leipzig: Reclam, 1980), 312 f; letter from Strauss to Wieland Wagner of June 18, 1946. Strauss mentioned the comparison to Sulla even earlier in a letter to Anton Kippenberg, September 24, 1945 ("Richard Strauss und Anton Kippenberg: Briefwechsel," 142).

25 "Mein künstlerisches Leben ist jedenfalls mit dem 1. September abgeschlossen und ich komme mir vor wie ein lebendig Begrabener." Grasberger, *Der Strom der Töne*, 436; letter from Strauss to Wolfgang Golther of April 5, 1945.

26 "Ich verstehe nichts von den Pflichten des Bibliothekars, mir scheint nur das thematische Verzeichniß viel zu viel Unnützes an wertlosem Skizzenmaterial und uninteressanten Jugendwerken zu enthalten. Schade um das Papier für solche Nichtigkeiten!" *Richard Strauss und Joseph Gregor: Briefwechsel*, 269; letter from Strauss of February 7 and 8, 1945.

basket. Please offer heartfelt thanks to our diligent author and ask him to clear away all superfluous elements from his work.[27]

Such gruffness followed from the composer's will to situate his creations precisely where they achieved historical significance—and then lost it again. In 1944, the same outlook prompted Strauss to settle scores with the Hegelian philosophy of history (and the notion of progress it entailed) in a manner bordering on rage. In an inscribed copy of *Griechisches Erbe* (Greek Legacy) by the pedagogical reformer Fritz Klatt (1888–1945), which had appeared the previous year, he noted (October 27):

> The final word about this a[nd] similarly well-intentioned fabulation, which wanders around in the fog of imperfect human "knowledge" and vainly deems itself Platonic "reason," has already been pronounced by music: by Ritter von Gluck in his *Iphigenia* pieces and *Orpheus*—and Richard Strauss in *Elektra* (fifth century BC), *Die ägyptische Helena* (fourth century), *Ariadne*, *Daphne*, and *Die Liebe der Danae*; here, the Greek soul sought in vain for so long turns into a direct revelation through the symbols of modern orchestration. [A?] Mozartian, Beethovenian, Schubertian melody casts away all the cloying phrases of works by the likes of Stefan George or Rilke, just as the eight bars from *Tristan* grind the amateurish [*dilettantisch*]—if you will: *dile-titanic*—rebellion of Nietzschean impotence and hopelessly bombastic Brucknerian symphonies to dust! These ingenious literati, with their philosophical education reaching back to Hegel, always forget that the music that has been discovered for the last two hundred years is the highest peak of gestalt culture.[28]

However—and contrary to what Strauss's pessimistic words suggest—taking leave from "gestalt" did not lead to silence so much as new,

---

27 "Hälfte leider wertloser Philologenstaub," "2 Drittel der angeführten, unveröffentlichten Jugendarbeiten lohnen nicht der Erwähnung und vor allem das Skizzenzeug ist reiner Papierkorb. Bitte dem fleißigen Verfasser bestens zu danken und ihm zu empfehlen, seine Arbeit gründlich von allem Überflüssigen zu reinigen." Ibid., 280; letter from Strauss of February 17, 1946.

28 "Das Schlußwort zu diesem u. ähnlichen gutgemeinten, im Nebel unvollkommenen menschlichen 'Wissens' u. vergeblich sich wähnender platonischer 'Vernunft' herumirrenden Fabulieren hat die Musik geschrieben u. zwar Ritter von Gluck in seinen Iphigenien, Orpheus – Richard Strauss in Elektra (5. Jahrhundert v. Chr.) Ägyptische

amorphously floral structures that did away with all definition. In the composer's very last years, there are signs that the loss Strauss lamented was not absolute, after all. After "de-Nazification" in 1947, Strauss was considered untainted by the past. From Montreux, he traveled again to give concerts in England. In spring 1949, still bearing the scars of a 1946 operation in Lausanne, he returned to Garmisch. After the war, Strauss could discern a new beginning, albeit one in which he no longer had a share. With a view to his grandchildren's education (and in light of plans for *Des Esels Schatten*), he thought that the new beginning should affirm European tradition—if in a way that differed from his own upbringing. This unsentimental assessment of the limited nature of his own life's work and the circumstances attending it stands as one of the composer's most irritating qualities. Such an outlook had already been in evidence when Strauss was quite young, and it persisted to the end. At no point did the composer offer a reckoning of the decisions he had made, which all displayed an abiding will to secure, or keep, his social position. Strauss never spoke about doubts, questionable choices, or compromises, even when they cast a shadow over his life after 1933. Yet this same refusal to make absolute aesthetic claims is what defines his status in modernity and modernism, with all the points of rupture, peril, and friction that it entails. A final paradox in the life and character of a figure already rich in paradoxes, this attitude demonstrates a will to occupy the present in strictly aesthetic terms. In turn—and in an enduring, dynamic process— it exercises greater and greater plastic force the more it fades away into history.

Helena (4. Jahrhundert), Ariadne, Daphne, die Liebe der Danae, in denen die bisher verzweifelt gesuchte griechische Seele durch die Symbole des modernen Orchesters zur unmittelbaren Offenbarung geworden ist. [Eine?] Mozartsche, Beethovensche, Schubertsche Melodie bläst die süßlichen Phrasen sämtlicher Werke der Herrn Stefan George, Rilke übern Haufen, gleichwie 8 Takte des Tristan das dilettantische sagen wir dile-titanische Aufbäumen Nietzscher Impotenz gleich den hoffnungslosen Steigerungen Brucknerscher Sinfonien zu Staub zermürben! Diese geistreichen Literaten mit ihrer hin zu Hegel reichenden philosophischen Bildung vergessen stets dass die seit 2 Jahrhunderten erfundene Musik der letzte Gipfel der Gestaltkultur ist." Fritz Klatt, *Griechisches Erbe: Das Urbild der Antike im Widerschein des heutigen Lebens* (Berlin: der Gruyter, 1943), handwritten dedication on the title; the document (acquired in 2006) is now in Vienna, Österreichische Nationalbibliothek, Mus. Hs. 43836. It was formerly property of Erna Handstaengl (1885–1981).

APPENDIX A

Biographical Timeline

1864   Richard Georg Strauss born on June 11 in Munich, Altheimer Eck 16, in the so-called Pschorr House (partially destroyed during the Second World War; the remaining structure was torn down in 1963; a commemorative plaque marks the site). Parents: Franz Strauss (1822–1905) and Josepha Strauss, *née* Pschorr (1838–1910).
Franz Joseph Strauss came from Parkstein (Upper Palatinate) and was the illegitimate son of Maria Anna Kunigunde Walter (father: Urban Strauss). In 1845, he became a citizen of Munich and two years later a member of the Bavarian Court Orchestra. In 1851, marriage to Elise Maria Seiff (born 1821); the couple's son, Johann Franz, died within a year of birth (1852); their daughter Klara Franziska, born 1853, and her mother died in a cholera epidemic in 1854. In 1863, remarriage to Josepha Pschorr; around 1870, the Strauss and Pschorr families joined the Old Catholic Church (which Ludwig II also promoted).

1867   Birth of Johanna Strauss († 1966), the couple's only other child, on June 9.

1868   Richard Strauss begins piano lessons (with August Tombo [1842–1878], harpist in the Court Orchestra); from 1872 on, violin lessons with Benno Walter [1847–1901], concertmaster at the Court Theater).

1870   Enrollment at the Munich Cathedral School; earliest extant compositions.

1874   Attendance at the Royal Ludwig-Gymnasium, Munich; lessons in composition begin the following year, with Friedrich Wilhelm Meyer (1818–1893).

1881   First public performances, including String Quartet Op. 2 and Symphony in D major, conducted by Hermann Levi; the former work appeared with the Munich publishing house Joseph Aibl, managed by Eduard Spitzweg (1811–1884, brother of the painter Carl Spitzweg) and his son Eugen Spitzweg (1840–1914). The firm published all of Strauss's songs up to the Lieder comprising Op. 37, with the exception of 1 (1881, Breitkopf & Härtel), 4, 15, 17, 22, 31, and 33; it was sold to Universal Edition in 1904.

1882   *Abitur*; visit (with his anti-Wagnerian father) to Bayreuth for the premiere of *Parsifal*; first performances outside of Munich (Op. 7 in Dresden, directed by Franz Wüllner; Op. 8 adapted for piano in Vienna, played by Benno Walter and

Strauss himself); university study in Munich: aesthetics, cutural history, and philosophy; prominent instructors include the conservative Hegelian Moriz Carrière (1817–1895), idealist philosopher and logician Carl von Prantl (1820–1888), and Wilhelm Heinrich von Riehl (1823–1897), professor of cultural history and statistics.

1883 Participation in *Wilde Gungíl* (Wild Swing), an orchestra directed by his father, until about 1885. In autumn, end of university studies (without taking a degree), followed by several months in Berlin that led to significant acquaintances, especially with Hans von Bülow (1830–1894). Performance of Op. 4 in Meiningen; Bülow conducts.

1884 Spectacular performances, including the Symphony in F minor in New York, conducted by Theodor Thomas (1835–1905); likely inception of an intense but difficult affair with a married woman, Dora Wihan (1860–1938).

1885 Through the mediation of Bülow, Strauss is named musical director at the court of Duke Georg II von Sachsen-Meiningen (reign: 1866–1914) at Meiningen on October 1 (alongside Bülow until December 1); although small, the court orchestra and theater enjoy renown throughout Europe. First encounters with Johannes Brahms (1833–1897) and Alexander Ritter (1833–1896), a violinist and fervent Wagnerian engaged by Bülow in 1882. Beginning of lifelong engagement with Wagner's *oeuvre*. Josepha Strauss spends a lengthy period at a psychiatric clinic (Oberbayerische Kreisirrenanstalt Giesing; from 1894 on, stays become more frequent)—likely because of her marriage to Franz Strauss (whom his son would later descibed as embittered, prone to rage, and tyrannical).

1886 First journey to Italy (April/May), which yields the "symphonic fantasia," *Aus Italien*, Op. 16. Summer visit to Bayreuth and first meetings with Cosima Wagner. Awarded the *Verdienstkreuz für Kunst und Wissenschaft* in Meiningen. In August, named third Kapellmeister at the Munich court opera, shortly after removal of Ludwig II, who is declared mad; Prince Luitpold takes power (imperial guardianship proclaimed).

1887 Premiere of *Aus Italien*, Op. 16 (dedicated to Hans von Bülow) in Munich; *Wandrers Sturmlied*, Op. 14, premieres in Cologne; first meeting with Gustav Mahler (1860–1911); occasional teaching activity in Munich, pupils include the soprano Pauline de Ahna (1863–1950), daughter of the Bavarian major general Adolf de Ahna (1830–1906) and his wife Marie, née Huber (1837–1923).

1888 Second voyage to Italy (May/June).

1889 On October 1 (an appointment renewed October 1, 1890), Strauss is named Second Kapellmeister at the Grand Duchy of Saxe-Weimar-Eisenach in Weimar; resides Erfurter Strasse 19 (where there is now a commemorative plaque). Contract with Pauline de Ahna and premiere of *Don Juan*, Op. 20, in Weimar. Close association with Cosima Wagner (1837–1930) and passing proximity to her increasingly *völkisch* and antisemitic circle; musical assistant in Bayreuth.

1890 *Tod und Verklärung*, Op. 24, premieres in Eisenach, as does *Burleske* (published without opus number), performed by Eugen d'Albert. Premiere of second version of *Macbeth*, Op. 23, in Weimar.

1891 In May, serious illness that does not heal properly (pulmonary inflammation). In August, engagement in Bayreuth as assistant, with Pauline de Ahna playing

Elisabeth (*Tannhäuser*). *Mädchenblumen* (Op. 22) published, the first work to appear at the press of Adolph Fürstner (1833–1908); all the composer's important works from 1900 on, in particular the operas (up to *Die Schweigsame Frau*), will be published here. (The press was operated by his son, Otto Fürstner [1886–1958], until he fled Germany in 1935; Johannes Oertel took over until the beginning of the 1940s, operating the firm under his own name.)

1892　Musical and stage rehearsal of *Tristan und Isolde* in Weimar (January 17). In May, collapse and life-threatening illness (pleurisy). Strauss resigns his duties in November; lengthy recovery trip financed by Georg Pschorr (uncle) to Egypt, via Greece, and returning through Sicily. Extensive journal (sustained engagement with Nietzsche); travel lasts until June the next year, during which Strauss completes his first opera, *Guntram*.

1893　Return in June and resumption of duties in Weimar. Premiere of *Macbeth*, Op. 23, in Berlin (third version). On December 23, conducts the premiere of Engelbert Humperdinck's *Hänsel und Gretel* in Weimar.

1894　First version of *Guntram*, Op. 25, premieres in Weimar. The same day (May 10), engagement to Pauline de Ahna (who is playing the role of Freihild). The couple is married on September 10 in Marquartstein (Chiemgau), at the summer home of the de Ahna family (commemorative plaques, Burgstrasse and castle chapel). On October 10, appointed royal Kapellmeister in Munich, at first under the physically infirm Hermann Levi (1839–1900), who retires in 1896. That winter, takes over the duties of Hans von Bülow, who died in Cairo, at the Berlin Philharmonic. First engagement conducting in Bayreuth (*Tannhäuser*); mounting distance from Cosima Wagner and her circle.

1895　Premiere of *Till Eulenspiegels lustige Streiche*, Op. 28, in Cologne.

1896　*Also sprach Zarathustra*, Op. 30, premieres in Frankfurt am Main. Break with Bayreuth, both for ideological reasons and because of irreconcilable differences with Wagner's son Siegfried (1869–1930); henceforth, Strauss is a *persona non grata* at the festival.

1897　*Enoch Arden*, Op. 38, premieres in Munich. Birth, in Munich, of Strauss's only child, Franz (1897–1980). (Pregnancy and delivery life-threatening for Pauline.)

1898　*Don Quixote*, Op. 35, premieres in Cologne. On October 1, appointed first Prussian Kapellmeister at the Court Opera House in Berlin, alongside Carl Muck (1859–1940); a twenty-year period of institutional ties to Berlin follows (until 1919); relocation to Charlottenburg (Knesebeckstraße 30). On September 30, together with jurist and musician Friedrich Rösch (1862–1925) and mathematician Hans Sommer (1837–1922), Strauss founds the *Genossenschaft deutscher Komponisten* for the purpose of influencing copyright law; in 1903, the organization is renamed *Genossenschaft deutscher Tonsetzer* (headed by Strauss); in 1915, members break off and found the *Genossenschaft zur Verwertung musikalischer Aufführungsrechte* (GEMA).

1899　Premiere of *Ein Heldenleben*, Op. 40, in Frankfurt am Main; contacts with Berlin Secession; first encounter with Hugo von Hofmannsthal (1874–1929).

1901　*Feuersnot*, Op. 50, premieres in Dresden, directed by Ernst von Schuch (1846–1914); a lifelong association with the Dresden Opera begins; elected chairman of the *Allgemeiner Deutscher Musikverein*.

1903   Honorary doctorate in philosophy from the University in Heidelberg; from now on, Strauss uses this title; premiere, on the same occasion, of *Taillefer*, Op. 52, at the municipal hall. First Strauss festival is held in London.

1904   *Symphonia domestica*, Op. 53, premieres in New York; Strauss founds and edits a monograph series, *Die Musik*; honorary membership in the *Vereinigung schaffender Tonkünstler* in Vienna; honorary citizenship in Cincinnati and Morgantown. Strauss takes up residence at Joachimsthaler Straße 17, Berlin (destroyed during the Second World War).

1905   Father's death in Munich. *Salome*, Op. 54, premieres in Dresden; public controversy ensues.

1906   Collaboration with Hugo von Hofmannsthal begins; plans for a villa in Garmisch.

1907   *Salome* produced in Paris; named officer of the *Legion d'Honneur*; co-editorship of the journal *Morgen*.

1908   Named General Music Director in Berlin (alongside Carl Muck); takes over managing concerts of the Royal Court Orchestra; already in 1905, the residency requirement is reduced (October to April), then a year off is granted—albeit with the ongoing duty of presiding over concerts given by the Hofkapelle. In May, Strauss moves into the Garmisch villa (Zoeppritzstraße) designed by Emanuel Seidl (1856–1919).

1909   Strauss Week in Dresden, including the premiere of *Elektra*, Op. 58; membership in the *Akademie der Künste*, Berlin; honorary chairmanship of the *Allgemeiner Deutscher Musikverein*.

1910   Mother's death in Munich. Strauss requests leave of absence as General Music Director, but still serves as guest conductor at the Hofkapelle. Receives the *Bayerischer Maximiliansorden für Wissenschaft und Kunst*. Strauss Weeks in Frankfurt and Munich.

1911   Premiere of *Der Rosenkavalier*, Op. 59, in Dresden. Engagement as General Music Director in Berlin comes to an end; ongoing engagement as standing conductor of the Hofkapelle and guest conductor at the Royal Opera. Publication of a biography by the conductor Max Steinitzer (1864–1936).

1912   Premiere, in Stuttgart, of *Ariadne auf Naxos/Der Bürger als Edelmann*, Op. 60, inspired by Max Reinhardt (1873–1943); Strauss moves into a luxurious apartment at Kaiserdamm 39 (today, Heerstraße 2) in Berlin (commemorative plaque).

1913   Premiere of *Festliches Präludium*, Op. 61, in Vienna for the opening of the new Konzerthaus; *Deutsche Motette*, Op. 62, premieres in Berlin.

1914   *Josephs Legende*, Op. 63, premieres in Paris; honorary doctorate from Oxford University; membership in the *Deutsche Gesellschaft 1914* headed by Wilhelm Solf; unveiling of a commemorative plaque where Strauss was born in Munich and naming of a street in his honor. London bank accounts blocked when war begins.

1915   *Eine Alpensinfonie*, Op. 64, premieres in Berlin (performed by the Dresden Hofkapelle).

1916   Premiere of *Ariadne auf Naxos—Neue Bearbeitung*, Op. 60, in Vienna; honorary membership in the *Gesellschaft der Musikfreunde* in Vienna.

1917   Reluctantly directs a master class in composition at the Berlin *Akademie der Künste* (until 1920); founding of the *Salzburger Festspiel-Gemeinde* in Vienna by Friedrich Gehmacher (1866–1942) and Heinrich Damisch (1872–1961); its artistic advisory board includes Hofmannsthal, Reinhardt, Strauss, Franz Schalk (1863–1931), and Alfred Roller (1864–1935).

1918 Final concert of the Berlin Hofkapelle on November 8, the evening before Wilhelm II abdicates; Strauss named interim director of the Berlin Opera; Strauss Week in Vienna; appointed director of the Vienna Opera (together with Franz Schalk), despite objections; after the war's end in November, confiscation of London assets.

1919 Premiere of *Die Frau ohne Schatten*, Op. 65, in Vienna; Strauss assumes duties here despite mounting resistance and moves to the city; temporary residence at Löwelstraße 8 (Mozartplatz), then Mozartgaße 4 (commemorative plaque); plans for a villa in the so-called chamber garden (*Kammergarten*) of the Belvedere, leased from the city for ninety years.

1921 Premiere of *Drei Hymnen* (Hölderlin), Op. 71, in Berlin; first Donaueschingen Chamber Music Festival, with Strauss as honorary chair; tour in the United States because of enduring financial difficulties; patron of the *Internationale Kammermusikaufführungen* in Salzburg, the forerunner of the *Internationale Gesellschaft für Neue Musik* (IGNM; Strauss is honorary president).

1922 Honorary membership in the *Salzburger Festspiel-Gemeinde*; first opera productions in Salzburg (Mozart).

1923 Honorary membership in the Academy of Fine Arts in Vienna and the Vienna Philharmonic.

1924 *Intermezzo*, Op. 72, premieres in Dresden; Strauss Festival in Vienna, including the premiere of *Schlagobers*, Op. 70; honorary citizenship in Munich, Vienna, and Salzburg; honorary president of the Salzburg Festival; membership in the *Orden pour le mèrite für Wissenschaften und Künste*; the Vienna contract is dissolved; Franz Strauss (son) marries Alice Grab (1904–1991).

1925 Premiere of *Parergon zur Symphonia domestica*, Op. 73, in Dresden. In December, Strauss moves into the new villa designed by Michael Rosenauer (1884–1971) in Vienna, Jacquingasse (commemorative plaque); honorary citizenship in Weimar.

1926 Film version of *Der Rosenkavalier* premieres in Dresden. Travel to Greece and plans for a festival hall in Athens; granted honorary citzenship in Naxos. Correspondence between Hofmannsthal and Strauss, reviewed by both parties and edited by Franz Strauss, is published.

1927 Birth of grandson, Richard († 2007).

1928 Premiere of *Die ägyptische Helena*, Op. 75, in Dresden; premiere of *Panathenäenzug*, Op. 74, in Dresden; premiere of *Die Tageszeiten*, Op. 76, in Vienna.

1929 Hofmannsthal dies unexpectedly in Rodaun (July 15), leaving the libretto of *Arabella* incomplete.

1932 Strauss Week in Munich. Through the mediation of Anton Kippenberg (1874–1950), first meeting with Stefan Zweig (1881–1942). Strauss's second grandson, Christian, is born.

1933 *Arabella*, Op. 79, premieres in Dresden on July 1, about half a year after Hitler becomes Reichskanzler; in light of the forced resignation of Fritz Busch (1890–1951) and SA attacks on theater manager Alfred Reucker (1868–1958), it represents a test of the dictatorship's power. Beginning of collaboration with Clemens Krauss (1893–1954). On April 16, Strauss signs the Munich letter of protest (*Protest der Richard-Wagner-Stadt München*) against Thomas Mann, forcing him into exile. That summer, Strauss returns to Bayreuth; for the last productions of *Parsifal* in the original staging, he replaces Arturo Toscanini, who has refused to perform in protest of National Socialist Germany. On November 15 (and following internal controversy), named president of the newly created Reichsmusikkammer; dedication of a Lied, *Das Bächlein* (based on an apocryphal Goethe poem, posthumously Op. 88, No. 1) to Joseph Goebbels.

1934 Honorary member of the Dresden State Opera; honorary citizen of the city. Named president of the *Ständiger Rat für die Internationale Zusammenarbeit der Komponisten*, a National Socialist organization founded to compete with the IGNM. Conducting engagement in Bayreuth (new staging of *Parsifal*). Awarded the *Adlerschild des Deutschen Reiches* (an honor dating to 1922, but continued throughout the National Socialist period). Named Knight Commander (*Großoffizier*) of the Order of Orange-Nassau by the Queen of the Netherlands. Receives Johannes Brahms Medal.

1935 *Die schweigsame Frau*, Op. 80, premieres in Dresden amidst great controversy; after four productions, the work is banned; because of contact with Zweig (and following the interception of a letter criticizing the government), Strauss is forced to resign his position at the Reichsmusikkammer; Hitler forbids further appearances at Bayreuth. Strauss continues to fail to appreciate the nature of the regime (in April, he still gave an autograph copy of *Arabella* to Göring as a wedding gift).

1936 Premiere of the *Olympische Hymne* (already commissioned in 1932 by the Olympic Committee) at the Olympic Stadium in Berlin for the opening of the Games on August 1. (In March 1935, Strauss already presided over a performance for Hitler.) Gold Medal from the Philharmonic Society in London.

1938 Premiere of *Friedenstag*, Op. 81, in Munich; premiere of *Daphne*, Op. 82, in Dresden. Despite massive reservations on the part of Goebbels, Strauss and his music are promoted to a kind of "state art." After "Kristallnacht" and the annexation of Austria, grave danger for the (Jewish) Grab family; at the last minute, arrangements are made for Alice's mother to flee to Switzerland; other family members emigrate, especially to the United States; in 1941, Elly Grab (aunt) dies following deportation to Łódź; confiscation of the family's assets.

1940 *Guntram*, Op. 25 (second version), premieres in Weimar.

1942 Premiere of *Capriccio*, Op. 85, in Munich; Vienna Beethoven Prize; Stefan Zweig commits suicide in Brazil.

1943 Premiere of Horn Concerto No. 2 in Salzburg. Brief internment of son and daughter-in-law in Vienna (ended by the intervention of Baldur von Schirach); failure of the spectacular effort (unattested in documents) to free Alice's grandmother from Theresienstadt by making a personal appearance at the camp.

1944 Semi-public dress rehearsal of *Die Liebe der Danae*, Op. 83, in Salzburg after performance ban is lifted (the actual premiere occurs in 1952). Premiere of *Aus der Werkstatt eines Invaliden* in Dresden. Strauss Weeks in Vienna and Dresden for the composer's eightieth birthday. Another letter criticizing the regime is intercepted in Garmisch, leading the composer to be declared a *persona non grata* in the National Socialist state; Strauss loses all privileges and his villa in Vienna.

1945 Following the end of the war, Strauss immediately relocates to Switzerland (with the assistance of Willi Schuh, 1900–1986): first to Baden (near Zurich), then, after a falling-out with the proprietor of the hotel *Verenahof*, to Montreux (Hotel Palace; monument).

1946 *Metamorphosen* premieres in Zurich; Sonatina No. 2 premieres in Winterthur; Oboe Concerto premieres in Zürich; operation in Lausanne (bladder stone).

1947 Symphonic Fantasia from *Die Frau ohne Schatten* premieres in Vienna; Austrian citizenship granted on January 31; on June 7, Strauss is cleared by the denazification tribunal in Garmisch. Conducts in England. Recordings with the *Orchestra della Radio della Svizzera Italiana*.

1948 Premiere of *Duett-Concertino* in Lugano; honorary membership in the IGNM (awarded in 1923) is revoked; another operation in Lausanne.

1949 Premiere of the Symphonic Fragment from *Josephs Legende* in Cincinnati. In May, Strauss returns from Montreux to Garmisch and is honored by the newly founded Free State of Bavaria; honorary citizen of Garmisch and Bayreuth; honorary doctorate from the University of Munich. On July 13, conducts publicly for the last time at the Munich Prinzregententheater. Dies September 8 in Garmisch. Funeral ceremonies in Munich (under the musical directorship of Georg Solti); many years later, the urn is transferred to the cemetery in Garmisch.

APPENDIX B

Catalog of Works

Drawing up a catalog of Strauss's works either in traditional, generic terms or along chronological lines proves difficult because the composer always insisted on the dichotomous relationship between tone poems and works for the stage; thereby, he adhered to a hierarchy of genres that was entirely his own. In Strauss's own estimation, the early, instrumental works preceded his *oeuvre*, properly speaking. By the same token, he viewed his late work—which did not merit being assigned opus numbers—as an afterthought. Accordingly, the following attempts to adhere to the composer's own hierarchy (while, at the same time, setting apart the Lieder in a traditional fashion, as Strauss himself did). For the genesis of a given work, the date of fair copy is used. Premieres (P) are indicated only in the case of orchestral works, operas, and large-scale vocal compositions; for unnumbered works, the date of initial publication (I) is provided. Information here relies on the catalogs established by Erich H. Mueller von Asow (1959–1974), the second edition of Franz Trenner's edition of the Lieder, as well as the encyclopedia entries by Bryan Gilliam (*New Grove 2*, 2001) and Walter Werbeck (*MGG 2*, 2006); that said, the forthcoming critical edition of Strauss's works will likely make considerable revisions necessary.

The most important editions are:
   Der junge Richard Strauss. Frühe Klaviermusik. 3 vols. Mainz 2003–2006.
   Richard Strauss Edition: Sämtliche Bühnenwerke. Sämtliche Orchesterwerke. 30 vols. Vienna 1996–1999.
   Richard Strauss: Lieder. Gesamtausgabe. Ed. Franz Trenner. London 1964.
   Willi Schuh (ed.). *Richard Strauss: Nachlese. Lieder aus der Jugendzeit und verstreute Lieder aus späten Jahren.* London and Bonn 1968.

Tone Poems
Aus Italien: Symphonic Fantasia [G major] for Large Orchestra, Op. 16 (1886), TrV 147.

   Piccolo, 2 flutes, 2 oboes (second also English horn), 2 clarinets, 2 bassoons, contrabassoon, 4 horns, 2 trumpets, 3 trombones, timpani, percussion (4 players), harp, strings
   Dedication: Hans von Bülow
   P: March 2, 1887, Munich, Odeon, Hofkapelle (Richard Strauss)

Macbeth: Tone Poem for Large Orchestra (after Shakespeare), Op. 23, TrV 163. Three versions (January 9, 1888, February 8, 1888, March 4, 1891).

3 flutes (third also piccolo), 2 oboes, English horn, 2 clarinets, bass clarinet, 2 bassoons, contrabassoon, 4 horns, 3 trumpets, bass trumpet, 3 trombones, tuba, timpani, percussion (4 players), strings (third version).
Dedication: Alexander Ritter
P: October 13, 1890, Weimar, Hoftheater, Hofkapelle (Richard Strauss) [second version]; February 29, 1892, Berlin, Philharmonie, Berliner Philharmoniker, Richard Strauss (third version).

Don Juan: Tone Poem (after Lenau) for Large Orchestra, Op. 20, TrV 156.

September 30, 1888
3 flutes (third version also piccolo), 2 oboes, English horn, 2 clarinets, 2 bassoons, contrabassoon, 4 horns, 3 trumpets, 3 trombones, tuba, timpani, percussion (3 players), harp, strings.
Dedication: Louis Thuille
P: November 11, 1889, Weimar, Hoftheater, Hofkapelle (Richard Strauss)

Tod und Verklärung: Tone Poem for Large Orchestra, Op. 24, TrV 158.

November 18, 1889
3 flutes, 2 oboes, English horn, 2 clarinets, bass clarinet, 2 bassoons, contrabassoon, 4 horns, 3 trumpets, 3 trombones, tuba, timpani, tam-tam, 2 harps, strings.
Dedication: Friedrich Rösch
P: June 21, 1890, Eisenach, Stadttheater, Hofkapelle Weimar (Richard Strauss)

Till Eulenspiegels lustige Streiche, nach alter Schelmenweise—in Rondeauform: Tone Poem for Large Orchestra, Op. 28, TrV 171.

May 6 1895
Piccolo, 3 flutes, 3 oboes, English horn, 3 clarinets, bass clarinet, 3 bassoons, contrabassoon, 8 horns, 6 trumpets, 3 trombones, tuba, timpani, percussion (3 players), 16 first violins, 16 second violins, 12 violas, 10 cellos, 8 contrabasses
Dedication: Arthur Seidl
P: November 5, 1895, Cologne, Gürzenich, Gürzenich-Orchester (Franz Wüllner)

Also sprach Zarathustra: Tone Poem (freely after Nietzsche) for Large Orchestra, Op. 30, TrV 176.

August 24, 1896
Piccolo, 3 flutes (third also second piccolo), 3 oboes, English horn, 3 clarinets, bass clarinet, 3 bassoons, contrabassoon, 6 horns, 4 trumpets, 3 trombones, 2 tubas, timpani, percussion (3 players), 2 harps, 16 first violins, 16 second violins, 12 violas, 12 cellos, 8 contrabasses, organ.
No dedication
P: November 27, 1896, Frankfurt am Main, Oper, Orchester der Museumsgesellschaft (Richard Strauss)

Don Quixote: Fantastic Variations on a Theme of Knightly Character for Large Orchestra, Op. 35, TrV 184.

December 29, 1897
Piccolo, 2 flutes, 2 oboes, English horn, 2 clarinets, bass clarinet, 3 bassoons, contrabassoon, 6 horns, 3 trumpets, 3 trombones, 2 tubas, timpani, percussion (2 players), harp, 16 first violins, 16 second violins, 12 violas, 10 cellos, 8 contrabasses
Dedication: Joseph Dupont
P: March 8, 1898, Cologne, Gürzenich, Gürzenich-Orchester (Franz Wüllner)

Ein Heldenleben: Tone Poem for Large Orchestra, Op. 40, TrV 190.

December 27, 1898 (final version)
Piccolo, 3 flutes, 3 oboes, English horn (also fourth oboe), 3 clarinets, bass clarinet, 3 bassoons, contrabassoon, 8 horns, 5 trumpets, 3 trombones, tenor tuba, tuba, timpani, percussion (4 players), 2 harps, 16 first violins, 16 second violins, 12 violas, 12 cellos, 8 contrabasses
Dedication: Willem Mengelberg and Concertgebouw Orchestra Amsterdam
P: March 3, 1899, Frankfurt am Main, Oper, Orchester der Museumsgesellschaft (Richard Strauss)

Symphonia domestica: For Large Orchestra, Op. 53, TrV 209.

December 31, 1903
Piccolo, 3 flutes, 2 oboes, oboe d'amore, English horn, 4 clarinets, bass clarinet, 4 saxophones, 4 bassoons, contrabassoon, 8 horns, 4 trumpets, 3 trombones, tuba, timpani, percussion (2 players), 2 harps, 16 first violins, 16 second violins, 12 violas, 10 cellos, 8 contrabasses
Dedication: Pauline and Franz Strauss
P: March 21, 1904, New York, Carnegie Hall, New York Philharmonic Orchestra (Richard Strauss)

Eine Alpensinfonie: For Large Orchestra, Op. 64, TrV 233.

February 8, 1915
4 (6) flutes (third and fourth also piccolo), 2 (4) oboes, English horn (also third oboe), heckelphone, 4 (6) clarinets (fourth also bass clarinet), 4 bassoons (fourth also contrabassoon), 8 horns (half also tenor tuba), 4 trumpets, 4 trombones, 2 tubas, timpani (2 players), percussion (3 players), 4 harps, celesta, at least 18 first violins, 16 second violins, 12 violas, 10 cellos, 8 contrabasses, organ. Offstage: 12 horns, 2 trumpets, 2 trombones
Dedication: Count Nicolaus von Seebach and the Royal Opera of Dresden (Königliche Kapelle Dresden)
P: October 28, 1915, Berlin, Philharmonie, Berliner Philharmoniker (Richard Strauss)

Stage Works, Music for Ballet

Guntram: Opera in Three Acts, Op. 25, TrV 168.

Libretto: Richard Strauss
September 5, 1893; revised several times; new version in 1934

The Old Duke (bass)—Freihild, *his daughter* (soprano)—Duke Robert, *her husband* (baritone)—Guntram, singer (tenor)—Friedhold, singer (bass)—The Duke's Jester (tenor)—Poor People: Old Woman (contralto), Old Man (tenor), Two Younger Men (bass)—A Boy (mute role)—Three Vassals (bass)—Messenger (baritone)—Four Minnesingers (two tenors, two basses)—Vassals of the Duke, Minnesingers, Four Monks, Servants, and Mercenaries

3 flutes (third also piccolo), 3 oboes (third also English horn), 3 clarinets (third also bass clarinet), 3 bassons, contrabassoon, 4 horns, 3 trumpets, bass trumpet, 3 trombones, tuba, timpani, percussion, lute (only first version), 2 harps, 16 first violins, 16 second violins, 12 violas, 10 cellos, 8 contrabasses. Stage music: 4 horns, 4 alto horns, 4 trumpets, 3 trombones, and 4 bugles

Dedication: Franz and Josepha Strauss

P: May 10, 1894, Weimar, Herzogliches Theater (Richard Strauss/Ferdinand Wiedey)/ October 29, 1940, Weimar, Deutsches Nationaltheater (Paul Sixt/Rudolf Hesse)

Feuersnot: Sung Poem in One Act, Op. 50, TrV 203.

Libretto: Ernst von Wolzogen (1855–1934).

May 22, 1901

Schweiker von Gundelfingen, The Bailiff (low tenor)—Ortolf Sentlinger, The Mayor (low bass)—Diemut, *his daughter* (high soprano)—Her Friends: Elsbeth (mezzo-soprano), Wigelis (low contralto)—Margret (high soprano)—Kunrad, *sorceror* (high baritone)— Jörg Pöschel, *innkeeper* (low bass)—Hämerlein, *grocer* (baritone)—Kofel, *blacksmith* (bass)—Kunz Gilgenstock, *baker and brewer* (bass)—Ortlieb Tulbeck, *master cooper* (high tenor)—Ursula, *his wife* (contralto)—Ruger Aspeck, *potter* (tenor)—Walpurg, *his wife* (high soprano)—[A large girl [soprano)]—Townsfolk [chorus], Children [chorus], Ducal Servants

3 flutes (third also piccolo), 3 oboes (second and third also English horn), 3 clarinets (third also bass clarinet), 3 bassoons (third also contrabassoon), 4 horns, 3 trumpets, 3 trombones, tuba, timpani, percussion, 2 harps, 12 first violins, 12 second violins, 8 violas, 8 cellos, 6 contrbasses; stage music with harmonium, harp, glockenspiel, 2 piccolo trumpets, solo violin, solo cello

Dedication: Friedrich Rösch

P: November 21, 1901, Dresden, Königliches Opernhaus (Ernst von Schuch/ Maximilian Moris)

Salome: Music Drama in One Act after Hedwig Lachmann's Translation of Oscar Wilde's Eponymous Work, Op. 54, TrV 215.

June 20, 1905 (without dance)

Herodes (tenor)—Herodias (mezzo-soprano)—Salome (soprano)—Jochanaan (baritone)—Narraboth (tenor)—A Page of Herodias (contralto)—5 Jews (4 tenors, 1 bass)—2 Nazarenes (tenor, bass)—2 Soldiers (base)—A Cappadocian (bass)—A Slave (soprano)

Piccolo, 3 flutes, 2 oboes, English horn, heckelphone, 5 clarinets, bass clarinet, 3 bassoons, contrabasson, 6 horns, 4 trumpets, 4 trombones, tuba, timpani, small timpani, percussion (6–7 players), 2 harps, celesta, 16 first violins, 16 second violins, 10–12 violas, 10 cellos, 8 contrabasses; stage music with harmonium and organ

Dedication: Edgar Speyer

P: December 9, 1905, Dresden, Königliches Opernhaus (Ernst von Schuch/Willi Wirk)

Elektra: Tragedy in One Act by Hugo von Hofmannsthal, Op. 58, TrV 223.

September 22, 1908

Clytemnestra (mezzo-soprano)—*her daughters* Elektra (soprano) and Chrysotemis (soprano)—Aegisthus (tenor)—Orestes (baritone)—Tutor of Orestes (bass)—Confidante (soprano)—Trainbearer (soprano)—Young Servant (tenor)—Old Servant (bass)—Overseer (soprano)—5 Maids (1 contralto, 2 mezzo-soprano, 2 soprano)—Men and women of the household

Piccolo, 3 flutes (third also piccolo), 3 oboes (third also English horn), heckelphone, 5 clarinets, 2 basset horns, bass clarinet, 3 bassoons, contrabassoon, 4 horns, 4 tubas (also horns), 6 trumpets, bass trumpet, 3 trombones, contrabass trombone, contrabass tuba, timpani (2 players), percussion (4 players), celesta, 4 harps, 8 first violins, 8 second violins, 8 third violins, 6 first violas (also fourth violin), 6 second violas, 6 third violas, 6 first cellos, 6 second cellos, 8 contrabasses

Dedication: Willy and Natalie Levin

P: January 25, 1909, Dresden, Königliches Opernhaus (Ernst von Schuch / Georg Toller)

Der Rosenkavalier: Comedy for Music in Three Acts by Hugo von Hofmannsthal, Op. 59, TrV 227.

September 26, 1910

The Marschallin, Princess von Werdenberg (soprano)—Baron Ochs auf Lerchenau (bass)—Octavian, *called Quinquin, a young gentleman from a prominent family* (mezzo-soprano)—Herr von Faninal, *a rich, newly ennobled merchant* (high baritone)—Sophie, *his daughter* (high soprano)—Marianne Leitmetzerin, *the Duenna* (high soprano)—Valzacchi, *an intriguer* (tenor)—Annina, *his accomplice* (contralto) – A Police Inspector (bass) – Major-Domo to the Princess (tenor)—Major-Domo to Faninal (tenor)—A Notary (bass)—An Innkeeper (tenor)—A Singer (high tenor)—A Scholar—A Flute-Player—A Hairdresser—His Assistant—A Noble Widow (mute roles)—Three Noble Orphans (soprano, mezzo-soprano, contralto)—A Milliner (soprano)—An Animal-Seller (tenor)—4 Lackeys (2 tenor, 2 bass)—4 Waiters (1 tenor, 3 bass)—A small negro, soldiers, cooks, guests, musicians, guards, small children, and assorted suspicious characters.

3 flutes (third also piccolo), 3 oboes (third also English horn), 3 clarinets, basset horn (also bass clarinet), 3 bassons (third also contrabassoon), 4 horns, 3 trumpets, 3 trombones, tuba, timpani, percussion (3 players), celesta, 2 harps, 16 first violins, 16 second violins, 12 violas, 10 cellos, 8 contrabasses; stage music with 2 flues, oboe, C clarinet, 2 B♭ clarinets, 2 bassoons, 2 horns, trumpet, piccolo trumpet, harmonium, piano, strings (solo or "amply doubled" [*in reichlicher Verdopplung*])

Dedication: Pschorr family

P: January 26, 1911, Dresden, Königliches Opernhaus (Ernst von Schuch/Georg Toller—[Max Reinhardt])

Ariadne auf Naxos: Opera in One Act by Hugo von Hofmannsthal. For Performance after Molière's *Bourgeois Gentleman*, Op. 60, TrV 228.

July 22, 1912

Ariadne (soprano)—Bacchus (tenor)—Naiad (high soprano)—Dryad (contralto)—Echo (soprano)—Zerbinetta (high soprano)—Harlequin (baritone)—Scaramuccio (tenor)—Truffaldino (bass)—Brighella (tenor)
2 flutes, 2 oboes, 2 clarinets, 2 bassoons, 2 horns, trumpet, trombone, timpani, percussion (3 players), 2 harps, piano, harmonium, celesta, 6 violins, 4 violas, 4 cellos, 2 contrabasses (the stage music also includes 2 piccolos, omitting celesta and harmonium)
Dedication: Max Reinhardt
P: October 25, 1912, Stuttgart, Königliches Hoftheater—Kleines Haus (Richard Strauss/Max Reinhardt)

Ariadne auf Naxos: Opera in One Act, besides a Prelude, by Hugo von Hofmannsthal. New Version, Op. 60, TrV 228a.

June 20, 1916
Prelude: Major-Domo (spoken)—Music teacher (baritone)—Composer (soprano)—The Tenor/Bacchus (tenor)—An Officer (tenor)—The Dancing Master (tenor)—A Wigmaker (high bass)—A Lackey (bass)—Zerbinetta (high soprano)—Primadonna/Ariadne (Sopran)—Harlequin (baritone)—Scaramuccio (tenor)—Truffaldino (bass)—Brighella (high tenor)—Opera: Ariadne (soprano)—Bacchus (tenor)—Najade (high soprano)—Dryad (contralto)—Echo (soprano) –Intermezzo: Zerbinetta (high soprano), Harlequin (baritone), Scaramuccio (tenor), Truffaldino (bass), Brighella (tenor)
2 flutes, 2 oboes, 2 clarinets (second also bass clarinet), 2 bassoons, 2 horns, trumpet, trombone, percussion (3 players), 2 harps, piano, harmonium, celesta, 6 violins, 4 violas, 4 cellos, 2 contrabasses
Dedication: Max Reinhardt
P: October 4, 1916, Vienna, K. K. Hofoperntheater (Franz Schalk/Wilhelm von Wymetal)

Josephs Legende [*La Légende de Joseph*]: Ballet in One Act by Harry Graf von Kessler and Hugo von Hofmannsthal, Op. 63, TrV 231.

February 2, 1914
Potiphar—Potiphar's Wife—Her Favorite Slave—Potiphar's Guests- Potiphar's Major-Domo—Potiphar's Servants, Guards, and Slaves—A Sheik—His Eight Attendants—His Young Servant—Three Veiled Women—Three Unveiled Women—The Veiled Women's Servants—Two Overseers—Sulamith, a Dancer—Six Boxers—Their Companions—Joseph, *a fifteen-year-old shepherd* —Six boys, *his friends* –Potiphar's Henchman—A Male Angel, *clad entirely in gold armor.*
Piccolo, 4 flutes (fourth also piccolo), 3 oboes (third also English horn), heckelphone, 3 clarinets, bass clarinet, contrabass clarinet, 4 bassoons (fourth also contrabassoon), 6 horns, 4 trumpets, 4 trombones, tenor tuba, bass tuba, timpani (2 players), percussion (3 players), celesta, 4 harps, piano, 10 first violins, 10 second violins, 10 third violins, 8 first violas, 8 second violas, 6 first cellos, 6 second cellos, 8 contrabasses; stage music: organ
Dedication: Edouard Hermann
P: May 14, 1914, Paris, Théâtre National de l'Opéra—Ballets Russes de Serge Diaghilev (Richard Strauss/Michel Fokine)

Die Frau ohne Schatten. Opera in Three Acts by Hugo von Hofmannsthal, Op. 65, TrV 234.

> June 24, 1917
>
> The Emperor (tenor)—The Empress (high dramatic soprano)—The Nurse (dramatic mezzo-soprano)—The Spirit-Messenger (high baritone)—The Guardian at the Threshold of the Temple (soprano or countertenor)—The Apparition of a Youth (high tenor)—The Voice of a Falcon (soprano)—A Voice from Above (contralto)—Barak the Dyer (bass-baritone)—His Wife (high dramatic soprano)—*The dyer's brother*, the One-Eyed Man (high bass)—*his brother*, the One-Armed Man (bass)—*his brother,* The Hunchback (high tenor)—Voices of Six Children (three soprano, three contralto)— *Voices of the City's Watchmen* (three high basses)—*Imperial Servants, Foreign Children, Spirit-Servants, Spirit-Voices*
>
> 4 flutes (third and fourth also piccolo), 3 oboes (third also English horn), 5 clarinets (fourth also basset horn, fifth also bass clarinet), 4 bassoons, (fourth also contrabassoon), 8 horns (fourth–eighth also tuba), 4 (6) trumpets, 4 trombones, bass tuba, timpani, percussion (4 players, including glass harmonica, 5 Chinese gongs, switch, and bells), 2 celestas, 2 harps, 16 first violins, 16 second violins, 6 first violas, 6 second violas, 6 first cellos, 6 second cellos, 8 contrabasses; stage music with 2 flutes, oboe, 2 clarinets, bassoon, horn, 6 trumpets (the first two at the end of Act Three, in the orchestra), 6 trombones, wind machine, thunder machine, organ, 4 tam-tams
>
> P: October 10, 1919, Vienna, Operntheater—Staatsoper (Franz Schalk/Hans Breuer)

Schlagobers: Gay Vienna Ballet in Two Acts, Op. 70, TrV 243.

> Libretto: Richard Strauss
>
> September 16, 1922
>
> Princess Pralinee—Prince Nicolo, *her major-domo*—Princess Teeblüte—Prince Kaffee—Prince Kakao—Don Zuckero—Mademoiselle Marianne Chartreuse— Liqueurs: Ladislav Slivovitz, Boris Wutki—A Doctor—Candidates for Confirmation and their Sponsors—Princess Pralinee's Royal Attendants: Firecrackers, Little Pralines, Quince Sausages—Four Heralds with Trumpets—Chorus of Giant Gugelhupfs, *Baumkuchen*, Christmas Stollen, Soft Pretzels, Dumplings, Puff Pastries, *Kaffeestriezel*— Oriental Mages—The Army of Marzipan, Gingerbread, and Plum Men—Whipped Cream (*Schlagobers*)
>
> Piccolo (also fourth flute), 3 flutes, 2 oboes, English horn, 3 clarinets, bass clarinet (also fourth clarinet), 3 bassoons, contrabassoon (also fourth bassoon), 4 horns, 3 trumpets, 3 trombones, tuba, timpani, percussion, celesta, 2 harps, 12 first violins, 12 second violins, 8 violas, 8 cellos, 6 contrabasses
>
> Dedication: Ludwig Karpath
>
> P: May 9, 1924, Vienna, Operntheater—Staatsoper (Richard Strauss/Heinrich Kröller)

Intermezzo: A Bourgeois Comedy with Symphonic Interludes in Two Acts, Op. 72, TrV 246.

> Libretto: Richard Strauss
>
> August 21, 1923
>
> Christine (soprano)—Little Franzl (eight years old), her son [speaking part]— Hofkapellmeister Robert Storch, her husband (baritone)—Anna, her lady-in-waiting

(soprano)—Baron Lummer (tenor)—The Notary (baritone)—His Wife (soprano)—A Kapellmeister (tenor)—Robert's Fellow Card Players: A Counsellor of Commerce (baritone), A Chamber Counsellor (baritone), A Chamber Singer (bass)—(A Young Girl [speaking part]—Chambermaids, Housemaids, Cook

2 flutes (second also piccolo), 2 oboes (second also English horn), 2 clarinets (second also bass clarinet), 2 bassoons, 3 horns, 2 trumpets, 2 trombones, timpani, percussion, harp, piano, large harmonium, strings (11 first violins, 9 second violins, 5 violas, 5 cellos, 3 contrabasses)

Dedication: Franz Strauss

P: November 4, 1924, Dresden, Sächsische Staatstheater—Schauspielhaus (Fritz Busch/Alois Mora)

Die ägyptische Helena: Opera in Two Acts by Hugo von Hofmannsthal, Op. 75. TrV 255.

October 8, 1927

Helen (soprano)—Menelaus (tenor)—Hermione, *their child* (soprano)—Aïthra, *daughter of an Egyptian king: a sorceress* (soprano)—Altaïr (baritone)—Da-Ud, *his son* (tenor)—Aithra's First Servant (soprano)—Aithra's Second Servant (mezzo-soprano)—First Elf (soprano)—Second Elf (soprano)—Third Elf (contralto)—The All-Knowing Seashell (contralto)—Elves, Warriors, Slaves, Eunuchs

4 flutes (third and fourth also piccolo), 2 oboes, English horn, 3 clarinets, bass clarinet, 3 bassoons (third also contrabassoon), 6 horns, 6 trumpets, 3 trombones, bass tuba, timpani, percussion, celesta, organ, 2 harps, 16 first violins, 16 second violins, 10 violas, 10 cellos, 8 contrabasses. Stage music: 6 oboes, 6 clarinets, 4 horns, 2 trumpets, 4 trombones, timpani, 4 triangles, 2 tambourines, wind machine

Dedication: Heinz Tietjen (1931)

P: June 6, 1928, Dresden, Sächsische Staatstheater—Opernhaus (Fritz Busch/Otto Erhardt)

Arabella: Lyric Comedy in Two Acts by Hugo von Hofmannsthal, Op. 79. TrV 263.

October 12, 1932

Count Waldner, *a retired cavalry officer* (bass)—Adelaide, *his wife* (mezzo-soprano)—Their Daughters: Arabella (soprano), Zdenka (soprano)—Mandryka (baritone)—Matteo, *a young officer* (tenor)—Arabella's Suitors: Count Elemer (tenor)—Count Dominik (baritone)—Count Lamoral (bass)—The Fiakermilli (coloratura soprano)—A Fortune-Teller (soprano)—Welko, *Mandryka's military attendant* [*Leibhusar*] [speaking role/tenor]—Mandryka's Servants: Djura [speaking role], Jankel [speaking role]—A Room Waiter [speaking role]—Arabella's Attendant [mute role]—Three Card Players [3 basses]—A Doctor [mute role]—Groom [mute role]—Cab Driver, Ball Guests, Hotel Guests, A Waiter

3 flutes (third also piccolo), 2 oboes, English horn, 3 clarinets, bass clarinet, 3 bassoons (third also contrabassoon), 4 horns, 3 trumpets, 3 trombones, tuba, timpani, harp, strings

Dedication: Alfred Reucker, Fritz Busch

P: July 1, 1933, Dresden, Sächsische Staatstheater—Opernhaus (Clemens Krauss/Josef Gielen)

Die schweigsame Frau: Comic Opera in Three Acts, freely after Ben Jonson, by Stefan

Zweig, Op. 80, TrV 265.

January 17, 1935
Sir Morosus (bass)—His Housekeeper (contralto)—The Barber (high baritone)—Actors: Henry Morosus (tenor)—Aminta, *his wife* (coloratura soprano)—Isotta (coloratura soprano)—Carlotta (mezzo-soprano)—Morbio (baritone)—Vanuzzi (deep bass)—Farfallo (deep bass)—Chorus of Actors and Neighbors
3 flutes (third also piccolo), 2 oboes, English horn, 3 clarinets, bass clarinet, 3 bassoons (third also contrabassoon), 4 horns, 3 trumpets, 3 trombones, bass tuba, timpani, percussion (4 players), celesta, harp, 14 first violins, 12 second violins, 8 violas, 8 cellos, 5–6 contrabasses. Stage music: organ, harpsichord, trumpets, bagpipes, drums
P: June 24, 1935, Dresden, Sächsische Staatstheater—Opernhaus (Karl Böhm/Josef Gielen)

Friedenstag: Opera in One Act by Joseph Gregor [in collaboration with Stefan Zweig], Op. 81, TrV 271.

June 14, 1936
Commandant of the Besieged Town (baritone)—Maria, *his wife* (soprano)—Military men: Sergeant (bass), Marksman (tenor), Constable (baritone), Musketeer (bass), Hornist (bass), Officer (baritone), Front-Line Officer (baritone)—A Piedmontese (tenor)—The Holsteiner, *commander of the besieging army* (bass)—Mayor of the Besieged Town (tenor)—Bishop of the Besieged Town (baritone)—A Woman of the People (soprano)—Soldiers on both sides, Town Elders, Women of the Deputation to the Commandant, Townspeople
3 flutes (third also piccolo), 2 oboes, English horn, 3 clarinets, bass clarinet, 3 bassoons, contrabassoon, 6 horns, 4 trumpets, 4 trombones, tuba, timpani, percussion, 16 first violins, 16 second violins, 12 violas, 10 cellos, 6 contrabasses. Stage music: organ, clarion, bells
Dedication: Viorica Ursuleac, Clemens Krauss
P: July 24, 1938, Munich, Bayerische Staatsoper—Nationaltheater (Clemens Krauss/Rudolf Hartmann)

Daphne: Bucolic Tragedy in One Act by Joseph Gregor, Op. 82, TrV 272.

December 24, 1937
Peneios (bass)—Gaea (contralto)—Daphne (soprano)—Leukippos (tenor)—Apollo (tenor)—First Shepherd (baritone)—Second Shepherd (tenor)—Third Shepherd (bass)—Fourth Shepherd (bass)—First Maid (soprano)—Second Maind (soprano)—Shepherds, Masked Members of the Bacchic Procession, Maids
3 flutes (third also piccolo), 2 oboes, English horn, 3 clarinets, basset horn, bass clarinet, 3 bassoons, contrabassoon, 4 horns, 3 trumpets, 3 trombones, tuba, timpani, percussion, 2 harps, 16 first violins, 16 second violins, 12 violas, 10 cellos, 8 contrabasses. Stage music: organ, alphorn
Dedication: Karl Böhm
P: October 15, 1938, Dresden, Sächsische Staatstheater—Opernhaus (Karl Böhm/Max Hofmüller)

Die Liebe der Danae: Gay Mythology in Three Acts by Joseph Gregor [based on a scenario by Hugo von Hofmannsthal], Op. 83, TrV 278.

June 28, 1940

Jupiter (baritone)—Mercury (tenor)—Pollux, *King of Eos* (tenor)—Danae, *his daughter* (soprano)—Xanthe, *Danae's servant* (soprano)—Midas (tenor)—Four Kings, *nephews to Pollux* (2 tenors, 2 basses)—Four Queens: Semele (soprano), Europa (soprano), Alkmene (mezzo-soprano), Leda (contralto)—Four Guards (basses)—Chorus of Creditors (tenors and basses)—Servants and Attendants to Pollux—Servants and Attendants to Danae—The People

Piccolo, 3 flutes (second and third also piccolo), 2 oboes, English horn, 3 clarinets, basset horn, 3 bassoons, contrabassoon, 6 horns, 4 trumpets, 4 trombones, tuba, timpani, percussion (2 players), 2 harps, celesta, piano, 16 first violins, 16 second violins, 12 violas, 10 cellos, contrabass

Dedication: Heinz Tietjen

P: August 14, 1952, Salzburg, Festspielhaus [dress rehearsal August 16, 1944] (Clemens Krauss/Rudolf Hartmann)

Capriccio: A Conversation-Piece for Music in One Act by Clemens Krauss and Richard Strauss [in collaboration with Hans Swarowsky], Op. 85, TrV 279.

August 3, 1941

The Countess (soprano)—The Count, *her brother* (baritone)—Flamand, *a musician* (tenor)—Olivier, *a poet* (baritone)—La Roche, *theater director* (bass)—Clairon, *actress* (contralto)—Monsieur Taupe (tenor)—An Italian Singer (soprano)—An Italian Tenor (tenor)—A Young Dancer—The Major-Domo (bass)—Eight servants (4 tenors, 4 basses)—Three Musicians (violinist, cellist, harpsichordist)

3 flutes (third also piccolo), 2 oboes, English horn, 3 clarinets, basset horn, bass clarinet, 3 bassoons (third also contrabassoon), 4 horns, 2 trumpets, 3 trombones, timpani, percussion, 2 harps, harpsichord, strings, 16 first violins, 16 second violins, 10 violas, 10 cellos, 6 contrabasses. Stage music: string sextet, violin, cello, harpsichord

Dedication: Clemens Krauss

P: October 28, 1942, Munich, Bayerische Staatsoper—Nationaltheater (Clemens Krauss/Rudolf Hartmann)

Excerpts from the Operas

Salomes Tanz, Op 54, TrV 215a.

before August 30, 1905 (premiere with the opera)

Der Rosenkavalier: Waltz Sequence No. 2 [from Act Three], Op. 59, TrV 227a.

1910/11
P: probably 1911.

Der Rosenkavalier: Suite for Orchestra, Op. 59, 1945.

P: September 28, 1946, Vienna, Konzerthaus (Hans Swarowsky)

Der Rosenkavalier: Waltz Sequence No. 1 [from Acts One and Two], Op. 59, TrV 227c.

November 15, 1944

P: August 4, 1946, London, Queen's Hall (Erich Leinsdorf)

Militärmarsch from the film version of *Der Rosenkavalier,* Op. 59. TrV 227b.

October 18, 1925 (premiere with the film)

Der Bürger als Edelmann: Suite, Op. 60, TrV 228c.

October 11, 1917, revised 1920
P: January 31, 1920, Vienna, Prinz-Eugen-Palais (Richard Strauss)

Four Symphonic Interludes from *Intermezzo,* TrV 246a.

August 21, 1923, arranged 1924
P: January 15, 1924, Vienna (Adapted for two pianos for the marriage of Franz Strauss [son])

Suite from *Schlagobers,* TrV 243a.

September 16, 1922
P: November 8, 1932, Mannheim, Konzerthaus (Richard Strauss)

Sextet from *Capriccio,* TrV 279a.

August 3, 1941, excerpted from the opera 1943.

Dances from *Capriccio* for violin, cello, and harpsichord, TrV 279b.

August 3, 1941, excerpted from the opera 1943.

An den Baum Daphne ("Geliebter Baum") for nine-voice chorus (Gregor), TrV 272a.

November 13, 1943, dedicated to the chorus of the Vienna State Opera
[I: London 1958]
P: January 5, 1947, Vienna, Konzerthaus (Felix Prohaska)

Suite from *Capriccio* for harpsichord, TrV 279c.

June 5, 1944
P: November 6, 1946, Vienna, Konzerthaus (Isolde Ahlgrimm)

Andante on a Theme from *Daphne* for Solo Violin [*Daphne*-Etude], TrV 272b.

February 27, 1945 (composed for Christian Strauss)

Symphonic Fantasia from *Die Frau ohne Schatten,* TrV 234a.

May 30, 1946
P: June 26, 1947, Vienna, Konzerthaus (Karl Böhm)

Symphonic Fragment from *Josephs Legende,* TrV 231a.

February 4, 1947
P: March 1949, Cincinnati, Music Hall (Fritz Reiner)

Adaptations of Stage Works and Film

Romeo und Julia: Four Pieces of Incidental Music for Shakespeare's Play (1887), TrV 150.

P: Munich, Königliches Hof- und Nationaltheater, October 23, 1887

Fanfare, for Large Orchestra, for Ernst von Wildenbruch's Scenic Epilogue to August Wilhelm Iffland's *Die Jäger* (1891), TrV 165.

P: Weimar, Großherzogliches Hoftheater, May 7, 1891 (Richard Strauss)

Christoph Willibald Gluck's *Iphigénie en Tauride* arranged for Orchestra (1890), TrV 161.

New translation and stage adaptation
P: Weimar, Großherzogliches Hoftheater, June 9, 1900 (Rudolf Krzyzanowski)

Acht Lebende Bilder: Three Pieces of Incidental Music Celebrating the Golden Wedding Anniversary of His Royal Highness, Grand Duke Carl Alexander, and Wife, Grand Duchess Sophie von Sachsen-Weimar-Eisenach (1892), TrV 167.

P: Weimar, Großherzogliches Hoftheater, October 8, 1892 (Richard Strauss)
The other compositions for the occasion were authored by Eduard Lassen and Hans von Bronsart; Weimar materials have been preserved only in fragmentary form. In 1895, Strauss reworked his second contribution ("Begegnung und Friedensschluß zwischen Moritz von Oranien und Marquis von Spinola [1609]") as "Bismarck-Festmarsch"; in 1931, he rewrote the third part ("Herzog Bernhard der Große von Weimar in der Schlacht bei Lützen [1632]") as "Kampf und Sieg."

Der Bürger als Edelmann. Comedy, with Dances, by Molière. Freely adapted for the stage in three acts by Hugo von Hofmannsthal. Op. 60, TrV 228b.

Dedication: Max Reinhardt
P: April 9, 1918, Berlin, Deutsches Theater (Einar Nilson/Max Reinhardt)

Ludwig van Beethoven/August von Kotzebue: *Die Ruinen von Athen*. A Festival with dances and choruses. Music partially incorporating Ludwig van Beethoven's ballet *Die Geschöpfe des Prometheus*, newly adapted by Hugo von Hofmannsthal and Richard Strauss (1924). TrV 249.

P: September 20, 1924, Vienna, Operntheater (Staatsoper), September 20, 1924 (Richard Strauss/Josef Turnau)

Der Rosenkavalier, TrV 227b.

Film 1925
Screenplay: Hugo von Hofmannsthal; Sets and Costumes: Alfred Roller et al.; Directed by Robert Wiene
P: January 10, 1926, Dresden, Sächsische Staatstheater—Opernhaus (Richard Strauss)

Wolfgang Amadeus Mozart: *Idomeneo, rè di Creta*, KV 366.

New adaptation by Lothar Wallerstein and Richard Strauss (1930), TrV 262.
[Dedication: Franz Schneiderhan and Clemens Krauss]
P: April 16, 1931, Vienna, Operntheater—Staatsoper—(Richard Strauss/Lothar Wallerstein)

Dance Music

Dance Suite after François Couperin, arranged and adapted for a small orchestra (1923), TrV 245.

P: February 17, 1923, Vienna, Theater im Redoutensaal der Hofburg (Clemens Krauss)

Verklungene Feste. Dance Visions from Two Centuries. Choreography based on historical models by Pia and Pino Mlakar. Music after François Couperin for a small orchestra (1940/41), TrV 245a.

P: April 5, 1941, Munich, Bayerische Staatsoper—Nationaltheater (Clemens Krauss)

Symphonies and Concertos

Symphony [No. 1] in D minor (1880), TrV 94.

2 flutes, 2 oboes, 2 clarinets, 2 bassoons, 4 horns, 2 trumpets, 3 trombones, timpani, strings
P: March 30, 1881, Munich, Odeon (Hermann Levi)

Symphony [No. 2] in F minor, Op. 12 (1884), TrV 126.

2 flutes, 2 oboes, 2 clarinets, 2 bassoons, 4 horns, 2 trumpets, 3 trombones, tuba, timpani, strings
P: December 13, 1884, New York, Philharmonic Society (Theodore Thomas)

Festliches Präludium, Op. 61 (1913), TrV 229.

Piccolo, 4 flutes, 4 oboes, heckelphone, 5 clarinets, 4 bassoons, contrabassoon, 8 horns, 4 trumpets, 4 trombones, tuba, timpani (2 players), percussion, 20 first violins, 20 second violins, 12 first violas, 12 second violas, 10 first cellos, 10 second cellos, 12 contrabasses, organ. Offstage: 12 trumpets.
P: October 19, 1913, Vienna, Konzerthaus (Ferdinand Löwe)

Divertimento [after François Couperin], Op. 86 (1940/41), TrV 245b.

2 flutes, 2 oboes (second also English horn), 2 clarinets, 2 bassoons, 2 horns, trumpet, trombone, timpani, percussion, celesta, harpsichord, harp, 3–6 first violins, 3–6 second violins, 2–4 violas, 2–4 cellos, contrabass, organ (harmonium)
P: January 31, 1943, Vienna, Musikverein (Clemens Krauss)

Romance in E♭ major for Clarinet and Orchestra (1879), TrV 80.

Solo clarinet, 2 oboes, 2 bassoons, 2 horns, strings
P: Summer 1879, Munich, Ludwigsgymnasium

Violin Concerto in D minor, Op. 8 (1882), TrV 110.

Solo violin, 2 flutes, 2 oboes, 2 clarinets, 2 bassoons, 4 horns, 2 trumpets, timpani, strings
P: December 5, 1882, Vienna, Bösendorfersaal (piano excerpt); March 4, 1890, Cologne, Gürzenich (Benno Walter/Franz Wüllner)

Horn Concerto in E♭ major [No. 1], Op. 11 (1883), TrV 117.

Solo French horn, 2 flutes, 2 oboes, 2 clarinets, 2 bassoons, 2 horns, 2 trumpets, timpani, strings
P: Early 1883, Munich, Tonkünstlerverein (piano excerpt); March 4, 1885, Meiningen, Hoftheater (Gustav Leinhos/Hans von Bülow)

Romance in F major for Cello and Orchestra (1883), TrV 118.

Solo cello, 2 flutes, 2 oboes, 2 clarinets, 2 bassoons, 2 horns, strings
P: probably February 15, 1884, Baden-Baden

Burleske in D minor for Piano and Orchestra (1886), TrV 145.

Solo piano, piccolo, 2 flutes, 2 oboes, 2 clarinets, 2 bassoons, 4 horns, 2 trumpets, timpani, strings
P: June 21, 1890, Eisenach, Stadttheater (Eugen d'Albert/Richard Strauss)

Parergon zur Symphonia Domestica for Piano and Orchestra, Op. 73 (1925), TrV 209a.

Solo piano (left hand), 2 flutes, 2 oboes, English horn, 2 clarinets, bass clarinet, 2 bassoons, contrabassoon, 4 horns, 2 trumpets, 3 trombones, tuba, timpani, harp, 12 first violins, 12 second violins, 8 violas, 8 cellos, 6 contrabasses
P: October 6, 1925, Dresden, Gewerbehaus (Paul Wittgenstein/Fritz Busch)

Panathenäenzug: Symphonic Etudes in Passacaglia Form for Piano and Orchestra, Op. 74 (1927), TrV 254.

Solo piano (left hand), 3 flutes (third also piccolo), 2 oboes, English horn, 2 clarinets, bass clarinet, 3 bassoons, 4 horns, 3 trumpets, 3 trombones, tuba, timpani, percussion, harp, celesta, strings
P: January 16, 1928, Berlin, Philharmonie (Paul Wittgenstein/Bruno Walter)

Smaller Orchestral Works

Overture to *Hochlands Treue* (ca. 1873), TrV 17.
   Concert Overture in B minor (1876), TrV 41, "Arranged with the assistance of Herr Kapellmeister Meyer"
   Festmarsch in E♭ major, Op. 1 (1876), TrV 43 (P: Munich 1881, Franz Strauss)
   Serenade in G major for orchestra (1877), TrV 52 (P: Munich 1878 [?], Franz Strauss).
   Overture in E♭ major (1878), TrV 69.
   Overture in A minor (1879), TrV 83.
   Concert Overture in C minor (1883), TrV 125 (P: Munich 1883, Hermann Levi).
   Festmarsch in D major (1884, rev. 1887), TrV 135 (P: Munich 1885, Franz Strauss).
   Festmarsch in C major for large orchestra (1888/89), TrV 157 (P: Munich 1889, Franz Strauss).
   Two Military Marches for Large Orchestra, Op. 57 (1906), TrV 221 (P: Berlin 1907, Richard Strauss).
   München, A Commemorative Waltz for Large Orchestra (1939, revised in 1945 as *Ein Gedächtniswalzer*), TrV 274 (P: Munich, 1939, Carl Ehrenberg; Vienna 1951, Fritz Lehmann).
   Festival Music, Op. 84. To celebrate 2,600 years of Imperial Japan. For Large Orchestra (1940), TrV 277. (P: Tokyo 1940, Helmut Fellmer).

Chamber Music

Etudes for solo Horns in E♭ and E (ca. 1873), TrV 15.
Concertante for piano quartet (ca. 1875), TrV 33.
Piano Trio [No. 1] in A major (1877), TrV 53.
Introduction, Theme, and Variations in E♭ major for hunting horn and piano (1878), TrV 70.
Piano Trio [No. 2] in D major (1878), TrV 71.
Introduction, Theme, and Variations in G major for flute and piano (1879), TrV 76.
String Quartet in A major, Op. 2 (1880) TrV 95 (P: Munich 1881, Benno Walter-Quartett).
Serenade in G major for piano quartet (1882?), TrV 114.
Serenade in E♭ major, Op. 7, for 13 wind instruments (1881), TrV 106 (P: Dresden 1882, Franz Wüllner).
Variations on "s'Deandl is harb auf mi" for string trio (1882), TrV 109 (P: Munich, 1882).
Sonata in F major, Op. 6, for cello and piano (1883), TrV 115 (P: Nuremberg 1883).
Fantasia on a Theme by Giovanni Paisiello for bassoon, flute, and guitar (1883), TrV 116 (P: Munich 1883).
Variations on a Dance by Cesare Negri (1604) for string quartet (1883), TrV 123.
Suite in B major, Op. 4, for 13 wind instruments (1884), TrV 132 (P: Munich 1884, Richard Strauss).
Piano Quartet in C minor, Op. 13 (1885), TrV 137 (P: Weimar 1885, Halir-Quartett and Richard Strauss).
Festmarsch in D major for piano quartet (ca. 1885), TrV 136.
Sonata in E♭ major, Op. 18, for violin and piano (1887), TrV 151 (P: Elberfeld 1888).
Two Pieces for piano quartet (1893), TrV 169.
Festive Procession of the Knights of the Order of Saint John for brass and timpani [Investiture march] (1909), TrV 224 (P: probably Vienna 1909).
Wedding Prelude for two harmoniums (1924), TrV 247 (P: Vienna 1924).
Vienna Philharmonic Fanfare (1924), TrV 248 (P: Vienna 1924).
Fanfare for the Opening of the *Musikwoche der Stadt Wien*, September 1924, for brass and timpani (1924), TrV 250. (P: Vienna 1924).

Piano Music

Schneiderpolka (1870), TrV 1; also arranged for orchestra (P: Munich 1873).
Panzenburg-Polka (1872), TrV 11 (P: Munich 1872, orchestrated by Franz Strauss).
[*Langsamer Satz*] in G major (ca. 1872), TrV 12.
Five Small Pieces (ca. 1873), TrV 18.
Six Sonatinas for piano (C major, F major, B major, E major, E♭ major, D major) (1874), TrV 22–27 (TrV 25 is incomplete; TrV 27 lost).
Fantasia in C major (ca. 1874), TrV 29.
Two Small Pieces (ca. 1875), TrV 30.
Sonata [No. 1] in E major (1877), TrV 47.
Twelve Variations in D major (1878), TrV 68.
Aus alter Zeit. Gavotte for Piano (1879), TrV 72.

Andante in C minor (1879), TrV 73.
Sonata ("Grosse Sonate") [No. 2] in C minor (1879), TrV 79.
Skizzen, Five Small Pieces for Piano (1879) TrV 82 (P of the fifth, arranged for orchestra: Munich 1880).
Scherzo in B minor (ca. 1879), TrV 86.
Two Small Pieces (1879–1880), TrV 93.
Scherzando in G major (1880), TrV 96.
Fugue for piano (1880), TrV 99.
Sonata [No. 3] in B minor, Op. 5 (1880–1881), TrV 103.
Five Piano Pieces, Op. 3: Andante, Allegro vivace scherzando, Largo, Allegro molto, Allegro marcatissimo (1881), TrV 105.
Albumblatt in F major (1882), TrV 111.
Largo in A minor (ca. 1883), TrV 120.
Stiller Waldespfad in B major (1883), TrV 121.
Stimmungsbilder, Op. 9: *Auf stillem Waldespfad, An einsamer Quelle, Intermezzo, Träumerei, Heidebild* (1884), TrV 127 (P Nos. 3/4: Berlin 1884).
Introduction, Theme, and Fugue in A minor (14 improvisations and a fugue) (1884), TrV 130 (dedicated to Hans von Bülow; I of the fugue: Munich 1898).
Intermezzo in F Major, for piano four hands (1885), TrV 138.
Parade March for the Regiment of Mounted *Königs-Jäger*, No. 1, in E♭ major (1905), TrV 213 (P: Berlin 1907 [adapted for military ensemble], Richard Strauss).
De Brandenburgsche Mars. Präsentiermarsch (1905), TrV 214 (P: Berlin 1907 [adapted for military ensemble], Richard Strauss).
Military *Festmarsch* in E♭ major (1905), TrV 217 (P: Berlin 1906 [arranged for orchestra], Richard Strauss; I: Berlin 1906 [for piano, as "royal march," and for orchestra]).
Parade March for Cavalry, No. 2, in D♭ major (1907), TrV 222.

Orchestral Lieder

Der Spielmann und sein Kind (Hoffmann von Fallersleben) (1878), TrV 63. (Dedicated to Caroline von Mangstl; piano version 1878) (I: London, Bonn 1968).
Vier Gesänge für eine Singstimme mit Begleitung des Orchesters, Op. 33 (1896–97): *Verführung* (Mackay); *Gesang der Apollo-priesterin* (Bodmann); *Hymnus* (attributed to Schiller); *Pilgers Morgenlied* (Goethe), TrV 180 (P: 1/2: Berlin, 1896; 4: Elberfeld 1897; 3: Cologne 1898).
Zwei größere Gesänge, for alto or bass voice and orchestra, Op. 44 (1899): *Notturno* (Dehmel); *Nächtlicher Gang* (Rückert), TrV 197 (Dedicated to Anton von Rooy (1) and Karl Scheidemantel (2); P: Berlin 1900).
Zwei Gesänge, for bass voice and orchestra, Op. 51 (1903, 1906): *Das Tal* (Uhland); *Der Einsame* (Heine) (1902/1906), TrV 206 (Dedicated to Paul Knüpfer; P: Berlin 1903 [1] and 1906 [2]).
Drei Hymnen von Friedrich Hölderlin, for soprano or tenor and a large orchestra, Op. 71 (1921): *Hymne an die Liebe; Rückkehr in die Heimat; Liebe*, TrV 240 (Dedicated to Minnie Untermyer; P: Berlin 1921).

Cäcilie (Hart), Op. 27, No. 2 (1894), TrV 170/2 (arranged for orchestra 1897; P: Brussels 1897).

Morgen (Mackay), Op. 27, No. 4 (1894), TrV 170/4 (arranged for orchestra 1897; P: Brussels 1897).

Liebeshymnus (Henckell), Op. 32, No. 3 (1896), TrV 174/3 (arranged for orchestra 1897; P: Brussels 1897).

Das Rosenband (Klopstock), Op. 36, No. 1 (1897), TrV 186/1 (arranged for orchestra 1897; P: Brussels 1897).

Meinem Kinde (Falke), Op. 37, No. 3 (1897), TrV 187/3 (arranged in G♭ major ca. 1900; P: Elberfeld 1900).

Wiegenlied (Dehmel), Op. 41, No. 1 (1899), TrV 195/1 (arranged for orchestra 1900; P: Elberfeld 1900).

Muttertändelei (Bürger), Op. 43, No. 2 (1900), TrV 196/1 (arranged for orchestra 1900; P: Elberfeld 1900).

Die heiligen drei Könige aus Morgenland (Heine), Op. 56, No. 6 (1906), TrV 220/6 (arranged for orchestra 1906).

Der Arbeitsmann (Dehmel), Op. 39, No. 3 (1898), TrV 189/3 (arranged for orchestra 1918; P: Berlin 1919).

Five Lieder with orchestral accompaniment (1918): *Des Dichters Abendgang* (Uhland), Op. 47, No. 2 (1900), TrV 200/2 (arranged for orchestra in D♭ major, 1918); *Waldseligkeit* (Dehmel), Op. 49, No. 1 (1901), TrV 204/1 (arranged for orchestra 1918); *Winterweihe* (Henckell), Op. 48, No. 4 (1900), TrV 202/4 (arranged for orchestra 1918); *Winterliebe* (Henckell), Op. 48, No. 5 (1900), TrV 202/5 (arranged for orchestra 1918); *Freundliche Vision* (Bierbaum), Op. 48, No. 1 (1900), TrV 202/1 (arranged for orchestra 1918).

Mein Auge (Dehmel), Op. 37, No. 4 (1898), TrV 187/4 (arranged for orchestra 1933; P: Berlin 1933).

Befreit (Dehmel), Op. 39, No. 4 (1898), TrV 189/4 (arranged for orchestra 1933; P: Berlin 1933).

Frühlingsfeier (Heine), Op. 56, No. 5 (1906), TrV 220/5 (arranged for orchestra 1933; P: Berlin 1933).

Sechs Lieder, after poems by Clemens Brentano, Op. 68, TrV 235: *Lied der Frauen* (No. 6; arranged for orchestra 1933; P: Berlin 1933); *Ich wollt' ein Sträußlein binden* (No. 2; arranged for orchestra 1940); *An die Nacht* (No. 1; arranged for orchestra 1940); *Als mir dein Lied erklang* (No. 4; arranged for orchestra 1940); *Säusle, liebe Myrthe* (No. 3; arranged for orchestra 1940); *Amor* (No. 5; arranged for orchestra 1940) (P of the cycle [in the original sequence]: Düsseldorf 1941).

Das Bächlein (attributed to Goethe), Op. 88, No. 1 (1933), TrV 264 (arranged for orchestra 1935; P: Berlin 1942).

Zueignung (Gilm), Op. 10, No. 1 (1885), TrV 141/1 (arranged for orchestra 1940; P: Rome 1940).

Ich liebe dich (Liliencron), Op. 37, No. 2 (1898), TrV 187/2 (arranged for orchestra 1943).

Ruhe, meine Seele (Henckell), Op. 27, No. 1 (1894), TrV 170/1 (arranged for orchestra 1948).

Collections of Lieder

Acht Gedichte aus "Letzte Blätter" (Gilm), Op. 10 (1885), TrV 141: *Zueignung; Nichts; Die Nacht; Die Georgine; Geduld; Die Verschwiegenen; Die Zeitlose; Allerseelen* (dedicated to Heinrich Vogl).

Fünf Lieder für eine mittlere Singstimme, Op. 15 (1886), TrV 148: *Madrigal* (Michelangelo); *Winternacht* (Schack); *Lob des Leidens* (Schack); *Lieder der Trauer* (No. 4): *"Dem Herzen ähnlich"* (Schack); *Heimkehr* (Schack) (dedicated to Victoria Blank [1, 3, 4]) and Johanna Pschorr [2, 5]).

Sechs Lieder für eine hohe Singstimme (Schack), Op. 17 (1886–1887), TrV 149: *Seitdem dein Aug' in meines schaute; Ständchen; Das Geheimnis; Lieder der Trauer* (No. 3): *"Von dunklem Schleier umsponnen"; Nur Mut!; Barcarole.*

Sechs Lieder aus "Lotosblätter" (Schack) for voice and piano, Op. 19 (1888), TrV 152: *Wozu noch, Mädchen, soll es frommen; Breit' über mein Haupt dein schwarzes Haar; Schön sind, doch kalt die Himmelssterne; Wie sollten wir geheim sie halten; Hoffen und wieder verzagen; Mein Herz ist stumm, mein Herz ist kalt* (dedicated to Emilie Herzog).

Mädchenblumen, Four Poems (Dahn) for voice and piano, Op. 22 (1888), TrV 153: *Kornblumen; Mohnblumen; Efeu; Wasserrose* (dedicated to Hans Giessen).

Schlichte Weisen, Five Poems (Dahn) for voice and piano, Op. 21 (1889–90), TrV 160: *All' mein Gedanken, mein Herz und mein Sinn; Du meines Herzens Krönelein; Ach Lieb, ich muß nun scheiden; Ach weh, mir unglückhaftem Mann; Die Frauen sind oft fromm und still* (dedicated to Johanna Strauss).

Two Lieder (Lenau) for voice and piano, Op. 26 (1891), TrV 166: *Frühlingsgedränge; O wärst du mein* (dedicated to Heinrich Zeller).

Four Lieder for voice and piano, Op. 27 (1894), TrV 170: *Ruhe, meine Seele* (Henckell); *Cäcilie* (Hart); *Heimliche Aufforderung* (Mackay); *Morgen* (Mackay) (dedicated to Pauline Strauss).

Three Lieder (Bierbaum) for a high voice, Op. 29 (1895), TrV 172: *Traum durch die Dämmerung; Schlagende Herzen; Nachtgang* (dedicated to Eugen Gura).

Three Lieder (Busse) for a high voice, Op. 31 (1895–96), TrV 173: *Blauer Sommer; Wenn; Weißer Jasmin* (dedicated to Johanna Rauchenberger, the composer's sister, for her wedding); added to later editions: *Stiller Gang* (Dehmel, 1895), TrV 173/4 (dedicated to Marie Ritter); the piece also exists in an arrangement with vila or vilin *ad lib.*

Five Lieder for voice and piano, Op. 32 (1896), TrV 174: *Ich trage meine Minne* (Henckell); *Sehnsucht* (Liliencron); *Liebeshymnus* (Henckell); *O süßer Mai* (Henckell); *Himmelsboten zu Liebchens Himmelbett* (*Des Knaben Wunderhorn*) (dedicated to Pauline Strauss).

Four Lieder for a high voice, Op. 36 (1897–98), TrV 186: *Das Rosenband* (Klopstock); *Für funfzehn Pfennige* (*Des Knaben Wunderhorn*); *Hat gesagt—bleibt's nicht dabei* (*Des Knaben Wunderhorn*); *Anbetung* (Rückert) (dedicated to Marie Riemerschmid [1] and Raoul Walter [2–4]).

Six Lieder for a high voice, Op. 37 (1898), TrV 187: *Glückes genug* (Liliencron); *Ich liebe dich* (Liliencron); *Meinem Kinde* (Falke); *Mein Auge* (Dehmel); *Herr Lenz* (Bodmann); *Hochzeitlich Lied* (Lindner) (dedicated to Pauline Strauss).

Five Lieder for voice and piano, Op. 39 (1898), TrV 189: *Leises Lied* (Dehmel); *Junghexenlied* (Bierbaum); *Der Arbeitsmann* (Dehmel); *Befreit* (Dehmel); *Lied an meinen Sohn* (Dehmel) (dedicated to Fritz Sieger).

Five Lieder for voice and piano, Op. 41 (1899), TrV 195: *Wiegenlied* (Dehmel); *In der Campagna* (Mackay); *Am Ufer* (Dehmel); *Bruder Liederlich* (Liliencron); *Leise Lieder* (Morgenstern) (1–4 dedicated to Marie Ritter).

Drei Gesänge älterer deutscher Dichter, Op. 43 (1899), TrV 196: *An sie* (Klopstock); *Muttertändelei* (Bürger); *Die Ulme zu Hirsau* (Uhland) (dedicated to Ernestine Schumann-Heink).

Five Poems (Rückert) for voice and piano, Op. 46 (1899–1900), TrV 199: *Ein Obdach gegen Sturm und Regen; Gestern war ich Atlas; Die sieben Siegel; Morgenrot; Ich sehe wie in einem Spiegel* (dedicated to Adolf und Maria de Ahna).

Five Lieder (Uhland) for voice and piano, Op. 47 (1900), TrV 200: *Auf ein Kind; Des Dichters Abendgang; Rückleben; Einkehr; Von den sieben Zechbrüdern* (dedicated to Carl Johann Pflüger).

Five Lieder (Bierbaum and Henckell) for voice and piano, Op. 48 (1900), TrV 202: *Freundliche Vision* (Bierbaum); *Ich schwebe* (Henckell); *Kling!* (Henckell); *Winterweihe* (Henckell); *Winterliebe* (Henckell).

Eight Lieder for voice and piano, Op. 49 (1901), TrV 204: *Waldseligkeit* (Dehmel); *In goldener Fülle* (Remer); *Wiegenliedchen* (Dehmel); *Das Lied des Steinklopfers* (Henckell); *Sie wissen's nicht* (Panizza); *Junggesellenschwur* (Des Knaben Wunderhorn); *Wer lieben will, muß leiden* (Mündel); *Ach, was Kummer, Qual und Schmerzen* (Mündel) (six different dedications).

Six Lieder for voice and piano, Op. 56 (1903–06), TrV 220: *Gefunden* (Goethe); *Blindenklage* (Henckell); *Im Spätboot* (Meyer); *Mit deinen blauen Augen* (Heine); *Frühlingsfeier* (Heine); *Die heiligen drei Könige aus Morgenland* (Heine) (dedicated to Pauline Strauss [1] and Josephine Strauss [2–6]).

Six Lieder (Brentano) for voice and piano, Op. 68 (1918), TrV 235: *An die Nacht; Ich wollt ein Sträußlein binden; Säusle, liebe Myrthe!; Als mir dein Lied erklang; Amor; Lied der Frauen* (dedicated to Elisabeth Schumann).

Krämerspiegel, Twelve Songs (Kerr) for voice and piano, Op. 66 (1918), TrV 236: *Es war einmal ein Bock; Einst kam der Bock als Bote; Es liebte einst ein Hase; Drei Masken sah ich am Himmel stehn; Hast du ein Tongedicht vollbracht; O lieber Künstler sei ermahnt; Unser Feind ist, großer Gott; Von Händlern wird die Kunst bedroht; Es war mal eine Wanze; Die Künstler sind die Schöpfer; Die Händler und die Macher; O Schöpferschwarm, o Händlerkreis* (dedicated to Friedrich Rösch).

Five Small Lieder, Op. 69 (1918), TrV 237: *Der Stern* (Arnim); *Der Pokal* (Arnim); *Einerlei* (Arnim); *Waldesfahrt* (Heine); *Schlechtes Wetter* (Heine).

Six Lieder for a high voice, Op. 67, in two parts (1918), TrV 238: *Drei Lieder der Ophelia* (Simrock, after Shakespeare): *Wie erkenn' ich mein Treulieb / Guten Morgen, 's ist Sankt Valentinstag / Sie trugen ihn auf der Bahre bloß; Aus den Büchern des Unmuts des Rendsch Nameh* (Goethe, *West-östlicher Divan*): *Wer wird von der Welt verlangen / Hab' ich euch denn je geraten / Wanderers Gemütsruhe*.

Gesänge des Orients (Bethge) for voice and piano, Op. 77 (1928), TrV 257: *Ihre Augen; Schwung; Liebesgeschenke; Die Allmächtige; Huldigung* (dedicated to Elisabeth Schumann and Karl Alwin).

Four Songs for Bass Voice, Op. 87 (1929, 1929, 1922, 1935), TrV 260, 244, 258, 268: *Vom künftigen Alter* (Rückert); *Erschaffen und Beleben* (Goethe); *Und dann nicht mehr* (Rückert); *Im Sonnenschein* (Rückert) (dedicated to Hans Hotter [1], Michael Bohnen, then Hans Hotter [2], Hans Hermann Nissen [3] and Georg Hann [4]).

Three Lieder, Op. 88 (1933, 1942, 1942), TrV 264, 280, 281: *Das Bächlein* (attributed to Goethe); *Sankt Michael* (Weinheber); *Blick vom oberen Belvedere* (Weinheber), posthumously (1964) collected and published (dedicated to Joseph Goebbels [1], Alfred Poell [2], and Viorica Ursuleac [3]).

Piano Lieder

Weihnachtslied (Schubart) (1870), TrV 2.
Einkehr (Uhland) (1871), TrV 3.
Winterreise (Uhland) (1871), TrV 4.
Der böhmische Musikant (Pletzsch) (ca. 1871), TrV 7.
Der müde Wanderer (Hoffmann von Fallersleben) (ca. 1873), TrV 16.
Husarenlied (Hoffmann von Fallersleben) (1876), TrV 42.
Der Fischer (Goethe) (1877), TrV 48.
Die Drossel (Uhland) (1877), TrV 49.
Laß ruhn die Toten (Chamisso) (1877), TrV 50.
Lust und Qual (Goethe) (1877), TrV 51.
Spielmann und Zither (Körner) (1878), TrV 58.
Wiegenlied (Hoffmann von Fallersleben) (1878), TrV 59.
Abend- und Morgenrot (Hoffmann von Fallersleben) (ca. 1878), TrV 60.
Im Walde (Geibel) (1878), TrV 62.
Nebel (Lenau) (ca. 1878), TrV 65.
Soldatenlied (Hoffmann von Fallersleben) (ca. 1878), TrV 66.
Ein Röslein zog ich mir im Garten (Hoffmann von Fallersleben) (ca. 1878), TrV 67.
Waldgesang (Geibel) (1879) TrV 75/1 [see "Lost Works"]
In Vaters Garten heimlich steht ein Blümelein (Heine) (1879), TrV 88.
Aus der Kindheit (Sturm) (1879).
Die erwachte Rose (Sallet) (1880), TrV 90.
Begegnung (Gruppe) (1880), TrV 98.
John Anderson (Freiligrath, after Burns) (1880), TrV 101.
Rote Rosen (Stieler) (1883), TrV 119.
Wer hat's getan? (Gilm) (1885), TrV 142.
Wir beide wollen springen (Bierbaum) (1896), TrV 175.
Weihnachtsgefühl (Greif) (1899), TrV 198.
Sinnspruch (Goethe) (1919), TrV 239.
Durch allen Schall und Klang (Goethe) (1925), TrV 251.
Spruch: Wie etwas sei leicht (Goethe) (1930), TrV 261.
Zugemessene Rhythmen (Goethe) (1935), TrV 269.
Xenion (Goethe) (1942), TrV 282.

Melodramas (with Piano)

Tennyson's Enoch Arden. Melodrama for narrator and piano (after Adolf Strodtmann's translation), Op. 38 (1897), TrV 181 (P: March 24, 1897, Munich [Ernst von Possart/ Richard Strauss]).
Das Schloß am Meere. Melodrama after Uhland's poem (1899), TrV 191 (P: March 23, 1899, Berlin [Ernst von Possart/Richard Strauss]).

Choral Works
a) A Cappella

Two Lieder (Eichendorff) for four voices (1876), TrV 37: *Morgengesang; Frühlingsnacht*.
Kyrie, Sanctus, Benedictus, Agnus Dei for four voices (1877), TrV 54 (dedicated to Franz Strauss, Sr.).
Seven Lieder for four voices (1880), TrV 92: *Winterlied* (Eichendorff); *Spielmannsweise* (Gensichen); *Pfingsten* (Böttger); *Käferlied* (Reinick); *Waldessang* (Böttger); *Schneeglöcklein* (Böttger); *Trüb blinken nur die Sterne* (Böttger) (dedicated to Franz Strauss, Sr.).
Schwäbische Erbschaft (Löwe) for male chorus (1884), TrV 134.
Two songs for sixteen-part chorus, Op. 34 (1897), TrV 182: *Der Abend* (Schiller); *Hymne* (Rückert) (dedicated to Julius Buths [1] und Philipp Wolfrum [2]).
Richard Till Khnopff: Er lebe hoch! [birthday felicitations for four voices, June 14, 1898], TrV 188.
Soldatenlied (Kopisch) for male chorus (1899), TrV 192.
Drei Männerchöre (Herder), Op. 45 (1899), TrV 193: *Schlachtgesang; Lied der Freundschaft; Der Brauttanz* (dedicated to Franz Strauss, Sr.).
Zwei Männerchöre (Herder), Op. 42 (1899), TrV 194: *Liebe; Alt-deutsches Schlachtlied* (P: Vienna 1899).
Hans Huber in Vitznau sei schönstens bedankt (1903), TrV 208 (four-voice canon, likely in thanks to Hans Huber for the latter's dedication of his Third Symphony, 1903].
S-c-a-t spielen wir fröhlich bei Willy Levin (1903), TrV 210 (four-voice canon welcoming the New Year, for Willy Levin).
Sechs Volksliedbearbeitungen für Männerchor (1905), TrV 216: *Geistlicher Maien; Mißlungene Liebesjagd; Tummler; Hüt du dich!; Wächterlied; Kuckuck*.
Deutsche Motette (Rückert) for four solo voices and sixteen-part chorus, Op. 62 (1913), TrV 230 (dedicated to Hugo Rüdel and the Berlin Hoftheatersingchor; P: Berlin 1913).
Cantata (*Tüchtigen stellt das schnelle Glück*, Hofmannsthal) for male chorus (1914), TrV 232 (dedicated to Nicolaus Graf Seebach).
Die Göttin im Putzzimmer (Rückert) for eight-part chorus (1935), TrV 267.
Drei Männerchöre (Rückert) (1935), TrV 270: *Vor den Türen; Traumlicht; Fröhlich im Maien* (dedicated to Eugen Papst and the Cologne Men's Chorus; P: Cologne 1936).
Durch Einsamkeiten (Wildgans) for male chorus (1938), TrV 273 (dedicated to the Vienna Schubertbund; P: Vienna 1939).

b) Vocal Ensembles and Solos

Der weiße Hirsch (Uhland) for contralto, tenor, bass, and piano (ca. 1871), TrV 6.
Alphorn (Kerner) for solo voice, horn, and piano (1878), TrV 64 (dedicated to Franz Strauss, Sr.).
Utan svafvel och fosfor [writing on a box of Swedish matches] for two tenors and two basses (1889), TrV 159.
Two Lieder from *Der Richter von Zalamea* (Calderón) (1904), TrV 211: *Liebesliedchen*, for tenor, guitar, and harp; *Lied der Chispa* for mezzo-soprano, male chorus, guitar, and two harps (P: Berlin 1904).
Hymne auf das Haus Kohorn (Strauss) for two tenors and two basses (1925), TrV 252 (dedicated to Oscar Kohorn).
Hab' Dank, du güt'ger Weisheitsspender (Strauss) für eine Bassstimme (1939), TrV 275 (dedicated to Anton Kippenberg).
Notschrei aus den Gefilden Lapplands (Strauss) for solo voice (1940), TrV 276 (dedicated to Walter Funck).
Wer tritt herein (Strauss) for solo voice (1943), TrV 289 (dedicated to Hans Frank) (I: Los Angeles 1945).

c) With Accompaniment

Chorus from *Electra* (Sophocles) for male chorus and orchestra (ca. 1881), TrV 104 (P: 1881, Munich, Ludwigsgymnasium).
Wandrers Sturmlied (Goethe), Op. 14 for six-part chorus and large orchestra (1885), TrV 131 (dedicated to Franz Wüllner) (P: March 8, 1887, Cologne, Gürzenich [Strauss]).
Hymn (*Licht, du ewiglich Eines*, Schiller) for brass band, large orchestra, and female chorus (1897), TrV 183 (P: June 1, 1897, Munich, Glaspalast [Strauss]).
Taillefer (Uhland) for mixed chorus, soloists, and orchestra, Op. 52 (1903), TrV 207 (dedicated to the philosophical faculty at the University of Heidelberg) (P: October 26, 1903, Heidelberg, Stadthalle [Strauss]).
Bardengesang (*Herbei, herbei, wo der Kühnsten Wunde blutet*, Klopstock) for three four-part males choruses and orchestra, Op. 55 (1906), TrV 219 (dedicated to Gustav Wohlgemuth) (P: February 6, 1907, Dresden, Saal Große Brüdergasse(?) [Friedrich Brandes]).
Die Tageszeiten (Eichendorff). Song-cycle for male chorus, orchestra, and organ, Op. 76 (1927), TrV 256 (dedicated to the Vienna Schubertbund and its conductor Viktor Keldorfer) (P: July 21, 1928, Vienna, Konzerthaus [Viktor Keldorfer]).
Austria (Wildgans), for large orchestra and male chorus, **Op. 78** (1929), TrV 259 (dedicated to the Vienna Men's Chorus) (P: January 10, 1930, Vienna, Musikverein, Großer Saal [Strauss]).
Olympic Hymn ("Völker! Seid des Volkes Gäste"; Lubahn) for four-part chorus and orchestra (1934), TrV 266 (I: Berlin 1936; P: August 1, 1936, Berlin, Olympiastadion [Strauss]).

Late Works

Horn Concerto No.2 in E♭ major, TrV 283.

> November 28, 1942
> Solo horn, 2 flutes, 2 oboes, 2 clarinets, 2 bassoons, 2 horns, 2 trumpets, timpani, strings
> Dedication: "To the memory of my father"
> P: August 11, 1943, Salzburg, Festspielhaus (Gottfried von Freiberg/Karl Böhm).

Festival Music for the City of Vienna, for brass and timpani, TrV 286.

> January 14, 1943 (greatly shortened and reworked as *Wiener Fanfare* TrV 287, April 17, 1943)
> 10 trumpets, 7 trombones, 2 tubas (bass tuba), 5 timpani
> Dedication: "To the municipal council"
> P: April 9, 1943, Vienna, Festsaal des Rathauses (Richard Strauss)

Sonatina [No. 1] in F major, *Aus der Werkstatt eines Invaliden*, for sixteen wind instruments, TrV 288.

> July 22, 1943
> 2 flutes, 2 oboes, 3 clarinets, basset horn, bass clarinet, 2 bassoons, contrabassoon, 4 horns
> P: June 18, 1944, Dresden, Gewerbehaus (Karl Elmendorff)

Metamorphosen, Study for twenty-three solo strings, TrV 290.

> April 12, 1945
> 10 violins, 5 violas, 5 cellos, 3 contrabasses
> Dedication: Paul Sacher and Collegium Musicum Zürich
> P: January 25, 1946, Zurich, Tonhalle—Kleiner Saal (Paul Sacher)

Sonatina No. 2 in E♭ major, Fröhliche Werkstatt. Den Manen des göttlichen Mozart am Ende eines dankerfüllten Lebens, for 16 wind instruments, TrV 291.

> June 22, 1945
> 2 flutes, 2 oboes, 3 clarinets, basset horn, bass clarinet, 2 bassoons, contrabassoon, 4 horns
> Dedication: Werner Reinhart
> P: March 25, 1946, Winterthur, Stadthaus (Hermann Scherchen)

Oboe Concerto in D major, TrV 292.

> October 25, 1945
> Solo oboe, 2 flutes, English horn, 2 clarinets, 2 bassoons, 2 horns, strings
> Dedication: Volkmar Andreae and the Tonhalle-Orchester Zürich
> P: February 26, 1946, Zurich, Tonhalle—Großer Saal (Marcel Saillet/Volkmar Andreae)

Duet-Concertino for Clarinet, Bassoon, Harp, and Strings in F major, TrV 293.

> December 16, 1947
> Solo clarinet, solo bassoon, 2 violins, viola, cello, contrabass, harp, strings
> Dedication: Hugo Burghauser
> P: April 4, 1948, Lugano, Radio Monte Ceneri (Armando Basile/Bruno Bergamaschi/Otmar Nussio)

Allegretto in E major for violin and piano, TrV 295.

August 5, 1948
I: Giebing 1969

[Four Last Songs] for soprano and orchestra, TrV 296.

Frühling (Hesse; July 18, 1948)
September (Hesse; September 20, 1948)
Beim Schlafengehen (Hesse; August 4, 1948)
Im Abendrot (Eichendorff; May 6, 1948)
Various orchestrations
Dedication: Willi Schuh and wife (I), Maria Jeritza and husband (II), Adolf Jöhr and wife (III), Ernst Roth (IV)
P: May 22, 1950, London, Royal Albert Hall (Kirsten Flagstad/Wilhelm Furtwängler)

Malven (Knobel), song for voice and piano, TrV 297.

November 23, 1948
Dedication: "To dear Maria [Jeritza], this final rose!"
P: January 10, 1985, New York, Avery Fisher-Hall (Kiri Te Kanawa/Martin Katz)

Adaptations

Ludwig van Beethoven. *Zwei Lieder: Zärtliche Liebe (Ich liebe dich)* WoO 123 (Herrosee); *Wonne der Wehmut (Trocknet nicht)*, Op. 83, No. 1 (Goethe), arranged (1898), TrV 185.
Revision of an aria from François-Adrien Boieldieu's *Jean de Paris*, Opéra comique 1812 (1922), TrV 242.
Alexander Ritter. *Nun hält Frau Minne Liebeswacht*, Op. 4, No. 8, arranged (1891), TrV 164.
Franz Lachner. Nonett in F major for four hands piano (1881), TrV 108.
Joachim Raff. Two marches arranged from *Bernhard von Weimar* for piano four hands (1885), TrV 143.
Alexander Ritter. Overture to *Der faule Hans*, piano excerpt (1886), TrV 140.
Franz Schubert. *Ganymed* (Goethe) D 544, "arranged for a small orchestra" (1897), TrV 179.
Franz Schubert (attributed). Waltz in G♭ major, the so-called Kupelwieser-Walzer, arranged for piano by ear (1943), TrV 285
Addition music for Richard Wagner's *Die Feen*, Act II (1888), TrV 154

Writings

The basis for the following is the third part of the catalog of works compiled by Müller von Asow, who also republished many of the texts [Müller von Asow]. In addition, most of Strauss's writings can be found in Franz Trenner (ed.), *Richard Strauss. Dokumente seines Lebens und Schaffens* (Munich 1954) [Trenner] and Willi Schuh (ed.), *Richard Strauss: Betrachtungen und Erinnerungen* (Zurich, second edition 1957) [Schuh].

Only authorized texts and essay manuscripts have been included, not excerpts from correspondence (with the exception of the letter to Karl Böhm published in 1950 as

"Künstlerisches Vermächtnis"); reference to initial publication is provided with as much bibliographical precision as available information permits.

Books

Hector Berlioz. *Instrumentationslehre: Ergänzt und revidiert von Richard Strauss* (Leipzig n.d. [1904]).

Essays and Commentary

"Brief eines deutschen Kapellmeisters über das Bayreuther Orchester." *Bayreuther Blätter* 15 (1892), 126–132. [Schuh]
Rundschreiben über die Parsifal-Schutzfrage (Munich 1894). [Lithographed circular]
["Biographical Sketch." In James Huneker: *Overtones* (New York 1904). 1–64 (in part with original quations); German version in *Die Musik* 4 (1905). 79–92].
"Bemerkungen über amerikanische Musikpflege." *Allgemeine Musikzeitung* 35 (1908). 337.
"Rechtfertigung der Aufführung der *Symphonia Domestica* im Warenhaus Wannemaker in New York." *Allgemeine Musikzeitung* 35 (1908). 363f.
"Gibt es für die Musik eine Fortschrittspartei?" *Morgen: Wochenschrift für deutsche Kultur* 1 (1907). 15–18. [Schuh]
["Die hohen Bach-Trompeten."] *Zeitschrift für Instrumentenbau* 30 (1909). 194f.
"Persönliche Erinnerungen an Hans von Bülow." *Neue Freie Presse*, December 25, 1909, 33. [Schuh]
["Gustav Mahler."] Paul Stefan (ed.). *Gustav Mahler: Ein Bild seiner Persönlichkeit in Widmungen* (Munich 1910). 66. [Schuh]
"Die Grenzen des Komponierbaren." *Der Merker* 1 (1910). 106.
"Der Rosenkavalier." *Allgemeine Musikzeitung* 37 (1910). 819–822. [Müller von Asow]
"Mozarts *Così fan tutte*. Geschrieben anläßlich der Neueinstudierung nach dem Original in München." *Neue Freie Presse*, December 25, 1910, 35f. [Schuh]
"Antwort auf die Rundfrage 'Worin erblicken Sie die entscheidende Bedeutung Franz Liszts für die Entwicklung des deutschen Musiklebens?'" *Allgemeine Musikzeitung* 38 (1911). 1020.
"Städtebund-Theater. Eine Anregung." *Vossische Zeitung*, February 22, 1914 (morning edition). [Schuh]
"Novitäten und Stars (Spielplanerwägungen eines modernen Operndirektors)." *Neues Wiener Journal*, June 22, 1922. [Schuh]
"Über Johann Strauß." *Neues Wiener Tagblatt*, October 25, 1925. [Schuh]
"Die Münchener Oper." Arthur Bauckner/Emil Preetorius (eds.). *150 Jahre Bayerisches Nationaltheater* (Munich 1928). 207. [Schuh]
"Über Komponieren und Dirigieren." *Berliner Börsen-Courier*, June 8, 1929 (evening edition). [Schuh]
"Die schöpferische Kraft des Komponisten." *Chemnitzer Allgemeine Zeitung*, June 11, 1929. [Trenner, excerpts]
"Über Richard Wagner." *Neue Zeitschrift für Musik* 100 (1933). 743.
"Zeitgemässe Glossen für Erziehung zur Musik." *Musik im Zeitbewußtsein* 1(1) (1933). 6f. [Schuh]

"Zehn goldne Regeln. Einem jungen Kapellmeister ins Stammbuch geschrieben."
Dresdner Anzeiger. April 29, 1934. [Schuh]
["Über die Besetzung der Kurorchester."] *Musik im Zeitbewußtsein* 2(1) (1934). 10.
"Mozart, der Dramatiker." *Dramaturgische Blätter der Intendanz der Bayerischen Staatsoper* 3 (1941/42). 26f.
"Über Mozart." *Schweizerische Musikzeitung* 84 (1944). 223. [Schuh]
Letter to Karl Böhm, April 27, 1945. Published as "The Artistic Testament of Richard Strauss. Translated and with an Introduction by Alfred Mann." *The Musical Quarterly* 36 (1950). 1–8. [Schuh]

Prologues, Speeches, Interviews

Introduction to August Göllerich, *Beethoven* [. . .]. Berlin 1904. I–IV. [Schuh]
"Zum Geleit." Leopold Schmidt. *Aus dem Musikleben der Gegenwart. Beiträge zur zeitgenössischen Kunstkritik.* Berlin 1909. V–VIII. [Schuh]
["Offener Brief an Ludwig Karpath zum Parsifal-Schutz; Antwort auf eine Rundfrage"]. *Hamburger Fremdenblatt,* August 1912. [Schuh]
"Offener Brief an einen Oberbürgermeister." *Berliner Tageblatt.* December 23, 1913 (evening edition). [Schuh]
["Telegramm an Ludwig Karpath."] *Neues Wiener Tagblatt.* April 14, 1919.
"Erwiderung zu Franz Schalks 'Begrüßung des Direktors Dr. Richard Strauß im Operntheater.'" *Neue Freie Presse,* May 17, 1919 (evening edition). 3.
["The Composer Speaks (1921)"]. In: David Ewen (ed.). *The Book of Modern Composers* (New York 1945). 54f.
["Gedächtnisrede auf Friedrich Rösch (1925)."] [Schuh]
"Die 10 goldenen Lebensregeln des hochfürstlichen bayerischen Kammerkappellarius Hans Knappertsbusch, Monachia." *Allgemeine Musikzeitung* 55 (1928). 491.
Preface to Hans Diestel. *Ein Orchestermusiker über das Dirigieren. Die Grundlagen der Dirigiertechnik aus dem Blickpunkt des Ausführenden. Mit einem Vorwort von Richard Strauß* (Berlin 1931). 5–7. [Schuh]
"Gedenkworte für Alfred Roller [1933]." *Neue Zürcher Zeitung,* June 11, 1964.
"An die Schriftleitung." *Musik im Zeitbewußtsein* 1(1) (1933). 3.
"Appell zum Schutz der ideellen Interessen am Kunstwerk [1933/34]." *GEMA-Nachrichten* 1949: 3f. [Trenner]
["Ansprache bei der öffentlichen Musikversammlung am 17. Februar 1934 in der Berliner Philharmonie."] *Musik im Zeitbewußtsein* 2.8 (1934). 1–3.
["Ansprache am ersten deutschen Komponistentag am 18. Februar 1934 in Berlin."] *Die Einheit* 1 (1934). 5–9.
"Musik und Kultur." In: Fred Hamel/Martin Hürlimann (eds.). *Das Atlantisbuch der Musik* (Berlin/Zurich 1934). 5f.
"Zur Urheberrechtsreform. Ansprache des Führers des Berufsstandes der deutschen Komponisten [. . .] in der Sitzung des Ausschusses: Urheber- und Verlagsrecht der Akademie für Deutsches Recht am 21. April 1934." *Die Einheit* 2 (1934). 13–15.
["Ansprache zur Eröffnung der Versammlung des Berufsstandes der deutschen Komponisten am 8. November 1934 in Berlin."] *Die Einheit* 3 (1934). 1f.
"Vorwort/Preface [1941]." In: Willi Schuh. *Das Bühnenwerk von Richard Strauss / The Stage Works of Richard Strauss* (Zurich and London 1954). 4–7.

"Glückwunsch für die Wiener Philharmoniker." In: Wilhelm Jerger (ed.). *Briefe an die Wiener Philharmoniker* (Vienna 1942). 141–146. [Schuh]
"Glückwunsch für die Sächsische Staatskapelle." *Musica* 2 (1948). 251. [Schuh]
"Garmischer Rede am 85. Geburtstag." June 11, 1949. [Trenner]

Introductions to Compositions

"Aus Italien. (op. 16). Sinfonische Fantasie (G-Dur) für Orchester." (Analysis by the composer.) *Allgemeine Deutsche Musik-Zeitung* 16 (1889). 263–266. [Müller von Asow]
"Analyse der Sinfonie f-Moll." *Programmbuch der Concert-direction Wolff IV. Hamburg 1889/90*. (Reprinted in Jürgen Schaarwächter, *Richard Strauss und die Sinfonie*. [Cologne 1994]. 155–162)
"Interview zu *Elektra*." *Allgemeine Musikzeitung* 35 (1908). 669.
"Einleitung." Richard Strauss. *Schlagobers* (Berlin 1924).
"Vorwort zu *Intermezzo*." Richard Strauss. *Intermezzo. Eine bürgerliche Komödie mit sinfonischen Zwischenspielen* (Berlin 1924). [Schuh]
Ludwig Karpath. "Richard Strauß über seine neue Oper *Die ägyptische Helena*." *Neue freie Presse*. May 27, 1928. 14. [Schuh]
"Die ägyptische Helena." *Blätter der Staatsoper Berlin* 11 (1931). [Müller von Asow]
"Arabella." *Blätter der Staatsoper Dresden* 2 (1937).
"Meine Josephslegende." *Dramaturgische Blätter der Bayerischen Staatsoper* 11 (1940/41). 117. [Schuh]
"Geleitwort zu *Capriccio*." Richard Strauss: *Capriccio: Ein Konversationsstück für Musik in einem Aufzug von Clemens Krauss und Richard Strauss* (Berlin 1942). [Schuh; partially reprinted as "Die Bedeutung des Wortes in der Oper." *Dramaturgische Blätter der Bayerischen Staatsoper* 3 (1941/42). 2–4.]
"Vorwort zu *Divertimento*." Richard Strauss. *Divertimento op. 86* (Berlin 1942). [Trenner, excerpts]

Manuscripts

Das Tagebuch der Griechenland- und Ägyptenreise (1892). Ed. Willi Schuh. *Richard Strauss-Jahrbuch* 1954. 89–96 [excerpts].
["Über mein Schaffen"], ca. 1895. Walter Werbeck: *Die Tondichtungen von Richard Strauss* (Tutzing 1996). 534–539. (*Dokumente und Studien zu Richard Strauss 2*.) [Ibid. (p. 534) a report on publication history.]
"Handschreiben zur Reform des Urheberrechts-Gesetzes von 1870. München 1898." *Musik und Dichtung: 50 Jahre Deutsche Urheberrechtsgesellschaft* (Munich 1953). 14–16.
[*Salomes Tanz*, 1908?]. *Theater-Zeitung des Stadttheaters Basel* 37 (1952). 4.
Preface to *Intermezzo*. [First version, 1924. Schuh]
["Der Dresdner Staatsoper zum Jubiläum." 1928].
["Über Schubert," ca. 1928. Schuh].
"Dirigentenerfahrungen mit klassischen Meisterwerken." [1934. Schuh]
["Anmerkungen zur Aufführung von Beethovens Symphonien," ca. 1934.] *Neue Zeitschrift für Musik* 125 (1964): 250–260.
["Geschichte der *Schweigsamen Frau*, 1935"]. In: Willi Schuh (ed.). *Richard Strauss. Stefan Zweig. Briefwechsel*. (Frankfurt 1957). 155–159.

["Bemerkungen zu Richard Wagners Gesamtkunstwerk und zum Bayreuther Festspielhaus," 1940. Schuh].
["Bemerkungen zu Richard Wagners *Oper und Drama*," ca. 1940. Schuh].
["Vom melodischen Einfall," ca. 1940. Schuh].
["Meine Werke in guter Zusammenstellung," ca. 1940. Schuh].
"Aus meinen Jugend- und Lehrjahren" [ca. 1940?. Schuh].
"Erinnerungen an meinen Vater" [ca. 1940?. Schuh].
"Erinnerungen an die ersten Aufführungen meine Opern" [1942. Schuh].
"Über Wesen und Bedeutung der Oper (1943)." Franz Grasberger. *Richard Strauss. Hohe Kunst, erfülltes Leben* (Vienna 1965). 11.
"Brief über das humanistische Gymnasium. An Professor Reisinger" [1945. Schuh].
"Pauline Strauss-de Ahna" [1947. Schuh].
["Letzte Aufzeichnung, 1949." *Gestalt und Gedanke. Ein Jahrbuch* [der Bayerischen Akademie der Schönen Künste] (Munich 1951). 32–39. [Schuh]

Etudes

Skizzen zu Klaviersonaten (1873/74) TrV 28
Vierstimmige Studien (2 ca. 1875, 2 1876) TrV 31, 32, 38, 39
Kontrapunktstudien (1875–76, 1877–78, 1878–79, 1879–80) TrV 36, 57, 81, 91

Unfinished Works, Fragments

Waldkonzert (Vogel) (ca. 1871), TrV 5 [I: 1968].
Herz, mein Herz (Geibel), song for voice and piano (1871), TrV 8.
Moderato in C major, for piano (ca. 1871) TrV 9.
Gute Nacht (Geibel), song for voice and piano (1871), TrV 10.
Two small pieces for violin and piano (1873), TrV 21.
Sonata in E major for piano (1874), TrV 25.
Allegro assai in B major for piano (1875), TrV 34.
String Quartet in C minor (one movement) (1875), TrV 35.
Six Scenes for a Singspiel, for voices and piano (1876), TrV 40.
Overture in E minor for *Ein Studentenstreich* (1876), TrV 45.
Overture to *Dom Sebastian* in E♭ major (1876), TrV 46.
Andante cantabile in D major, for orchestra (1877), TrV 55.
Andante in B major for orchestra (1877), TrV 56.
Lila (after Goethe, 1878), TrV 61 (3 parts: *Lied der Lila*; Almaide's aria; ensemble, *Auf aus der Ruh*).
String Quartet in E♭ major (one movement) (1879), TrV 85.
Melody in G♭ major, for piano (ca. 1883), TrV 122.
Lied ohne Worte in E♭ major for soloist and orchestra (1883), TrV 124.
Rhapsody in C♯ minor, for piano and orchestra (1886), TrV 146.
Andante in C major, for horn and piano (1888), TrV 155 [I: London 1973].
Vorüber ist der Graus der Nacht (Arent), song for piano (1896), TrV 178.
Kythere: Ballett in drei Akten nach Watteau (1900) TrV 201.
Der Graf von Rom, Two versions for voice and piano, without text; dedicated to Georg von Hülsen-Haeseler (1906), TrV 218 [I: Berlin 1961].
Waltz for an operette by Maximiliano Niederberger (1921), TrV 241.

Symphony on Three Themes in E♭ major (ca. 1925), TrV 253.
Die Donau, for orchestra, chorus, and organ (1941–42), TrV 284.
Des Esels Schatten. Comedy in Six Scenes (Wieland) (1947–48), TrV 294.
Besinnung (Hesse), for chorus and orchestra (1949), TrV 298.

Lost Works

Des Alpenhirten Abschied (Schiller), song for voice and piano (ca. 1872), TrV 13.
Polka, Waltz, and other short piano works (ca. 1872), TrV 14.
Sonatina [No. 1] in C major for piano (ca. 1873), TrV 19.
Sonatina [No. 2] in E major for piano (ca. 1873), TrV 20.
Sonata in D major (1874), TrV 27.
Für Musik (Geibel), song for voice and piano (1879), TrV 74.
Drei Lieder (Geibel): *Waldgesang; O, schneller mein Roß; Die Lilien glühn in Düften* (1879) TrV 75 (the first has been preserved in its entirety, and the beginning of the second).
Frühlingsanfang (Geibel), song for voice and piano (1879), TrV 77.
Das rote Laub (Geibel), song for voice and piano (1879), TrV 78.
Wedding Music for piano and toy instruments (1879), TrV 84.
Die drei Lieder (Uhland), song for voice and piano (1879), TrV 87.
Der Morgen (Sallet), song for voice and piano (1880), TrV 89.
Immer leiser wird mein Schlummer (Lingg), song for voice and piano (1880), TrV 97.
Festival Chorus with piano accompaniment (ca. 1880), TrV 102.
Mutter, o sing mir zur Ruh (Hemans), song for voice and piano (1880), TrV 100.
Geheiligte Stätte (Fischer), song for voice and piano (1881), TrV 107.
Waldesgang (Stieler), song for voice and piano (1882), TrV 112.
Ballade (Becker), song for voice and piano (1882), TrV 113.
Mein Geist ist trüb (Böttger after Byron), song for voice and piano (1884), TrV 128.
Der Dorn ist Zeichen der Verneinung (Bodenstedt), song for voice and piano (1884), TrV 129.
Cadenzas. Wolfgang Amadé Mozart: Concerto in C minor KV 491 (1885), TrV 139.
Bardengesang (*Wir litten menschlich seit dem Tage*, Kleist) for male chorus, brass, and harp (1886), TrV 144.
Three Excerpts from Richard Wagner: *Rienzi* (1890), TrV 162.
Herbstabend, song for voice and piano (before 1910), TrV 226.

Misattributed

Der Zweikampf. Polonaise for flute, bassoon, and orchestra (1884), TrV 133.

APPENDIX C

Personalia

Ahna, Pauline de See Strauss, Pauline

Albert, Eugen d' (1864–1932). Composer and pianist. D'Albert was considered one of the most important performers of his day; in 1882, he received the honor of being named Weimar Court Pianist. In 1903, his opera *Tiefland* enjoyed vast international success. D'Albert stood especially close to Engelbert Humperdinck, belonged to the advisory board of the *Genossenschaft deutscher Tonsetzer*, and authored works conducted by Strauss himself. He also played piano at the premiere of the latter's *Burleske,* a piece demanding utmost technical mastery.

Annunzio, Gabriele d' (1863–1938). Poet. The son of a wealthy family known for his extravagant lifestyle, D'Annunzio—who stood under Wagner's spell—became one of the most important poets around the turn of the century, especially after meeting Eleonora Duse in 1894. Among his works for the stage, *Le Martyre de Saint-Sébastien* holds a key position. In 1911, Debussy set the work to music, and the poet contacted Strauss to propose a joint venture; plans for collaboration did not come to fruition, however.

Bahr, Hermann (1863–1934). Poet. Bahr hailed from Linz; following a brief sojourn in Berlin, he became a central figure in Vienna Modernism, especially as his artistic program sought to move beyond Naturalism. After converting to Catholicism and relocating to Salzburg (1912), he gradually lost his prominent status. Ten years later, Bahr moved to Munich. Around 1900, he was one of the leading lights at Max Reinhardt's theater and also involved in early plans for the Salzburg Festival. Bahr and Strauss knew each other well, and the composer's late work still shows an appreciation for the poet: Strauss sought to enlist him for *Intermezzo* when Hofmannsthal rejected the commission. Bahr dedicated his successful comedy, *Das Konzert* (which premiered in Berlin, 1909), to Strauss.

Beethoven, Ludwig van (1770–1827). Composer. Strauss's relationship to Beethoven was quite complicated. On the one hand (and wholly in line with nineteenth-century sensibilities), he considered the latter's symphonies to represent the peak of instrumental music and conducted them regularly. Strauss first conducted the *Pastorale* in Weimar in 1889; in 1895–1896, he conducted all nine symphonies in Munich. On the other hand, Strauss held that the idea of autonomous instrumental music exemplified by Beethoven could no longer continue in productive manner. On several occasions, he took issue with his forebear in compositional terms, especially in *Ein Heldenleben, Festliches Präludium,* and *Metamorphosen*—to say nothing of plans, with Hofmannsthal, to rework *Geschöpfe des Prometheus* and *Ruinen von Athen*.

Bekker, Paul (1892–1937). Music critic. Bekker started out as a violinist and conductor, but in 1906 he turned to criticism, first in Berlin and then in Frankfurt. In 1934, Bekker was forced to emigrate. His 1919 study, *Neue Musik*, coined the title for the new movement. Bekker paid due attention to Strauss all his life, albeit from a critical standpoint. In 1932, in a fictive letter to the composer, he drew up a summary balance taking issue with, and showing appreciation for, Strauss's work in equal measure.

Bellincioni, Gemma (1864–1950). Singer. Hailing from Como, Bellincioni began her career as an acclaimed singer of Verdi; with her starring role in the sensational premiere of Mascagni's *Cavalleria rusticana* (1890), she turned to *verismo*. Bellincioni was the first Salome in Italy (Turin, 1906, in a production directed by the composer) and played the role more than one hundred times. In 1911, she officially retired from the stage after playing this same role for the last time. The following year, she published *Scuola di Canto*, dedicated to Strauss "*con profonda ammirazione*."

Berg, Alban (1885–1935). Composer. Significantly younger than Strauss, Berg studied the latter's works thoroughly and numbered among guests at the 1906 production of *Salome* in Graz. In 1922, he was one of the founding members of the *Internationale Gesellschaft für Neue Musik* (headed by Strauss). In 1924, Berg received the *Kunstpreis der Stadt Wien*, especially for his *Wozzeck*. Strauss was foreman of the jury.

Berlioz, Hector (1803–1869). Composer. Strauss, who professed adherence to Lisztian tradition (especially during his tenure in Weimar), took Berlioz's works seriously—starting, in 1889, with *Symphonie fantastique*. Strauss was loath to comment systematically on his activity as conductor or composer, but he made an (indirect) exception in his 1905 treatment of Berlioz's *Traitè d'instrumentation*, commissioned by the Peters Verlag (Leipzig).

Bierbaum, Otto Julius (1865–1910). Poet. A native of Silesia, Bierbaum lived in Munich until 1893 and then in Berlin; he returned to Munich in 1903. He was one of the most important figures of incipient literary modernism in both cities. In Berlin, Bierbaum belonged to the artistic circle that regularly met at the Café des Westens (Kurfürstendamm), which Strauss, who lived nearby, also frequented. Bierbaum and Strauss first met in Munich, then in Berlin; here, Bierbaum edited the journals *PAN* and *Moderner Musenalmanach*. The composer held the poet in high esteem and set a number of his works to music: Bierbaum is the only contemporary author to whom Strauss devoted an entire book of songs (*Liederheft*). Plans for collaborative works for the stage never came to fruition.

Blech, Leo (1871–1958). Conductor. Blech, who hailed from Aachen, came via Prague to the Royal Opera in Berlin, where he worked alongside Strauss. In 1913, he was appointed General Music Director in Prussia. Including a brief interlude at the Charlottenburg Opera, his time in Berlin lasted until 1937. Fleeing to Riga, he managed to escape deportation and murder thanks to the intervention of Heinz Tietjens. He then served as royal Kapllmeister in Stockholm. At Tietjen's request, Blech returned to Berlin in 1949. Blech and Strauss held each other in high regard; it was Blech's idea to make the part of the composer in *Ariadne* a trouser role.

Böhm, Karl (1894–1981). Conductor. Böhm studied law before switching to music. After executive positions in Darmstadt and Hamburg, he went to the Dresden Opera in 1934, where he assumed the position vacated by Fritz Busch, whom National Socialist pressure had driven away. At least in part, Böhm rose to prominence as a conductor thanks to his fervent support for the regime. During the 1930s, he and Strauss were on close and friendly terms; when the latter died, he entrusted his "legacy" to the conductor. Böhm directed the premieres of *Die Schweigsame Frau* and *Daphne* (which was dedicated to him), as well as the Symphonic Fantasia from *Die Frau ohne Schatten*. He also played a key role during the composer's late period, conducting the premiere of Horn Concerto No. 2 and encouraging work on *Metamorphosen*.

Brahm, Otto (1856–1912). Critic and director. Brahm (born Abrahamsohn) came from Hamburg and moved to Berlin. His journal, *Freie Bühne für modernes Leben*, was an important mouthpiece for Naturalism; in particular, Gerhart Hauptmann numbered among the authors he supported. In 1894, Brahm took over the Deutsches Theater (which Strauss later frequented); the ensemble included Max Reinhardt. Brahm counts as one of the founders of psychological representation on the stage. In 1892, he published the letters of the painter Karl Stauffer (from the estate of Lydia Welti); the story of Stauffer's life represents one of the most significant sources for *Eine Alpensinfonie*.

Brahms, Johannes (1833–1897). Composer. Although Franz Strauss (Richard's father) participated in all the premieres of Wagner's works from *Tristan* on, he made no secret of his contempt for the composer's music. Musical luminaries esteemed in the Strauss household included Mendelssohn and Brahms. When Richard Strauss served as Kapellmeister in Meiningen, he met Brahms at the premiere of the latter's Fourth Symphony (October 1885). Relations gradually cooled, proving increasingly difficult in light of the critical reception Eduard Hanslick gave to Strauss's tone poems.

Brecher, Gustav (1879–1940). Conductor and critic. Brecher hailed from Bohemia; in 1914, after holding numerous positions, he was appointed General Music Director in Leipzig. At the opera here, he made a name for himself conducting the premieres of works by Weill and Krenek. In 1933, Brecher was forced to flee, eventually winding up in Belgium; as German troops approached, he and his wife committed suicide in May 1940. Strauss conducted the premiere of Brecher's *Rosmerholm* in 1896; in 1900, Brecher published a monograph on his contemporary and his orchestral works.

Brian, Havergal (1876–1972). Composer. The son of Staffordshire laborers, Brian began his career as a choral composer. Later, he devoted himself a vast series of symphonies, the last of which he completed at the age of more than ninety. His first symphony, *Gothic*, was written between 1919 and 1927, although it did not premiere until 1961. The gigantic work, with a playing time of 110 minutes and featuring extravagant orchestration (32 woodwinds, 56 brass instruments, organ, celesta, percussion, 2 harps, 82 strings, soloists, and adult and children's choirs), was dedicated to Richard Strauss, who deemed the composition "magnificent" (*großartig*).

Bruckner, Anton (1824–1896). Composer. All his life, Strauss displayed skepticism and reserve about Bruckner's music. Contact between the two men was sporadic, although Max Auer reports a performance, together with August Göllerich, of the slow movement of the Seventh Symphony on piano. The composers' final meeting occurred in Vienna in 1896, when *Till Eulenspiegel* and the Fourth Symphony were produced together. Strauss conducted Bruckner, whom he called a "stammering cyclops," very rarely, and only during his time in Berlin. He devoted sustained attention to the Third Symphony alone;

the First, Fourth, and Ninth featured only once in his programs, and he never performed the others.

Bülow, Hans von (1830–1894). Pianist and conductor. Born in Dresden, Bülow was decisively influenced by Richard Wagner, whom he followed to Zurich in 1850. After the scandal of his wife Cosima's adulterous liaison with the composer in Munich, Bülow lay down his appointment as royal Kapellmeister. He numbered among the most important patrons of the young Strauss, conducting premieres and supporting the composer despite an increasingly critical view of his work after *Macbeth* and *Don Juan*. Despite his own reservations, Strauss always showed Bülow the greatest respect, to whom he felt indebted.

Busch, Fritz (1890-1951). Conductor. A native of Siegen, Busch experienced a meteoric rise and became one of the most important conductors of his generation. At the age of 22, he already served as musical director in Aachen; a position in Stuttgart followed. In 1922, Busch was appointed music director at the Dresden State Opera. During this period, he and Strauss developed close personal ties, and he was responsible for the premieres of *Intermezzo* and *Die ägyptische Helena*. Known for his grueling rehearsals, Busch harbored great skepticism about the conventions of repertory orchestras. The National Socialists vigorously sought to win him over, but he unambiguously rejected their advances. After clamorous SA henchmen interfered with his production of *Rigoletto* on March 7, 1933, Busch went into exile. His relationship with Strauss, who had dedicated *Arabella* to him, was damaged beyond repair.

Carrière, Moriz (1817–1895). Philosopher. Carrière, from Hessen, taught at the university in Munich from 1853 on; starting the following year, he also lectured at the Academy of Fine Arts. A founding member of the literary society *Die Krokodile*, Carrière professed a theistic worldview derived from Hegel; his lectures on aesthetics focused on the interaction between form and expression. Strauss attended his courses in 1882 and 1883.

Corinth, Lovis (1858–1925). Painter. Corinth hailed from East Prussia. After a spell in Munich, he moved to Berlin in 1887—and then back to Munich in 1891. In 1901 Corinth settled in Berlin once again and became member of the Secession; subsequently, he returned to Bavaria. It is likely that Corinth and Strauss first met in Munich. In 1902 and 1903, the artist worked for Max Reinhardt, designing the sets for both Oscar Wilde's *Salome* (1902) and Hofmannsthal's *Elektra* (1903). Corinth is also responsible for the artwork on the title page of the piano treatment of *Elektra*.

Debussy, Claude (1862–1918). Composer. It is not possible to say when, exactly, Strauss became acquainted with Debussy. At any rate, in 1907 he conducted the *Prélude* in Vienna (together with his own *Symphonia domestica* and Wagner's *Faust*-overture). Strauss failed to appreciate *Pelléas et Mélisande* (which he heard in Paris in 1907)—even though the basic concept underlying his *Salome* resembles that of Debussy's opera. The French composer sent his counterpart the score for *La Mer* with a dedication; Strauss continued to voice support for Debussy's music during the 1930s.

Dehmel, Richard (1863–1920). Poet. A native of Brandenburg with a PhD in economics, Dehmel lived in Hamburg following divorce in 1901. As co-founder of the journal *PAN* and one of the most important representatives of nascent literary modernism, he also occasioned scandal (his poem *Venus consolatrix* was condemned in court). From the 1890s on, Strauss corresponded with Dehmel, whose poems he admired, and set eleven of them to music. Close contact lasted until at least 1910. In 1900, the poet also proposed a work for dance, *Lucifer*; Strauss evidently intended to set it to music, although he never did so.

Diaghilev, Sergej (1872–1929). Impresario. How contact arose between Diaghilev, who came from Novgorod, and Strauss cannot be said with certainty. At any rate, in 1912 Hofmannsthal and Count Harry Kessler were already working on a ballet for his *Ballets russes*. Strauss immediately agreed to the plan. The score of *Josephs Legende* was finished in February 1914. Whereas Hofmannsthal and Kessler dedicated the libretto to Diaghilev, Strauss dedicated the music to his patron Édouard Hermann. The premiere occurred in 1914 in Paris; attendees included Gabriele d'Annunzio and Romain Rolland.

Draeseke, Felix (1835–1913). Composer. A vigorous advocate of Wagner, Draeseke left Germany but returned to Dresden in 1876, where he eventually taught composition at the conservatory. In 1906, with *Salome* in mind, he published a polemical article, *Die Konfusion in der Musik*, which triggered a journalistic controversy about musical modernism in general and Richard Strauss in particular.

Dukas, Paul (1865–1935). Composer and scholar. Dukas belonged to the same generation as Strauss and admired his music. In turn, Strauss had great respect for Dukas's work, especially *Ariane et Barbe-Bleue* (1907). He also intervened on his behalf when the National Socialists sought to have the Jewish composer's works removed from programming. This led to a public dispute at the 1935 Music Festival of the Standing Council for the International Cooperation of Composers (*Musikfest des Ständigen Rats für die internationale Zusammenarbeit der Komponisten*) in Hamburg; Strauss sought to arrange a performance of *Ariane* and was forbidden from doing so. At the music festival in Vichy that same year, Strauss made a point of including the work to honor Dukas, who had died in the interim.

Eysoldt, Gertrud (1870–1955). Actress. In 1890, Eysoldt made her debut in Munich; from this point on, she was a key figure in Max Reinhardt's ensemble. Among other roles, she played Salome (Wilde) and Elektra (Hofmannsthal), epitomizing the type of the "psychological" and "nervous" woman. Strauss saw her perform in Berlin on many occasions; her acting style had effects reaching far beyond *Salome* and *Elektra*.

Fanto, Leonhard (1874–1940). Set designer. A native of Vienna, from 1902 on Fanto worked as director of costuming at the Dresden Royal Opera. In this capacity he was responsible for most premieres of Strauss's operas in the city. Together with Emil Rieck, and then Alfred Roller, Fanto played a decisive role in exemplary productions. He also made a name for himself as painter and drew a portrait of Strauss in 1927.

Franze, Johannes (1889–1968). Music critic. Franze hailed from the Rhineland. In 1920, he emigrated to Argentina and did much to promote German works at the Teatro Colón (founded in 1857), where Strauss also conducted. Strauss's correspondence with Franze affords important insight into the composer's view of his own works, especially during the late period.

Fürstner, Adolph (1833-1908) and Otto (1886–1958). Publishers. Strauss's first works appeared with the Joseph Aibl Verlag, owned by Eugen Spitzweg (1840-1914). In 1891, Strauss's lifelong business relationship with the Fürstner publishing house began; almost all his other works for the stage appeared here, and Fürstner provided his most important composer a yearly income from 1900 until 1903. In 1935, Otto Fürstner fled the National Socialist regime, to London, and leased the German publishing rights to Johannes Oertel, who became the press's proprietor in 1939. The relationship between Strauss and the publisher did not survive events. The latter sold international rights to the composer's works to Boosey & Hawkes in 1943. In 1966, remaining rights were obtained by Schott.

Furtwängler, Wilhelm (1886–1954). Conductor. During the 1920s, Furtwängler, the son of archeologist Adolf Furtwängler, became one of the most important conductors in Germany. When he succeeded Artur Nikisch at the Berlin Philharmonic, his pre-eminence was uncontested. Furtwängler never numbered among conductors close to Strauss (unlike Ernst von Schuch, then Fritz Busch, and finally Clemens Krauss or Karl Böhm). When Strauss was appointed president of the Reichsmusikkammer, he took the place of Furtwängler, who directed the Berlin State Opera. Strauss had to resign the position in the controversy surrounding Stefan Zweig in 1935; Furtwängler had already done so the previous year in support of Paul Hindemith. Although his bearing during the National Socialist period was contradictory, Furtwängler—in contrast to Böhm or Krauss—never voiced sympathy or support for the regime.

Gehmacher, Friedrich (1866–1942). Jurist. Gehmacher, from Frankenmarkt, was president of the *Arbeiter-Versicherungsanstalt*. As a member of the board of trustees at the Salzburg Mozarteum, he played a key role in the construction of its concert hall, which opened in 1914. At his instigation, Mozart's house of birth was bought by the state in 1917. The same year, Gehmacher founded the *Salzburger Festspielgemeinde*, together with the journalist Heinrich Damisch (1872–1961). The artistic advisory board included Reinhardt, Hofmannsthal, Roller, Schalk, and Strauss; the first festival took place in 1920 on the Cathedral Square. In the economic crisis following the war, the festival hall designed by Hans Poelzig (for which Strauss laid the foundation stone in 1922) could not be built; this led to the redesign of the royal mews as a performance space.

Georg II (1826–1914). Duke of Sachsen-Meiningen (1866–1914). After his father Bernhard II abdicated, Georg II assumed the regency in Meiningen and systematically reformed the state. In this context, he also promoted the arts, especially theater and music. The realistic style of representation on the Meiningen stage proved exemplary—as did the orchestral work begun under Hofkapellmeister Hans von Bülow (from 1880 on). In 1885 Georg II, on Bülow's recommendation, named Strauss musical director at court; here, the composer also met Alexander Ritter. The duke awarded Strauss the *Verdienstkreuz für Kunst und Wissenschaft* in 1866.

Gnecchi, Vittorio (1876–1954). Composer. Gnecchi composed his opera *Cassandra* in 1903, based on a libretto by Luigi Illica. The piece debuted in 1905 at the Teatro Communale of Bologna, with Arturo Toscanini conducting. In 1909, following the premiere of *Elektra*, Giovanni Tebaldini published an article, *Telepatia musicale*, in which he pointed out similarities between the two works. Discussions of possible plagiarism ensued. Gnecchi had sent his score to Strauss in 1906 and given him another copy in December that same year; the charge of plagiarism does not withstand philological scrutiny, however.

Goebbels, Joseph (1897–1945). National Socialist politician. The relationship between Goebbels and Strauss was complicated—and rocky. Goebbels' *Diaries* reveal a combination of attraction and repulsion from the 1920s on. During the second half of the 1930s, dislike and hatred are evident; in 1941, Goebbels went so far as to insult Strauss in person. Until 1944, the composer was tolerated only for the sake of maintaining appearances. Strauss, who was far from the ideal candidate, had been appointed president of the Reichsmusikkammer in 1933 with reluctance. He offered thanks by dedicating an apocryphal text by Goethe, *Das Bächlein*, to Goebbels—thereby expressing sarcastic distance on multiple levels.

Goethe, Johann Wolfgang von (1749–1832). Poet. Mindful of his own historical position, Strauss attached more and more importance to his relationship to Goethe, starting with a large-format musical adaptation in 1887 (*Wandrers Sturmlied*, Op. 14). In this context, a productive sense of rivalry also developed—evident in, for example, *Die Frau ohne Schatten*. Strauss owned the Weimar edition of Goethe's works, which he read intensively and annotated. Late in life, inspired by the biography authored by Herman Grimm (a pupil of Ranke), the composer came to concentrate on the reconciliation of antiquity and modernity along the lines of Goethe's conception of metamorphosis. The same idea also informs his late, instrumental work, especially the string arrangements.

Grab, family. The Grab family had roots in Bohemia going back to the eighteenth century, the oldest known ancestor being Herrschel Isaak, also known as Hebron Grab. The family became prosperous through oilcloth manufacture and eventually settled in Prague. Hermann Grab, grandfather of Alice (who married Strauss's son), expanded factory operations and provided workers an incomparable retirement fund. In 1915, Kaiser Franz Josef I elevated his son Emanuel (1868–1929), who had moved to Vienna before 1914, to the hereditary nobility as Ritter Grab von Hermannswörth; after the end of the monarchy, he went by Grab-Hermannswörth. A son of Emanuel's brother Hugo was the author Hermann Grab. Many members of the family managed to survive National Socialism by emigrating in time.

Gregor, Joseph (1888–1960). Librarian and author. Gregor hailed from Czernowitz and received his doctorate in Vienna. After a brief engagement as assistant director to Max Reinhardt, he secured a position at the Austrian National Library in 1911, where he started the theater collection in 1922. When Stefan Zweig stopped working with Strauss, he eventually suggested Gregor as a collaborator. The latter was never the composer's equal, however; Strauss engaged him only to carry out plans already made with others. The "partnership" was difficult—humiliating, even—and ended during work on *Capriccio*. Gregor's *Weltgeschichte des Theaters* (1944) reflects this difficult collaboration in some respects.

Halbe, Max (1862–1944). Writer. Halbe came from West Prussia; after studying and completing his doctorate, he settled in Munich in 1895, where he founded the *Intimes Theater*. Halbe's *Jugend* (1893) was a pioneering work of Naturalism for the stage. However, Halbe soon distanced himself from the movement and emerged as a key player in Munich modernism. Strauss witnessed the opening of the *Intimes Theater*, which provided the model for Max Reinhardt's Kleines Theater in Berlin not long thereafter. In

1897—together with Halbe, Ernst von Wolzogen, and Ludwig Ganghofer—the composer founded a literary society in Munich.

Hanslick, Eduard (1825–1904). Musicologist and music critic. Hanslick took note of Strauss early on, but he harbored major reservations about the tone poems, ultimately rejecting them altogether. (In contrast, he appreciated Pauline de Ahna's singing.) For Strauss, the critic's name became synonymous with the formalist aesthetics he deemed unproductive from the 1880s on.

Hartmann, Rudolf (1900–1988). Manager. Hartmann, who was born in Ingolstadt, held his first appointments in Bamberg and Altenburg; in 1928, he moved to Nuremberg, where he first met Strauss, and became senior director (*Oberspielleiter*). In 1934, Heinz Tietjen hired Hartmann as senior director at the Berlin State Opera, where he worked closely with Clemens Krauss, then followed him to Munich in 1937. Following denazification, Hartmann became the manager there in 1952 and played a key role in rebuilding the hall, which had been destroyed during the war. Thanks to the involvement of Strauss and Krauss, productions in Munich were considered exemplary. Hartmann staged the premieres of *Friedenstag, Capriccio,* and *Die Liebe der Danae*.

Hauptmann, Gerhart (1862–1946). Novelist and playwright. In 1880s Berlin, Hauptmann became the most important representative of Naturalism, first at Otto Brahm's theater, then at Max Reinhardt's. From 1901 on, he resided at his estate in Agnetendorf and was considered the leading author of the German Empire—and, in turn, the Weimar Republic. An honorary member of the Berlin Secession, Hauptmann met Strauss during the 1890s. Both men belonged to the *Verein zur Förderung der Kunst* as honorary chairmen. When Strauss was commissioned to compose the Olympic Hymn in 1932, he immediately thought of Hauptmann. Respectful and amicable correspondence between the composer and writer continued until 1944.

Hausegger, Siegmund von (1872–1948). Composer, conductor, and author. He was the son of music critic and philosopher Friedrich von Hausegger, whose *Die künstlerische Persönlichkeit* (1897) contains a rare example of Strauss commenting on his own works. Siegmund von Hausegger held conducting positions in Munich, Frankfurt am Main, and Hamburg; in 1920, he returned to Munich and became director of the Academy of Music. Strauss occasionally conducted his works in Berlin, but relations were always formal.

Henckell, Karl (1864–1929). Writer. A native of Hanover, Henckell relocated to Zurich and made a name for himself writing poetry and prose with a socially critical bent. Strauss and Henckell met in 1895. Along with Otto Julius Bierbaum, he was the most important poet for the composer before his collaboration with Hofmannsthal. Strauss had set nine of Henckell's poems to music by 1906. The relationship was close, and they planned a joint tour of musical and poetic performances (which never occurred). Strauss also selected a number of Henckell's poems for adaptation, but only completed some of them.

Hesse, Hermann (1877–1962). Writer. Hesse, a native of Calw, relocated to Ticino, Switzerland, in 1919. At an early date, Strauss already considered setting his poems to music, but he did not do so. The composer came back to the poet in three of his late orchestral Lieder. Hesse kept his distance from Strauss, disapproving of his accommodating attitude toward National Socialism and preferring the musical adaptations of his works by Othmar Schoeck.

Hindemith, Paul (1895–1963). Composer. Hindemith and Strauss probably first met in Donaueschingen, where Strauss headed the honorary committee of the festival and Hindemith belonged to its working committee. At Donaueschingen, Strauss heard Hindemith's Second String Quartet appreciatively, even though its style was foreign to his sensibility. Further encounters occurred rarely—for instance in 1938, following a production of Lortzing's *Wildschütz* conducted by Hans Swarowsky in Zurich.

Hitler, Adolf (1889–1945). Dictator. Hitler's relationship to music has been studied at length. While possessed of a veritable mania for Wagner—which most of the composer's family repaid in kind—Hitler held an ambivalent view of contemporary music. He had attended *Salome* in Graz in 1906, but Strauss did not enjoy the dictator's favors either in personal terms or for his compositions. Hitler originally wanted Max von Schillings, a strict man of the party, to head the Reichsmusikkammer. Following the premiere of *Die Schweigsame Frau* and Strauss's forced resignation from the Reichsmusikkammer, Hitler wanted nothing more to do with the composer, who retained his commission for the Olympic Hymn so that political appearances would be preserved. The document signed by Martin Bormann declaring Strauss a *persona non grata* in January 1944 went back to a personal decision made by Hitler himself.

Hochberg, Hans Heinrich XIV. Bolko von (1843–1926). Diplomat and manager. Following his *Abitur*, Hochberg busied himself primarily with composition; in 1886, he was called to Berlin to be General Manager of the Royal Theater (*Generalintendant der königlichen Schauspiele*). In this position, which he held until a grave conflict arose in 1902, he was responsible for all the state stages in Prussia, that is, also outside of Berlin. It was essentially his decision to engage Strauss in 1898. Hochberg was granted regular audiences with the kaiser to inform him of theater business, which he managed through a finely spun network of connections. In 1909, Strauss conducted the premiere of Hochberg's Third Symphony.

Hofmannsthal, Hugo Laurenz August Edler von (1874–1929). Poet. Hofmannsthal studied in Vienna; already at a young age, he numbered among the stars of modernism in the city. In 1901, he married Gertrud Schlesinger, withdrew from literary circles, and settled in Rodaun. From this point on, Hofmannsthal adopted an increasingly critical view of the *fin de siècle* and sought a new artistic beginning. In this context, the Deutsches Theater in Berlin—under first Otto Brahm, then Max Reinhardt—played a major role. Strauss and Hofmannsthal met for the first time in 1899; closer contact began after the premiere of *Elektra* in 1903. Setting the drama to music yielded a multilayered, multifaceted, and remarkably systematic work, defining opera as the fitting artistic response to the challenges of modernity. Collaboration often proved difficult and almost dissolved on more than one occasion, but the poet and composer continued working together until Hofmannsthal's sudden death. With the exception of *Die Schweigsame Frau*, Strauss's projects during the 1930s all stemmed from collaboration with Hofmannsthal. By personal agreement, royalties went to both composer and librettist.

Hülsen-Haeseler, Georg von (1858–1922). Hülsen-Haeseler, son of the royal theater manager (*Hoftheaterintendant*) Botho von Hülsen, pursued a military career before switching to the theater in 1903, when he assumed the position formerly held by Bolko von Hochberg. In this capacity, Hülsen-Haeseler enjoyed great freedom, even when the kaiser was of a different opinion. Berlin theater experienced a heyday at the beginning of the twentieth century in large part thanks to his efforts. Relations with Strauss were not easy as the latter took great liberties in his works. Hülsen-Haeseler held the office until the monarchy collapsed in 1918.

Humperdinck, Engelbert (1854–1921). Composer. Personal contact between Strauss and Humperdinck started in 1890, based on shared enthusiasm for Wagner (for whom Humperdinck had been an assistant in the production of *Parsifal*). Friendship with composers was otherwise rare for Strauss. In 1893, he conducted the premiere of *Hänsel und Gretel*, the universally admired high point of Humperdinck's career, in Weimar. Following a position in Frankfurt, Humperdinck moved to Berlin in 1900 in order to found a course in composition at the Academy of Arts. In Berlin, where Strauss conducted the premiere of another opera, their relations were especially close. Humperdinck also wrote music for Max Reinhardt's stage. He resigned from all appointments in 1920, due to enduring difficulties following a stroke.

Jeritza, Maria (1887–1982). Singer. Born Marie Jedličková, Jeritza adopted her stage name in 1913. The previous year, she sang the title role in the premiere of *Ariadne* in Stuttgart and soon became a celebrated ensemble member at the Vienna Court Opera. Here, her roles included the part of the Empress in the premiere of *Die Frau ohne Schatten*. With a style shaped by work with Max Reinhardt, Jeritza was an exemplary singer and actress in Strauss's eyes. The composer dedicated *Malven*, his 1948 Lied for piano, to her: "To dear Maria, this final rose"; until her death, Jeritza safeguarded the work.

Kerr, Alfred (1867–1948). Poet and journalist. Alfred Kempner, who went by "Kerr" from 1909 on, hailed from Breslau. In the theatrical world around the turn of the century, he was a precise observer, formidable critic, and committed fellow traveler. During the 1910s he displayed increasing reserve about modernist tendencies. His highly ironic *Krämerspiegel*, written in 1918 for Strauss, represents an exception among the composer's works. Kerr, who was Jewish, resolutely opposed National Socialism and numbered among the intellectuals facing immediate persecution under the regime. In February 1933, he fled Germany—returning, in 1948, on a lecture tour.

Kessler, Count Harry (1868–1937). Art collector and writer. Kessler, who was ennobled in 1881, was officially the son of a Hamburg banker; it is possible, however, that he was the illegitimate child of Kaiser Wilhelm I. After completing his studies, Kessler went to Berlin in 1893; a decade later, he became director of the Museum for Art and Trade (*Museum für Kunst und Gewerbe*) in Weimar. In 1898, he met Hofmannsthal, and the two men became fast friends. Kessler played a decisive role in the genesis of *Der Rosenkavalier* and *Josephs Legende*. A firm believer in European culture, he welcomed republican government after 1918. His relationship with Strauss remained difficult to the end.

Knappertsbusch, Hans (1888–1965). Conductor. Following appointments in Elberfeld, Leipzig, and Dessau, Knappertsbusch held the position of General Musical Director in Munich until he was forced to resign for political reasons in 1935. He and Strauss had personal dealings with each other from 1922 on; in 1927, the composer even wrote his "Ten Golden Rules of Conducting" for him. That said, the relationship was difficult.

The "Protest of the Richard Wagner City of Munich" (*Protest der Richard-Wagner-Stadt München*), which was published April 16, 1933 and led to threats to Thomas Mann's very life, was essentially Knappertsbusch's idea. Signatories included Strauss, although he had not read the document. A falling-out took place in 1935; no personal interaction occurred after this point.

Knobel, Betty (1904–1998). Journalist. Although a vocational teacher by trade, Knobel was also active as a journalist and writer from 1936 on, primarily in Glarus. In 1948, Strauss struck upon her poem *Malven* by chance and set it to music.

Krauss, Clemens (1893–1954). Conductor. Krauss succeeded Franz Schalk at the Vienna State Opera in 1929; in 1935, he was appointed General Music Director of the Berlin State Opera, which started his meteoric rise under the National Socialist regime. In 1937, at the express request of Hitler, he became General Music Director in Munich; following the annexation of Austria, he was also rector of the Mozarteum and manager of the Salzburg Festival. When Fritz Busch emigrated, Krauss took over conducting the premiere of *Arabella*, beginning his relationship to Strauss, which lasted until the composer died. Strauss dedicated *Friedenstag* to Krauss, who conducted the premiere of this work and *Capriccio*, as well as the dress rehearsal (and later premiere) of *Die Liebe der Danae*. When collaboration between Strauss and Joseph Gregor fell apart, Krauss collaborated on the libretto for *Capriccio*, which was also dedicated to him. In 1945, the conductor was prohibited from further performances and no longer had a foothold in the German-speaking world.

Lehmann, Lotte (1888–1976). Singer. A native of Perleberg, Lehmann belonged to the ensemble of the Vienna Court Opera from 1916 on. Here she played the Dyer's Wife in the premiere of *Die Frau ohne Schatten*; at the 1924 premiere of *Intermezzo*, in Dresden, she played the part of Christine. Lehmann's roles in Vienna included Sophie and Octavian, and finally the Marschallin, for which she was best known. Until 1937, Lehmann was also a member of the ensemble at the Salzburg Festival; Max Reinhardt and Strauss played key parts in casting members. When courted by the National Socialists, she opted for exile in New York, where she became one of the most important personalities of the Metropolitan Opera.

Levi, Hermann (1839–1900). Conductor. The son of a chief rabbi (*Landesrabbiner*), Levi held various positions before being appointed Court Music Director in Karlsruhe from 1864 to 1872; from here, contact with Richard Wagner was established. Levi assisted in rehearsals for the premiere of the *Ring* and directed *Parsifal* in 1882 and following years. From 1872 on, he held the position of Court Kapellmeister in Munich; he stepped down in 1896 for health reasons. Levi exercised a formative influence on the young Strauss; in 1894, while the elder man was still in office, the composer came to Munich to fill the position. Levi conducted the premieres of a number of Strauss's early works.

Liebermann, Max (1847–1935). Painter. Liebermann counted as the most important painter of Berlin modernism. As the chief officer of the Berlin Secession, he also exercised considerable influence in artistic politics. From 1920 until 1932, Liebermann was President of the Prussian Academy of the Arts, then Honorary President until the National Socialists came to power. Strauss commissioned Liebermann to paint two portraits: one for a public collection (today in Berlin), the second for private display (now in Garmisch). The latter—which Pauline Strauss did not like—is the most important likeness of Strauss to have been made.

Lindner, Anton (1874–1928). Writer and translator. Linder was born in Lviv, but his family relocated to Vienna when he was a child. In Vienna, Linder worked as a writer and journalist—and became known for opposing the *fin de siècle*. In 1913, he moved and became editor of the *Neue Hamburger Zeitung*. Strauss set one of Lindner's poems to music (and had—unrealized—plans for more). The writer first drew the composer's attention to Wilde's *Salome* and sent him his own treatment of the work; Strauss opted for the original (in German translation), instead.

Liszt, Franz (1811–1886). Composer and pianist. When Strauss attended *Parsifal* rehearsals with his father, he is likely to have seen Liszt, too. His relationship to the latter was largely shaped by his proximity to the Bayreuth circle. Strauss regularly included Liszt's orchestral works up into his Berlin period. In 1911, responding to questions from the *Allgemeine Musik-Zeitung* on the occasion of Liszt's hundredth birthday, Strauss emphasized that his forebear had been the first to "understand Beethoven correctly" before Wagner. Liszt's concept of symphonic poetry was important for Strauss, even if he disagreed on key points (especially the extent to which form admits generalization). When Strauss abandoned orchestral composition, he consigned Liszt to the historical past.

Ludwig II (1845–1886). King of Bavaria (1864–1886). With Ludwig's accession the same year that Strauss was born, Munich fell entirely under the spell of Richard Wagner. City planning, the project for a festival hall, and productions were all organized with an eye to fusing art and life in keeping with a Wagnerian vision. During his childhood and youth, Strauss witnessed Ludwig's grand scheme at every turn. His father's appointment at court also familiarized him with the inner workings of the Hofkapelle. Strauss received his Munich appointment in 1886 at the monarch's behest.

Luitpold Karl Joseph Wilhelm von Bayern (1821–1912), Prince Regent of Bavaria (1886-1912). Luitpold already had to assume public duties during the reign of his nephew Ludwig II, who was often absent from the capital. When the latter was declared legally incompetent (June 9, 1886), Luitpold governed as prince regent for three days. After Ludwig's death, his brother Otto succeeded him officially, but he was mentally ill. A vice-regency was proclaimed (July 28, 1886), and Luitpold remained in power. While he held this position, preparations were made to turn the state into a parliamentary monarchy. Luitpold was also a patron of the arts; during his tenure, Munich became a center for nascent modernism, exercising a magnetic pull on painters, poets, and musicians. Strauss's terms as royal Kapellmeister in Munich (1894–1898) coincided with this heyday.

Mackay, John Henry (1864-1933). Writer. Hailing from Scotland, Mackay spent almost his whole life in Germany—especially in Berlin, where he was close to the Friedrichshagen circle of poets. Mackay, who was homosexual and endorsed pedophilia, provoked scandal when he published *Die Anarchisten*, a novel celebrating radical individualism with a socialist color. Strauss first met Mackay in 1891—a "stimulating acquaintance" [*reizende Bekanntschaft*], as he told his father. Mackay inspired the composer to engage with Max Stirner's philosophy. Strauss also set four of Mackay's poems to music. The writer's influence on the conception of the subject in *Zarathustra* and *Guntram* was significant.

Mahler, Gustav (1860–1911). Composer and conductor. Contact between Mahler and Strauss started in 1888 and lasted until the former's death. Strauss esteemed his contemporary greatly, even though the two men's ideas differed fundamentally. Strauss, who dismissed metaphysics from music, deemed Mahler, who affirmed the deep connection between music and worldview, his opposite. Strauss facilitated productions (the First Symphony in Weimar [1895], then excerpts from the Second in Berlin [1895]), and also conducted his works. When Mahler—who had played a key role in the final form that *Eine Alpensinfonie* assumed—died in 1911, Strauss directed the Third Symphony in his honor. For his part, Mahler had conducted several works by Strauss in Vienna, starting with the preludes to Acts One and Two of *Guntram*; he also backed the performance of *Salome* in Graz when the work ran into difficulties with censors (1906).

Mann, Thomas (1875–1955). Writer. Like many young intellectuals, Mann was drawn to Munich during the so-called *Prinzeregentenzeit*. It is unclear whether he and Strauss met there, although the composer occasionally paid social calls to the Pringsheim family until 1898. Biographical parallels (one patrician parent and the other with an artistic bent) and productive differences with Wagner are striking. Likewise, Strauss and Mann were both interested in achieving a fusion of life and art. Relations broke off in 1933, when Strauss signed the *Protest der Richard-Wagner-Stadt München* against Mann. *Doktor Faustus*, which contains a literary monument to the 1906 production of *Salome* in Graz, implicitly engages with Strauss (whose music for *Der Rosenkavalier* the author failed to appreciate). As part of the occupying forces after the Second World War, Klaus Mann interviewed Strauss in Garmisch for the U.S. army newspaper; his autobiography contains an account of the meeting.

Mariotte, Antoine (1875–1944). Composer. Mariotte set out to compose a *Salomé* of his own in the belief that the complicated circumstances surrounding Wilde's estate ensured his rights to the play. However, the Fürstner Verlag had secured rights for Strauss. In 1908, after lengthy legal disputes, Mariotte's *Salomé* premiered in Lyon. Meanwhile, Strauss undertook a French version, which he intended to write in collaboration with Romain Rolland.

Mengelberg, Willem (1871–1951). Conductor. In 1895, Mengelberg became head conductor of the Concertgebouw Orkest in Amsterdam, a position he held until 1945. He also had major visiting appointments in Frankfurt (1908 to 1920) and New York (1921 to 1930). An uncompromising experimenter, Mengelberg counted as one of the foremost personalities in the conducting world. His engagement on behalf of Gustav Mahler and Richard Strauss, with whom he enjoyed friendly relations to the end, bore particular weight. The composer dedicated *Ein Heldenleben* to Mengelberg, who directed the work with major changes to the instrumentation. The conductor openly sympathized with the National Socialists during the occupation of the Netherlands. In 1944, he relocated to Switzerland; following the war, he was no longer permitted to perform in his native country.

Meysenheim, Cornelie (1853–1923). Singer. Born in the Netherlands, Meysenheim joined the Munich Royal Court Opera in 1872. Apart from a brief engagement in Karlsruhe, she stayed here until 1896, after which she made appearances only in a guest capacity. On April 16, 1881, Meysenheim performed an evening of Lieder that included three songs by Strauss—the first time his vocal works had a public audience.

Moralt, Rudolf (1902–1958). Conductor. Theodor Moralt (1817–1877), who came from an artistic family in Switzerland and served as treasurer for the Royal Theater, married Maria Louisa Pschorr (1834–1889), sister of Georg and Josephine Pschorr. The marriage produced three sons. The son of the second son was named Rudolf, like his father, and became a conductor. Following various appointments, this grand-nephew of Richard Strauss became first Kapellmeister of the Vienna State Opera in 1940—a position he held until his unexpected death (after a rehearsal of *Josephs Legende*). Moralt counted as major conductor of Strauss and Wagner; his family was also related to Strauss's first publisher, Eugen Spitzweg.

Mottl, Felix von (1856–1911). Conductor. A native of Vienna, Mottl had formative experiences in Bayreuth, where he worked as an assistant in 1876 and then conducted regularly until 1906. In 1907, following engagements in Karlsruhe and New York, Mottl became Royal Kapellmeister in Munich. Here, in 1911, he experienced a heart attack during a production of *Tristan* and died soon thereafter. Strauss held Mottl in high regard, and he directed the premiere of his opera *Fürst und Sänger* in 1894 (even though he viewed him as a competitor at the time). In turn, Mottl regularly conducted Strauss's works, including *Der Rosenkavalier* one week after its premiere in 1911.

Mozart, Wolfgang Amadeus (1756–1791). Composer. Strauss engaged productively with Mozart's works all his life with different points of emphasis (and notwithstanding his admiration for Wagner). Time and again, he conducted Mozart, whom he credited with having created new sonic textures (*Klangbilder*). At his very first concert in Meiningen (which was also his first concert as Kapellmeister, October 18, 1885), Strauss performed as the soloist in Mozart's Concerto in C minor K 491 (October 18, 1885); Bülow conducted. Mozart's collaboration witth Da Ponte served as a model for Strauss's work together with Hoffmansthal; *Le Nozze di Figaro* provided a point of reference for *Der Rosenkavalier*. Strauss, Hofmannsthal, and Reinhardt deemed it important that the Salzburg Festival be held in Mozart's native city. *Die Zauberflöte* played a key role in the conception underlying *Die Frau ohne Schatten*, and the adaptation of *Idomeneo* (made together with Lothar Wallerstein) offered a source of legitimation for Strauss's view of antiquity. Finally, Mozart's works represent a vanishing point for the composer's late works, especially the sonatinas for woodwinds.

Muck, Carl (1859–1940). Conductor. Muck, who had earned a doctorate in classical philology, held appointments in Zurich, Salzburg, Brünn, and Graz; in 1886, he came to the attention of the impresario Angelo Neumann, especially for conducting Wagner. In 1892, Muck was appointed Kapellmeister at the Royal Opera in Berlin. In 1908, he and Strauss jointly held the position of General Music Director. Muck left for the Boston Symphony four years later and finally retired in 1933.

Nietzsche, Friedrich (1844–1900). Philosopher. It is difficult to say when Strauss started to engage with Nietzsche's works in earnest, but the process likely began in the early 1890s. Reading Nietzsche proved a formative experience and shaped the composer's outlook at least until he began working with Hofmannsthal. Against the backdrop of reading Schopenhauer, Strauss took interest in Nietzsche for a number of reasons: atheistic self-affirmation of the subject, productive nihilism, the critique of morality, forging a productive distance from Wagner, and the rejection of systematicity. In contrast to the generation that followed him, Strauss was put off by the totalitarian aspects of Nietzsche's celebration of "leadership" (*Führerschaft*). Starting with *Guntram*, engagement with the philosopher played an implicit role in the composer's work—and an explicit one in *Zarathustra* and *Alpensinfonie*. The former abandons coherent logic in favor of an aphoristic structure that proceeds paratactically. Productive distance to Nietzsche is evident in the failure of the "deed" in *Elektra* and Strauss's turn to comedy—first in *Feuersnot*, then in *Der Rosenkavalier*.

Panizza, Oskar (1853–1921). Writer and journalist. Following unsuccessful musical efforts, Panizza studied medicine and briefly practiced psychiatry. In 1890s Munich, he became a scandalous literary figure, writing atheistic, blasphemous, and pornographic satires in a phonetic writing system of his own devising. Panizza had contracted syphilis in 1878; his radically individualistic anarchism resembled Mackay's. Panizza's play *Das Liebeskonzil* (1894) was condemned in a sensational trial, and the author served a prison term. Strauss, who set one of his poems to music in 1901, stood under his spell for at least a while; Panizza also inspired aspects of the composer's adaptation of *Salome*.

Pfitzner, Hans (1869–1949). Composer. Strauss's relationship with Pfitzner was difficult, if not doomed, from the outset. The reasons lay in the latter's personality and sense of artistic destiny—which was particularly pronounced at the celebrated Munich premiere of his *Palestrina* (1917). Strauss failed to appreciate the work (or anything else that tied music to metaphysical claims). Pfitzner's adherence to tradition, along with his increasing nationalism, struck his contemporary as ridiculous to the end.

Possart, Ernst von (1841–1921). Actor and manager. Possart, who hailed from Berlin, was first active in Munich from 1873 until 1888. From 1893 on, he served as general director and manager of the Royal Theater and enjoyed the favor of Prince Regent Luitpold; he retired in 1905. Strauss's relationship with Possart was less than warm at first, but it ultimately proved fruitful. Possart loved the genre of melodrama, and Strauss composed *Enoch Arden*, Op. 38, for him; the two men collaborated in the work's premiere and numerous touring performances (followed by *Das Schloss am Meer* [1899]). Possart played an important role in reviving appreciation for Mozart in Munich, where Strauss conducted the restored version of *Così fan tutte* in 1897. He was also involved in the construction of the *Prinzregententheater*, by Max Littmann (1901).

Prantl, Carl von (1820–1888). Philosopher. Prantl was an adjunct (1847), then a full (1859), professor at the university in Munich, teaching first philology, then philosophy. During his brief studies in 1882–1883, Strauss attended lectures by Prantl, who professed a version of objective idealism; soon, the composer would vehemently criticize this outlook.

Pringsheim, Klaus (1883–1972). Conductor and composer. The son of Alfred and Hedwig Pringsheim, Klaus was the twin brother of Katia, who later married Thomas Mann. In the 1890s, Strauss became acquainted with the siblings at the family home in the Munich Arcisstrasse. Pringsheim, who studied music after his *Abitur* in 1901, resolutely sided with Strauss in the *Salome*-controversy started by Felix Draeseke; in his eyes, an entirely new mode of composition was in evidence.

Pschorr, family. Originally from Ammersee, the Pschorrs resided in Munich from the late eighteenth century on, where the family operated a brewery. When Josef Pschorr (1770–1841) married Maria Theresia Hacker, he came into possession of another brewery owned by his father-in-law. Thanks to a complicated cooling technique that enabled beer to be preserved for longer periods, the breweries became leading commercial enterprises, and the family joined the ranks of wealthy and influential Munich society. Josef Pschorr willed the businesses to his brothers Georg (1798–1867), who took over the Pschorr brewery, and Matthias (1800–1879), who inherited the Hacker brewery. The latter's son, also named Matthias (1834–1900), had no heirs; he turned the enterprise into a public limited company in 1881. Georg's son, who had the same name as his father (1830–1894), transformed the Pschorr brewery into an industrial concern. Their sister Josephine (in fact, Josepha [1838–1910]) married Franz Strauss, a musician at court, in 1863. The union produced two children: Richard (1864–1949) and Johanna (1867–1966). From 1894 on, three of Georg's sons co-owned the Pschorr company; in 1922, the firm became a stock corporation. In 1972, the Hacker and Pschorr breweries merged once and for all. Strauss dedicated *Der Rosenkavalier* to the Pschorr family.

Raabe, Peter (1872–1945). Conductor and journalist. A native of Frankfurt an der Oder, Raabe trained as a conductor. In 1920, he was named General Music Director in Aachen, where Herbert von Karajan succeeded him when he left for Weimar in 1935. Upon Strauss's resignation from the presidency of the Reichsmusikkammer, Goebbels appointed Raabe. Although a genuine agent of the regime, he increasingly came into conflict with the party line on fundamental matters; in consequence, the Ministry of Propaganda restricted his discretionary power and monitored his activities. Relations between Raabe and Strauss were businesslike. In early 1935—and likely with ironic intent—Strauss dedicated to him an adaptation of Goethe, *Zugemessne Rhythmen*.

Reger, Max (1873–1916). Composer. Strauss and Reger occasionally had personal meetings, and each man followed the other's works. Strauss also put Reger in touch with the publisher Eugen Spitzweg. At a 1915 Strauss concert, Reger conducted his Mozart variations and *Vaterländische Ouvertüre*. The following year, in memory of his departed contemporary—who had stepped in on his behalf in the controversy surrounding *Salome*—Strauss conducted the *Sinfonischer Prolog*. All in all, however, the two composers kept their distance.

Reinhardt, Max (1873–1943). Actor and manager. Reinhardt, whose real name was Max Goldmann, was born in Baden near Vienna. In 1894, he was called by Otto Brahm to Berlin, where his meteoric career began. Reinhardt became the most important theatrical figure in the German Empire and Weimar Republic, directing the Kleines Theater, Deutsches Theater, and Theater am Schiffbauerdamm. His authors of choice included Hofmannsthal, and he seems to have done much to facilitate collaboration between the poet and Strauss. Reinhardt's psychologizing theater, which exercised a strong force of attraction on the composer, departed from Brahm's naturalism; Hofmannsthal's term for the effect was "the social." The conception of comedy at work in *Der Rosenkavalier* would have been unthinkable without Reinhardt. When Dresden rehearsals of the opera threatened to fall apart, Strauss made a point of insisting on Reinhardt's involvement. To express his gratitude, the composer also dedicated the music of *Ariadne* (in all four versions) to him. In 1911, Hofmannsthal's *Jedermann* premiered at the Berlin *Zirkus*

Schumann under the direction of Reinhardt, who also played a decisive role in establishing the Salzburg Festival. The director emigrated to the United States in 1937.

Reinhart, Werner (1884–1951). Patron. The third of five children born to the wealthy Winterthur merchant Theodor Reinhart and his wife Lilly, Reinhart focused all his energy on promoting music and made his native city—where he was also responsible for engaging Hermann Scherchen—a center for contemporary music. Reinhart supported many composers (including Braunfels, Hindemith, Stravinsky, and Webern) and played a key role in the founding of the *Internationale Gesellschaft für Neue Musik*. His relationship with Strauss started in 1934, when the latter conducted *Eine Alpensinfonie* in Winterthur. Reinhart was instrumental in the composer's move to Switzerland and a key figure for his late work. Strauss's Sonatina No. 2, which premiered in Winterthur, is dedicated to him.

Reucker, Alfred (1868-1958). Actor and manager. Reucker, from Bergisches Land, managed the opera and stage in Zurich from 1901 to 1921, where he made a mark both in terms of music (for instance, a production of *Parsifal*) and drama (when Gertrud Eysoldt debuted, in particular). In 1921, he was called to manage the theater in Dresden; here, he worked continuously with Strauss, beginning with *Ariadne* and *Die Frau ohne Schatten*. In conjunction with Fritz Busch, *Intermezzo* and *Helena* premiered; Strauss dedicated *Arabella* to the latter and Reucker. In March, one day after Busch was forced to leave, Reucker was fired by the National Socialist administration and retreated to private life in Dresden.

Rheinberger, Joseph Gabriel (1839–1901). Composer. A native of Vaduz, Rheinberger came to Munich at a young age. He first taught piano at the Conservatory, then, from 1876 on, was professor of composition and organ at the newly founded Royal School of Music. In Strauss's eyes, Rheinberger represented a "strictly conservative direction," but he still played a mentor's role for the young composer. At the instigation of Franz Strauss, Rheinberger evaluated the young Strauss's compositions on several occasions. In 1894, Strauss premiered Rheinberger's Organ Concerto No. 2.

Riehl, Wilhelm Heinrich von (1823–1897). Cultural historian. From Biebrich, Riehl held the position of full professor of cultural history in Munich beginning in 1859. In marked contrast to contemporary neoliberalism, which focused on urban life, he advanced a model of society that focused on ethical, not economic, factors in human affairs. Strauss attended his lectures In 1882–1883; the views he encountered in this context may have informed his later collaborations with Hofmannsthal.

Ritter, Alexander (1833–1896). Violinist and composer. Ritter was born in Estonia. Through his mother Julie, who actively supported Wagner from 1849 on, he fell under the spell of the latter's music. In 1854, Ritter married a niece of the composer. In 1882, through Bülow's mediation, he was appointed concertmaster of the Hofkapelle at Meiningen. Ritter met Strauss here and passed along his love for Wagner to him. He followed Strauss to Munich in 1886. The relationship between the two men was close, and Strauss acknowledged his friend's formative influence all his life. The composer owed his turn to dramatic music to Ritter, even though *Guntram* led to disagreements that were never resolved. In 1890, Strauss conducted the premiere of Ritter's opera *Wem die Krone* in Weimar.

Rösch, Friedrich (1862–1925). Conductor and jurist. Hailing from Memmingen, Rösch was co-founder of the *Genossenschaft deutscher Tonsetzer*; beginning in 1919, he served as chairman for the *Allgemeiner Deutscher Musikverein*. Strauss and Rösch first met during the 1880s. He was the composer's most important ally and adviser in matters of musical copyright. Strauss dedicated *Feuersnot* to Rösch and delivered the eulogy at his funeral in 1925.

Rohlfs, Christian (1849–1938). Painter. In artistic terms, Rohlfs stood close to Expressionism. It is likely that Strauss made his acquaintance in Weimar; he especially admired his canvases, and acquired several of his works.

Rolland, Romain (1866–1944). Writer. Rolland, who was awarded the 1915 Nobel Prize in literature, championed European humanist culture. Strauss and Rolland met in Bayreuth in 1891; their correspondence proved intensive and remarkably candid, even though Rolland had reservations. Strauss's plans for a French version of *Salomé* would not have been possible without his assistance.

Roller, Alfred (1864–1935). Set designer. A native of Brno, Roller joined the Vienna Royal Opera in 1903 at Gustav Mahler's instigation. He remained true to the city all his life. Strauss's work with Roller likely occurred thanks to Max Reinhardt, and it played a formative role from *Der Rosenkavalier* on. (*Die Frau ohne Schatten* posed a particular challenge.) Roller also belonged to the founding circle of the Salzburg Festival, where he made the set designs for Hofmannsthal's *Jedermann*. His admirers included Hitler, who had wanted to be apprenticed to him in 1908. In 1934, when the original staging of *Parsifal* in Bayreuth was changed (and Strauss directed the opera), Roller provided the set designs at the dictator's express request.

Rosenauer, Michael (1884–1971). Architect. Born in Weis, Rosenauer moved to Vienna in 1909; here, he became an advocate of *Neue Sachlichkeit*. His design for Strauss's villa (made in close collaboration with the composer) in 1922 was his first major private commission. Rosenauer emigrated to London in 1928.

Sacher, Paul (1906–1999). Conductor and patron. Contact between Sacher and Strauss was struck in the 1940s—and possibly involved competition with Werner Reinhart. Sacher played a decisive role facilitating Strauss's composition of *Metamorphosen*, and he conducted the work's premiere in Zurich. Relations did not extend further, however.

Schalk, Franz (1863–1931). Conductor. A native of Vienna, Schalk numbered among the foremost conductors of his generation. After appointments in Graz and Prague, as well as guest engagements in London and New York, he went to Berlin in 1898; from here, Gustav Mahler recruited him for the Vienna Court Opera. From 1919 to 1924, he directed the opera together with Strauss, and from 1929 alone. Schalk was somewhat notorious for his adaptations of symphonies by Brucker, whom he knew personally, but proved a conductor of significant influence. His work with Strauss, which began when he conducted *Die Frau ohne Schatten*, went smoothly at first, then, after two years, became increasingly difficult—especially since Strauss did not bother much with day-to-day responsibilities. All the same, the period of their joint activity represented the institution's heyday once it was no longer under courtly patronage.

Schillings, Max von (1868–1933). Composer and conductor. Schillings and Strauss met during the 1880s; over time, agreement gave way to distance. In 1919, Schillings succeeded

Strauss as director of the Prussian State Opera. He was a doctrinaire National Socialist and party member. In spring 1933, in the capacity of president of the Prussian Academy of the Arts, he saw to it that all racially and politically unsuitable individuals were dismissed. Schillings was the ideal candidate for heading the Reichsmusikkammer, but he died from cancer in July 1933.

Schirach, Baldur von (1907–1974). National Socialist politician. Schirach joined the National Socialist movement early; in October 1931, Hitler appointed him National Youth Leader of the NSDAP (*Reichsjugendführer der NSDAP*). In 1940, he was promoted to *Gauleiter* and *Reichsstatthalter* of Vienna. From here, he fled in April 1945, but was arrested and condemned at the Nuremberg trials. Schirach prided himself in his musical knowledge and numbered among Strauss's admirers; in this respect, he stood at odds with Hitler and Goebbels. When the situation in Vienna became increasingly perilous for Alice Strauss and her children Richard and Christian, Schirach, although a fanatical antisemite all his life, protected the family. Schirach also made public festivities for Strauss's eightieth birthday possible.

Schoenberg, Arnold (1874–1951). Composer. Schoenberg was Kapellmeister at Ernst von Wolzogen's Berlin cabaret *Überbrettl,* where he first came to Strauss's attention. Personal contact began in 1902, when Schoenberg approached Strauss for assistance. Strauss put him in touch with the Stern Conservatory and the Franz Liszt Foundation, and Schönberg secured a stipend for two years. Strauss facilitated a production of his contemporary's String Quartet No. 1 (1907) in Vienna but rejected the orchestral pieces comprising Op. 16. During the 1910s Strauss helped Schoenberg obtain additional stipends, even though he disapproved of his turn towards atonality. Their last personal meeting occurred in Berlin, 1912. Strauss used Schoenberg's *Harmonielehre* when giving lessons to his grandson Richard.

Schopenhauer, Arthur (1788–1860). Reading Schopenhauer was a central experience for Strauss; his personal copy of *World as Will and Representation* (displaying traces of intensive use) has been preserved. At first, the composer's encounter with the philosopher's radical pessimism was colored by his fondness for Wagner. In turn, reading Nietzsche gave a certain vitalism the upper hand, which is evident in the finale of *Guntram. Feuersnot* moved the radical affirmation of individual selfhood through erotic consummation to the fore—in open contradiction to Schopenhauer. This figure of thought also set the course for Strauss's collaboration with Hofmannsthal; only in the composer's final works did it yield to a vision of (failed) human interaction.

Schuch, Ernst von (1846–1914). Conductor. Schuch, who hailed from Graz, became the director of the Dresden Royal Opera in 1872, a position he held for more than forty years. The advocate of new Italian and German music, he induced Strauss to agree to a long-term engagement in the city. From *Feuersnot* up to *Der Rosenkavalier* Schuch premiered all of the composer's operas in Dresden. With a reputation for being a sober and exacting perfectionist, he enjoyed Strauss's highest esteem all his life.

Schuh, Willi (1900–1986). Music critic. A native of Basel, Schuch worked as a music critic for the *Neue Zürcher Zeitung* from 1928 on. In this capacity, he also displayed political commitment—emphatically intervening on behalf of Thomas Mann in 1933, for instance. In 1935, Schuh and Strauss struck up a personal relationship, which grew stronger over time (especially after the journalist helped the composer relocate to Switzerland). In conscious parallel to Goethe and Eckermann, Schuh became Strauss's official biographer, although his account stops in 1898. Schuh also edited the composer's correspondence with Hofmannsthal.

Seidl, Emanuel von (1856–1919). Architect. Around the turn of the century, Seidl was one of the leading architects in his native Munich. His most important building is the German Museum, a project started by his brother. In 1907, following the success of *Salome,* Strauss commissioned Seidl to design an imposing villa in Garmisch (even though he still lived in Berlin).

Specht, Richard (1870–1932). Music critic. Born in Vienna, Specht spent his entire life in his native city, editing *Der Merker* and various other publications. In 1921, Strauss's third year of appointment in Vienna, Specht published a two-volume work, the most sustained popular discussion of the composer to date.

Stauffer, Karl (1857–1891). Painter. When Otto Brahm published the biography of Stauffer—whom Strauss had met during his first Berlin sojourn—his life became an exemplary fable of the modern artist. Following a scandalous liaison with Lydia Welti, Stauffer had been arrested in Italy at her family's urging. He committed suicide after his release, and Welti did the same the following year. Although references were ultimately removed, Stauffer's biography played a central role in Strauss's conception of *Eine Alpensinfonie.*

Steinitzer, Max (1864–1936). Music critic. Starting in 1911, Steinitzer worked for *Leipziger Neueste Nachrichten,* and he remained in Leipzig for the rest of his life. His monograph on Richard Strauss (1911) is an invaluable resource—among other reasons, because its catalog includes materials that are now lost.

Stirner, Max (1806–1856). Philosopher. Born Johann Caspar Schmidt, Stirner published his main work, *Der Einzige und sein Eigentum,* in 1844. A proponent of radically anarchist atheism, Stirner was a Left Hegelian who, in response to philosophical idealism, came to stand in stark opposition to Hegel himself. Stirner's work represented a formative experience for Nietzsche-readers at the turn of the century—including Strauss, who learned about the philosopher from reading *Die Anarchisten,* a novel by John Henry Mackay, an ardent admirer. *Till Eulenspiegel* and *Zarathustra* were conceived in the wake of Stirner, whose influence is still evident in *Eine Alpensinfonie.*

Strauss, Alice (1904–1991). Alice Grab was the oldest daughter of Emanuel Grab (1868–1929) and his second wife, Marie Henriette Neumann (1883–1954). The Grab family attached great importance to philanthropy and culture; Alice's prematurely deceased brother, Paul Friedrich (1906–1924), aspired to a career as a pianist. The father's side of the family remained true to the Jewish faith, but Alice agreed to baptism when she married Franz Strauss (the composer's only son) in 1924. She served as a kind of private secretary to Richard Strauss and founded the composer's archive. In 1938, they managed to help Marie Henriette flee Vienna to Switzerland at the last minute. In 1940, the dangers facing Alice and her sons became increasingly perilous, and they eventually had to go into hiding. Following Strauss's death, she managed his archive in Garmisch.

Strauss, Pauline (1863–1950). Singer. Daughter of Major General Adolf de Ahna, Pauline met her future husband 1887 in Munich and followed him to Weimar. There, in 1890, she made her debut and became a celebrated singer; the high points of her career were playing Isolde in Weimar and Elisabeth in Bayreuth. At the premiere of *Guntram*, Pauline was cast as Freihild. In 1894, the couple married at her family's country house in Maquartstein. Pauline assiduously pursued a singing career, even after the difficult birth of her son, Franz. In 1905—much to her husband's regret—she stopped performing. Pauline Strauss counted as extremely difficult and forthright woman; the couple's relationship was puzzling to others, and Hofmannsthal avoided her altogether. Their extensive correspondence has been preserved but is not available for consultation.

Strauss, family. Franz Strauss (1822–1905) hailed from Parkstein, the illegitimate son of Urban Strauss and Maria Anna Kunigunde Walter. His musical gifts attracted notice at a young age; eventually, he played horn as a member of the Munich Hofkapelle. In May 1851, he married Maria Seiff (1821–1854). The union produced a son, also named Franz, who died the same year he was born (1852), as well as a daughter, Klara Franziska (1853); in 1854, both mother and daughter succumbed to a cholera epidemic. In 1863, Franz Strauss married Josepha Pschorr, thereby joining one of Munich's wealthiest and most influential families. The Wagner-mania gripping the city meant that the musician had to participated in premieres from *Tristan* on, even though he despised Wagner's music. Josepha was very unstable; starting in 1885, she made repeated visits to psychiatric institutions. The marriage brought forth Richard and Johanna (1867–1966). Richard Strauss's marriage to Pauline de Ahna produced only one child, Franz (1897–1980). Strauss always spoke of his father respectfully and composed his Horn Concerto No. 1 for the instrument that he played; at the same time, he acknowledged that he had been a difficult man prone to fits of rage.

Swarowsky, Hans (1899–1975). Conductor. Swarowksy came from Budapest and held numerous engagements before reaching Zurich, through Strauss's mediation. From there, he moved to Berlin in 1940. In 1944–1945, Swarowsky was General Music Director in Cracow; in turn, he taught at the Vienna Academy, where he became one of the most influential pedagogues of the twentieth century. Swarowsky played a particularly significant role in the final version of *Capriccio*.

Thuille, Ludwig (1861–1907). Composer. A native of Bolzano, Thuille first moved to Innsbruck. He made Strauss's acquaintance in 1877; two years later, he relocated to Munich, where he served first as teacher (1883) and then professor (1890) at the Royal School of Music. In 1893, Thuille obtained the position of his former teacher Rheinberger. Relations between Strauss and Thuille were especially close and heartfelt, comparable only to those between Strauss and Humperdinck or Ritter. Both men agreed that it was necessary to take distance from nineteenth-century models in a productive way. On many occasions, Strauss conducted the works of Thuille, who died at the age of just forty-five.

Tietjen, Heinz (1881–1967). Director and manager. During the 1920s, Tietjen, who was born in Morocco, rose to become the most important man of the theater in Prussia. The high point of his career was appointment as *Generalintendant* of the Prussian State Theater, a position he held until 1944. In 1931, Winifred Wagner called him to Bayreuth to direct the festival there. A protégé of Göring, Tietjen had no rivals during the National Socialist period. After completing the course of denazification in 1947, he worked first in Berlin, then in Hamburg. When Toscanini canceled his Bayreuth engagement in 1933 and 1934, Tietjen recruited Strauss to conduct; the composer dedicated *Liebe der Danae* to him.

Tombo, August (1842–1878). Harpist. Tombo, from Erfurt, joined the Munich Hofkapelle in 1861; in this capacity, he participated in the earliest performances of Wagner conducted by Bülow, as well as in Bayreuth. The young Strauss received his first piano lessons from him.

Toscanini, Arturo (1867–1957). Conductor. The most important Italian conductor of his generation, Toscanini advocated for Strauss early on; engagement on his behalf included the premiere of *Salome* at the Scala. Otherwise, however, he viewed the operas with skepticism, although he continued to direct the composer's orchestral works (both in Europe and the United States). In 1933, in an act of protest against the Nazi regime, Toscanini refused to perform in Bayreuth. (In 1937, he conducted Wagner's *Meistersinger* in Vienna to counter the National Socialists' appropriation of the work.) Heinz Tietjen wanted Fritz Busch to replace Toscanini for the staging of *Parsifal,* but he also declined. In turn, Strauss accepted, although he declined payment.

Ursuleac, Viorica (1893–1995). Singer. Ursuleac held her first engagement at the Vienna *Volksoper* in 1922; in 1926, she moved to Franfurt am Main and married Clemens Krauss (her second husband). Fritz Busch recruited the singer for the ensemble in Dresden in 1931; in 1935, Wilhelm Furtwängler induced her to come to Berlin. Guest engagements brought the singer to Vienna, then Munich (1937–1945). Following Krauss's death (1954), she no longer performed. In 1959, Ursuleac began teaching at the Salzburg Mozarteum. After performing in the premiere of *Arabella* (1933), she had become one of Strauss's favorite singers. The composer wrote for her the female leads in *Die Liebe der Danae, Capriccio,* and *Friedenstag* (which he dedicated to the couple). Ursuleac ultimately played twelve different roles in Strauss's works.

Wagner, Cosima (1837–1930). Manager. With his father, Strauss paid his first visit to Bayreuth in 1882; he returned in 1886 and 1887. In March 1889, his first encounter with Cosima Wagner occurred, who immediately engaged him—first as assistant (1889 and 1891), then as conductor (1894). Their correspondence was quite extensive, with Cosima playing the role of musical educator early on. Following Strauss's tone poems—in particular, *Zarathustra,* but also *Guntram*—the relationship became strained. In 1896, the composer broke with Bayreuth and the Wagner clan, and he did not return while Cosima was still alive.

Wagner, Richard (1813–1883). Composer. Strauss grew up at a time when Munich stood in thrall to Wagner (whom Ludwig II championed). Beginning with *Tristan,* the composer's father participated in all the premieres, even though he made no secret of his dislike for Wagner. During the 1880s, Strauss came to appreciate his forebear, especially through the influence of his friend Alexander Ritter; his primary conducting interest eventually came to be Wagner. At the same time, Strauss followed Nietzsche and deemed it impossible to continue along Wagnerian lines. He was also disgusted to see Bayreuth transform into a shrine of *völkisch* chauvinism. Finally, Strauss's conception of music and drama was based on clear demarcations: separate roles for librettist and composer, a preference for comedy (or "broken," refracted tragedy), a classical turn marking distance from the past, ancient mythological themes (similarly "broken"), and motifs with a psychological thrust conveyed by counterpoint. Strauss staged *Tristan* in Weimar, but he was convinced that Wagner represented the culmination—and end—of a cultural epoch.

Wagner, Siegfried (1869–1930). Composer. Beginning in 1891, Siegfried Wagner and Strauss interacted on a first-name basis—a favor the composer showed few others. However, the relationship soon soured as Strauss disapproved of developments in Bayreuth and, despite initial enthusiasm, came to have considerable doubts about his contemporary's talents. In turn—and not without reason—Siegfried held that *Guntram* and Strauss's turn to Nietzsche amounted to a rejection of his father's vision. Strauss broke with the Wagner family once and for all in 1896; that summer, apropos of Siegfried's conducting, he wrote to his wife: "O Bayreuth, pigsty of all pigsties."

Wallerstein, Lothar (1882–1949). Director. Wallerstein had already collaborated with Clemens Krauss in Frankfurt during the 1920s. From 1927 until 1938, when he fled the Nazi regime, he acted as senior director at the Vienna State Opera; beginning in 1929, he was also involved in the Salzburg Festival. Strauss esteemed Wallerstein very highly; following the treatment of Beethoven undertaken with Hofmannsthal, he worked with him on the new adaptation of Mozart's *Idomeneo* (1931).

Walter, Benno (1847–1901). Violinist. A native of Munich, he joined the Royal Court Opera in 1862; in 1870, he was appointed concertmaster. He gave Strauss his first lessons in violin and later performed the premiere of his student's Violin Concerto.

Walter, Bruno (1876–1962). Conductor. Bruno Walter Schlesinger came from Berlin; Hans von Bülow exercised a formative influence on him. During Mahler's Hamburg period, Walter was employed at the opera as a répétiteur. After holding various positions, he was recruited by Mahler to be Kapellmeister at the Vienna Court Opera in 1901. In 1913, he was appointed General Music Director in Munich. From 1925 to 1929, Walter directed the Charlottenburg Opera, then became Kapellmeister at the Leipzig Gewandhaus Orchestra. When the National Socialists removed him from office, he initially returned to the Vienna State Opera before leaving for France in 1938, then the United States. Walter conducted Strauss regularly, but he viewed his music with skepticism. In March 1933, he stepped down from a concert with the Berlin Philharmonic when the SA threatened violence, and he requested that Wolff & Sachs, the leading agency, engage Strauss to take his place. The latter declined at first, but finally accepted at the urging of Hugo Rasch and Julius Kopsch. Strauss refused payment and insisted that he be announced as Walter's replacement; nevertheless, this step sent a political signal with disastrous effects.

Weis, Dora (1864–1938). Strauss fell madly in love with Dora Weis, a Jewish pianist married to the cellist Hans Wihan (to whom the composer dedicated his Cello Sonata, Op. 6). They first met in Berlin, in 1883. Although few records exist, it seems that the relationship was difficult, despite an uncharacteristic level of devotion on Strauss's part. The couple grew more distant in 1890 and reverted to formal modes of address. The relationship ended in 1893, with a final letter from Dora. It is impossible to say whether any contact occurred after this point. With one exception, all of Strauss's letters were destroyed in 1938 by Weis, who now lived in Dresden and faced grave danger.

Wilhelm II (1859–1942). King of Prussia and German Emperor (1888–1918). Strauss's longest appointment, lasting almost twenty years, was in Berlin. During this time, he served Wilhelm II, under whom cultural politics were decidedly liberal, making Berlin a magnet for artists of all stripes. In the words of Max Reinhardt's dramaturg, Arthur Kahane, the capital became "a center of culture, a global market." (Reinhardt's career illustrates as much.) Although the Kaiser did not care for Strauss's music, the composer enjoyed great privileges and liberties; even when he ran into difficulty with censors (as in the case of *Feuersnot*), it yielded useful publicity. Strauss's time in Berlin was also his most productive period of composition.

Wilhelm, Kurt (1923–2009). Director. A native of Munich, Wilhelm was arrested by the Gestapo after his first engagement in Stuttgart. Following the war, he returned to Munich and took a managerial position at *Bayerischer Rundfunk*. Wilhelm conducted a radio interview with Strauss in 1949 and also published previously unavailable materials.

Wittgenstein, Paul (1887–1961). Pianist. Wittgenstein's distinguished career was interrupted in gruesome fashion when he lost an arm in the First World War. However, his personal fortune allowed him to continue during the 1920s, when he commissioned a series of compositions for the left hand. From 1931 to 1938, Wittgenstein was a professor in Vienna, finally escaping to the United States. He knew Strauss personally and engaged him to compose two pieces (which occupy a singular position in his output): *Parergon zur Symphonia domestica* and *Panathenäenzug*.

Wolzogen, Ernst von (1855–1934). Writer. Born into the Austrian aristocracy, Wolzogen lived first in Berlin, then in Munich (1892 to 1899), where he met Strauss. In 1901, on the suggestion of Otto Julius Bierbaum (among others), he founded a Berlin cabaret with the ironically Nietzschean name of *Überbrettl* (Alexanderstrasse). In the German capital, Wolzogen and Strauss collaborated on *Feuersnot*, which sent up Wagner with mildly obscene eroticism. Plans for a second project were made, but never carried out. Wolzogen left Berlin and eventually settled in Bavaria, where he became a resolute opponent of the Weimar Republic.

Wüllner, Franz (1832–1902). Conductor. Hailing from Münster, Wüllner eventually landed in Munich, where he conducted the premieres of *Rheingold* and *Walküre* (among other works) and became Hofkapellmeister. After appointments in Dresden (where he worked alongside Ernst von Schuch) and Berlin, Wüllner succeeded Ferdinand Hiller as Kapellmeister of the Gürzenich Orchestra Cologne in 1884. He and Strauss had met the previous year, in Dresden. From this point on, Wüllner was one of the composer's most important advocates, organizing chamber music recitals as well as the German premiere of the Symhony in F minor. Strauss dedicated *Wandrers Sturmlied*, Op. 14, to him; Wüllner also conducted the premieres of *Till Eulenspiegel* and *Don Quixote*.

Zweig, Stefan (1881–1942). Writer. Zweig came from a prosperous family in Vienna, where he wrote his first literary works. Emerging from the First World War a convinced pacifist, he relocated first to Zurich, then to Salzburg, where he bought the *Paschinger Schlössl* (a majestic residence on the Kapuzinerberg). Zweig was an ardent admirer of Strauss, who learned of the writer through the publisher Anton Kippenberg. After a period of hesitation, the two men enjoyed a deep understanding and worked together wholeheartedly. *Die Schweigsame Frau* represented a new beginning for comedy in music.

When the National Socialists came to power, Zweig faced vicious persecution immediately. Strauss sought to continue work together, but the premiere of *Die Schweigsame Frau* prompted a scandal—the opera was ultimately banned—and he had to resign from his position as president of the Reichsmusikkammer. (Zweig's works, copies of which had already been burned, were forbidden for good in 1935; in the meanwhile, the author had fled to London.) Despite Strauss's efforts, Zweig declined further collaboration, although he was still involved with the completion of *Friedenstag* from abroad; ultimately, he suggested that the composer enlist the assistance of Joseph Gregor. Correspondence continued under pseudonyms for a spell, then ceased. In February 1942, Zweig committed suicide in Brazil.

Select Bibliography

Richard Strauss attracted extensive journalistic and scholarly interest from the late-nineteenth century on. Necessarily, then, the following represents a selection of significant editions, collections of sources, and research. Newer studies receive preference, since the bibliography compiled by Oswald Ortner provides a ready overview of older items; only a few studies devoted to particular works are included. Further resources include the electronic bibliography managed by the Richard-Strauss-Institut in Garmisch-Partenkirchen (http://www.richard-strauss-institut.de) and the extensive catalog of secondary literature in the German edition of the present book (http://www.reclam.de/richard_strauss_literatur).

Catalogs of Sources and Works; Bibliographies

Brosche, Günter and Karl Dachs. *Richard Strauss Autographen in München und Wien. Verzeichnis.* Tutzing 1979.

Müller von Asow, Erich H. *Richard Strauss: Thematisches Verzeichnis.* 3 vols. Vienna 1959, 1966, 1974.

Ortner, Oswald. *Richard-Strauss-Bibliographie. Teil 1. 1882–1944. Aus dem Nachlass hrsg. von Franz Grasberger.* Vienna 1964.

Specht, Richard (ed.). *Vollständiges Verzeichnis der im Druck erschienenen Werke von Richard Strauss.* Vienna 1910.

Trenner, Florian (ed.). *Richard Strauss. Chronik zu Leben und Werk.* Vienna 2003.

Trenner, Franz. *Die Skizzenbücher von Richard Strauss.* Tutzing 1977.

Trenner, Franz. *Richard Strauss. Werkverzeichnis (TrV).* Second edition. Vienna 1999.

Editions of Works

Hofmannsthal, Hugo von. "Ungeschriebenes Nachwort zum 'Rosenkavalier.'" *Der Merker* 2 (1911). 488f.

Hofmannsthal, Hugo von. *Dramen 5. Operndichtungen.* Ed. Bernd Schoeller in consultation with Rudolf Hirsch. Frankfurt 1979.

Hofmannsthal, Hugo von. *Operndichtungen 1.* Ed. Dirk O. Hoffmann and Willi Schuh. Frankfurt a. M. 1986; contains *Der Rosenkavalier.*

Hofmannsthal, Hugo von. *Operndichtungen 3, 1.* Ed. Hans-Albrecht Koch. Frankfurt a.M. 1998; contains *Die Frau ohne Schatten, Danae oder Die Vernunftheirat.*

Hofmannsthal, Hugo von. *Operndichtungen 3, 2.* Ed. Ingeborg Beyer-Ahlert. Frankfurt a. M. 2001; contains *Die ägyptische Helena, Aus dem Nachlaß, Opern- und Singspielpläne.*

Hofmannsthal, Hugo von. *Operndichtungen 4.* Ed. Hans-Albrecht Koch. Frankfurt a. M. 1976; contains *Arabella, Lucidor, Der Fiaker als Graf.*

Hofmannsthal, Hugo von and Count Harry Kessler. *Josephslegende: Handlung. Musik von Richard Strauss.* Berlin [1914].

Schlötterer, Reinhold. *Die Texte der Lieder von Richard Strauss: Kritische Ausgabe.* Pfaffenhofen 1988.
Strauss, Richard. *Sämtliche Bühnenwerke.* Vienna 1996.
Strauss, Richard. *Orchesterwerke.* Vienna and Frankfurt 1999.
Strauss, Richard. *Lieder. Gesamtausgabe.* 4 vols. London 1964f.
First editions are used when operas are not available in critical editions.

Exhibition Catalogs, Reference Works, Collected Volumes, and Iconography

Del Mar, Norman. *Richard Strauss. A Critical Commentary on his Life and Works.* 3 vols. London, corrected edition. 1978.
Edelmann, Bernd, Birgit Lodes, and Reinhold Schlötterer (eds.). *Richard Strauss und die Moderne. Bericht über das Internationale Symposium. München, 21. Bis 23. Juli 1999.* Berlin 2001.
Gilliam, Bryan (ed.). *Richard Strauss and His World.* Princeton 1992.
Gilliam, Bryan (ed.). *Richard Strauss: New Perspectives on the Composer and His Work.* Durham 1992.
Grasberger, Franz, Franz Hadamowsky, and Géza Rech (eds.). *Richard Strauss und Salzburg: Ausstellung anläßlich seines 100. Geburtstages und 15. Todestages in den Räumen der Residenz.* Salzburg 1964.
Grasberger, Franz and Franz Hadamowsky (eds.). *Richard-Strauss-Ausstellung zum 100. Geburtstag: Österreichische Nationalbibliothek 23. Mai bis 15. Oktober 1964.* Vienna 1964.
Heinemann, Michael, Matthias Herrmann, Stefan Weiss, and Hans John (eds.). *Richard Strauss: Essays zu Leben und Werk.* Laaber 2002.
Mühlegger-Henhappel, Christiane and Alexandra Steiner-Strauss (eds.). *"Trägt die Sprache schon Gesang in sich . . ." Richard Strauss und die Oper.* [Catalog to the Vienna exhibition in the Theatermuseum 2014.] Salzburg 2014.
Ott, Alfons (ed.). *Katalog der Ausstellung Richard Strauss und seine Zeit.* Munich 1964.
Restle, Konstantin and Dietmar Schenk (ed.). *Richard Strauss im kaiserlichen Berlin.* Berlin 2001.
Schaefer, Hartmut (ed.). *Richard Strauss. Autographen. Porträts. Bühnenbilder. Ausstellung zum 50. Todestag.* Munich 1999.
Schmid, Mark-Daniel (ed.). *The Richard Strauss Companion.* Westport, CT and London 2003.
Schuh, Willi (ed.). Richard Strauss. *Betrachtungen und Erinnerungen.* Second edition. Zurich and Freiburg. 1957.
Trenner, Franz. *Richard Strauss. Dokumente seines Lebens und Schaffens.* Munich 1954.
Youmans, Charles (ed.). *The Cambridge Companion to Richard Strauss.* Cambridge 2010.
Werbeck, Walter (ed.). *Richard Strauss Handbuch.* Stuttgart, Weimar, Kassel etc. 2014.

Letters

No single collection of Strauss's correspondence, nor even a catalog of his correspondents, exists. The most important exchanges have been published in different formats. These include letters to and from Volkmar Andreae, Karl Böhm, Hans von Bülow, Fritz Busch, Joseph Gregor, Rudolf Hartmann, Gerhart Hauptmann, Hugo von Hofmannsthal, Ludwig Karpath, Alfred Kerr, Anton Kippenberg, Clemens Krauss, Karl von Lion, Gustav Mahler, Werner Reinhart, Alexander Ritter, Romain Rolland, Franz Schalk, Max von Schillings, Arnold Schönberg, Ernst von Schuch, Willi Schuh, Ludwig Thuille, Heinz Tiessen, Heinz Tietjen, Giuseppe Verdi, Cosima Wagner, Ernst von Wolzogen, Franz Wüllner, and Stefan Zweig.

Individual Volumes

[Böhm] Martina Steiger (ed.). *Richard Strauss—Karl Böhm: Briefwechsel 1921–1949*. Mainz 1999.
[Gregor] Roland Tenschert (ed.). *Richard Strauss und Joseph Gregor: Briefwechsel. 1934–1949*. Salzburg 1955.
[Hartmann] Roswitha Schlötterer (ed.). *Richard Strauss—Rudolf Hartmann: Ein Briefwechsel. Mit Aufsätzen und Regiearbeiten von Rudolf Hartmann*. Tutzing 1984.
[Hofmannsthal] Willi Schuh (ed.). *Richard Strauss. Hugo von Hofmannsthal: Briefwechsel*. Fifth edition. Zurich and Freiburg 1978. First edition 1926.
[Krauss] Günter Brosche (ed.). *Richard Strauss. Clemens Krauss: Briefwechsel. Gesamtausgabe*. Tutzing 1997.
[Schalk] Günter Brosche (ed.). *Richard Strauss—Franz Schalk: Ein Briefwechsel*. Tutzing 1983.
[Schuh] Willi Schuh (ed.). *Richard Strauss: Briefwechsel mit Willi Schuh*. Zurich and Freiburg 1969.
[Zweig] Willi Schuh (ed.). *Richard Strauss—Stefan Zweig: Briefwechsel*. Frankfurt 1957.
Additionally, excerpts of Strauss's letters to his parents exist, as do the following important collections.
Brosche, Günter (ed.). "Strauss, Sie sind ja so ein göttlicher Kerl! Brief an und von Emil Struth, Hugo Becker, Wilhelm Bopp und Helmut Grohe." *Richard-Strauss-Blätter*. New series 1 (1979). 15–37.
Grasberger, Franz (ed.). *Der Strom der Töne trug mich fort: Die Welt um Richard Strauss in Briefen. In Zusammenarbeit mit Franz und Alice Strauss*. Tutzing 1967.
Schuh, Willi (ed.). *Richard Strauss: Briefe an die Eltern. 1882–1906*. Zurich and Freiburg 1954.
Strauss, Gabriele (ed.). *Lieber Collega! Richard Strauss im Briefwechsel mit zeitgenössischen Komponisten und Dirigenten*. Vol. 1. Berlin 1996.
Strauss, Gabriele and Monika Reger (eds.). *Ihr aufrichtig ergebener: Richard Strauss im Briefwechsel mit zeitgenössischen Komponisten und Dirigenten*. Vol. 2. Berlin 1998.

Biographical Material

General

Boyden, Matthew. *Richard Strauss: Die Biographie*. Munich, Vienna 1999.
Ender, Daniel. *Richard Strauss: Meister der Inszenierung*. Vienna 2014.
Gilliam, Brian. *The Life of Richard Strauss*. Cambridge 1999.
Gilliam, Brian and Charles Youmans. "Strauss, Richard." In Stanley Sadie and John Tyrrel (eds.). *New Grove Dictionary of Music*. Vol. 24 (2001). 497–527.
Holden, Raymond. *Richard Strauss: A Musical Life*. New Haven, CT and London 2011.
Kennedy, Michael. *Richard Strauss: Man, Musician, Enigma*. Cambridge 1999.
Krellmann, Hanspeter (ed.). *Wer war Richard Strauss? Neunzehn Antworten*. Frankfurt and Leipzig 1999.
Messmer, Franzpeter. *Richard Strauss. Biographie eines Klangzauberers*. Zurich and St. Gallen 1994.
Schuh, Willi. *Richard Strauss: Jugend und frühe Meisterjahre. Lebenschronik 1864–1898*. Zurich 1976.
Strauss, Gabriele and Barbara Wunderlich (eds.). *Der Patriarch: Richard Strauss und die seinen*. Leipzig 2014.
Walter, Michael. *Strauss und seine Zeit*. Laaber 2001.
Werbeck, Walter. "Strauss, Richard." *Die Musik in Geschichte und Gegenwart*. Personenteil 16 (2006). Columns 55–115.

Individual Studies

Adorno, Theodor W. "Richard Strauss, Geboren am 11. Juni 1864." *Neue Rundschau* (1964), 572–583. Reprinted in *Musikalische Schriften*. Vol. 3. (Frankfurt, 1978). 565–606.

Adamy, Bernhard. "Schopenhauer bei Richard Strauss." *Schopenhauer-Jahrbuch* 61 (1980). 195–198.

Adamy, Bernhard. "'. . . Hundertfache Bemühung.' Zum künstlerischen Selbstverständnis von Richard Strauss." *Richard Strauss-Blätter*. New series 36 (1991). 3–50.

Dorschel, Andreas (ed). *Gemurmel unterhalb des Rauschens. Theodor W. Adorno und Richard Strauss*. Vienna 2004.

Ebbenhorst Tengbergen, Marijke. *De Richard Straussvilla in Wenen: 50 Jaar Nederlandse Residentie*. St. Pölten 1999.

Finscher, Ludwig. "Richard Strauss and Jugendstil. The Munich Years, 1894–1898." In: Andrew MacCredie (ed.). *Art Nouveau and Jugendstil and the Music of the Early 20th Century*. Adelaide 1984. 169–180.

Gerlach, Reinhard. "Richard Strauss. Prinzipien seiner Kompositionstechnik (mit einem Brief von Strauss)." *Archiv für Musikwissenschaft* 23 (1966). 277–288.

Gilliam, Bryan. "'Friede im Innern.' Strauss' Public and Private Worlds in the Mid- 1930s." *Journal of the American Musicological Society* 57 (2005). 565–597.

Hanke Knaus, Gabriella. *Aspekte der Schlussgestaltung in den sinfonischen Dichtungen und Bühnenwerken von Richard Strauss*. Tutzing 1995.

Katzenberger, Günter. "Vom Einfall zur harten Arbeit. Zum Schaffen von Richard Strauss." In: Hermann Danuser and Günter Katzenberger (eds.). *Vom Einfall zum Kunstwerk: Der Kompositionsprozeß in der Musik des 20. Jahrhunderts*. Laaber 1993. 65–83.

Liebscher, Julia. "Richard Strauss und Friedrich Nietzsche." *Richard-Strauss-Blätter*. New series 27 (1992). 10–38.

Riethmüller, Albrecht. "Stefan Zweig and the Fall of the Reichs Music Chamber President, Richard Strauss." In: Michael H. Kater and Albrecht Riethmüller (eds.). *Music and Nazism. Art under Tyranny, 1933–1945*. Laaber 2003. 269–291.

Satragni, Giangiorgio. *Richard Strauss dietro la maschera: Gli ultimi anni*. Turin 2015.

Schmidt, Manuela Maria. *Die Anfänge der musikalischen Tantiemenbewegung in Deutschland: Eine Studie über den langen Weg bis zur Errichtung der Genossenschaft Deutscher Tonsetzer (GDT) im Jahre 1903 und zum Wirken des Komponisten Richard Strauss (1864–1949) für Verbesserungen des Urheberrechts*. Berlin 2005.

Splitt, Gerhard. *Richard Strauss 1933–1935: Ästhetik und Musikpolitik zu Beginn der nationalsozialistischen Herrschaft*. Pfaffenweiler 1987.

Splitt, Gerhard. "Richard Strauss' Idee vom Ende der deutschen Musik 1945." *Musik in Bayern* 41 (1990). 37–61.

Splitt, Gerhard. "Richard Strauss' Brief vom 17. Juni 1935 an Stefan Zweig." *Die Musikforschung* 58 (2005). 406–414.

Vaget, Hans Rudolf. "Thomas Mann und Richard Strauss. Zeitgenossenschaft ohne Brüderlichkeit." *Thomas Mann Jahrbuch* 3 (1990). 50–85.

Werbeck, Walter. *Richard Strauss: Facetten eines neuen Bildes*. Munich 2014.

Wagner-Trenkwitz, Christoph. *Durch die Hand der Schönheit. Richard Strauss und Wien*. Vienna 2014.

Wolf, Christian and Jürgen May. *Bei Richard Strauss in Garmisch-Partenkirchen: Fotos von Anton Brandl*. Munich, etc. 2008.

Youmans, Charles. "The Role of Nietzsche in Richard Strauss's Artistic Development." *The Journal of Musicology* 21 (2004). 309–342.

Tone Poems

General

Hansen, Mathias. *Richard Strauss: Die sinfonischen Dichtungen.* Kassel, etc. 2003.
Kennedy, Michael. *Strauss's Tone Poems.* London 1984.
Werbeck, Walter. *Die Tondichtungen von Richard Strauss.* Tutzing 1996.
Youmans, Charles. *Richard Strauss's Orchestral Music and the German Intellectual Tradition: The Philosophical Roots of Musical Modernism.* Bloomington 2005.

Individual Works

Bartók, Béla. "Strauss. Symphonia Domestica Op. 53." In: Benjamin Suchoff (ed.). *Béla Bartók. Essays.* London 1976. 437–445.
Bayreuther, Rainer. *Richard Strauss' Alpensinfonie. Entstehung, Analyse und Interpretation.* Hildesheim 1994.
Bayreuther, Rainer. "Der Held des 'Heldenleben.'" *Archiv für Musikwissenschaft* 62 (2005). 286–302.
Büttner, Fred. "Ein Heldenleben, op. 40, von Richard Strauss. Sujet und Musik." *Musik in Bayern* 34 (1987). 27–58.
Gerlach, Reinhard. "Die Orchesterkomposition als musikalisches Drama. Die Teil-Tonalitäten der 'Gestalten' und der bitonale Kontrapunkt in 'Ein Heldenleben' von Richard Strauss." *Musiktheorie* 6 (1991). 55–78.
Liebscher, Julia. *Richard Strauss: Also sprach Zarathustra. Tondichtung (frei nach Friedr. Nietzsche) für großes Orchester. Op. 30.* Munich 1994.
Nieden, Hans-Jörg. *Richard Strauss: Till Eulenspiegels lustige Streiche. Sinfonische Dichtung op. 28.* Munich 1991.
Schmid, Bernhold. "Richard Strauss' Macbeth." *Musik in Bayern* 35 (1987). 25–53.
Unger, Annette. *Welt, Leben und Kunst als Themen der 'Zarathustra-Kompositionen' von Richard Strauss und Gustav Mahler.* Frankfurt etc. 1992.
Werbeck, Walter. "'Macbeth' von Richard Strauss. Fassungen und Entstehungsgeschichte." *Archiv für Musikwissenschaft* 50 (1993). 232–253.
Wilde, Denis. *The Development of Melody in the Tone Poems of Richard Strauss.* Lewiston etc. 1990.

Opera and Ballets

General

Birkin, Kenneth. "Stephan Zweig—Richard Strauss—Joseph Gregor." *Richard-Strauss-Blätter.* New series 10 (1983). 3–37.
Brzoska, Matthias. "Richard Strauss und Max Reinhardt: Kontinuität und Traditionswechsel im Musiktheater der Moderne." In: Jean Gribenski, Marie-Clair Mussat and Herbert Schneider (ed.). *D'un opéra l'autre: Hommage à Jean Mongrédien.* Paris 1996. 67–76.
Gilliam, Bryan. "Strauss's Preliminary Opera Sketches. Thematic Fragments and Symphonic Continuity." *19th-Century Music* 9 (1985/86). 176–188.

Gilliam, Bryan. *Rounding Wagner's Mountain: Richard Strauss and Modern German Opera.* Cambridge 2014.
Hartmann, Rudolf. *Richard Strauss: Die Bühnenwerke von der Uraufführung bis heute.* Munich and Zurich 1980.
Heisler, Wayne. *Freedom from the Earth's Gravity: The Ballett Collaborations of Richard Strauss.* Rochester 2009.
Liebscher, Julia (ed.). *Richard Strauss und das Musiktheater: Bericht über die internationale Fachkonferenz Bochum 2001.* Berlin 2005.
Lütteken, Laurenz. *Richard Strauss: Die Opern.* Munich 2013.
Messmer, Franzpeter (ed.). *Kritiken zu den Uraufführungen der Bühnenwerke von Richard Strauss.* Pfaffenhofen 1989.
Rowat, Malcolm. *The Origins and Roles of Instrumental Music in the Operas of Richard Strauss: From Concert Hall to Opera House. With a Foreword by John Deathridge.* Lewiston 2012.
Schuh, Willi. *Das Bühnenwerk von Richard Strauss in den unter Mitwirkung des Komponisten geschaffenen letzten Münchner Inszenierungen.* Zurich 1954.
Winterhager, Wolfgang. *Zur Struktur des Operndialogs: Komparative Analysen des musikdramatischen Werks von Richard Strauss.* Frankfurt 1984.

Strauss and Hofmannsthal

Bayerlein, Sonja. *Verkörperte Musik: Zur Dramaturgie der Gebärde in den frühen Opern von Strauss und Hofmannsthal.* Hamburg 2006.
Bottenberg, Julian. *Shared Creation: Words and Music in the Hofmannsthal-Strauss Operas.* Frankfurt etc. 1996.
Dürhammer, Ilja and Pia Janke (eds.). *Richard Strauss—Hugo von Hofmannsthal: Frauenbilder.* Vienna 2001.
Fetting, Hugo (ed.). *Max Reinhardt. Leben für das Theater: Briefe, Reden, Aufsätze, Interviews, Gespräche, Auszüge aus Regiebüchern.* Berlin 1989.
Hottmann, Katharina. *"Die anderen komponieren. Ich mach' Musikgeschichte": Historismus und Gattungsbewußtsein bei Richard Strauss. Untersuchungen zum späteren Opernschaffen.* Tutzing 2005.
Kech, Adrian. *Musikalische Verwandlung in den Hofmannsthal-Opern von Richard Strauss.* Munich 2015.
Kohler, Stephan. "Das Singspiel als dramatischer Formtypus. Goethe-Strauss-Hofmannsthal." In: Wolfgang Wittkowski (ed.). *Goethe im Kontext: Kunst und Humanität, Naturwissenschaften und Politik von der Aufklärung bis zur Restauration. Ein Symposium.* Tübingen 1984. 181–192.
Lütteken, Laurenz. "Das andere 20. Jahrhundert. Der 'Rosenkavalier' und der Auftakt der Moderne." In: Susanne Schaal-Gotthardt, Giselher Schubert, Luitgard Schader, and Heinz-Jürgen Winkler (ed.): *". . . dass alles auch hätte anders kommen können." Beiträge zur Musik des 20. Jahrhunderts.* Mainz etc. 2009. 82–93.
Rutsch, Bettina. *Leiblichkeit der Sprache—Sprachlichkeit des Leibes: Wort, Gebärde, Tanz bei Hugo von Hofmannsthal.* Frankfurt etc. 1998.
Schmid, Martin E. *Symbol und Funktion der Musik im Werk Hugo von Hofmannsthals.* Heidelberg 1968.
Salvan-Renucci, François. *Ein "Ganzes von Text und Musik": Hugo von Hofmannsthal und Richard Strauss.* Tutzing 2001.

Uhlmann-Radke, Gyburg. "Die Krise des Modernen und der Mythos von der plastischen Antike." In: Laurenz Lütteken (ed.). *Musik und Mythos—Mythos Musik um 1900. Zürcher Festspiel-Symposium 2008.* Kassel etc. 2009. 72–91.

Vogel, Juliane. "Erscheinung und Zeremonie: Ankunftsszenen bei Hugo von Hofmannsthal." Aage A. Hansen-Löve, Annegret Heimann, and Inka Mülder-Bach (eds.). *Ankünfte: An der Epochenschwelle um 1900.* Munich 2009. 161–172.

Ward, Philip. *Hofmannsthal and Greek Myth: Expression and* Performance. Bern 2002.

Individual Works

Aringer-Grau, Ulrike. "'. . . daß es zum Besten gehört, was ich je geschrieben habe.' Zur Konzeption des III. Aktes der 'Liebe der Danae' und seiner Stellung im Spätwerk von Richard Strauss." Peter Csobádi et al. (ed.). *Das Fragment im (Musik-)Theater: Zufall und/oder Notwendigkeit?* Anif and Salzburg 2005. 614–639.

Axt, Eva-Maria. *Musikalische Form als Dramaturgie: Prinzipien eines Spätstils in der Oper "Friedenstag" von Richard Strauss und Joseph Gregor.* Munich and Salzburg 1989.

Berghahn, Cord Friedrich. "'Wir werden nur bestehen, sofern wir uns eine neue Antike schaffen': Beethovens Prometheus bei Hofmannsthal und Strauss." In: Laurenz Lütteken (ed.). *Der entfesselte Prometheus: Der antike Mythos in der Musik um 1900. Zürcher Festspiel-Symposium 2014.* Kassel etc. 2015. 133–161.

Birkin, Kenneth. *"Friedenstag" and "Daphne": An Interpretative Study of the Literary and Dramatic Sources of Two Operas by Richard Strauss.* New York and London 1989.

Birkin, Kenneth. *Richard Strauss: Arabella.* Cambridge 1989.

Edelmann, Bernd. "'Mit Haut und Haar komponiert'? Die Arbeit am Textbuch der 'Schweigsamen Frau' und Strauss' erste Musikideen." *Richard-Strauss-Jahrbuch* 2009. 37–68.

Erwin, Charlotte E. "Richard Strauss' Presketch Planning for 'Ariadne auf Naxos.'" *The Musical Quarterly* 47 (1981). 348–365

Fischer, Jens Malte. "Der 'arme Guntram' und der 'reiche Heinrich': Zwei Erstlingsopern am Ende des 19. Jahrhunderts." *Vom Wunderwerk der Oper.* Vienna 2007. 156–184.

Forsyth, Karen. *"Ariadne auf Naxos" by Hugo von Hofmannsthal and Richard Strauss: Its Genesis and Meaning.* Oxford 1982.

Fritz, Rebekka. "'Die ägyptische Helena' von Hofmannsthal und Richard Strauss—ein vergessenes Juwel?" *Jahrbuch des Freien Deutschen Hochstifts* (1997). 299–312.

Gerlach, Reinhard. *Don Juan und Rosenkavalier.* Bern 1966.

Gerlach, Reinhard. "Die Tragödie des inneren Menschen. 'Elektra'-Studien." Joseph Kuckertz et al. (eds.). *Neue Musik und Tradition. Festschrift Rudolf Stephan zum 65. Geburtstag.* Laaber 1990. 389–416.

Gersthofer, Wolfgang. "Leitmotivtechniken in der 'Frau ohne Schatten.'" *Richard-Strauss-Blätter.* New series 42 (1999). 121–144.

Gilliam, Bryan. *Richard Strauss' "Elektra."* Oxford 1991.

Gilliam, Bryan. "'Ariadne,' 'Daphne,' and the Problem of Verwandlung." *Cambridge Opera Journal* 15 (2003). 67–81.

Hoppe, Manfred. "Hofmannsthals 'Ruinen von Athen': Das Festspiel als 'konservative Revolution.'" *Jahrbuch der Deutschen Schillergesellschaft* 26 (1982). 325–356.

Jahn, Bernhard. "Zwischen Ochs und Übermensch: Übergang und Gabe als Dimensionen der Zeit im 'Rosenkavalier' von Hofmannsthal und Strauss." *Deutsche Vierteljahrsschrift für Literaturwissenschaft und Geistesgeschichte* 73 (1999). 419–456.

Jefferson, Alan (ed.). *Richard Strauss: Der Rosenkavalier*. Cambridge 1985.
Kohler, Stephan. "Die 'Idomeneo'-Bearbeitung von Lothar Wallerstein und Richard Strauss." In: Robert Münster (ed.). *Wolfgang Amadeus Mozart: Idomeneo. 1781–1981*. Munich 1981. 158–179.
Konrad, Claudia. *"Die Frau ohne Schatten" von Hugo von Hofmannsthal und Richard Strauss: Studien zur Genese, zum Textbuch und zur Rezeptionsgeschichte*. Hamburg 1988.
Konrad, Ulrich. "'All Wärme quillt vom Weibe, All Licht von Liebe stammt.' Mythos und Gegenwart in der *Feuersnot* von Richard Strauss." In: Laurenz Lütteken (ed.). *Musik und Mythos—Mythos Musik um 1900: Zürcher Festspiel-Symposium 2008*. Kassel etc. 2009. 111–133.
Kramer, Lawrence. "Fin-de-siècle Fantasies. Elektra, Degeneration and Sexual Science." *Cambridge Opera Journal* 5 (1993). 141–165.
Krebs, Wolfgang. *Der Wille zum Rausch: Aspekte der musikalischen Dramaturgie von Richard Strauss' Salome*. Munich 1991.
Kristiansen, Morten. *Richard Strauss's 'Feuersnot' in Its Aesthetic and Cultural Context. A Modernist Critique of Musical Idealism*. Diss. Yale University 2000.
Kunze, Stefan. "'Ein Schönes war . . .': Strauss' 'Capriccio' – Rückspiegelungen im Einakter." Winfried Kirsch and Sieghard Döhring (eds.). *Geschichte und Dramaturgie des Operneinakters*. Laaber 1991. 285–299.
Leibnitz, Thomas. *Richard Strauss. 100 Jahre Rosenkavalier*. Vienna 2010.
Lenz, Eva-Maria. *Hugo von Hofmannsthals mythologische Oper "Die Ägyptische Helena."* Tübingen 1972.
Lütteken, Laurenz. "'Leupold, wir gehen!' Der Walzer als Chiffre im 'Rosenkavalier' von Hofmannsthal und Strauss." Günter Schnitzler and Achim Aurnhammer (ed.). *Wort und Ton*. Freiburg etc. 2011. 403–422.
Lütteken, Laurenz. "'Geheimnis der Stunde': Das Spiegelgespräch im Finale des 'Capriccio' von Richard Strauss." In: Jan Standke (ed.). *Gebundene Zeit: Zeitlichkeit in Literatur, Philologie und Wissenschaftsgeschichte. Festschrift für Wolfgang Adam*. Heidelberg 2014. 605–613.
Mehring, Reinhard. "'Bei Ariadne aber ist Unendliches zu leisten und zu zeigen': Hugo von Hofmannsthals 'Vision' der Ariadne auf Naxos." *Weimarer Beiträge* 57 (2011). 165–179.
Piribauer, Kerstin. "Spätwerk für die Jugend: Das unvollendete Singspiel 'Des Esels Schatten.'" *Richard-Strauss-Blätter*. New series 38 (1997). 115–129.
Puffett, Derrick (ed.). *Richard Strauss: Elektra*. Cambridge 1989.
Puffett, Derrick (ed.). *Richard Strauss: Salome*. Cambridge 1989.
Saxer, Marion. "Zeit der Oper—Zeit des Films: Der Rosenkavalier im Stummfilm." *Musik und Ästhetik* 15 (2011). 42–61.
Schlötterer, Roswitha (ed.). *Musik und Theater im "Rosenkavalier" von Richard Strauss*. Vienna 1985.
Schmidt, Wolf Gerhard. "'. . . wie nahe beisammen das weit Auseinanderliegende ist': Das Prinzip der Metamorphose in der Oper 'Die Ägyptische Helena' von Hugo von Hofmannsthal und Richard Strauss." *Jahrbuch zur Kultur und Literatur der Weimarer Republik* 7 (2002). 169–223.
Schnitzler, Günter. "Libretto, Musik und Inszenierung: Der Wandel der ästhetischen Konzeption in 'Ariadne auf Naxos' von Hofmannsthal und Strauss." Michael von Albrecht and Werner Schubert (eds.). *Musik und Dichtung: Neue Forschungsbeiträge. Viktor Pöschl zum 80. Geburtstag gewidmet*. Frankfurt 1990. 373–408.
Schuh, Willi. "Das Szenarium und die musikalischen Skizzen zum Ballett 'Kythere.'" *Richard-Strauss-Jahrbuch* (1959/60). 59–98.

Shirley, Hugo. "Melancholy and Allegory in 'Die Frau ohne Schatten.'" *Cambridge Opera Journal* 24 (2012). 67–97.
Splitt, Gerhard. "Oper als Politikum. 'Friedenstag' (1938) von Richard Strauss." *Archiv für Musikwissenschaft* 55 (1998). 220–251.
Splitt, Gerhard. "Calderóns Drama 'Die Beglagerung von Breda,' Velzaquez' Gemälde 'Die Übergabe von Breda' und das Libretto zu Strauss' Oper 'Friedenstag.' Bezüge, Divergenzen und Legenden." In: Günter Schnitzler and Edelgard Spaude (eds.). *Intermedialität: Studien zur Wechselwirkung zwischen den Künsten.* Freiburg 2004. 481–517.
Steiger, Martina. *"Die Liebe der Danae" von Richard Strauss: Mythos, Libretto, Musik.* Mainz etc. 1999.
Tadday, Ulrich (ed.). *Richard Strauss. Der griechische Germane.* Munich 2005.
Walter, Michael and Andrea Zedler (eds.). *Richard Strauss' Grazer Salome: Die österreichische Erstaufführung im theater- und sozialgeschichtlichen Kontext.* Vienna 2014.
Werbeck, Walter. "'Schlagobers.' Musik zwischen Kaffeehaus und Revolution." *Richard-Strauss-Blätter.* New series 42, 1999. 106–120.
Wilhelm, Kurt. *Fürs Wort brauche ich Hilfe: Die Geburt der Oper 'Capriccio' von Richard Strauss und Clemens Krauss.* Munich 1988.

Instrumental Music

Schaarwächter, Jürgen. *Richard Strauss und die Sinfonie.* Cologne 1994.
Werbeck, Walter. "Richard Strauss und Paul Wittgenstein: Zu den Klavierkonzerten für die linke Hand 'Parergon zur Symphonia domestica' op. 73 und 'Panathenäenzug' op. 74." *Österreichische Musikzeitschrift* 54 (1999). 16–25.

Late Work

Danuser, Hermann. "Über Richard Strauss' 'Metamorphosen.'" In: Volker Kalisch et al. (eds.). *Festschrift Hans Conradin: Zum 70. Geburtstag.* Bern and Stuttgart 1983. 179–193.
Gellermann, Bernd. "Die Donau: Betrachtungen zum Fragment der letzten Symphonischen Dichtung von Richard Strauss." *Richard Strauss Blätter.* New series 6 (1982). 21–43.
Lodes, Birgit. "Richard Strauss' Skizzen zu den 'Metamorphosen' und ihre Beziehung zu 'Trauer um München.'" *Die Musikforschung* 47 (1994). 234–252.
Lütteken, Laurenz. "'Eine 3000jährige Kulturentwicklung abgeschlossen': Biographie und Geschichte in den 'Metamorphosen' von Richard Strauss." Winterthur 2004.
Lütteken, Laurenz. *Werkstatt-Musik: Die Zweite Sonatine und das Spätwerk von Richard Strauss.* Winterthur 2014.

Lieder and Choral Works

Borchmeyer, Dieter. "'Die Genies sind eben eine große Familie . . .': Goethe in Kompositionen von Richard Strauss." *Goethe-Jahrbuch* 116 (1999). 206–223.
Dümling, Albrecht. "Zwischen Autonomie und Fremdbestimmung: Die Olympische Hymne von Robert Lubahn und Richard Strauss." *Richard-Strauss-Blätter.* New series 38 (1997). 68–99.
Petersen, Barbara A. *Ton und Wort: The Lieder of Richard Strauss.* Ann Arbor 1980.
Wajemann, Heiner. *Die Chorkompositionen von Richard Strauss.* Tutzing 1986.

Reception, Influence, and Effect

Fuß, Hans-Ulrich. "Richard Strauss in der Interpretation Adornos." *Archiv für Musikwissenschaft* 45 (1988). 67–85.

Jefferson, Alan. *The Operas of Richard Strauss in Great Britain 1910–1963*. London 1964.

Lesnig, Günther. *Die Aufführungen der Opern von Richard Strauss im 20. Jahrhundert: Daten, Inszenierungen, Besetzungen*. 2 vols. Tutzing 2008, 2010.

Schütte, Jens-Peter. "Anmerkungen zur Letzten Aufzeichnung von Richard Strauss." *Musik in Bayern* 65/66 (2003). 85–106.

Wattenbarger, Richard. "A 'Very German Process': The Contexts of Adorno's Strauss-Critique." *19th-Century Music* 25 (2002). 313–336.

Index

Page references followed by *f*, or *t* refer to figures, and tables respectively.

Adorno, Theodor W., 6–8
Ahna, Pauline de. *See* Strauss, Pauline
Albert, Eugen d', 32–33, 167–68, 241
Allgemeiner Deutscher Musikverein, 167–68
Altmann, Gustav, 8–9
Annunzio, Gabriel d', 177–78, 241
antiquity, ix, 114–20, 136–41
aristocratic world, collapse of, 79. *See also* courtly appointments
Arnim, Achim von, 56*t*
art
    and "the social," 130–31
    Strauss on, 108–9, 129–30
artistic will, 91–92, 94–95
Asow, Erich Hermann Müller von, 202, 212, 235
atonal music, 5–6, 81–82
Auber, Daniel Francois Esprit, 76–78
authorial rights, 167–69
autobiography, aspects of, in tone poems, 98–100, 102–5

Bach, Johann Sebastian, 76–78
Bahr, Hermann, 190–91, 241
Batka, Rudolf, 2–4
Bausznern, Waldemar von, 34–35
Beethoven, Ludwig van
    biography of, 241–42
    Eroica, 103, 194–96
    and *Intermezzo*, 154–55
    Ruinen von Athen, 141
    and sonata form, 43–44
    symphony no. 9, 124–25
Bekker, Paul, vii, 242
Bellincioni, Gemma, 78–79, 242
Berg, Alban, 6–8, 242
Berlin
    program of the Royal Orchestra's Third Symphony Evening in, 80*f*
    Reinhardt's theater in, 111–14
    Strauss's apartment in, 77*f*
    Strauss's employment in, 73–79, 166

Berlioz, Hector
    biography of, 242
    Treatise on Instrumentation, 83–84, 94–95
Bethge, Hans, 56*t*
Bie, Oskar, 2–4
Bierbaum, Otto Julius, 4, 55–60, 70, 242
Binding, Rudolf, 180–81
Bithorn, Willi, 128*f*
Bizet, Georges, 76–78, 82–83
Blech, Leo, 242
Bodenhausen, Eduard von, 126–27
Bodmann, Emanuel von, 56*t*
Böhm, Karl, 194, 242–43
Brahm, Otto, 112–13, 243
Brahms, Johannes, 72–73, 206, 243
Braun, Lily, 30, 71
Brecher, Gustav, 2–4, 243
Brian, Havergal, 78–79, 243
Bruckner, Anton, viii–ix, 243–44
Bülow, Hans von
    biography of, 244
    on Strauss's conducting skills, 70
    and Strauss's dismissal of traditional genres, 43–44
    Strauss's letter to, 43–44, 45*f*
    summoned to Munich, 20–21
    on Symphony in F minor, Op. 12, 44–46
    Wagner and, 69–70
Busch, Fritz, 145–46, 172–73, 175, 244
Busoni, Ferruccio, 152–53
Busse, Carl, 56*t*

cabaret, 109–12
Calderón de la Barca, Pedro, 110–11
Carrière, Moriz, 28–29, 244
Chabrier, Emmanuel, 76–78
chamber music, 42–48, 226
choral compositions, 61–66, 232–33
coloration, 41, 131–32, 148–49
comedies, 131–33, 139–40, 179–80
communication
    music as, 41

communication (*Cont.*)
    Strauss and Hofmannsthal on, 127–31
    tonality and, 147–51
    waltz and faltering, 135–36
composing
    conditions for, 92–94
    and copyright, 166–69
    at Garmisch villa, 162–64
    method for, 123*f*
conducting
    composition and, 69–70
    and inspiration and technique, 40–41
    of premieres by Strauss, 88*t*
    Strauss's approach to, 83–90
    Strauss's career in, 70
copyright, 166–69
Corinth, Lovis, 114–16, 126–27, 244
Couperin, François, 34–35
courtly appointments, 71–79, 166, 206

Dahn, Felix, 56*t*
Damisch, Heinrich, 157–58, 159
dance. *See* ballet and stage works
Debussy, Claude, 42, 106, 152–53, 244
    La Mer, 76–78
    Pelléas et Mélisande, 115
Dehmel, Richard, 55–57, 58–60, 244–45
Deutsches Theater, 111–13
Diaghilev, Serge, 133–34, 245
Donaueschingen Chamber Music
    Festival, 152–53
Dopper, Cornelis, 80*f*, 88*t*
Dostoevsky, Fyodor, 30–31
Draeseke, Felix, 1–2, 245
Dukas, Paul, 132–33, 245

Eichendorff, Joseph von, 56*t*, 60–61
Elgar Edward, 76–78
Eysoldt, Gertrud, 112, 114–15, 126–27, 245

Falke, Gustav, 56*t*
Fanto, Leonardo, 7*f*, 245
"festive, the," 112–14, 122, 124–25, 187
Flotow, Friedrich von, 33
fluency, and inspiration and technique, 38–40
Franze, Johannes, 189–90, 245
Freud, Sigmund, 108
Friedrich-Schack, Adolf, 58–60
Fürstner, Adolph, 166, 245–46
Furtwängler, Wilhelm, 5–6, 246

Garmisch villa, 162–64
Gehmacher, Friedrich, 157–58, 246
Geibel, Emanuel, 56*t*
Genossenschaft Deutscher Komponisten,
    166–68, 207
Genossenschaft Deutscher Tonsetzer (GDT),
    167–68, 173, 207
Genossenschaft zur Verwertung musikalischer
    Aufführungsrechte (GEMA), 168, 207
Georg II, 206, 246
George, Stefan, 55–57
Gilm, Hermann von, 56*t*
Gnecchi, Vittorio, 120, 246
Goebbels, Joseph, 6, 50–53, 159, 173–76,
    209–10, 247
Goethe, Johann Wolfgang von, 56*t*, 60–61,
    196–99, 247
    Wilhelm Meisters Wanderjahre, 107
Göring, Hermann, 170–71, 175
Grab, Alice. *See* Strauss, Alice
Grab, Elly, 210
Grab family, 210, 247
Gregor, Joseph, 180–87, 247
Greif, Martin, 56*t*
Grimm, Herman, 196–98
Gruppe, Otto Friedrich, 56*t*

Hacker-Pschorr brewing empire, 25–26
Hackländer, Friedrich Wilhelm von, 154
Halbe, Max, 115–16, 247–48
Hanslick, Eduard, 33, 248
harmony
    dissolution of melody and, 147–48
    distinction between melody and, 4
    simultaneity of melody and, 118–19
Hart, Heinrich, 56*t*
Hartmann, Rudolf, 248
Hauff, Wilhelm, 141–42
Hauptmann, Gerhart, 30–31, 65–66,
    177–78, 248
Hauptmotive, 148–49
Hausegger, Friedrich von, 36–37
Hausegger, Siegmund von, 30, 36–37,
    39–40, 248
Havemann, Gustave, 173–74
Haydn, Joseph, 188.P.23
Heine, Heinrich, 56*t*, 58–60
Henckell, Karl, 56*t*, 58–60, 248
Hesse, Hermann, 56*t*, 60–61, 67–68, 248–49
Hindemith, Paul, 152–53, 155, 249
Hitler, Adolf, 144*f*, 173–74, 175–76, 181–82,
    199, 249
Hochberg, Hans Heinrich XIV Bolko, 74–76,
    109–10, 249
Hofmannsthal, Hugo von.
    on *Die ägyptische Helena*, 139–40
    biography of, 249
    on bonding power of music, 112–13
    "Chandos Letter," 15–16, 128–29, 183–84
    on contemporary music, 129–30
    on conventional theater, 112–13
    death of, 177–78, 209

influence of, 74–76
and *Intermezzo*, 153–55
on *Josephs Legende*, 134
on operetta, 143–46
on production of *Die Frau ohne Schatten*, 79–81
on Reinhardt, 112
and *Der Rosenkavalier*'s afterword, vii
on *Salome* and *Elektra*, 118
and Salzburg Festival, 157–58
with Strauss, 128*f*
Strauss's collaboration with, 60–61, 177–78, 208
Strauss's first meeting with, 207
Strauss's relationship with, 126–28
on understanding Strauss's *oeuvre*, vii–viii
on waltz, 135–36
Hölderlin, Friedrich, 56*t*
Hoffmann von Fallersleben, August Heinrich, 56*t*
Huber, Hans, 78–79
Hülsen-Haeseler, Georg von, 74–76, 249–50
Humperdinck, Engelbert, 30, 36–37, 63, 106, 167–68, 250

individualized form, 93–94
inherited genres, left behind by Strauss, 42–48
inspiration, and technique, 36–41
instrumental music
  end of, 120–25
  restrictions of, 129–30
  return to, 191–94
intentional communicability, 130–31, 132–33, 150
International Society for New Music, 152–53
Internationale Kammermusikaufführung, 152–53
"intimate, the," 115–16
"Intimate Theater," 115–16
Italy, Strauss travels to, 106–7

Jeritza, Maria, 50–53, 250

Kahane, Arthur, 73–74
Kapp, Julius, 155–56
Kerr, Alfred, 56*t*, 60–61, 73–74, 250
Kessler, Count Harry, 160–61, 177–78, 250
Kippenberg, Anton, 179, 209
Kleines Theater, 111–13, 114–16
Kleist, Heinrich von, 185–86
Knappertsbusch, Hans, 171–72, 250–51
Knobel, Betty, 251
Klopstock, Friedrich Gottlieb, 56*t*
Kokoschka, Oskar, 79–81
Kopsch, Julius, 170–71
Korngold, Erich Wolfgang, 78–79
Krauss, Clemens, 145–46, 172–73, 209–10, 251

Künstleropern, 106–10
Kusche, Ludwig, 200

Lachmann, Hedwig, 114–15
Lachner, Franz, 32–33
language
  dance as mediator between music and, 133–34
  order by means of, 129
Lehmann, Lotte, 79–81, 251
Leitmotivik, 148–49
Lenau, Nikolaus, 56*t*, 97–98
Leoncavallo, Ruggero, 76–78
Lernet-Holenia, Alexander, 180–81
Levi, Hermann, 22, 23–25, 207, 251
Lieberman, Max, 251–52
  Strauss portraits painted by, 74, 75*f*
Lied(er)
  catalog of, 227–32
  chronology of, 51*t*
  as form of musical thought, 49–61
  poetry set to, 55–61
  Strauss's return to, 66–68
Liliencron, Detlev von, 56*t*
Lindner, Anton, 58–60, 114–15, 252
Liszt, Franz, 94–95, 252
Littmann, Max, 20
Loewe, Carl, 94–95
love, Strauss on, 107–8
Ludwig I, 19–20
Ludwig II, 19–21, 206, 252
Luitpold Karl Joseph Wilhelm von Bayern, 23–24, 206, 252
Lully, Jean-Baptiste, 34–35
Lützel, Karl, 3*f*
lyric, and choral compositions, 61–66

Mackay, John Henry, 55–57, 252
Mahler, Gustav, 8–9, 69–70, 71–72, 206, 253
Mann, Thomas, 21–22, 23–25, 30–31, 161–62, 171–72, 199, 209–10, 253
Marchi, Emilio de, 155–56
Mariotte, Antoine, 115, 253
Mascagni, Pietro, 76–78
Maximilian II, 19–20
Meiningen court, 70–71, 72–73
melody
  dissolution of harmony and, 147–48
  distinction between harmony and, 4
  simultaneity of harmony and, 118–19
Mendelssohn, Felix, 46–47
Mengelberg, Willem, 85–87, 253
Meyer, Friedrich Wilhelm, 23, 56*t*
Meyerbeer, Giacomo, 76–78
Meysenheim, Cornelie, 22, 66, 253–54
modernity, Hofmannsthal and Strauss on, 127–30

Molière, 112, 223
Moralt, Rudolf, 254
Morgenstern, Christian, 56t
motifs, 109, 147–50
Monteverdi, Claudio, 34–35, 179–80
Mottl, Felix von, 73–74, 254
Mozart, Wolfgang Amadeus, 47–48, 254
  Gran Partita, 191–92
  Idomeneo, 141, 178
  Manen, 195–96
Muck, Carl, 74, 254
Müller von Asow, Erich Hermann, 202
Muncker, Franz, 28–29
Mündel, Curt, 56t
Munich, 19–22, 23–24
music
  autonomy of, 14–15
  as communication, 41
  dance as mediator between language and, 133–34
  function of, 131–33
  Nietzsche on, 13–14
  and poeticization, 14–16
  Schopenhauer on, 11–13
  Strauss's conception of, 15–18, 169
  Strauss's understanding of contemporary, 152–53
Musikdrama, 93–94

National Socialism
  Strauss as head of Reichsmusikkammer under, 170–76, 180–81, 209–10
  Strauss declared *persona non grata* under, 165–66, 176, 188, 210
  Strauss misinterpreted under, 5–6
  Strauss's entanglement in, ix, 161
  Zweig and, 181–82
nervous counterpoint, 63–64, 94–95, 114–20, 179–80, 191–92
Newman, Ernest, 2–4
Niest, Carl, 23
Nietzsche, Friedrich
  biography of, 254–55
  on foreignness of Greek antiquity, 116
  Gay Science, 192–93
  influence of, on Strauss, 29–30, 33–34, 37–38
  on *Macbeth*, 96–97
  on music, 13–14
  on plasticity of Greek art, 136–38
  and transvaluation of values, 121
  and understanding *Don Quixote* and *Ein Heldenleben*, 104
Nilson, Einar, 112–13

Oertel, Johannes, 206–7
Offenbach, Jacques, 139–40
Olympic Games (1936), 65–66, 210

opera(s)
  catalog of, 221–22
  comic, 179–80
  Künstleropern and turn to, 106–10
  "un-Wagnerian," 131–32
operetta, 110–11, 143–46
orchestra
  limitations in, 92–94
  orchestral autonomy, 149–50
orientalism and Oriental antiquity, 114–20, 134

Panizza, Oskar, 25–26, 56t, 255
petrification, 141–42
Pfitzner, Hans, 24–25, 255
plasticity
  of antiquity, 136–41
  and comprehensibility, 40–41, 130–31, 135–36
  in conducting, 87
  of Lieder, 53, 54, 60–61
  and motif, 147–48
  of music, 17
poetry, set to Lieder, 55–61
Possart, Ernst von, 58–60, 255
Prantl, Carl von, 28–29, 255
present
  effort to take position vis-à-vis, 153–57
  founding life in, 151
Pringsheim, Klaus, 41, 255
Pschorr, August, 25–26
Pschorr, Georg, 25–26
Pschorr, Joseph, 25–26
Pschorr, Robert, 25–26
Pshorr family, 256
psychic polyphony, 40–41, 94–95, 117, 148–50, 180–81
Puccini, Giacomo, 76–78

Raabe, Peter, 174–75, 256
Rasch, Hugo, 170–71
Ravel, Maurice, 32–33, 152–53
  La Valse, 76–78
realism, in Strauss's tone poems, 98–100
Reger, Max, 69–70, 78–79, 95, 256
Reichsmusikkammer, 170–76, 180–81, 209–10
Reinhardt, Max, 74–76, 110–14, 144f, 157–58, 256–57
Reinhardt, Werner, 192–93, 257
religion, Strauss on, 29–30
Remer, Paul, 55–57
Reucker, Alfred, 145–46, 172–73, 257
Rheinberger, Joseph Gabriel, 30, 257
Rieck, Emil, 119f
Riehl, Wilhelm Heinrich von, 28–29, 198–99, 257
Rimsky-Korsakov, Nikolai, 82–83
Ritter, Alexander, 27–28, 29–30, 78–79, 98–99, 206, 257

Index • 281

Rögely, Fritz, 78–79
Rohlfs, Christian, 258
Rolland, Romain, 103–4, 258
Roller, Alfred, 79–81, 144f, 258
Rösch, Friedrich, 166–68, 258
Rosenauer, Michael, 164f, 165, 258
Rubiner, Ludwig, 117
Rückert, Friedrich, 56t, 58–60

Sacher, Paul, 194, 258
Saint-Saëns, Camille, 76–78
Sallet, Friedrich von, 56t
Salzburg Festival, 141, 142–43, 157–59
Schack, Adolf Friedrich, 56t, 58–60
Schalk, Franz, 79–81, 82–83, 157–58, 258
"Schall und Rauch," 111–12
Scherchen, Hermann, 66
Schiller, Friedrich von, 61t, 96–97
Schillings, Max von, 32–33, 69–70, 173–74, 258–59
Schirach, Baldur von, 165–66, 210, 259
Schoeck, Othmar, 60–61
Schoenberg, Arnold, 42, 106, 259
Schopenhauer, Arthur, 11–13, 107–8, 259
Schubart, Friedrich Christian Daniel, 22, 56t
Schubert, Franz, 76–78, 80f,
Schuch, Ernst von, 152f, 259
Schuh, Willi, vii–viii, 183–84, 194, 197f, 259–60
Schwarzenbach, Alfred, 170f
Schwarzenbach-Wille, Renée, 170f
Seidl, Anton, 74
Seidl, Emanuel von, 162–64, 260
Shakespeare, William, 28–29, 56t, 222
Shaw, George Bernard, 78–79
Skat, 28
"social, the," 5–6, 27–28, 64–65, 112–14, 122, 124–25, 130–31, 185–86
Society of Friends of Music, 152–53
Solti, Georg, 200
Sombart, Werner, 91
Sommer, Hans, 166–67
sonata form, brushed aside by Strauss, 42–48
Sophocles, 61t
Specht, Richard, 2–4, 260
Spengler, Oswald, 13–14
Spieloper, 143–44
Staatlich genehmigte Gesellschaft zur Verwertung musikalischer Aufführungsrechte (STAGMA), 168
stage works. See ballet and stage works
Ständiger Rat für die Internationale Zusammenarbeit der Komponisten, 174–75
Stanford, Charles Villiers, 76–78
Stauffer, Karl, 121–22, 260
Steiner, Rudolf, 71
Steinitzer, Max, 2–4, 260

Stieler, Karl, 56t
Stirner, Max, 260
  Der Einzige und sein Eigentum, 100–1
Stranski, Josef, 155–56
Strauss, Alice, 81, 161, 165–66, 175, 210, 260
Strauss, Berta Johanna, 26
Strauss, Franz Joseph (father)
  biography of, 205, 261
  death of, 208
  dislike of, for Wagner, 20–21
  employment of, 20–21
  influence of, 49
  marriage of, 21–22
  personality of, 26
  social standing of, 21–22, 25, 26
Strauss, Franz (son), 50–53, 81, 161, 207, 210
Strauss, Johann, Die Fledermaus, 32–33
Strauss, Johanna, 205
Strauss, Josephine "Josepha" Pschorr, 20, 21–22, 25–26, 206, 208
Strauss, Pauline, 27–28, 50–53, 155–56, 160–61, 206, 207, 261
Strauss, Richard Georg. See also Strauss works
  biographical timeline for, 205–11
  birth of, 20, 205
  "bourgeois mask" of, 161–64
  bust portrait en face, 7f
  as car driver, 170f
  composition method of, 123f
  conducting at rehearsal, 85f
  conducting habits of, 85–86
  conflicted perceptions of, 1–9
  death of, 200, 211
  declared persona non grata under National Socialist leadership, 165–66, 176, 188, 210
  early career of, 69–73
  early success of, 1–2, 22–23
  education and readings of, 23, 28–31, 55–61, 205
  family of, 25–28, 261
  first public performances of, 205
  with Hofmannsthal, 128f
  illness of, 106–7, 207
  influences on, 49
  Munich's impact on, 24–25
  as object of caricature and satire, 152f
  portraits of, 3f, 74, 75f
  private life of, 160–62
  reception and historical placement of, vii–x
  renown of, 32–33
  rupture in oeuvre of, 5–6
  scholarship on, ix–x, 2–4
  self-perception and historical placement of, 200–4
  tensions in career of, 5
  travels of, 106–7
  upper-class propriety of, 27–28
  writings of, 235–40

Strauss family, 261
Strauss works. *See also* Lied(er); tone poems
  adaptations, 222–23, 235
  Idomeneo (Mozart), 34–35, 223
  Iphigènie en Tauride (Gluck), 34–35, 223
  Die Ruinen von Athen (Beethoven), 34–35, 223
  Die ägyptische Helena, Op.75, 5–6, 81–82, 139–40, 145–46, 153–54, 209, 219
  Eine Alpensinfonie, Op.64, 74–76, 120–25, 208, 214
  Also sprach Zarathustra, Op.30, 100–3, 213
  Arabella, Op.79, 132–33, 145–46, 172–73, 175–76, 177–78, 209–10, 219–14
  Ariadne auf Naxos, Op.60, 9–11, 12f, 13–14, 17–18, 34–35, 39, 72–73, 79–81, 136–40, 141–42, 143–44, 149–50, 186, 187, 208, 216–17
  Aus der Werkstatt eines Invaliden, 191–93, 210
  Aus Italien, Op.16, 95–96, 206, 212
  Das Bächlein, Op.88, 209–10, 247
  Befreit, Op.39, 53, 228
  Burleske in D minor for Piano and Orchestra, 46, 206, 225
  Capriccio, Op.85, 34–35, 40–41, 54–55, 68, 84, 85–86, 139–40, 147–48, 169, 176, 181, 182–84, 186–87, 188–91, 210, 221
  catalog of, 212–40
  Cello Sonata, Op.6, 46–47, 263
  chamber music, 42–48, 226
  choral compositions, 61–66, 232–33
  Daphne, Op.82, 68, 141, 150–51, 176, 182–84, 185–86, 210, 220
  Deutsche Motette, Op.62, 63–64, 208
  Dirigentenerfahrungen (Experiences of a Conductor), 84
  Divertimento, Op.86, 224
  Don Juan, Op.20, 97–98, 213
  Don Quixote, Op.35, 103–5, 207, 214
  Die Donau, 81–82, 120–21, 191–92
  Duet-Concertino for Clarinet, Bassoon, Harp, and Strings in F Major, 211, 234
  early, in "major" genres, 43t
  Elektra, Op.58, 111–12, 118–20, 126–27, 133, 134, 150, 151, 162–64, 208, 216
  Enoch Arden, Op.38, 58–60, 207
  Festliches Präludium, Op.61, 124–25, 208, 224
  Feuersnot, Op.50, 15–16, 109–10, 207, 215
  Four Lieder for voice and piano, Op.27, 50–53, 229
  Four Last Songs, 67t
  Die Frau ohne Schatten, Op.65, 79–81, 139–40, 141–44, 149–50, 209, 211, 218
  Friedenstag, Op.81, 175–76, 181, 182–85, 186, 210, 220
  Fünf Lieder, Op.39, 53
  Guntram, Op.25, 15–16, 26–28, 29–30, 106–7, 108–10, 207, 210, 214–15
  Ein Heldenleben, Op.40, viii–ix, 35–36, 85–87, 103–5, 120–21, 195–96, 207, 214
  Hochzeitlich Lied, Op.37, 59f
  Horn Concerto in E♭ major, Op.11, 46, 188, 191–92, 210, 224–25
  Intermezzo, Op.72, vii–viii, 40–41, 81, 145–46, 148–50, 153–57, 209, 218–19
  Josephs Legende, Op.63, 133–35, 149–50, 165, 208, 211, 217
  Krämerspiegel, Op.66, 60–61, 230
  late, 188–94, 234–35
  Leises Lied, 53
  Die Liebe der Danae, Op.83, 5–6, 41, 68, 141, 145–46, 159, 176, 182–84, 186, 210, 220–21
  lost, 240
  Macbeth, Op.23, 41, 96–98, 206, 207, 213
  Mädchenblumen, Op.22, 206–7, 229
  "Malven," 50–53, 235
  Metamorphosen, 41, 66–67, 189–90, 194–99, 211, 234
  misattributed, 240
  Oboe Concerto, 211
  Olympische Hymne, 65–66, 210
  Op.57, 74–76
  Orest und die Furien, 134–35
  Panathenäenzug: Symphonic Etudes in Passacaglia Form for Piano and Orchestra, Op.74, 209, 225
  Parergon zur Symphonia Domestica for Piano and Orchestra, Op.73, 209, 225
  Piano Trio in D major, 47–48
  Prometheus, 81–82
  Romance in E♭ major for Clarinet and Orchestra, 224
  Romance in F Major for Cello and Orchestra, 225
  Der Rosenkavalier, Op.59, vii, 26–27, 28–29, 41, 111–13, 126–27, 132–33, 135, 136–38, 143–44, 148–50, 159, 164–65, 208, 209, 216
  Salome, Op.54, vii, 114–20, 133, 150, 151, 152f, 162–64, 166, 199, 208, 215–16
  Schlagobers, Op.70, 133–34, 164–65, 209, 218
  Die schweigsame Frau, Op.80, 34–35, 179–80, 181–82, 210, 219–20
  Semiramis, 182–84
  Serenade in E♭ major, Op.7, 23, 47–48
  Sonatina No. 2 in E♭ major, *Fröhliche Werkstatt*, 35–36, 191–93, 211
  String Quartet, Op.2, 23, 205
  Suite in B♭ major, Op.4, 23, 47–48
  Symphonia domestica, Op.53, 105, 120–21, 208, 214
  Symphony in D minor, 22, 224
  Symphony in F minor, Op.12, 23, 44–46, 151, 224

Die Tageszeiten, Op.76, 60–61, 64–65, 209, 233
Taillefer, Op.52, 63*f*, 208, 233
"Ten Golden Rules," 84
Till Eulenspiegels lustige Streiche, nach alter Schelmenweise, Op.28, 100–1, 207, 213
Tod und Verklärung, Op.24, 98–99, 100, 102–3, 206, 213
Über Komponieren und Dirigieren (On Composition and Conducting), 84
unfinished, 239–40
Violin Concerto in D minor, Op.8, 23, 46, 224–14
Vision der Semiramis, 177–78
Wandrers Sturmlied, Op.14, 62, 206, 233
Zueignung, Op.10, No. 1, 53, 66
Stravinsky, Igor, 134, 152–53
Strindberg, August, 115–16
Sturm, Julius, 56*t*
Sudermann, Hermann, 114–15
Suk, Josef, 78–79
Swarowsky, Hans, 186, 261
sword-motif, 148–49
symphonic unity, 149–50
symphony form, brushed aside by Strauss, 42–48

Tchaikovsky, Pyotr Ilyich, 76–78, 95
technique
  artistic will and, 91–92, 94–95
  inspiration and, 36–41
Tennyson, Alfred, 58–60, 232
Thuille, Ludwig (Louis), 30, 78–79, 261
Tietjen, Heinz, 172–73, 261–62
Tiessen, Heinz, 78–79
Tombo, August, 23, 205, 262
tonality, and new musical communicability, 147–51. *See also* atonal music
Tondichtung, 94–95
tone poems
  anti-metaphysical conception of, 98–102
  aspects of autobiography in, 98–100, 102–5
  catalog of, 212–14
  and distancing from Wagner, 91–98
  plasticity in, 138–39
  realism in, 98–100
Toscanini, Arturo, 82–83, 209–10, 262
tradition
  left behind by Strauss, 42–48
  Strauss's view of, 32–36

Überbrettl, 110–11
Uhde, Franz von, 98–99
Uhland, Ludwig, 56*t*, 58–60
Ursuleac, Viorica, 66, 262

Verdi, Giuseppe, 76–78
Vienna Court Opera, 79–83
Vienna Hofoper, 33
Vienna Music Prize, 152–53
Vienna Ringtheater, 33
Vienna villa, 164–65

Wagner, Cosima, 20–21, 101–2, 206, 262
Wagner, Richard
  biography of, 262–63
  Bülow and, 69–70
  Franz Strauss's dislike for, 20–21
  influence of, 20, 49
  and metamorphosis music, 198–99
  on motifs, 109
  Parsifal, 76–78, 82–83, 159, 168–69, 209–10
  Rheingold, 148–49
  Strauss distances himself from, 29–30, 91–98, 109–10
  Strauss's affinity for, 23
  and Strauss's view of music and theater, 147–48
  Die Walküre, 148–49
Wagner, Siegfried, 207, 263
Wallerstein, Lothar, 178, 263
Walter, Benno, 23, 205, 263
Walter, Bruno, 170–71, 263
waltzes, 135–36
Weber, Max, 91–92
Webern, Anton von, 152–53
Weinheber, Josef, 56*t*
Weis, Dora, 160–61, 206, 263
Welti, Lydia, 121
Wendel, Ernst, 170–71
Wilde, Oscar, *Salome*, 114–16
Wildgans, Anton, 61*t*
Wilhelm, Kurt, 264
Wilhelm II, 1–2, 209, 264
Wille, Bruno, 55–57
Witkowski, Georg, 98–99
Wittgenstein, Paul, vii–viii, 264
Wittich, Marie, 152*f*
Wolff, Herman, 74
Wolzogen, Ernst von, 109–11, 115–16, 264
World War II, 196–98
Wüllner, Franz, 23, 264

Zweig, Stefan
  biography of, 264–65
  and "bourgeois mask," 162–64
  Strauss's collaboration with, 173–76, 179–82
  Strauss's first meeting with, 193–94, 209
  on Strauss's self-perception, 200–1